Great Debates
in Jewish History

COURSE EDITOR
Rabbi Mordechai Dinerman

CONCEIVED AND DEVELOPED IN CONSULTATION WITH
Lawrence H. Schiffman, PhD
Judge Abraham Lieberman Professor of Hebrew and Judaic Studies,
Skirball Department of Hebrew and Judaic Studies, and
Director of the Global Network for Advanced Research in Jewish Studies,
New York University

LESSON AUTHORS
Rabbi Mordechai Dinerman
Rabbi Lazer Gurkow
Rabbi Eli Raksin
Rabbi Shmuel Super
Rabbi Yanki Tauber

EDITORIAL BOARD
Rabbi Zalman Gordon
Rabbi Shimon Posner
Rabbi Yisrael Rice
Mrs. Rivkah Slonim
Rabbi Avrohom Sternberg

COORDINATOR
Mrs. Rivki Mockin

ADMINISTRATOR
Mrs. Chana Dechter

Great Debates

in Jewish History

JEWISH LEARNING INSTITUTE

STUDENT TEXTBOOK

THE ROHR JEWISH LEARNING INSTITUTE

gratefully acknowledges
the pioneering support of

George and Pamela Rohr

Since its inception,
the Rohr JLI has been
a beneficiary of the vision, generosity,
care, and concern
of the Rohr family.

In the merit of
the tens of thousands of hours of Torah study
by JLI students worldwide,
may they be blessed with health,
Yiddishe nachas from all their loved ones,
and extraordinary success
in all their endeavors.

Endorsements

Disputation has been a cardinal feature of Jewish civilization since the very first Jew, Abraham, debated with God as recounted in the Book of Genesis. *Great Debates in Jewish History,* developed under the guidance and direction of one of America's foremost Jewish scholars, Prof. Lawrence H. Schiffman, introduces students to some of the most memorable and significant of these debates. Anyone who has ever followed a great debate, or engaged in one, will appreciate the historical and religious perspectives that this course offers.

JONATHAN D. SARNA, PHD
University Professor and Joseph H. & Belle R. Braun Professor of American Jewish History,
Brandeis University
Author, *The History of the Jewish People* and other titles

Great Debates in Jewish History touches on a central aspect of Jewish culture and society since its earliest days, already rooted in the Hebrew Bible, until today, and surely into tomorrow: how to respectfully disagree with and challenge one another (and God) on matters of existential importance without descending into sectarian enmity and mutual debilitation. Where better to begin this history than in the late Second Temple period, with the window provided by the discovery of the Dead Sea Scrolls seventy years ago? Here is a group that renounced other streams of Judaism, claiming alone to be the true Israel, even while placing great emphasis on procedures for its members to fulfill the biblical mandate to constructively reprove one another without engendering hatred. The early rabbis, in the aftermath of Rome's destruction of the Second Temple and suppression of the Bar Kokhba revolt, sought to find the right balance between modeling "argument for the sake of heaven" and rooting out "gratuitous hatred." Largely due to their success, we are here today to confront the same challenge. I applaud the Rohr Jewish Learning Institute for enriching us through serious engagement with these timely and timeless debates.

STEVEN D. FRAADE, PHD
Mark Taper Professor of the History of Judaism
Chair, Program in Judaic Studies,
Yale University
Author, *Legal Fictions: Studies of Law and Narrative in the Discursive Worlds of Ancient Jewish Sectarians and Sages* and other titles

Students of Jewish history at whatever level should, like all students of history, learn that in the past, just as in the present, women and men argued over texts and over changes in the political, economic, and cultural realities around them. Those who lived before us were no more united than we are as they faced new ideas and new circumstances. That is a lesson that this project imparts so well. Each one of these learning modules will allow students to view actors in history as people divided and therefore engaged in intense debates about the best ways to face to the future.

HASIA DINER, PHD
Paul S. and Sylvia Steinberg Professor of American Jewish History
Director, Goldstein-Goren Center for American Jewish History,
New York University
Author, *A New Promised Land: A History of Jews in America* and other titles

The Dead Sea Scrolls are the only writings of a Jewish group in the Second Temple period to have survived to modern times. Although the group was withdrawn from the larger society, they allow us to see firsthand what the group thought about key issues and often what their opponents believed about them. I am gratified to see the Rohr JLI present this topic to the public in *Great Debates in Jewish History*.

JAMES. C. VANDERKAM, PHD
Professor of Hebrew Scriptures and Biblical Studies,
University of Notre Dame
Author, *The Dead Sea Scrolls Today* and other titles

Disputation is an essential element in the learning process, and over the centuries, it has been much prized by scholars and educators of every background. Jewish scholars, especially, have earned renown for their contributions to Jewish learning because of their skills in making arguments and defending their views with equal energy and imagination. In *Great Debates in Jewish History,* some of the finest scholars of the Jewish experience will examine six perennial debates. Understanding the questions raised by the discovery of the Dead Sea Scrolls, the revolt at Masada, the tension between faith and reason in the life and works of Maimonides, among other topics, will offer rich illumination of Jewish history. This is an opportunity not to missed by all who value Jewish learning.

ALAN KRAUT, PHD
University Professor and Professor of History,
American University
Past President, Organization of American Historians
Author, *The Huddled Masses: The Immigrant in American Society* and other titles

The new initiative of the Rohr Jewish Learning Institute studying the *Great Debates in Jewish History* is truly innovative. By learning about these key moments in Jewish history, the participants will be enriched by an intellectual and spiritual experience that may guide their thinking in the years to come. This process will not only deepen their understanding of the past, but will also make them aware of some of the issues of the present. I cannot think of a better director of the program than the erudite and experienced Professor Lawrence H. Schiffman of New York University, who conceived the idea of the series and is an expert in all its themes.

EMANUEL TOV, PHD
J. L. Magnes Professor of Bible Emeritus,
Hebrew University
Former Editor in Chief, *International Publication Project of the Dead Sea Scrolls*

Designed in consultation with the distinguished New York University Professor Lawrence Schiffman, *Great Debates in Jewish History* explores six fractious moments in the Jewish past. Starting with the ancient Dead Sea sectarian community, the course ends in the twentieth century, as American Jews argue over whether displaying a menorah on public property violated the Constitution's wall of separation between church and state. Sponsored by the Rohr Jewish Learning Institute, which is dedicated to inspiring Jewish learning around the world,

Great Debates in Jewish History opens a window onto the distant and recent Jewish past.

PAMELA S. NADELL, PHD
Patrick Clendenen Chair in Women's and Gender History
Director, Jewish Studies Program,
American University
Past Chair, Academic Council of the American Jewish Historical Society
Author, *American Jewish Women's History* and other titles

The long way that led the Jewish people from antiquity to the present is, in fact, not a single route, but rather a series of ideological, political, halakhic, and theological junctions. The bitter struggles, fundamental debates, painful schisms, and fateful decisions that took place during and following turning points in Jewish history are all components of Jewish current identity, whether we are aware of it or not. Therefore, I highly endorse the fascinating course *Great Debates in Jewish History*, launched by the Rohr Jewish Learning Institute, which will explore six crucial debates of great historical significance, from the Second Temple era to recent Jewish American disputes, from issues of early halakhah through medieval philosophy, the rise of Hassidism and up to current political-ideological movements.

VERED NOAM, PHD
Professor of Talmud
Chair of the Chaim Rosenberg School of Jewish Studies and Archaeology,
Tel Aviv University
Author, *Megillat Ta'anit: Versions, Interpretation, History* and other titles

Great Debates in Jewish History guides students through significant moments when Jews vigorously disagreed. From each, our people emerged transformed. JLI's course was developed in consultation with Professor Schiffman, who brings the rigor of the scholar and the heart of the believing Jew to each and every debate.

STEVEN FINE, PHD
Dean Pinkhos Churgin Professor of Jewish History,
Yeshiva University
Founding Director, Yeshiva University Center for Israel Studies
Author, *Art, History and the Historiography of Judaism in Roman Antiquity* and other titles

Abraham Lincoln put it best: "If we could first know where we are, and whither we are tending, we could better judge what to do, and how to do it." The internal controversies that have marked Jewish history cast long shadows. Revisiting that history is a first step toward learning who we are and what we would wish to be.

RALPH LERNER, PHD
Benjamin Franklin Professor Emeritus,
The College, The University of Chicago
Author, *Maimonides' Empire of Light* and other titles

The JLI course on *Great Debates in Jewish History* is of interest to anyone who wants to understand some of the great moments in Jewish history. Six debates are planned, spanning the millennia and the continents. The scope is breathtaking, but the focus on six critical disputes ensures an engagement that will pique most intellectual curiosities. I can think of few others who could present the debates surrounding the Dead Sea Scrolls better than Professor Larry Schiffman. His book, *Reclaiming the Dead Sea Scrolls* (1994), marked a shift to rabbinics in the scholarly study of these most famous of manuscripts.

TIMOTHY H. LIM, PHD
Professor of Hebrew Bible and Second Temple Judaism,
University of Edinburgh
Author, *The Dead Sea Scrolls: A Very Short Introduction* (2017) and other titles

Over many millennia, Jews have made sense of Judaism and themselves by debating about meanings and practices. Rohr JLI's focus on six important debates in Jewish history is most welcome. I hope JLI course participants will learn that Jews are a people who fruitfully disagree about the meaning of their Judaism, while these very disagreements reinvigorate the Jewish people.

YOHANAN PETROVSKY-SHTERN, PHD
Crown Family Professor of Jewish Studies
Professor of Jewish History,
Northwestern University
Author, *The Golden Age Shtetl: A New History of Jewish Life in East Europe* and other titles

By revisiting controversies that help define Judaism, the Rohr Jewish Learning Institute's program *Great Debates in Jewish History* will enable participants to understand and grapple with some of the big questions that divide Jews to this day. I highly recommend it!

MICHAH GOTTLIEB, PHD
Associate Professor of Jewish Thought and Philosophy,
New York University
Author, *Faith, Reason, Politics: Essays on the History of Jewish Thought*

Foreword

LAWRENCE H. SCHIFFMAN, PHD

Judge Abraham Lieberman Professor of Hebrew
and Judaic Studies
Skirball Department of Hebrew and Judaic Studies
Director of the Global Network for Advanced Research
in Jewish Studies,
New York University

The sages taught in Ethics of the Fathers (5:17): "Any argument that is for the sake of Heaven, in the end will endure, but [any argument] that is not for the sake of Heaven, in the end will not endure." They cited the debates between the schools of Hillel and Shammai as examples of those that were for the sake of Heaven, and the revolt of Korach and his followers against Moses and Aaron as an example of an argument *not* for the sake of Heaven.

Indeed, debate and conflict have been a part of Jewish history throughout the ages. There have been debates that were "for the sake of Heaven," in which Jews debated about how to serve God and follow His Torah in various circumstances. There have also been those conflicts that resulted from petty jealousy or power struggles. The sages were convinced that genuine controversy could be a source of great inspiration, and that such controversies should therefore be preserved and studied, even once the halachic question in dispute was decided. In this way, both sides of the dispute continue in their role in making a positive contribution to Jewish identity and continuity. On the other hand, the sages were convinced that some controversies that stemmed from base motives could not serve such a purpose and that those controversies were better forgotten.

The course you are embarking on sees debate and controversy as an entry point to the study of important issues in Jewish history and thought. Some of the debates you will encounter are ancient; some are modern debates of the past; and some are set in our contemporary world. The assumption of the course is that studying these controversies can serve "for the sake of Heaven," in that participants will learn about important periods and events in Jewish history and central trends in Jewish thought. We also hope that you will come away with a sense of how dispute and debate can serve as a positive part of the Jewish tradition, but also about how they can sometimes be harmful.

When studying the topic of the Dead Sea Scrolls, you will learn about an ancient controversy crucial to understanding Second Temple Judaism, and how this controversy affected the eventual codification of the rabbinic tradition in the Mishnah. This topic is also important because it sheds light on the history of the Hasmonean period—the years of Jewish independence after the Maccabean Revolt. There are numerous modern controversies surrounding the Scrolls and their interpretation, and I hope that the interested student will explore these further.

The study of Masada will give you a wider view of the causes and effects of the Great Revolt of the Jews against Rome in 66–73 CE and the controversies among Jews as to whether to revolt or not. It should be noted, however, that there is a modern debate among scholars as to whether or not—and to what degree—the tragic but heroic events described by Josephus are historically accurate.

The course will then move to the medieval period, studying the controversy that surrounded the writings of Moses Maimonides (Rambam). Maimonides, the great codifier of Jewish law, leaned heavily on Greek philosophy in his *Guide for the Perplexed*. It may be hard to believe in retrospect, but the writings of this great sage touched off a controversy of enormous ferocity as to the religious legitimacy of the use of such sources and the interpretations that they engendered. These debates are still echoed both in the inner debates of the Jewish people and in the scholarly issues regarding how to understand Maimonides in light of his strict fealty to Jewish law and some of the daring theological concepts in his philosophical writings.

Moving to the late medieval/early modern period, the course will explore the nature of rabbinic authority through the lens of the attempt to reestablish the ancient form of rabbinic ordination and, in turn, the Sanhedrin—the central Jewish judicial and legislative assembly. This story is set in sixteenth-century Safed (Tzefat), where in the aftermath of the expulsion of the Jews from Spain in 1492, a group of Jewish scholars and mystics had gathered. Here you will learn both about a controversy that took place in the past but also about modern controversies surrounding the reestablishment of the Sanhedrin in the aftermath of the formation of the State of Israel.

At the very same time as the United States was coming into being in the late eighteenth and early nineteenth centuries, a new movement developed in Eastern Europe. The Hasidic movement would change the face of Judaism in Eastern Europe and, subsequently, in Israel, the United States, and elsewhere. But the coalescence of this movement led to an inner Jewish debate that sometimes reached very unfortunate heights. Here you will have a chance to see how what should have remained arguments about issues of Jewish law and mysticism set off political and economic struggles. With time, however, the excesses of this controversy were healed and Hasidism was able to make extremely important contributions to Jewish life and thought. Study of the rise of Hasidism will also make possible an understanding of some of the great events that shaped the emergence of the modern period for eastern European Jewry. The rise of Hasidism is a subject of scholarly controversy and I hope that the interested student will be moved to examine the different views held by researchers in this important area of Jewish history.

The final controversy to be studied in this course pertains to the lighting of public menorahs during Hanukkah, initially and still primarily by Chabad. Presentation of this dispute will enable discussion of some important matters pertaining to the American Jewish community, the emergence of Orthodoxy as a public "player," and the role of Jews and Judaism in our wider culture. You will dig into an American legal dispute of immense importance regarding the role of religion in American society and the division of Church and State. This will also be a chance to review the significance of Hanukkah and the notion of "making the miracle public" in observance of this remarkable holiday.

Hopefully, the discussion of all of these controversies will engender debate among those participating in this course. The ability to learn through discussion and debate is one of the hallmarks of Jewish tradition and one of the age-old methods of Jewish education. Through your study of these ancient, medieval, and modern controversies, and the resultant deepening of your Jewish knowledge, these historical debates, and your own debates, can join the ranks of those arguments that are truly "for the sake of Heaven" and provide for you an enduring link in the chain of Jewish tradition.

Contents

LESSON 1 1

The Dead Sea Scrolls
*Sectarianism and Jewish Law
in the Second Temple Era*

LESSON 2 49

Masada versus Yavneh
*Divergent Jewish Responses
to Roman Tyranny*

LESSON 3 105

The Maimonidean Controversy
*The Nexus of Faith and
Reason in Judaism*

LESSON 4 147

In the Wake of Expulsion
*Was the Time Ripe to
Reestablish the Sanhedrin?*

LESSON 5 193

Chasidic Renaissance
*Power and Controversy in the
Teachings of the Chasidic Masters*

LESSON 6 245

The Public Menorah
Is All Publicity Good Publicity?

Lesson

1

THE DEAD SEA SCROLLS

SECTARIANISM AND JEWISH LAW IN THE SECOND TEMPLE ERA

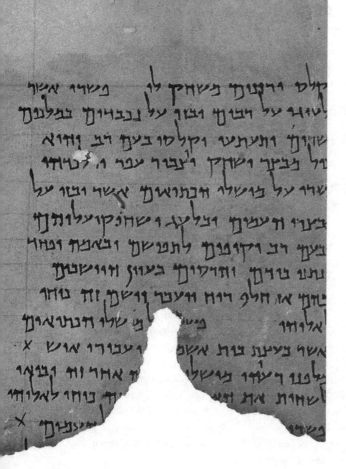

The Habakkuk Commentary (1QpHab), one of the Dead Sea Scrolls. (Photo Credit: Shrine of the Book Photo; The Israel Museum, Jerusalem)

The Dead Sea Scrolls are considered to be the most important archaeological find of the twentieth century. A considerable number of these scrolls are evidently sectarian and they reveal an intense debate from the Second Temple era over aspects of Jewish ritual and philosophy. Who were these sectarians? What were their beliefs? Against whom were they polemicizing? We will learn the underpinnings of this dispute by examining key passages in the scrolls and by searching for contrasts and analogues in rabbinic literature.

TEXT 1a

4Q169, COLUMN II, LINES 1–2
DONALD W. PARRY AND EMANUEL TOV, *THE DEAD SEA SCROLLS READER: EXEGETICAL TEXTS* (LEIDEN, NETHERLANDS: BRILL, 2004), P. 74*

Courtesy of the Israel Antiquities Authority, Photographer Najib Anton Albina

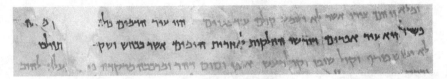

הוי עיר הדמים כולה כֹחֹשׁ פֶּרֶק מלאה פשרו היא עיר אפרים דורשי
החלקות לאחרית הימים אשר בכחש ושקריֹם יֹתהלכו

"Woe to the city of blood; it is all lies and full of robbery" (NAHUM 3:1). Its interpretation concerns the city of Ephraim, the seekers of falsehood at the end of days, who go by falsehoods and lies.

THE DEAD SEA SCROLLS

The first of the Dead Sea Scrolls were discovered by Bedouin shepherds on the northwest side of the Dead Sea in 1946 and became known to the public in 1947. Over the 10 years that followed, thousands of fragments, believed to be from approximately 900 different scrolls, were discovered in 12 caves in the vicinity of the ruins of the ancient settlement Qumran. The vast majority of these manuscripts are written in Hebrew or Aramaic, and many of them are copies of the Bible—the oldest copies known to be in existence. Archaeologists have dated the oldest of the scrolls to the 3rd century BCE, and the youngest to the 1st century CE.

---

* Many of the Dead Sea Scrolls are damaged or fragmentary, and many letters or words are unclear or missing. Scholars generally indicate probable letters with a dot above the letter; possible letters with a hollow circle above the letter; and full restorations, which are based on learned conjecture, in brackets. In this lesson, we indicate the scholarly restorations in the Hebrew with hollow letters, but we assume that the possible and probable letters are more or less definite and so we use a regular font for them. Moreover, in the case of full restorations, if a parallel manuscript confirms the restoration, we treat it as definite and use a regular font. With respect to the English translations, we do not indicate any restoration, in order to make the reading easier.

Before each quote from a scroll, we indicate whence we took the Hebrew text and restorations: either from Donald W. Parry and Emanuel Tov, *The Dead Sea Scrolls Reader* (Leiden, Netherlands: Brill, 2004); or from Devorah Dimant and Donald W. Parry, *Dead Sea Scrolls Handbook* (Leiden, Netherlands: Brill, 2014). When the Hebrew text is from Parry and Tov's books, we generally use their English translation as well. At times, though, we introduced minor revisions for an easier read and to more clearly convey the points of the lesson.

TEXT **1b**

4Q169, COLUMN II, LINES 8–9
DONALD W. PARRY AND EMANUEL TOV, IBID., P. 76

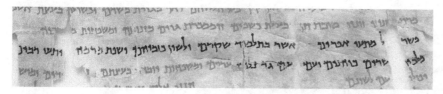

Courtesy of the Israel Antiquities Authority, Photographer Najib Anton Albina

פשרו על מתעי אפרים אשר בתלמוד שקרם ולשון כזביהם ושפת מרמה יתעו רבים מלכים שרים כוהנים ועם עם גר נלוה

Its interpretation concerns those who lead Ephraim astray, in whose teaching is their falsehood, and whose lying tongue and dishonest lips lead many astray— their kings, officers, priests, people, and the proselyte who converts.

A ritual bath (mikveh) at the Qumran site. (Photo Credit: Samuel Magal)

TEXT **2**

CD, COLUMN XIX, LINES 24–26, 31–32
DEVORAH DIMANT AND DONALD W. PARRY, *DEAD SEA SCROLLS HANDBOOK* (LEIDEN,
NETHERLANDS: BRILL, 2014), PP. 971–972

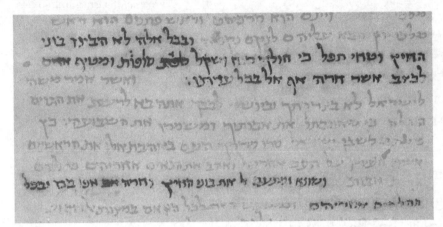

ובכל אלה לא הבינו בוני החיץ וטחי תפל כי הולך רוח ושקל סופות
ומטיף אדם לכזב אשר חרה אף א-ל בכל עדתו . . . ושונא ומתעב אל
את בוני החיץ וחרה אפו בם ובכל ההלכים אחריהם

All these things the builders of the wall and those who daub it with plaster have not understood. For one who takes wind and preaches falsehoods preached to them, for which reason God became angry with His entire congregation. . . . He hated the builders of the wall. He became angry with them and with all who follow them.

TEXT 3

4Q397, COLUMN IV, LINES 7–8

DONALD W. PARRY AND EMANUEL TOV, *THE DEAD SEA SCROLLS READER: TEXTS CONCERNED WITH RELIGIOUS LAW* (LEIDEN, NETHERLANDS: BRILL, 2004), P. 332

Courtesy of the Israel Antiquities Authority, Photographer unknown

ואתם יודעים שפרשנו מרוב העם ומכול טמאתם ומהתערב בדברים
האלה ומלבוא עמהם לגב אלה

You know that we have separated from the mainstream of the people, and from all their impurity, and from being involved in these things, and from participating with them regarding these matters.

TEXT 4

MISHNAH, YADAYIM 4:7 ⊕

MISHNAH

The first authoritative work of Jewish law that was codified in writing. The Mishnah contains the oral traditions that were passed down from teacher to student; it supplements, clarifies, and systematizes the commandments of the Torah. Due to the continual persecution of the Jewish people, it became increasingly difficult to guarantee that these traditions would not be forgotten. Rabbi Yehudah Hanasi therefore redacted the Mishnah at the end of the 2nd century. It serves as the foundation for the Talmud.

אוֹמְרִים צְדוֹקִין, קוֹבְלִין אָנוּ עֲלֵיכֶם פְּרוּשִׁים, שֶׁאַתֶּם מְטַהֲרִים אֶת
הַנִּצוֹק.

The Sadducees say: We complain to you Pharisees, for you regard an uninterrupted flow of liquid as pure.

TEXT 5

4Q394, COLUMN IV, LINES 5–8
DONALD W. PARRY AND EMANUEL TOV, *THE DEAD SEA SCROLLS READER: TEXTS CONCERNED WITH RELIGIOUS LAW* (LEIDEN, NETHERLANDS: BRILL, 2004), P. 330

Courtesy of the Israel Antiquities Authority, Photographer Najib Anton Albina

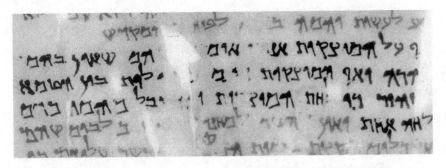

ואף על המוצקות אנחנו אומרים שהם שאין בהם טהרה ואף המוצקות
אינם מבדילות בין הטמא לטהור כי לחת המוצקות והמקבל מהמה
כהם לחה אחת

Also, concerning uninterrupted flows of liquid, we say that they are not pure, and that these flows do not separate between the impure and pure. For the liquid of uninterrupted flows and the liquid in the vessel are like a single liquid.

Pottery from Qumran, dated to the 1st century BCE. Some of the Dead Sea Scrolls were preserved in similar jars.

TEXT **6**

MISHNAH, MENACHOT 10:3 🙂

וְכָל הָעֲיָרוֹת הַסְּמוּכוֹת לְשָׁם, מִתְכַּנְּסוֹת לְשָׁם, כְּדֵי שֶׁיְּהֵא נִקְצָר בְּעֵסֶק גָּדוֹל.

כֵּיוָן שֶׁחֲשֵׁכָה אוֹמֵר לָהֶם בָּא הַשֶּׁמֶשׁ, אוֹמְרִים הֵן, בָּא הַשֶּׁמֶשׁ, אוֹמְרִים הֵן. מַגָּל זוֹ, אוֹמְרִים הֵן, מַגָּל זוֹ, אוֹמְרִים הֵן. קֻפָּה זוֹ, אוֹמְרִים הֵן, קֻפָּה זוֹ, אוֹמְרִים הֵן. בְּשַׁבָּת אוֹמֵר לָהֶם שַׁבָּת זוֹ, אוֹמְרִים הֵן, שַׁבָּת זוֹ, אוֹמְרִים הֵן. אֶקְצֹר, וְהֵם אוֹמְרִים לוֹ קְצֹר, אֶקְצֹר, וְהֵם אוֹמְרִים לוֹ קְצֹר.

שָׁלֹשׁ פְּעָמִים עַל כָּל דָּבָר וְדָבָר, וְהֵם אוֹמְרִים לוֹ הֵן הֵן הֵן.

וְכָל כָּךְ לָמָה? מִפְּנֵי הַבַּיְתוֹסִים שֶׁהָיוּ אוֹמְרִים אֵין קְצִירַת הָעֹמֶר בְּמוֹצָאֵי יוֹם טוֹב.

Residents from all cities that were near [the location of the reaping] would gather there so that the reaping would be carried out with great fanfare.

Once night fell, the reaper would say to those gathered, "Has the sun set?" and they would answer affirmatively. [He would ask again:] "Has the sun set?" and they would answer affirmatively.

"With this sickle?" and they would answer affirmatively. "With this sickle?" and they would answer affirmatively.

"This basket?" and they would answer affirmatively. "This basket?" and they would answer affirmatively.

If it were Friday night, he would say to them, "Is it Shabbat?" and they would answer affirmatively. "Is it Shabbat?" and they would answer affirmatively.

"Shall I reap?" and they would answer, "Reap!" "Shall I reap?" and they would answer, "Reap!"

He would ask each question three times, and they would respond affirmatively three times.

What was the purpose of this ritual? Because of the Baitusim who used to say that the *omer* was not reaped at the close of the festival.

TEXT 7

4Q320, COLUMN III, LINES 2–5
DONALD W. PARRY AND EMANUEL TOV, *THE DEAD SEA SCROLLS READER: CALENDRICAL AND SAPIENTIAL TEXTS* (LEIDEN, NETHERLANDS: BRILL, 2004), P. 21

Courtesy of the Israel Antiquities Authority, Photographer Najib Anton Albina

On the third day in the week of the sons of Ma'oziah falls the Passover. On the first day in Jeda'iah falls the Waving of the Omer. On the fifth day in Se'orim falls the Second Passover. On the first day in Jeshu'a falls the Festival of Weeks.

TEXT 8

LAWRENCE SCHIFFMAN, *QUMRAN AND JERUSALEM: STUDIES IN THE DEAD SEA SCROLLS AND THE HISTORY OF JUDAISM* (GRAND RAPIDS, MI: WM. B. EERDMANS PUBLISHING, 2010), PP. 335–336

The Qumran evidence reveals that, contrary to widespread scholarly opinion, tannaitic literature preserves reliable information about the pre-70 CE Pharisees. These Pharisees, as they are illustrated by the Qumran material, are truly similar to what is described in the later rabbinic texts, especially as regards the specifics of their legal rulings. . . .

One thing is certain: the rabbinic system was not invented *de novo* after the destruction of the temple and the nation in the Great Revolt against Rome in 66–73 CE. It was a continuation, albeit with numerous changes and innovations, that based itself on the long tradition of Pharisaic Judaism revealed more fully than ever before in the Dead Sea Scrolls.

LAWRENCE H. SCHIFFMAN, PHD
1948–

Noted historian and authority on the Dead Sea Scrolls. Schiffman is Professor of Hebrew and Judaic Studies at New York University and director of the Global Institute for Advanced Research in Jewish Studies. He is a specialist in the Dead Sea Scrolls, Judaism in late antiquity, the history of Jewish law, and Talmudic literature. He has authored many books and publications, and he is co-editor of the *Encyclopedia of the Dead Sea Scrolls*.

Learning Exercise 1

Read Texts 9–13 with a partner, and then summarize briefly in the chart below how many categories of Jewish law you have identified (in addition to the Written Torah).

TEXT 9

JOSEPHUS, *ANTIQUITIES OF THE JEWS* 13:10

The Pharisees *Sages* have passed on to the people a great many observances handed down by their fathers, which are not written down in the Law of Moses.

JOSEPHUS
CA. 37–100

Jewish historian. Born Yosef ben Matityahu Hakohen, he changed his name to Titus Flavius Josephus upon becoming a Roman citizen. His two principal works, *The Jewish War* and *Antiquities of the Jews*, are considered primary sources in documenting Jewish history during the Second Temple period. Despite surrendering his garrison to the Romans during the great revolt and later accepting Roman patronage, Josephus viewed himself as a faithful Jew.

TEXT 10

MAIMONIDES, INTRODUCTION TO THE MISHNAH

שֶׁכָּל מִצְוָה שֶׁנָּתַן הַקָּדוֹשׁ בָּרוּךְ הוּא לְמֹשֶׁה רַבֵּינוּ נִיתְּנָה לוֹ עִם פֵּירוּשָׁהּ. הָיָה הַקָּדוֹשׁ בָּרוּךְ הוּא אוֹמֵר לוֹ הַמִּקְרָא וְאַחַר כַּךְ אוֹמֵר לוֹ פֵּירוּשׁוֹ וּבִיאוּרוֹ וְכָל מַה שֶׁכָּלַל אוֹתוֹ הַמִּקְרָא הַמְחוּכָּם.

Every mitzvah that God gave to Moses was given with its explanation. God would tell Moses the verse and then tell him its meaning, explanation, and all that was contained in the ingenious wording of the verse.

RABBI MOSHE BEN MAIMON
(MAIMONIDES, RAMBAM) 1135–1204

Halachist, philosopher, author, and physician. Maimonides was born in Cordoba, Spain. After the conquest of Cordoba by the Almohads, he fled Spain and eventually settled in Cairo, Egypt. There, he became the leader of the Jewish community and served as court physician to the vizier of Egypt. He is most noted for authoring the *Mishneh Torah,* an encyclopedic arrangement of Jewish law, and for his philosophical work, *Guide for the Perplexed.* His rulings on Jewish law are integral to the formation of halachic consensus.

TEXT 11

JOSEPHUS, *THE JEWISH WAR* 2:8

The Pharisees *(sages)* are those who are considered most skillful in the exact explication of their laws, and are the leading school.

TEXT 12

RABBI YOSEF ALBO, *SEFER HA'IKARIM* 3:23 — *Spanish Rabbi & Philosopher*

נִתְּנוּ לְמֹשֶׁה בְּסִינַי עַל פֶּה דְרָכִים כּוֹלְלִים נִרְמָזוּ בַּתּוֹרָה בִּקְצָרָה, כְּדֵי שֶׁעַל יָדָם יוֹצִיאוּ הַחֲכָמִים שֶׁבְּכָל דּוֹר וָדוֹר הַפְּרָטִים הַמִּתְחַדְּשִׁים. וְהֵם הַדְּרָכִים שֶׁנִּזְכְּרוּ בְּתוֹרַת כֹּהֲנִים בִּתְחִלָּתוֹ בְּאוֹתָהּ בָּרַיְיתָא הַמַּתְחֶלֶת ר' יִשְׁמָעֵאל אוֹמֵר בִּשְׁלֹשׁ עֶשְׂרֵה מִדּוֹת הַתּוֹרָה נִדְרֶשֶׁת, מִקַּל וָחוֹמֶר, מִגְּזֵרָה שָׁוָה וְכוּ'. וְעַל יְדֵי אוֹתָן הַדְּרָכִים אוֹ אֶחָד מֵהֶן יוֹדֵעַ כָּל מַה שֶּׁלֹא נִמְצָא בַּתּוֹרָה בְּפֵירוּשׁ.

RABBI YOSEF ALBO
CA. 1380–1444

Spanish rabbi and philosopher. A student of Rabbi Chasdai Crescas, Albo is renowned for his philosophical work *Sefer Ha'ikarim* (*Book of Fundamentals*). The work stresses three fundamental aspects of Jewish belief: the existence of God, Torah from Sinai, and reward and punishment.

God gave to Moses, as part of the Oral Torah, pathways of derivation, hinted at in the Torah, so that sages of each generation can extract laws relevant for new developments. These pathways of derivation are the thirteen hermeneutic rules that are mentioned in the beginning of Midrash, *Torat Kohanim*. By using one or more of these principles, one can learn how to act in cases not addressed explicitly by the Torah.

TEXT 13

MISHNAH, AVOT 1:1

מֹשֶׁה קִבֵּל תּוֹרָה מִסִּינַי, וּמְסָרָהּ לִיהוֹשֻׁעַ, וִיהוֹשֻׁעַ לִזְקֵנִים, וּזְקֵנִים
לִנְבִיאִים, וּנְבִיאִים מְסָרוּהָ לְאַנְשֵׁי כְנֶסֶת הַגְּדוֹלָה.
הֵם אָמְרוּ שְׁלֹשָׁה דְבָרִים: הֱווּ מְתוּנִים בַּדִּין, וְהַעֲמִידוּ תַלְמִידִים הַרְבֵּה,
וַעֲשׂוּ סְיָג לַתּוֹרָה.

PIRKEI AVOT (ETHICS OF THE FATHERS)

A 6-chapter work on Jewish ethics that is studied widely by Jewish communities, especially during the summer. The first 5 chapters are from the Mishnah, tractate Avot. Avot differs from the rest of the Mishnah in that it does not focus on legal subjects; it is a collection of the sages' wisdom on topics related to character development, ethics, healthy living, piety, and the study of Torah.

Moses received the Torah from Sinai and gave it over to Joshua. Joshua gave it over to the Elders, the Elders to the Prophets, and the Prophets gave it over to the Men of the Great Assembly.

The Men of the Great Assembly would say these three things: "Be cautious in judgment. Establish many pupils. And make a fence around the Torah."

Qumran ruins, excavated during the 1950s.

TEXT 14

LAWRENCE SCHIFFMAN, *QUMRAN AND JERUSALEM: STUDIES IN THE DEAD SEA SCROLLS AND THE HISTORY OF JUDAISM* (GRAND RAPIDS, MI: WM. B. EERDMANS PUBLISHING, 2010), P. 341

It is important to examine the designation our text uses for the Pharisees. The Hebrew expression *dorshei hachalakot* is actually a pun. It begins with *chalakot*, literally "smooth things" (i.e., "falsehoods"), which appears in Isaiah 30:10, Psalms 12:3–4 and 73:18 and Daniel 11:32. This word is intended here as a play on the word *halachot*, a term attested otherwise only later, which refers to the Pharisaic-Rabbinic laws. While the noun *chalakot* appears in Isaiah with *dabru*, "to speak," it appears here, as well as in other sectarian documents, with *derash*, which by this time meant "to interpret." Accordingly, the expression *dorshei hachalakot* is a designation for the Pharisees who, in the view of the sect, are false interpreters of the Torah who derive incorrect legal rulings from their exegesis.

TEXT **15**

1QH, COLUMN XII (FORMERLY IV), LINES 10–12
DEVORAH DIMANT AND DONALD W. PARRY, *DEAD SEA SCROLLS HANDBOOK* (LEIDEN, NETHERLANDS: BRILL, 2014), P. 88

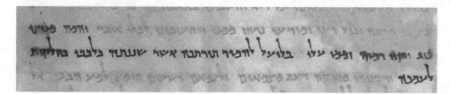

והמה מליצי כזב וחוזי רמיה זממו עלי בליעל להמיר תורתכה אשר
שננתה בלבבי בחלקות לעמכה

They are speakers of lies and seers of falsehoods. They planned evil against me to replace Your Torah that You taught in my heart with falsehoods to Your people.

Tefilin *found at Qumran, Cave 4, dated to the 1st century CE. (Photo Credit: Shrine of the Book Photo; The Israel Museum, Jerusalem)*

TEXT 16

TALMUD, TEMURAH 16A

שְׁלֹשֶׁת אֲלָפִים הֲלָכוֹת נִשְׁתַּכְּחוּ בִּימֵי אֶבְלוֹ שֶׁל מֹשֶׁה.

אָמְרוּ לוֹ לִיהוֹשֻׁעַ: שְׁאַל!

אָמַר לָהֶם: "לֹא בַשָּׁמַיִם הִיא" (דְּבָרִים ל, יב).

אָמְרוּ לוֹ לִשְׁמוּאֵל: שְׁאַל!

אָמַר לָהֶם: "אֵלֶּה הַמִּצְוֹת" (וַיִּקְרָא כז, לד) - שֶׁאֵין הַנָּבִיא רַשַּׁאי לְחַדֵּשׁ דָּבָר מֵעַתָּה.

BABYLONIAN TALMUD

A literary work of monumental proportions that draws upon the legal, spiritual, intellectual, ethical, and historical traditions of Judaism. The 37 tractates of the Babylonian Talmud contain the teachings of the Jewish sages from the period after the destruction of the 2nd Temple through the 5th century CE. It has served as the primary vehicle for the transmission of the Oral Law and the education of Jews over the centuries; it is the entry point for all subsequent legal, ethical, and theological Jewish scholarship.

Three thousand laws were forgotten during the mourning period for Moses.

The Jews asked Joshua: "Inquire of God!"

He responded: "It is not in Heaven" (DEUTERONOMY 30:12).

They said to Samuel: "Inquire of God!"

He responded: "'These are the commandments' (LEVITICUS 27:34)—meaning, from here on, no prophet can introduce anything novel."

QUESTIONS FOR DISCUSSION

1 What are the advantages/disadvantages of a system that relies on prophecy for legal rulings?

2 What are the advantages/disadvantages of a system that relies on reason to derive legal rulings from the Torah?

Qumran caves where some of the Dead Sea Scrolls were found.

TEXT **17a**

THE LUBAVITCHER REBBE, RABBI MENACHEM MENDEL SCHNEERSON, *LIKUTEI SICHOS* 19:5–6

דִי בַּײתּוֹסִים גְלוֹיבְּן נָאר אִין תּוֹרָה שֶׁבִּכְתָב, נִיט אִין תּוֹרָה שֶׁבַּעַל פֶּה. דֶער חִילוּק צְווִישְׁן תּוֹרָה שֶׁבִּכְתָב אוּן תּוֹרָה שֶׁבַּעַל פֶּה אִיז: תּוֹרָה שֶׁבִּכְתָב אִיז הַקָדוֹשׁ בָּרוּךְ הוּא אוֹמֵר וּמֹשֶׁה כּוֹתֵב, זִי אִיז גֶעגֶעבְּן גֶעוָוארְעֶן אִינגַאנצְן מִלְמַעֲלָה... תּוֹרָה שֶׁבַּעַל פֶּה אִיז עִנְיָנָה, וְוִי תּוֹרָה אִיז אַראָפְגֶעקוּמֶען בַּהֲבָנָה וְהַשָׂגָה, וְוִי זִי וֶוערְט נתְגַלֶה אוּן אִיבֶּערְגֶעגֶעבְּן דוּרְךְ דִי חַכְמֵי יִשְׂרָאֵל שֶׁבְּכָל דוֹר וָדוֹר, אוּן אִין אִיר דַאַרְף זַיין "לְאַפָּשָׁה לָהּ" - דֶער לוֹמֵד דַאַרְף הָאַרֶעוֶוען מִיט זַיין שֵׂכֶל צוּ אוֹפְטָאן אוּן מְחַדֵשׁ זַיין אִין תּוֹרָה...

דִי בַּײתּוֹסִים גְלוֹיבְּן נָאר אִין תּוֹרָה שֶׁבִּכְתָב, זֵיי הַאלְטְן אַז תּוֹרָה אִיז נָאר דָאס וָואס קוּמְט בְּגָלוּי מִלְמַעֲלָה. וְעַל דֶרֶךְ זֶה בְּמַתַּן תּוֹרָה. אוּן דָאס אִיז דִי טַעֲנָה פוּן דִי בַּײתּוֹסִים אַז... עֲצֶרֶת, מַתַּן תּוֹרָה, אִיז אַחַר הַשַׁבָּת - נָאךְ אַ טָאג וֶועלְכֶער אִיז אָן עָמָל וְיגִיעָה נָאר תַּעֲנוּג, מֶ׳גִיט אַלְץ מִלְמַעֲלָה.

RABBI MENACHEM MENDEL SCHNEERSON
1902–1994

The towering Jewish leader of the 20th century, known as "the Lubavitcher Rebbe," or simply as "the Rebbe." Born in southern Ukraine, the Rebbe escaped Nazi-occupied Europe, arriving in the U.S. in June 1941. The Rebbe inspired and guided the revival of traditional Judaism after the European devastation, impacting virtually every Jewish community the world over. The Rebbe often emphasized that the performance of just one additional good deed could usher in the era of Mashiach. The Rebbe's scholarly talks and writings have been printed in more than 200 volumes.

The Baitusim only believed in the Written Torah but rejected the other parts of Torah. The difference between the Written Torah and the other parts of Torah is that God spoke the Written Torah and Moses wrote it—it was completely from above . . . whereas the other parts of Torah are revealed through comprehension. The sages of each generation are tasked with toiling intellectually to introduce novel Torah ideas. . . .

The Baitusim, with their belief only in the Written Torah, believed that all of Torah is from above. It was through this prism that they regarded the giving of the Torah. And so their claim was that . . . Shavuot, the day celebrating the giving of the Torah, must be after Shabbat. It must be prefaced by a day that is without toil and that is given from above.

TEXT 17b

THE LUBAVITCHER REBBE, RABBI MENACHEM MENDEL SCHNEERSON, IBID.

דֶער אֱמֶת אִיז אָבֶּער אַז . . . אוֹיךְ דָאס וָואס נִבְרָאִים זַיינֶען מַשִׂיג מִיט זַייעֶר שֵׂכֶל אִין תּוֹרָה, אִיז עֶס - תּוֹרַת ה', נָאר דָאס אִיז וִוי תּוֹרָה אִיז אַרְאָפְּגֶעקוּמֶען בְּהִתְלַבְּשׁוּת לְמַטָה, בִּיז אַז אַ נִבְרָא זָאל עֶס קֶענֶען פַאְרשְׁטֵיין.

אוּן אִין דֶעם פִּירְט זִיךְ אוֹיס דֶער מְכוּוָן פוּן מַתַּן תּוֹרָה, אַז ס'זָאל זַיין דֶער חִיבּוּר "עֶלְיוֹן" וְ"תַּחְתּוֹן". וֶוען אַ מֶענְטְשׁ הָארֶעוֶועט אוֹיס מִיט זַיין שֵׂכֶל אַ סְבָרָא אִין תּוֹרָה, אִיז תּוֹרַת הוי' וֶוערְט נִקְרֵאת עַל שְׁמוֹ, תּוֹרָתוֹ, דָאס וֶוערְט זַיינֶער אַן עִנְיָן. ס'אִיז טַאקֶע נִיט אַזוֹיפִיל וִוי דֶער ט' קַבִּין שֶׁל חֲבֵירוֹ (וָואס מ'גִיט מִלְמַעֲלָה), דֶערְפַאר אָבֶּער אִיז עֶס קַב שֶׁלוֹ - אוּן דוּרְכְדֶעם וֶוערְט זַיין מְצִיאוּת מְיוּחָד בְּחָכְמָתוֹ יִתְבָּרֵךְ "בְּיִחוּד נִפְלָא" . . . אוּן דֶערִיבֶּער אִיז דָאס דִי רִיכְטִיקֶע הַכָנָה צו מַתַּן תּוֹרָה.

The truth is that . . . what people comprehend about the Torah with their own minds is also God's Torah. What we comprehend is a part of God's infinite wisdom that He made accessible to us in our finite world so that a human mind is able to comprehend it.

And thereby, the purpose of the giving of the Torah is realized—that there should be harmony between God and humankind. When we introduce Torah concepts using our own minds, God's Torah is attributed to us and becomes our Torah, our idea. This knowledge might be less than what we would have had if we received everything from above; but on the other hand, this knowledge is ours, and engaging in this process links us to God in a very intimate way. . . .

Thus, counting the forty-nine days is the proper preparation for the holiday of Shavuot.

TEXT 18

THE LUBAVITCHER REBBE, RABBI MENACHEM M. SCHNEERSON, CORRESPONDENCE, 1973, WWW.CHABAD.ORG/1274

If one wishes to know the secret of Jewish survival under circumstances which have obliterated larger and stronger nations . . . it is necessary to find the common factor, or factors, in all the various periods of Jewish history, which would then have to be taken as the basis of Jewish survival. . . . This factor was not language, nor country, nor anything else which is often associated with nationhood and nationalism; for in all these things there have been radical changes from one period to another, as anybody familiar with Jewish history knows. The single factor . . . which has preserved our Jewish people throughout the ages, under all kinds of circumstances, has been the fulfillment of the *mitzvot* in day-to-day life, such as the observance of Shabbat, the putting on of *tefillin*, and the Torah education of our children. . . .

There have always been deviationists; the Torah itself relates that immediately after the Torah was given at Sinai, there were the Golden Calf worshippers. Similarly, throughout the period of the Judges, Prophets and Kings, as well as in the post-Biblical period of the Second Beit Hamikdash, and later. These deviationists attempted to steer another course, away from traditional Judaism, but they could never take root within the Jewish people. Either these deviationists eventually realized their mistake and returned to the fold of observance of Torah and *mitzvot*, or they were completely assimilated among the nations of the world.

The Cheder, *Jacques Emile Eduard Brandon, 1870.*

KEY POINTS

1 The Qumran evidence confirms that the Mishnah preserves reliable information about the Judaism of Temple times, and it reinforces the notion that Mishnaic law was well established before the Temple's destruction.

2 One component of the Mishnah is the "Received Oral Torah," the explanations and specifics that Moses received from God along with the Written Torah. It is impossible to perform the *mitzvot* without the details of the Received Oral Torah.

3 A second component of the Mishnah is the "Derived Oral Torah," whereby the sages employed the power of logic, guided by principles of derivation, to apply the laws of the Torah to various legal questions.

4 A third component of the Mishnah is the "Legislated" rabbinic ordinances designed to safeguard against biblical transgression. The leaders during the Second Temple era sensed a period of religious weakening and thus advocated for "fences" to be erected around the Torah.

5 The evidence suggests that the Dead Sea Sect abandoned these three components of law, choosing instead to be guided by some means of continued divine inspiration. However, the sages taught that halachic rulings may not be reached by prophecy or divine inspiration.

6 In the sectarian approach, human creativity played no role in the realm of Torah. But the sages taught that human beings must lend their creative thinking to the development of Torah.

7 The world was created in order to allow for the harmonization of the Creator with the created. The goal is not to find God by eschewing our own personality, nor to be physical creatures with no spirituality; physical creatures and their personalities ought to express God and His ideals. This is accomplished when we intellectually strive to faithfully apply the Torah, following the principles of derivation, to address new circumstances or unanswered questions.

8 The survival of the Jews hinges on their attachment to Torah—the holistic system of the Written, Received, Derived, and Legislated.

Visit
facebook.com/myJLI
to vote on the following question:

What is the secret
of Jewish survival?

1 Antisemitism
2 Divine miracle
3 Torah observance
4 Jewish stubbornness
5 Jewish wisdom
6 The dispersion

Appendix

TEXT 19

MISHNAH, PARAH 3:7 ⊕

וְזִקְנֵי יִשְׂרָאֵל הָיוּ מַקְדִּימִים בְּרַגְלֵיהֶם לְהַר הַמִּשְׁחָה, וּבֵית טְבִילָה הָיָה
שָׁם. וּמְטַמְּאִים הָיוּ אֶת הַכֹּהֵן הַשּׂוֹרֵף אֶת הַפָּרָה, מִפְּנֵי הַצְּדוֹקִים שֶׁלֹּא
יִהְיוּ אוֹמְרִים בִּמְעוֹרְבֵי שֶׁמֶשׁ הָיְתָה נַעֲשֵׂית.

The elders of Israel would walk ahead to the Mount of Olives, where there was a place for immersion. The priest who was to burn the corpse of the cow was [deliberately] made impure by the elders [and he would then immerse in the *mikveh*]. This was done on account of the Sadducees, so that the people won't think as they did, that the cow could only be prepared by those for whom the sun had set.

TEXT **20**

4Q394, COLUMN I, LINES 16–19
DONALD W. PARRY AND EMANUEL TOV, *THE DEAD SEA SCROLLS READER: TEXTS
CONCERNED WITH RELIGIOUS LAW* (LEIDEN, NETHERLANDS: BRILL, 2004), P. 326

*Courtesy of the Israel Antiquities
Authority, Photographer Najib
Anton Albina*

ואף על טהרת פרת החטאת השוחט אותה והסורף אותה והאוסף
את אפרה והמזה את מי החטאת לכול אלה להעריבות השמש להיות
טהורים בשל שא יהיה הטהר מזה על הטמה

Also, concerning the cow of purification, he who slaughters it, he who burns it, he who gathers its ashes, and he who sprinkles the water of purification—all of them are to become pure at sunset, so that it is a pure person who sprinkles upon the impure one.

TEXT 21

MISHNAH, CHAGIGAH 2:4 📖

עֲצֶרֶת שֶׁחָל לִהְיוֹת . . . בַּשַּׁבָּת, שֶׁיּוֹם טְבוֹחַ אַחַר הַשַּׁבָּת. וְאֵין כֹּהֵן גָּדוֹל מִתְלַבֵּשׁ בְּכֵלָיו, וּמֻתָּרִין בְּהֶסְפֵּד וְתַעֲנִית, שֶׁלֹּא לְקַיֵּם דִּבְרֵי הָאוֹמְרִין עֲצֶרֶת אַחַר הַשַּׁבָּת.

If Shavuot falls out . . . on Shabbat, the day dedicated for bringing the holiday sacrifice is Sunday. However, the High Priest does not wear his vestments on this Sunday, and the populace is permitted to fast and deliver eulogies. These changes were instituted to undermine those who claim that Shavuot must be on Sunday.

Calendar for counting the omer, *the Netherlands, ca. 1700. (The Jewish Museum, New York)*

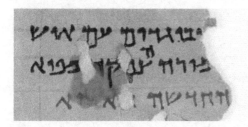

TEXT 22

1QPHAB, COLUMN II, LINES 1–3
DONALD W. PARRY AND EMANUEL TOV, *THE DEAD SEA SCROLLS READER: EXEGETICAL TEXTS* (LEIDEN, NETHERLANDS: BRILL, 2004), P. 80

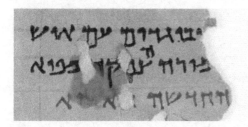
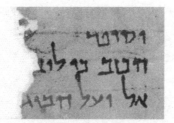

Shrine of the Book Photo © The Israel Museum, Jerusalem

פשרו הדבר על הבוגדים עם איש הכזב כי לוא האמינו בדברי מורה צדקה מפיא א-ל

This passage refers to the traitors with the Man of Lies, because they did not believe the words of the Teacher of Righteousness from the mouth of God.

TEXT 23

CD, COLUMN III, LINES 12–15
DEVORAH DIMANT AND DONALD W. PARRY, *DEAD SEA SCROLLS HANDBOOK* (LEIDEN, NETHERLANDS: BRILL, 2014), P. 962

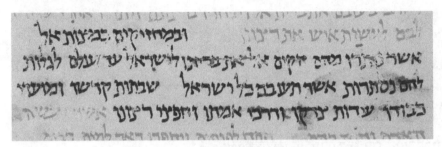

Reproduced by kind permission of the Syndics of Cambridge University Library

ובמחזיקים במצות א-ל אשר נותרו מהם הקים א-ל את בריתו לישראל
עד עולם לגלות להם נסתרות אשר תעו בם כל ישראל שבתות קדשו
ומועדי כבודו עידות צדקו ודרכי אמתו וחפצי רצונו

With those remaining who have held fast to God's commandments did God establish His covenant with the Jews forever—to reveal to them hidden matters about which all Jews have erred: His Shabbat, His festivals, His just commandments, His true paths, and the desires of His will.

TEXT **24**

TALMUD, BAVA BATRA 12A

וְחָכָם עָדִיף מִנָּבִיא, שֶׁנֶּאֱמַר (תְּהלִים צ, יב): "וְנָבִיא לְבַב חָכְמָה" - מִי
נִתְלֶה בְּמִי? הֱוֵי אוֹמֵר קָטָן נִתְלֶה בְּגָדוֹל.

A sage is greater than a prophet. This is alluded to by [an interpretation of] Psalms 90:12: "The prophet has the heart of the wise." Who is compared to whom? Obviously, the smaller is compared to the greater.

TEXT **25**

TALMUD, MEGILAH 6B

אִם יֹאמַר לְךָ אָדָם: יָגַעְתִּי וְלֹא מָצָאתִי - אַל תַּאֲמֵן, לֹא יָגַעְתִּי וּמָצָאתִי -
אַל תַּאֲמֵן, יָגַעְתִּי וּמָצָאתִי - תַּאֲמֵן.
הֲנֵי מִילֵי - בְּדִבְרֵי תּוֹרָה.

If a person says to you, "I have labored and not found success," do not believe this person.

If a person says to you, "I have not labored but nevertheless I have found success," do not believe this person.

If a person says to you, "I have labored and I have found success," believe this person.

And all this was said with regard to the study of Torah.

TEXT 26

RABBI DON YITSCHAK ABARBANEL, DEUTERONOMY 17 ⚏

אִם הָיוּ הַנְּבִיאִים מְבָאֲרִים סְפֵקוֹת הַתּוֹרָה וּמִצְוֹתֶיהָ הָיוּ הַחֲכָמִים מִתְרַשְּׁלִים בְּעִיּוּן הַתּוֹרָה וְלִמּוּדָהּ וַהֲבָנָתָהּ. וְלֹא הָיוּ שׁוֹקְדִים עַל דַּלְתוֹתֶיהָ יוֹם יוֹם. וְלֹא עֲמֵלִים עַצְמָם לְהַשִּׂיג תַּעֲלוּמוֹתֶיהָ בְּסָמְכָם עַל בִּיאוּר הַנְּבִיאִים וְהַכְרָעָתָם, וְגַם מַה שֶּׁיָּבִינוּ אַחֲרֵי הַחֲקִירָה וְהָעִיּוּן בְּדִבְרֵי הָאֱלֹקִים יְסַפְּקוּ בּוֹ, וְלֹא יִבְטְחוּ בְּעַצְמָם עַד בּוֹא דְּבַר הַנָּבִיא.

אָמְנָם כַּאֲשֶׁר לֹא יִהְיֶה לַנְּבִיאִים מָבוֹא בְּבֵאוּר הַתּוֹרָה וְהַמִּצְוֹת, יִתְעַצְּמוּ הַחֲכָמִים, וְיַפְלִיגוּ בְּעִיּוּנָם, וְיִבְטְחוּ בְּדַעְתָּם וְקַבָּלָתָם, כֵּיוָן שֶׁאֵין לָהֶם עַל מַה שֶּׁיִּסְמְכוּ כִּי אִם שִׂכְלָם וְדַעְתָּם הַטּוֹב.

RABBI DON YITSCHAK ABARBANEL
1437–1508

Biblical exegete and statesman. Abarbanel was born in Lisbon, Portugal, and served as a minister in the court of King Alfonso V of Portugal. After intrigues at court led to accusations against him, he fled to Spain, where he once again served as a counselor to royalty. It is claimed that Abarbanel offered King Ferdinand and Queen Isabella large sums of money for the revocation of their Edict of Expulsion of 1492, but to no avail. After the expulsion, he eventually settled in Italy where he wrote a commentary on Scripture, as well as other venerated works.

If the prophets were granted the authority to explicate matters of doubt about the *mitzvot* in the Torah, the sages would slacken in their learning, analysis, and comprehension of Torah. They would not study it assiduously on a daily basis, and they would not exert themselves to comprehend its mysteries, relying instead on the explanations and decisions of the prophets. Even with respect to those ideas that they would understand upon their studies, they would not be certain of their conclusions, and they would not rely on their ruling without hearing the word of a prophet.

Because, however, the prophet is not involved in explicating the Torah, the sages exert themselves to study profusely and trust their conclusions, because they have nothing to rely on other than their own competent minds.

Additional Readings

SCHEDULING THE *OMER*
THE TALMUDIC DISCUSSION

TALMUD, MENACHOT 65A–66A

Mishnah: How did they perform [the reaping of the omer, which took place on the night following the first day of the Pesach festival]? Agents of the court went out on the eve of the holiday and tied [the barley that was to be cut] in bunches while it was still attached to the earth, in order for it to be easily harvested. [On the first day of the holiday, toward nightfall,] all of the nearby towns gathered together there, in order for the harvest to be reaped with great fanfare.[1] *When it got dark, he [the harvester] would ask them [the crowd that assembled], "Has the sun set?" They would answer, "Yes." "Has the sun set?" They would answer, "Yes." "Using this sickle?" They would answer, "Yes." "Using this sickle?" They would answer, "Yes." "Using this basket?" They would say, "Yes." "Using this basket?" They would say, "Yes." On Shabbat he would ask [an additional question], "On this Shabbat?" They would say, "Yes." "On this Shabbat?" They would say, "Yes." "Should I harvest?" They would say, "Harvest." "Should I harvest?" They would say, "Harvest." [He would ask] three times for each item, and they would respond "yes" [to each question].*

BABYLONIAN TALMUD

A literary work of monumental proportions that draws upon the legal, spiritual, intellectual, ethical, and historical traditions of Judaism. The 37 tractates of the Babylonian Talmud contain the teachings of the Jewish sages from the period after the destruction of the 2nd Temple through the 5th century CE. It has served as the primary vehicle for the transmission of the Oral Law and the education of Jews over the centuries; it is the entry point for all subsequent legal, ethical, and theological Jewish scholarship.

Why did they go to such lengths? Because of the Baitusim [Boethusians] who would say that the omer should not be harvested on the night after the holiday.

Gemara: The Rabbis taught [in a *beraita* in *Megilat Ta'anit*]: These are the days on which it is not permissible to fast, and on some of them it is not [even] permissible to make a eulogy: From Rosh Chodesh Nisan through the eighth day of that month, the public *tamid* sacrifice was established, and there is to be no eulogizing [or fasting]; from the eighth of the month through the end of the holiday [of Pesach], the time of the Shavuot holiday was settled, and no fasting is allowed [but eulogizing is permitted].

[The *beraita* elaborates on the history behind the first period of days:] From Rosh Chodesh Nisan through the eighth day of that month, the public *tamid* sacrifice was established, and there is to be no eulogizing [or fasting]. For the Sadducees would say that an individual may volunteer and offer the public *tamid* sacrifice [instead of coming from communal funds]. How did they derive that [from Scripture]? [For the verse in the passage concerning the *tamid* sacrifice uses the singular form of 'you,'] "The one lamb you should do in the morning and the second lamb you should do in the afternoon" (Numbers 28:4). How did [the sages] rebut this argument? [For a couple of verses prior, the plural term for 'you should keep' is used,] "My offering of my bread for my fire…you should keep" (Numbers 28:2) — [to teach us] that they [the communal sacrifices] should all come from the *terumah* of [the half-shekel given by all, that is kept in] the Temple chamber.

[The *beraita* continues to elaborate on the next period:] From the eighth of the month through the end of the holiday, the time of the Shavuot holiday was settled, and fasting is not allowed. For the *Bait-usim* would say that *Atzeret* [Shavuot] would [always] come right after Shabbat.[2] Rabban Yochanan ben Zakai took up the argument against them and said to them: "Fools! From what text do you derive this?" There was not one person who could answer him save for a certain old man [amongst the *Baitusim*] who began a quibbling rejoinder and said, "Moses our teacher loved the people Israel. Knowing that Shavuot is a holiday of only one day [unlike Pesach and Sukkot which are seven days], he arose and established that it should come after Shabbat [on Sunday] so that Israel would be able to delight in a two-day celebration."

Rabban Yochanan ben Zakai quoted a text for him: "[There was a journey of only] eleven days from Horeb [where they received the Torah] by way of Mount Seir [until Kadesh-barnea]." (Deuteronomy 1:2) "If Moses was such a lover of the people of Israel, why did he keep them in the desert for forty years?"

The man replied: "Rabbi, you are dismissing me with this? [You have no other proof?]"

Rabban Yochanan ben Zakai said to him: "Fool, let our perfect Torah not be thought of like your vain prattle. One verse says, 'You should count fifty days' (Leviticus 23:16) and another verse says, 'They should be seven whole weeks' (Leviticus 23:15). How can both verses be maintained? [The first implies that the count can begin in the middle of the week, while the second requires the count to consist of complete weeks, i.e., beginning on Sunday?] [Rather,] one speaks of when the holiday of Pesach falls on Shabbat [and the count begins the next day, on Sunday,] and the other, when it falls in the middle of the week [and it is merely a count of 50 days]."

[The Gemara interjects with a mnemonic to remember the proofs that are going to be offered presently by the Tannaim in the *beraita*:] (Rabbi Eliezer's is *sofer*; Rabbi Yehoshua: *moneh*; Rabbi Yishmael: *meamer*; Rabbi Yehudah: *lematah*—a mnemonic.)

Rabbi Eliezer says: "This [line of argument] is unnecessary. For Scripture says, 'Count for yourselves' (Deuteronomy 16:9)—the count is dependent on [members of] the court, who know how to set the beginning of the months—'from the day after Shabbat'—that is, the day after the holiday of Pesach.[3] This excludes the possibility of the Shabbat of Creation [i.e., Saturday], whose count is within the ability of every person."

Rabbi Yehoshua says [offering another proof that "the day after Shabbat" refers to the day after the first day of Pesach]: "The Torah says, 'Count [twenty-nine] days and sanctify the new month,' [and the Torah also says,] 'Count [fifty] days and sanctify Shavuot.' [Thus, we can learn from one to the other.] Just as the new month is recognizable at the beginning of its count [i.e., when the "new moon" reappears], so too is Shavuot recognizable at the beginning of its count [for the count always begins on the sixteenth of the month]. And if you were to say that Shavuot must always come on Sunday, how could it be recognized at the start, [as in that case there is no set date for the count to begin]?"

Rabbi Yishmael says [offering another proof]: "The Torah says, 'Bring the *omer* on Pesach' and [it also says] '[Bring] the two loaves of leavened bread on Shavuot.' Just as the one [the two loaves] is brought on a festival and at its beginning, so must the other [the *omer*] be brought on a festival and at its beginning, [and were Shavuot always on a Sunday, then the offering of the *omer* and the fifty-day count would sometimes begin some days after Pesach began, and when Pesach fell on Sunday, it would be after the festival concluded]."

Rabbi Yehudah ben Beteira says [offering another proof]: "It says 'Shabbat' in an earlier text [regarding the *omer* being offered on the 'day after Shabbat'] and 'Shabbat' in a later text [that the two loaves are offered on the 'day after Shabbat']. Just as in the later text the ['day after Shabbat' has the] beginning of a holiday in immediate proximity to it, [i.e., the festival of Shavuot commences on the day after the seventh 'Shabbat,' meaning in this context after the conclusion of the seventh "week" of the seven-week count,] so too in this text [the 'day after Shabbat' must have] the beginning of a holiday in immediate proximity to it [i.e., the 'day after Shabbat' when the *omer* count begins, is immediately after the first day of Pesach, regardless of the day of the week.]"

Our rabbis taught [in a second *beraita*]: [The Torah states,] "You will count for yourselves" [in the plural]—that each person should count for himself—"from the day after Shabbat"—that is, the day after the [first day of the] holiday. But perhaps it really means the day after Shabbat commemorating Creation? Rabbi Yosi bar Yehudah says: The Torah says "You shall count fifty days"—your every count should be only fifty days. But if you are to say that Shavuot must come on the day after Shabbat, then sometimes the [end of the] count will be fifty-one days, sometimes fifty-two, fifty-three, fifty-four, fifty-five, or fifty-six [i.e., concluding up to six days later on the calendar relative to the previous year].

Rabbi Yehudah ben Beteira says: "This is unnecessary. The Torah says 'Count for yourselves'—the count is dependent on the court. This excludes the Shabbat that commemorates Creation, for that is [able to be] counted by all people."

Rabbi Yosi says: "[When the verse states,] 'From the day after Shabbat'—that is, the day after the holiday. You say, the day after the holiday, perhaps it really means the day after Shabbat? But could you maintain that? For the text does not say 'the day after the Shabbat that falls in the middle of Pesach', but only 'the day after Shabbat.' Why, the whole year is filled with Shabbats, so how would one know which one was meant? Moreover, it says 'Shabbat' in a later text [that the two loaves are offered on the 'day after Shabbat'] and 'Shabbat' in an earlier text [regarding the *omer* being offered on the 'day after Shabbat']. Just as in the later text the ['day after Shabbat' has the] beginning of a holiday [is in immediate proximity to it, i.e., the festival of Shavuot commences on the day after the seventh 'Shabbat,' meaning in this context after the conclusion of the seventh 'week' of the seven-week count,] so too in this text [the 'day after Shabbat' must have] the beginning of a holiday [in immediate proximity to it, i.e., the 'day after Shabbat' when the *omer* count begins, is immediately after the first day of Pesach, regardless of the day of the week]."

Rabbi Shimon ben Elazar says, "One text says, 'You shall eat matzot for six days' (Deuteronomy 16:8) and another text says, 'You shall eat matzot seven days' (Exodus 12:15). How can that be? [There is] matzah that you cannot eat all seven days because it is made from grain from the new crop [which still may not be eaten on the first day of Pesach], but you may eat on [the last] six days [of Pesach]."

[The *beraita* continues: The verse states,] "from the day you bring [the *omer*] . . . you will count" (Leviticus 23:15). You might think that one would harvest the *omer* of barley and bring it and then begin to count whenever one chooses. The text, however, says, "From the moment you first take the scythe to the standing crop you should begin to count" (Deuteronomy 17:16). If one begins the count from the moment you first take the scythe, you might think that one could harvest the barley and begin to count but bring the barley as an offering whenever one chooses. The text, however, says, "from the day that you bring [you should count]." If it is "from the day that you bring," one might think that one could harvest and count and bring the sacrifice all in the daytime. The text, however, says, "They should be seven complete weeks" (Leviticus 23:15). When is it that you find seven complete weeks? [Only] when you begin to count in the evening. You might think that one may harvest and bring the *omer* to the Temple and count all at night. The text, however, says, "From the day that you bring." How can that be? The harvesting and the counting are at night, and the offering of the *omer* at the Temple is by day."

Rava said: "All these arguments can be refuted except for the last two Tannaim of the first *beraita* and [the last two Tannaim] of the last *beraita*, which are irrefutable. Rabban Yochanan ben Zakai's proof may be refuted, for perhaps [the mention of days in one instance and weeks in another] is as Abbaye said, 'There is a mitzvah to count days and a mitzvah to count weeks.' The proofs of Rabbi Eliezer and Rabbi Yehoshua can [both] be refuted by asking, 'How do you know that the text is talking about the holiday of the first day of Pesach and not the holiday of its last day?' But the arguments of Rabbi Yishmael and Rabbi Yehudah ben Beteira are irrefutable.

"[Similarly regarding the second *beraita*:] If the proof was as advanced by Rabbi Yosi bar Yehudah, I could argue that maybe the fifty days are besides for the six [or fewer additional days prior to the actual start of the count, which are not included. The count itself will only be fifty days, even if it starts a few days later than the previous year]. If [the proof is] from Rabbi Yehudah ben Beteira's interpretation, it can be refuted thus: How does he know that it means the first day of the holiday? Perhaps it means the last day of the holiday! Rabbi Yosi also realized this same difficulty,

and he therefore added [the second interpretation, introduced by the word] 'Moreover.'"

The translation is based on the *Koren Talmud* (Jerusalem, Israel: Koren Publishers, 2015), with revisions by Rabbi Yaakov Gershon, Rabbi Shmuel Klatzkin, and Rabbi Shmuel Super.

Endotes

[1] The purpose of making a large ceremony was to negate the opinion of the *Boethusians* who did not agree to this timing of the harvest, as the Mishnah will explain shortly.

[2] They interpreted the words of the verse, "from the morrow of Shabbat" (in Leviticus 23:11, 15–16) literally, that the *omer* offering, as well as the beginning of the count, is to take place on a Sunday, thus the fiftieth day (Shavuot) would also fall on a Sunday.

[3] "Shabbat" in this context is understood as "day of rest," which can refer to a holiday as well.

THE DISCOVERY OF THE DEAD SEA SCROLLS

JAMES C. VANDERKAM AND PETER FLINT

The story of the discovery of the first Dead Sea Scrolls has become a part of Western lore. Who has not heard about the Bedouin shepherd who threw a rock into a cave, heard a crash, went in to explore, and found the scrolls? The story in that form may be accurate, but it turns out to be something of a simplification. As a matter of fact, much remains unknown about the exact circumstances under which those scrolls were discovered. The story of the discovery at first deals with just one cave; the other ten were located at later times.

The First Cave

What are our sources of information about the episode? The Bedouin shepherds (more than one) who

are the heroes have told their story, and that story has been retold and examined by the scholars who first had access to and worked on the scrolls. But different stories are attributed to the discoverers, who did not give a very precise indication of when the incident occurred. Also, a significant amount of time elapsed between the discovery and the first reports about it, and the cave in which the texts were found was not located by scholars until perhaps two years after the first scrolls were removed from it.[3]

The best, most complete source of information about the initial discovery is chapter 12 (supplemented by other parts) in John C. Trever's *The Untold Story*

JAMES C. VANDERKAM, PHD, 1946–

Professor and author. James C. VanderKam is a professor of Hebrew Scriptures at the University of Notre Dame and a member of the international team working to preserve and translate the Dead Sea Scrolls. His books include the award-winning *The Dead Sea Scrolls Today*, and *An Introduction to Early Judaism*.

PETER FLINT, PHD, 1951–2016

Professor and antiquities researcher. Peter Flint was a professor of religious studies at Trinity Western University, where he served as the Canada Research Chair in Dead Sea Scrolls Studies. He was a director of the Dead Sea Scrolls Institute, serving as the editor for the *Psalms Scrolls* as well as the largest intact scroll, the *Great Isaiah Scroll*.

of Qumran. Trever was the first American scholar to come into contact with the scrolls, and he took it upon himself to investigate as carefully as possible the circumstances under which they were found. His conclusions are based on interviews with the Bedouin and evidence from others.[1] The following summarizes the account given by the Bedouin as related by Trever; it is supplemented in places with other early evidence.

The Bedouin Tell Their Story

The discovery of the first scrolls and the long process of bringing them to scholarly and public attention took place at a time of great turmoil and violence in the Middle East. Tensions between Arabs and Jews were high during the British Mandate, and they grew higher and the mayhem increased as the United Nations debated the partition of Palestine. In 1946 or 1947, toward the end of the British Mandate in Palestine, which ended with the partition of the land in May 1948, three men from the Ta'amireh tribe of Bedouin-Khalil Musa, a younger cousin, Jum'a Muhammad Khalil, and a still younger cousin (fifteen years of age), Muhammad Ahmed el-Hamed, nicknamed edh-Dhib (the Wolf)—were tending their flocks of sheep and goats in the region of Ain Feshkha on the northwestern side of the Dead Sea. The tribe customarily moved about in that region between the Jordan River and Bethlehem and had done so for centuries. They had even proved to be a source of archeological discoveries from time to time. Jum'a, we are told, liked to explore caves in the hope of finding gold, and so, when the opportunity presented itself, he would check the nearby cliffs for caves. The key events happened at some point in the winter of 1946–47; Trever reports that "the Bedouin think it was November or December 1946."[2] He describes what happened in this way:

> Jum'a, it was, who happened upon two holes in the side of a rock projection above the plateau where the flocks were grazing. The lower of the two holes was barely large enough "for a cat to enter;" as Jum'a described it in several interviews; the one which was somewhat above eye level was large enough for a slender man to enter. Jum'a threw a rock through the smaller opening and was startled by the strange sound he heard; apparently the

rock shattered an earthenware jar within. Thinking there might be a cache of gold within, he summoned the two other herdsmen to show them the curious holes. In the gathering darkness of evening it was too late to attempt an entrance; the next day had to be devoted to watering their flocks at 'Ain Feshkha, so they agreed to explore the cave two days later.[3]

The youngest of the three, Muhammad Ahmed el-Hamed, returned to the cave openings a few days later while his relatives slept in the early morning; there he climbed into the cave through the larger opening. Returning to Trever's narrative:

> As his eyes became accustomed to the dim light, he saw about ten tall jars lining the walls of the cave, according to his own description. Several of them had covers. Some of the jars had small handles which apparently were used in tying down the covers to seal the contents. In addition, the Bedouins claim that there was a pile of rocks which had fallen from the ceiling, and much broken pottery on the floor of the cave. All but two of the jars proved to be empty. One was filled with reddish earth; from the other one, a jar with a cover, Muhammed pulled two bundles wrapped in cloth which he described as "greenish" in appearance. A third, the largest, was a roll of leather without any wrapping. From his description and hand motions during our interview, as well as from other evidence, it seems quite probable that the larger scroll was the now-famed Isaiah Scroll (lQIsa) and the two smaller ones, the Habakkuk Commentary (lQpHab) and the Manual of Discipline (lQS). Only these three manuscripts were taken by edh-Dhib from the cave that morning.[4]

According to Trever, the fact that the older cousins were angry with edh-Dhib for entering the cave without them and perhaps hiding treasure he may have found (he did show them the three bundles) accounts for his absence from later events. At any rate, a few days later Jum'a brought the scrolls to a Ta'amireh site southeast of Bethlehem, where the scrolls were reportedly left for weeks in a bag hanging on a tent pole. During this time, as they were shown to others, at least some of them suffered some damage: the cover broke off the Isaiah scroll, and the *Manual of Discipline*[5] was split in two.

Selling the Manuscripts

The chronology becomes a little more certain after this. In March 1947, the two older cousins brought the manuscripts to a Bethlehem carpenter and antiquities dealer named Ibrahim 'Ijha, who, after being advised they might have been stolen from a synagogue, returned them to Jum'a after several weeks (Trever calculates this was April 5, 1947) and declared them devoid of archeological worth. Jum'a next brought them to another Bethlehem antiquities dealer, Khalil Eskander Shahin (known as Kando), who was a cobbler by trade. The arrangement made was that Kando would put up a guarantee of five Jordanian pounds (a Jordanian pound was worth about $4 at the time) while George Isha'ya Shamoun, a member of the Syrian Orthodox Church whom Jum'a had met in Bethlehem, kept the scrolls. The Bedouin were to receive two-thirds of any amount that Isha'ya and Kando would be able to gain from selling them. The fact that Isha'ya was from the Syrian Orthodox Church leads us into the next stage in the story about the scrolls.

Metropolitan Athanasius Yeshue Samuel

It was during Holy Week (April 7-13, 1947) that Isha'ya contacted St. Mark's Syrian Orthodox Monastery in the Old City of Jerusalem in the hope of finding out what the manuscripts might be. He apparently thought the texts on them might be in the Syriac language…. The head of the monastery was Metropolitan (Archbishop) Athanasius Yeshue Samuel (1907–1995), who was to become a very important figure in identifying the scrolls and bringing them to the attention of scholars. The Metropolitan agreed to look at a scroll, and Isha'ya and Kando brought part of the Manual of Discipline to the monastery. After examining the piece and hearing the report about how the scrolls were found, he suspected that they might be old and indicated an interest in buying them. That sale was not to be concluded, however, for several months.

Before the sale took place Isha'ya was brought to the cave twice, once by both of the two older Bedouin and once by Khalil Musa alone. Four other scrolls were removed from the cave on the second of these visits, and one of them, apparently the one to be named the Genesis Apocryphon, was left with Kando. The other three[6] of this more recent lot of four manuscripts Khalil Musa and Jum'a kept. In June 1947 they sold the three to Faidi Salahi, also an antiquities dealer, for seven Jordanian pounds (about $28). He also purchased two of the jars from the cave.

The original three scrolls (the large Isaiah scroll, the *Commentary on Habakkuk*, and the *Manual of Discipline*), with the fourth one now in Kando's possession (the Genesis Apocryphon), were sold to Metropolitan Samuel on July 19, 1947. There is a familiar story about how the two Bedouin and Isha'ya, who were coming to deliver the manuscripts, were turned away from the monastery by a monk who knew nothing of their arrangements with Samuel. The mistake was rectified, however, and Kando, on behalf of the Metropolitan, then paid the Bedouin sixteen Jordanian pounds (about $64), since he had sold the four manuscripts to the cleric for twenty-four pounds. Isha'ya, at the Metropolitan's request, brought a priest of St. Mark's to the cave, thus verifying the story about the discovery told by the Bedouin.

While Mar[7] Samuel suspected the scrolls were very old, several individuals to whom he showed them (none of whom was an expert in such matters) doubted their antiquity. In late July Father J. van der Ploeg, an Old Testament scholar at the University of Nijmegen (the Netherlands) who was staying in Jerusalem at the Ecole Biblique, was shown the scrolls, and was the first to recognize that one of them was a copy of Isaiah. Yet he was not at all convinced of the scroll's antiquity and wanted to see the jar in which it was found. No one ever showed it to him and thus he had no convincing reason to accept the cleric's claim that the scrolls were two thousand years old.

Eleazar Sukenik

Mar Samuel continued to seek the advice of others about the age of the scrolls and even brought them with him on a trip to Lebanon and Syria. Despite his efforts, he had no success in confirming his hunch about the parchments. As his quest continued with regard to the four scrolls in his possession, the fate of the other three—the ones purchased by Faidi Salahi—soon took an interesting twist. An Armenian antiquities dealer in Jerusalem named Nasri Ohan contacted Eleazar Lipa Sukenik (1889–1953), professor of archeology at the Hebrew University of Jerusalem. They met on November 25, 1947,[8] in Zone B of partitioned Jerusalem (a neutral place), at the Jaffa Gate.

> *There, through the barbed-wire barricade, the eminent archeologist saw a ragged fragment of leather inscribed in strange Hebrew characters. The dealer told him of its discovery by Bedouins who were seeking to sell many such pieces to their mutual friend, Faidi Salahi. . . . When Sukenik noted a resemblance between the script on the fragment and that which he had often seen scratched on first-century ossuaries, his initial skepticism soon gave way to excited curiosity. He therefore offered to buy the fragments for the Hebrew University and urged the Armenian dealer to get more samples of them from the Bethlehem dealer.[9]*

In his diary entry for November 25, 1947, Sukenik wrote: "Today I met X [antiquity dealer]. A Hebrew book has been discovered in a jar. He showed me a fragment written on parchment. *Genizah*?!"[10] Later that week the dealer, who mentioned the Bedouin story about their discovery in a cave near the Dead Sea, showed Sukenik more fragments at his shop. This made Sukenik resolve to go on a dangerous trip to Bethlehem to see Faidi Salahi, with whom he had dealt in antiquities before. On November 29, 1947, the dealer and Sukenik took the bus to Bethlehem. Salahi told the story of the discovery and showed them his two jars and the scrolls and fragments in his possession. At Sukenik's request, Salahi allowed him to take two scrolls to Jerusalem so that he could make a decision whether to purchase them. He promised to decide within two days.

In a well-known and striking coincidence, as Sukenik was back in Jerusalem taking his first look at the scrolls (the *Thanksgiving Hymns* and the *War Scroll*, also called the *War Rule*),[11] he heard over the radio the news that the UN General Assembly, meeting at Lake Success on Long Island, had voted to partition Palestine and thus to form a Jewish and an Arab state.

In a diary entry for December 1, 1947, Sukenik wrote: "I read a little more in the 'parchments.' I'm afraid of going too far in thinking about them. It may be that this is one of the greatest finds ever made in Palestine, a find we never so much as hoped for."[12] When in December Sukenik mentioned the scrolls to a librarian at the university—who happened to have been one of the persons to whom Mar Samuel had earlier shown his scrolls—he informed Sukenik about the ones the Syrians had in their hands. So, by December 1947, Sukenik was aware of all the scrolls found, although the nature of the ones held by the Metropolitan was not clear to him.

At the request of Metropolitan Samuel, Anton Kiraz, a member of the Syrian Orthodox Church and a prosperous businessman, contacted Sukenik about the scrolls held at St. Mark's.[13] A meeting between Kiraz and Sukenik took place on February 4, 1948, at the YMCA. When the archeologist saw the script of the three texts shown to him, he recognized similarities with the ones he had bought from Salahi. He offered to buy the scrolls and asked that he be allowed to show them to the president of the university, Judah L. Magnes, and other interested individuals. He was permitted to borrow the three scrolls (apparently against Mar Samuel's wishes), and copied several chapters of the larger Isaiah scroll while he had it in his possession. At a meeting on February 6 Sukenik offered Kiraz a fairly large amount of money for the scrolls—500 Jordanian pounds and another 500 if Kiraz could convince the Metropolitan to sell. The Jewish Agency had promised to provide the money needed for the purchase. The sums mentioned tipped off Kiraz and the Metropolitan that they had valuable property, and they began to ponder how much they should ask for them.

John Trever, William Brownlee, and Millar Burrows

Rather than meeting again with Sukenik, Kiraz decided to seek expert opinion at the American School of Oriental Research (ASOR) in Jerusalem. Sukenik was forced to wait (although he and President Magnes tried by telephone to convince the Syrians to sell) while Mar Samuel and Kiraz worked out what they would do with the manuscripts. As Sukenik tells it, "Towards the end of February, I received a letter from him [Kiraz] saying that his co-religionists had decided to postpone selling the manuscripts until relations with the outside world were restored and they could ascertain their proper value. He assured me, however, that as soon as this was done the Hebrew University would have the option of first refusal of the manuscripts."[14] As a matter of fact, on February 18, 1948, Father Butrus Sowmy of St. Mark's had placed a telephone call to ASOR. The person who took the call was John Trever, one of only two scholars present there at the time. It happened that the director of the school, Millar Burrows, of Yale University, was on a trip to Baghdad and had appointed Trever acting director in his absence. Also at the school was William Brownlee, who, like Trever, was a recent Ph.D. and recipient of an annual ASOR fellowship. Ironically, all three had been at the Dead Sea near where the cave was on October 25, 1947, but their purpose then was pleasure and they had no idea they were so close to a place that would soon change their lives. Trever reports that the priest said over the phone that he was the librarian at the monastery and "had been organizing their collection of rare books to prepare a catalogue of them. Among the books he had found some scrolls in ancient Hebrew, which had been in the Monastery for about forty years, but he could find no information about them. He was inquiring, therefore, if our School could supply him with some data for the catalogue."[15] Trever asked him to bring the manuscripts to the school, and Sowmy agreed that he would do so the next day. Trever assumed the manuscripts were recent ones and did not think much about them.

Father Sowmy brought the four manuscripts to the school on February 19, 1948, and showed them to Trever, who happened to have a set of slides illustrating the history of the biblical text. He compared the script of one of Father Sowmy's manuscripts with the writing on several texts shown on the slides and found similarities between the manuscript letters and those on the Nash Papyrus, which dated to the second century BCE. He copied out some lines of one of the manuscripts, but told his visitors that it would take some time to do the careful analysis required to date

the script. Trever tells the story that, as he examined the scrolls, Father Sowmy's brother, Ibrahim, who was a customs official at the Allenby Bridge and who had accompanied his brother to the American school, related some of his thoughts:

> *Ibrahim remarked that while working at the Allenby Bridge he had studied about the history of Jericho and the Dead Sea area. From his studies he had learned about the Essenes who lived in that region during the time of Jesus. As a result he had become very interested in the Essenes. He suggested to the Syrians at the Monastery that these documents might have belonged to that ancient sect of Jews and been deposited by them in the cave during a period of persecution, perhaps when the Romans attacked Jerusalem in A.D. 70. Since the scrolls had been "wrapped like mummies" originally, he added, they must be very ancient, for mummification had long since become a lost art.[16]*

It is intriguing that Ibrahim had come to the conclusion, before knowing what the scrolls were, that they were connected with Essenes and predated the destruction of Jerusalem—views that were to become a near consensus among scholars. Trever, after the Syrians left, was able to identify the passage he had copied as coming from Isaiah. He informed Brownlee about the manuscripts and was understandably eager to see them again. Yet the fact that the parchments were now back in the Old City made access to them difficult under the trying circumstances for travel in Jerusalem at that time.

With considerable difficulty Trever was able to visit the monastery and meet with Father Sowmy and the Metropolitan on February 20, 1948. He told them that he was willing to photograph the manuscripts so that scholars could perform the necessary studies preparatory to determining a date for them. After some debate, they agreed to bring the scrolls to the school the next day. Trever was also allowed to examine the manuscript of Isaiah again. He was further convinced of its authenticity by the presence of scribal corrections in different hands and by repairs to the manuscript itself—procedures that he believed no forger would apply to a manuscript.

It is fortunate that Trever, one of the first scholars to see the scrolls, was also a photographer; the pictures he shot under difficult conditions and with whatever materials were available in war-torn Jerusalem have left the field forever in his debt. Metropolitan Samuel and Father Sowmy brought the manuscripts to the school the next day, where Trever had all the necessary equipment in place in the basement. He was concerned about the work because electricity could be cut off at any time in those days. The procedure took most of the day (February 21, 1948), but Trever and Brownlee, with Sowmy's assistance, succeeded in photographing the entire scroll of Isaiah and the *Commentary on Habakkuk*. At the end of the session and just before the Syrians had to leave, Trever says that he was "determined to take a few color shots. The special camera and plates had been carefully prepared for the purpose that morning, so the shift could be made quickly. Then it was that I made two exposures of Columns 32 and 33, with the rest of the scroll rolled on either side—a picture which has been published probably more often than any other one related to the scrolls."[17]

The Syrians agreed to leave the unphotographed scrolls at the school so that they, too, could be repaired and photographed. Trever later photographed what had appeared to be two manuscripts, but proved to be two parts of the same one (the *Manual of Discipline* [*Rule of the Community*]). Trever and Brownlee returned the manuscripts on February 24, when Trever urged the Syrians to move the scrolls to a safer place and to have experts in America attempt to open the one that could not be unrolled (the *Genesis Apocryphon*).

On February 25, 1948, Trever wrote to William Foxwell Albright, a scholar at Johns Hopkins University and the leading paleographer in the world, to inform him about the manuscripts and to say that, if Albright's dating of the Nash Papyrus to the second century BCE was accurate, the Isaiah scroll, whose script was similar to that of the papyrus, was the oldest biblical manuscript yet found. Meanwhile, Trever continued to work on his photographs as he and Brownlee studied the texts. Brownlee was the first to identify one of them as a commentary on Habakkuk, and was later to publish several important studies of the manuscript. When the director of the school, Millar Burrows, returned, the three studied the manuscript photographs intently. It was not until March 5 that the Syrians divulged to Trever that the manuscripts had not been kept in their library for forty years as first claimed; they admitted they had purchased them the previous year from Bedouin living near Bethlehem and that one of their monks had actually visited the cave where the scrolls had been found. They also indicated their desire to take Trever to the cave.

The complications involved in every move can hardly be overstated. Not only was there the constant danger and difficulty of travel from one part of Jerusalem to another, but the Syrians did not want to work with the Jordanian Department of Antiquities, although the American School was obligated to do so for any archeological work. Trever had already mentioned the scrolls to the director of antiquities, R. W. Hamilton, who encouraged him to visit the cave with the Syrians. They, however, now declined to guide him there out of concern for safety. The Metropolitan also informed Trever that he would soon be leaving Jerusalem to visit Syrian communities in the United States.

On March 15 Trever was cheered by the arrival of a letter from Albright which included the following words:

> My heartiest congratulations 'on the greatest MS discovery of modern times! There is no doubt whatever in my mind that the script is more archaic than that of the Nash Papyrus, standing very close to that of the third-century Egyptian papyri and ostraca in Aramaic. Of course, in the present state of our definite knowledge about Hebrew paleography it would be safe only to date it in the Maccabean period, i.e., not later than the accession of Herod the Great. I should prefer a date around 100 B.C.[18]

Albright added that he doubted the scroll would supply very significant corrections to the traditional Hebrew text of Isaiah, but thought it would "revolutionize our conception of the development of Hebrew orthography. And who knows what treasures may be concealed in the remaining rolls!" Albright's dating of the Isaiah scroll has withstood the test of time, his assessment of the text-critical value of the Isaiah scroll has largely been confirmed, and his hint about other treasures has proved to be prophetic.

After Trever tried unsuccessfully to find a route to the area of the cave that would avoid danger zones, the Americans decided that the time had come to let the Syrians know how important the manuscripts were. On March 17, 1948, Trever and Burrows prepared a statement meant to be a press release, and the next day they showed it to Metropolitan Samuel, who was pleased with it. The statement was then sent for release to the ASOR office in New Haven, Connecticut, although it was not issued until April 11. It was only after the press release was written that the Metropolitan told Trever about the interest of some Jews in the manuscripts, including President Magnes of the Hebrew University. Trever says the Syrians had alluded to this on March 5, when he assumed that Sukenik was one of the individuals involved. On this latter occasion Mar Samuel disclosed that Sukenik had seen the scrolls and wanted to buy them, while Trever informed him that he had let the director of antiquities know about the scrolls. But on March 25 the Metropolitan, after giving Trever another fragment of the Habakkuk Commentary that he happened to find in a book he had opened that morning(!), informed Trever that Father Sowmy had left earlier in the day for Lebanon and had taken the four scrolls with him. A controversy was later to erupt about this, because Trever wrote soon afterward about his happiness that the scrolls had been removed from the country—an act that was illegal. As he writes in his book: "It was a great relief to know that at last the scrolls were out of strife-ridden Jerusalem. By what route or means of transportation Sowmy had departed, I was not informed. That the manuscripts would be placed in a bank vault in Beirut was all the specific information revealed to me. The fact that removing antiquities from the country without an export license was technically illegal was foreign to my thoughts. I rejoiced to know that the scrolls were safe."[19] Soon after this the three scholars of the American School had to leave the country because of the mounting violence. Before departing, Trever and the Syrians agreed on a number of points that would go into a contract giving ASOR the right to publish the scrolls of which the Metropolitan claimed ownership. Through most of February and all of March, of course, Sukenik was left waiting for more word about these scrolls.

The office of ASOR issued the press release on April 11, and it appeared in print on April 12. *The Times* of London for that date carried the following announcement:

> *Yale University announced yesterday the discovery in Palestine of the earliest known manuscript of the Book of Isaiah. It was found in the Syrian monastery of St. Mark in Jerusalem, where it had been preserved in a scroll of parchment dating to about the first century BC. Recently it was identified by scholars of the American School of Oriental Research at Jerusalem.*
>
> *There were also examined at the school three other ancient Hebrew scrolls. One was part of a commentary on the Book of Habakkuk; another seemed to be a manual of discipline of some comparatively little-known sect or monastic order, possibly the Essenes. The third scroll has not been identified.*

The release says much about the four texts and already uses the name "a manual of discipline," which Burrows (reminded of a Methodist "discipline") had given to one of the scrolls. It is also interesting that already at this time a connection with Essenes is mentioned and that the American scholars, all of whom were Protestants, used the term "monastic order" for the group responsible for the texts. Yet what is most surprising about the statement is how the impression is left that the Isaiah scroll was discovered at St. Mark's. Although by the time the release was written the Syrians had told the Americans about the cave, the press release fails to mention it. Burrows wrote later about the release:

> *Unfortunately a mistake had somehow been introduced into the version given to the press. I had written, "The scrolls were acquired by the Syrian Orthodox Monastery of St. Mark." As released to*

the press in America the statement said that the scrolls had been "preserved for many centuries in the library of the Syrian Orthodox Monastery of St. Mark in Jerusalem."[20] Who inserted this I do not know. Professor Sukenik, on reading the published account, issued a statement to set the matter right, pointing out that the scrolls had been found in a cave near the Dead Sea within the previous year. From this statement, which I read in the Rome Daily American of April 28, 1948, when our ship stopped at Genoa, I first learned that the discovery included manuscripts other than those bought by Archbishop Samuel.[21]

With Sukenik's press release announcing the existence of the three scrolls he had purchased, it became public knowledge that seven manuscripts from the same cave were involved.

By this time apparently other texts had also turned up. In early September 1948, Mar Samuel showed the new director of the American School, Ovid Sellers of McCormick Theological Seminary in Chicago, some additional scroll fragments he had acquired. After he was appointed Apostolic Delegate to North America, the cleric brought the four manuscripts and these new pieces with him to the United States; he showed the new fragments to Trever in early February 1949. They had been removed from the cave by one of the men of St. Mark's whom Mar Samuel had sent there in the fall of 1948. Included were fragments from two copies of the book of Daniel. We will meet the Metropolitan again later in our story.

Locating and Excavating the Cave

By the end of 1948, nearly two years after the initial discovery, no scholar had yet located the manuscript cave. This is understandable when one remembers the dangers of travel in the area while the American trio were still in Jerusalem (they left in April). The British Mandate in Palestine ended on May 15, 1948, and war broke out immediately. Peace was not restored until November 1948, and in January 1949 restrictions on travel were removed so that it became possible to visit the area of the cave. Sellers tried to get the Syrians to keep their promise to help in reaching the cave, but Father Bulos, who was then in charge of St. Mark's,

demanded more money than Sellers could pay for the service. At this time Joseph Saad of the Palestine Archaeological Museum was also involved in the delicate efforts to learn about the location of the cave.

The person who was in large part responsible for rediscovery of the cave was a Belgian observer serving on the United Nations staff, Captain Philippe Lippens, who was staying in Jerusalem and became interested in finding the cave. He went around to the various institutions that had had something to do with the scrolls and gathered what information he could, from people and publications, about the location of the cave. Trever reports:

> *On January 24, 1949, he succeeded in obtaining an interview with Major General Lash, the British Commander of the 3rd Brigade of the Arab Legion at Ramallah. General Lash called Brigadier Ashton, his archeological advisor, who in turn contacted G. L. Harding, Chief Inspector of Antiquities, in Amman, Jordan [the area in question was now in Jordanian territory]. Harding confirmed the importance of the cave project. Thus, General Lash dispatched Brigadier Ashton with two Bedouins and Captain Akkash el-Zebn to search the area mentioned in my article.[22]*

Captain Akkash el-Zebn was the one who actually spotted the cave on January 28, 1949, only four days after Lippens had spoken with General Lash (see Figure 1.1). He saw that the earth in front of a cave was disturbed and thought it might be the result of excavating work. This proved to be correct, and Harding was then summoned. Despite some initial skepticism, he soon confirmed that the cave was the one in which the manuscripts had been found. What evidence suggested that this was the scrolls cave, when there were many other caves in the area? Pieces of the same sorts of scroll jars as those sold to Sukenik were found, as were fragments that had broken away from the scrolls we have been describing. An example is the War Scroll, one of Sukenik's three texts; several pieces of it were spotted in the cave by the excavators.[23]

From February 15 to March 5, 1949, a collaborative excavation of the cave was conducted under the auspices of the Jordan Department of Antiquities, the

Ecole Biblique, and the Palestine Archaeological Museum. The leaders were Harding and Roland de Vaux, the director of the Ecole Biblique. Something of the conditions under which they worked emerges from the thanks Harding later recorded to the Arab Legion "for their always willing co-operation and assistance: it is entirely due to the wonderful security which they maintain that archaeological work is possible even in the most remote parts of the country."[24]

The cave is some 8 meters long, 4 meters high, and its width varies from less than 1 meter to about 2 meters. The Bedouin and the Syrians had removed the complete or largely intact manuscripts and the bigger pieces from the cave, but the official excavators found about 600 fragments as well as "numerous scraps of cloth, fragments of wood, olive- and date-stones, palm fibre, leather phylactery cases, and a mass of broken pottery."[25] It turns out that the visitors to the cave who preceded the archeologists had enlarged the lower entrance. It is worthwhile to quote Harding's brief summary of the work of excavation and the finds:

The dump of the illegal excavations was first examined and produced large quantities of sherds and cloth and a few pieces of inscribed leather, including the first piece we had seen in the Phoenician [=paleo-Hebrew] script. The filling of the cave consisted of very fine powdery grey dust mixed with stones fallen from the sides and roof; there was about 50 cm. depth of this type of fill before undisturbed soil was reached. In view of the earlier clearance no stratification could be observed, but several large clumps of coagulated animal droppings made it clear that the cave had been used as a shelter by small wild animals for a considerable period of time.

The only tools it was possible to use in the clearance of the cave were penknives, brushes, tweezers, and fingers, for the fragments are brittle and easily damaged, and sieving was not possible because of the presence of the stones in the fill. Several hundred fragments of inscribed leather and a few fragments of papyrus were recovered, varying in size from pieces bearing one letter, or even half a letter, to a piece containing several lines of text in a column. After the two intact jars acquired by the

Hebrew University were re-moved the remainder were apparently broken up, for we found nothing but sherds. Very few other objects were found . . . apart from the linen; one scroll, or part of a scroll, was found still in its linen wrapper, stuck together to the neck of a jar. . . . Having been exposed to dampness for some time it was corroded to a solid black mass, and it was impossible to separate even a small portion of it.

Inscribed fragments were mounted between glass each day as they were found, and photographed on the spot for safe record. Infrared photographs taken in the studio of the Palestine Archaeological Museum later have revealed texts on pieces which to the naked eye present merely a blank black surface.[26]

His reference to photographing the finds is especially important; photos of the scrolls and fragments have not only preserved a record of what was found but have often proved to be the best way to read the texts they bear. Harding also mentions finding three phylactery cases and a wooden comb.

DeVaux reported on the large amount of pottery (twelve baskets full were taken from the cave), which included the remains of many (at least fifty) jars and covers, some bowls, a pot, a pitcher, and four lamps. In his initial publications on the subject, dating from 1949, de Vaux insisted that almost all of the pottery was from the second century BCE, but later, on the basis of more information, he dated it to the first century CE.[27] In his first report he also bemoaned the disaster left behind by those who had visited the cave after the Bedouin first entered it.[28] According to Mrs. G. M. Crowfoot, who wrote up the results of tests on the linens, they were cleaned "of thick dark brown dust mixed with rat and mouse droppings" and subjected to technical analysis.[29] She estimated that there were pieces from forty, perhaps well over fifty, cloths and divided them into three groups: those with deco ration of blue lines, plain cloths (some having fringes), and jar covers. Their uses seemed to be limited to two: as scroll wrappers and as jar covers.[30] Although admitting the difficulty in dating the linens and the lack of parallels to some features in them, she concluded that the dating suggested by a carbon-14 test on a linen piece from the cave (more on this later) and by coins found at Khirbet Qumran (near the end of the first century CE) was consistent with all the evidence pertinent to the linens.[31]

With hindsight, it is intriguing to read a footnote de Vaux attached to his second report about the cave. He reported that the site of ancient habitation nearest to the cave was Khirbet ["the ruin of"] Qumran, about one kilometer to the south: "We took the opportunity during our stay at the cave to examine the site anew. We will soon publish the results of this survey; it suffices to say here that no archeological clue places this human installation in relation with the cave where the manuscripts were hidden."[32] The statement is correct for that time: there was no archeological indication then connecting the cave and the site, after he and Harding had made only a surface examination and excavated just two tombs.[33] De Vaux was soon to change his mind when he excavated the site itself (see Chapter 3).

Once the cave had been found and it was clear that the Bedouin and Syrians had taken most of the written pieces out, it became important to learn whether any other texts they might have removed were now in other hands. Joseph Saad, under instructions from and with the support of Harding, went to considerable lengths to learn the identity of the Bethlehem antiquities dealer who had sold the scrolls. No informed person had been willing to divulge this information. Dealing in antiquities, which various individuals mentioned in this chapter had done, was illegal, but compromises at times seem unavoidable to ensure that valuable antiquities are properly preserved and so that they can be acquired by the authorities if necessary. Saad became acquainted with Kanda and worked out arrangements to purchase for 1,000 Jordanian pounds the additional manuscript fragments he had obtained.

Subsequent Fate of the Cave 1 Manuscripts

Before turning to subsequent discoveries, we should trace what happened to these famous manuscripts, the first of the Dead Sea Scrolls. Publication proceeded rapidly. Sukenik issued two Hebrew fascicles of a work he entitled *Hidden Scrolls from the Genizah Found in the Judean Desert*.[34] The first of these appeared already in 1948. It contained an introduction to the scrolls; parts of the *War Scroll*, the *Thanksgiving Hymns*, and the fragmentary Isaiah scroll; and several photographic plates of the manuscripts. The second (1949), which appeared after the cave had been found that year, offered more of the same, but also some treatment of the *Rule of the Community*, a copy of Leviticus, the longer Isaiah scroll, and the *Commentary on Habakkuk*, with a number of photographic plates. Sukenik died in 1953, but the Hebrew University appointed a committee to publish the material he had left behind. The posthumous volume completed the publication of his three texts, with more photographs, the introductions for the two earlier fascicles, and excerpts from Sukenik's diary.[35]

The American scholars, too, published the texts they had photographed with admirable promptness. The first publication in 1950 presented an introduction followed by photographs of the entire larger Isaiah scroll and the *Commentary on Habakkuk* with transcriptions of the text on the facing page.[36] The *Manual of Discipline* (the *Rule of the Community*) appeared the next year, again with photographic plates and facing transcriptions.[37]

Metropolitan Samuel, who had come to the United States in 1949, attempted to sell the manuscripts in his possession. The story about this is complicated, but his scrolls were displayed several times (including at the Library of Congress in October 1949). No buyer stepped forth, perhaps dissuaded by rumors about a high asking price or by continuing questions about who was the legal owner of these antiquities.[38]

To make a long story short, Mar Samuel placed an advertisement in *The Wall Street Journal* of June 1, 1954. It read: "'The Four Dead Sea Scrolls' Biblical Manuscripts dating back to at least 200 BC are for sale. This would be an ideal gift to an educational or religious institution by an individual or group. Box F 206, The Wall Street Journal" (p. 14). The ad, which ran for several days, was brought to the attention of Yigael Yadin, Sukenik's son, who was in the United States at the time. Working through intermediaries in order to keep his interest a secret, he arranged to have the authenticity of the scrolls verified and then purchased (July 1, 1954). The individual who made the purchase possible—the final price was $250,000—was the philanthropist D. S. Gottesman. Each of the four scrolls was flown in a separate plane to Israel, where, at a press conference on February 13, 1955, the prime minister of Israel announced what had happened.

This meant that the state of Israel now possessed all seven of the first scrolls discovered. The state decided at that time to set up the Shrine of the Book Foundation, a project that Gottesman agreed to fund as well. Eventually the Shrine of the Book was built at the Israel Museum in Jerusalem, with the inauguration taking place on April 20, 1965. There the seven manuscripts are housed, along with some other texts owned by Israel.[39]

The Other Caves

The scrolls cave that engendered so much publicity and excitement turned out not to be the only one containing written remains. In February 1952, Bedouin explorers found another cave, this time containing only fragments of manuscripts and no complete scrolls. The discovery occurred while Harding, de Vaux, and others were excavating caves farther south in the Wadi Murabba'at where material, including documentary texts, dating from the second Jewish revolt against Rome (132–35 CE) had been located by Bedouin in October 1951. The second scrolls cave is just a short distance south of the first, also in the cliffs on the northwest shore of the Dead Sea. In this case, Kando soon offered for sale the fragmentary manuscripts taken from the cave; with the agreement of the Jordanian Department of Antiquities, they were purchased by the Palestine Archaeological Museum and the Ecole Biblique.

After learning about the discovery of the cave, Harding called together William Reed, director of ASOR, Father Dominique Barthelemy of the Ecole Biblique, and Joseph Saad, and they quickly located the cave. An expedition was led by Reed and de Vaux, who were assisted by three others from the Ecole Biblique, three Arab leaders, and twenty-four Bedouin. The group, divided into seven teams, explored the cave and the surrounding region from March 10 to

March 29, 1952. De Vaux wrote that the purpose of the caves expedition was not only to verify that the fragments came from this cave, but also and especially to determine the area inhabited by the group who had left the manuscripts. He commented on how thoroughly the Bedouin had cleared the cave of its contents: of the written material, they had left behind only two small fragments, which the archeologists found and studied.[40] It is noteworthy that the debris left behind by the Bedouin also contained fragments of cylindrical jars, as the first cave did.

This cave expedition surveyed all the caves in an 8-kilometer stretch from Hadjar el-Asba in the north to a kilometer south of Ain Feshkha. Khirbet Qumran lies at approximately the midpoint in this stretch of land. De Vaux wrote about the work: "An exploration was made of the holes, caves, and crevices with which the cliffs are everywhere honeycombed. Of the soundings taken 230 proved barren, but 40 of these cavities contained pottery and other objects. These remains range in date from the Chalcolithic to the Arab period, but 26 of the sites explored yielded pottery which was identical with that of the first cave of Khirbet Qumran."[41] Most of the caves with objects in them were to the north of or adjacent to Khirbet Qumran; only a few were farther to the south. Also, two partially paved roads were detected, one connecting Qumran with the west and another leading south from it to Ain Feshkha. De Vaux admitted that the survey was not exhaustive. The heat became oppressive, the workers fell ill or quit, and so the project came to an end.[42] Its nonexhaustive character soon became evident when other text-bearing caves were found in the area.

In the course of the caves expedition, on March 14, the archeologists did find a third cave with inscribed fragments. This was the first time that an official group was able to spot such a cave before the Bedouin did. Cave 3 is located about a half kilometer to the north of Cave 1 and contained bits and pieces of what their editor Maurice Baillet later identified as fourteen manuscripts; the fifteenth text taken from Cave 3 is the famous Copper Scroll, a list of treasure sites inscribed on copper. Again, many cylindrical jars were found in the cave.[43]

In August 1952, Bedouin explorers, who were obviously carrying out their own major survey, made a most significant discovery. In July and August they had already found the sites known as Khirbet Mird and Nahal Hever, where important manuscripts had survived. Then also in August they came upon what is now known as Qumran Cave 4 (see Figure 1.2), the cave with the largest number of written remains in the area. De Vaux was to write later that, in conducting the cave survey in March 1952, "we restricted our research to the rock cliffs and did not examine the marl terrace stretching in front of them. The reason was that the nature of the terrain is such as to exclude in this marl terrace the presence of any natural caves suitable for human use. All that we noticed were cavities eroded by water which were archaeologically barren. In this we erred."[44]

It turns out that, according to the story they told,[45] the Bedouin were alerted to the presence of a cave near Khirbet Qumran by an older member of their tribe. One night, as some of the Ta'amireh were discussing their discoveries in the vicinity of the cave, he remembered that when he was young he had chased a partridge in the area of Khirbet Qumran. The partridge went into a hole that turned out to be the opening of a cave, which the Bedouin entered and where he found pottery and other objects. With the information supplied by the older man, younger Bedouin soon found the cave and the mass of fragments preserved in it.

They tried to sell about 15,000 of these in Jerusalem and gave false information about where the cave was in order to protect their treasure and profit. On September 20, 1952, Harding was contacted by de Vaux, who said that Bedouin had offered him a huge quantity of fragments and that he had purchased some of them for 1,300 pounds. Harding went to the area of Qumran (this much was at least clear about the cave's location) and caught the Bedouin at their work, who had apparently been removing material from the cave for three days before they were stopped. They made off with their valuable discoveries, meaning that what they had taken would have to be purchased from them (no small matter when thin budgets were already strained by the amounts that had been spent to acquire other manuscripts and fragments). An official

excavation of the cave was conducted September 22–29, 1952, and fragments from many more manuscripts were recovered. As de Vaux was later to write:

> The Bedouin had already removed more than half the fill of the cave and had worked so carefully that only a few small fragments were found in their debris. But the archeologists themselves explored the lower levels of the cave and a small underground room that the Bedouin had not reached, and they discovered the original entrance. They gathered almost a thousand fragments, belonging to one hundred different manuscripts which are almost all represented among the fragments bought from the Bedouin. This certifies the origin of the lot sold by them. On the other hand this scattering of the parts of the same manuscripts indicates an ancient upheaval.[46]

Eventually scholars were to identify the remains of almost 600 manuscripts in Cave 4.

This cave is located only a short distance from the building ruins at Qumran. It is an artificial cave hollowed out in the marl overlooking the Wadi Qumran. Although called Cave 4, it is actually an "oval chamber opening on to two smaller chambers which had been partially eroded away."[47] De Vaux commented that there was relatively little pottery found in it, although pieces from several jars and other objects were present. Texts were found in both chambers of the cave (called 4Qa and b), but they were mixed by the Bedouin, with the result that texts are identified simply as coming from Cave 4. However, almost all of the texts and pottery came from what de Vaux called the first room of Cave 4,4Qa.

The sheer number of fragments emerging from Cave 4 changed the way in which the Qumran discoveries were handled. Prior to this find, it was expensive but feasible to purchase all of the material and prepare it for swift publication. The Jordanian authorities had established a going rate of one pound per square centimeter of inscribed surface, and as the fragments poured in, the rate went down to half of that. With the arrival of the Cave 4 fragments, the financially strapped Jordanian government nevertheless made 15,000 pounds available for purchase.

When more money was soon needed but was not forthcoming from the treasury, the government, at Harding's suggestion, invited foreign institutions to purchase fragments with the stipulation that, after the work preparatory to editing them was finished, they would be given an equivalent number in quantity and quality to the ones they had purchased.[48] As things turned out, several institutions responded: McGill University (Montreal), the Vatican Library, the University of Manchester, the University of Heidelberg, McCormick Theological Seminary (Chicago), All Souls Church in New York, and Oxford University. In the end, the government reversed its decision and ordered that the texts remain in Jordan, but the institutions were reimbursed. In this way the perhaps 15,000 fragments from Cave 4 were, for the most part, kept in the country and not scattered over the world. John Allegro, one of the team of scholars appointed to work on the scrolls from Cave 4 and a scholar who wrote sensitively about the Bedouin and Jordanian side of things, has commented about the situation:

> The Ta'amireh jealously guarded their secrets now, and their cave hunting had become a thoroughgoing business, directed by the leaders of the tribe, and engaged in by all the able-bodied members. Nobody in the world knows that desolate area like these people, and it is certain that if it had not been for them the Dead Sea Scrolls would still have remained undiscovered. If the prices are high, the work is tedious and back-breaking in the extreme, and certainly no member of the expedition who scaled the cliffs and combed the hundreds of caves, sifting the dust between their finger-tips for days on end, in a stifling atmosphere which is just indescribable, would begrudge the Ta'amireh a penny of their gains.[49]

The fact that Cave 4 was so close to the ruins raised the question of a relation between Khirbet Qumran and the scrolls with a new urgency. If it had been plausible to wonder about a connection between the scrolls and the building ruins when only Caves 1–3 were known, it became more difficult to deny a connection with the discovery of Cave 4. One would almost have to pass through the structures to reach the cave.

While excavating Cave 4, the archeologists located Cave 5 some 25 meters farther north. It held fragmentary remains of what have been arranged by editor J. T. Milik into twenty-five units.[50] Although the yield from this cave was nothing like what Cave 4 had to offer, its location so close to the buildings again suggested a connection. Cave 5 was excavated September 25–28, 1952. The Bedouin, early in September, had found another manuscript cave in the cliffs directly west of Khirbet Qumran. Cave 6 held remains of thirty-one scrolls, a large number of which were papyrus rather than leather.[51]

After the excitement of 1952, no new manuscript caves were discovered until 1955, when during an official excavation lasting from February 2 until April 6, archeologists found four more caves during a survey of the entire side of the marl terrace near Khirbet Qumran. All four had been artificially carved out. This brought to six the number of caves immediately adjacent to the buildings. Caves 7–10 yielded few texts: Cave 7 had nineteen, Cave 8 had five, Cave 9 had one, and Cave 10 had only an ostracon. These caves had collapsed and suffered erosion. Though Cave 8 yielded very few texts, it did contain about one hundred leather thongs and leather tabs with eyelets in them—items used for fastening scrolls. It is possible, therefore, that this cave was where such items were made as part of a scroll-producing process; or perhaps their presence means only that Cave 8 was where they were hidden.[52]

The final discovery of a cave housing manuscripts came in 1956, this time by the Bedouin. In January a group of them cleared out the blocked entrance of the cave and found some rather well preserved manuscripts in it. Other than Cave 3, this is the northernmost of the caves. In Cave 11 were the remains of some thirty-one texts, including a long and interesting Psalms scroll and the *Temple Scroll*.[53]

The Meaning of the Dead Sea Scrolls: Their Significance for Understanding the Bible, Judaism, Jesus, and Christianity (London: T & T Clark, 2005), pp. 3–18
Reprinted with permission of the authors

Endnotes

1 Westwood, NJ: Revell, 1965. Trever refers to numerous interviews (between November 1961 and July 1964, i.e., about fourteen to seventeen years after the events in question) with the Bedouin involved. Specifically he mentions an interview with them conducted by Anton Kiraz (an individual whose name will appear in the story) and J. F. Docmac on November 24, 1961; the Bedouins' oral answers (tape recorded) to sixty-three questions formulated by Trever and put to them on November 25; Trever's interviews with them on July 29 and August 10, 1962, with Kiraz and Docmac as interpreters; and Kiraz's later questions to them and his report in letters about their answers.

2 *The Untold Story,* 103.

3 *The Untold Story,* 103–4.

4 *The Untold Story,* 104.

5 The scroll was called the *Manual of Discipline,* but is now named the *Rule of the Community.*

6 They were a second, more fragmentary copy of Isaiah, the *Thanksgiving Hymns,* and the *War Scroll.*

7 The word Mar is an ecclesiastical title of respect and means something like *Lord* or *Sir.*

8 This is the date Sukenik gives for the meeting (Sukenik, ed., *Dead Sea Scrolls of the Hebrew University* [Jerusalem: Magnes, 1955], 14). Trever implies it was November 24 (*The Untold Story,* 110).

9 Trever, *The Untold Story,* 110-11.

10 *Dead Sea Scrolls of the Hebrew University,* 17. A *genizah* is a storage place for old manuscripts no longer in use.

11 On December 21, 1947, Sukenik bought the third manuscript, the fragmentary Isaiah scroll, from Faidi Salahi.

12 *Dead Sea Scrolls of the Hebrew University,* 17.

13 Sukenik had earlier excavated some tombs found on property owned by Kiraz.

14 *Dead Sea Scrolls of the Hebrew University,* 16.

15 *The Untold Story,* 14.

16 *The Untold Story,* 25.

17 *The Untold Story,* 44. The famous picture can be seen in many places, such as opposite p. 129 in *The Untold Story.*

18 *The Untold Story,* 85.

19 *The Untold Story,* 94.

20 Note that this formulation differs from the one quoted above.

21 Burrows, *The Dead Sea Scrolls* (New York: Viking Press, 1955) 17–18.

22 *The Untold Story,* 121. Trever's article was "The Discovery of the Scrolls," *Biblical Archaeologist* 11 (1948) 46–57.

23 See *The Untold Story,* 203, n. 2, for a complete summary of the pieces of the individual manuscripts that were recovered in the cave.

24 "G. L. Harding, "The Archaeological Finds: Introductory: The Discovery, the Excavation, Minor Finds," *in* ed. D. Barthélemy and J. T. Milik, eds., *Discoveries in the Judaen Caves* (DJD) 1: *Qumran Cave I* (Oxford: Clarendon Press, 1955), 6.

25 R. de Vaux, *Archaeology and the Dead Sea Scrolls* (The Schweich Lectures, 1959; rev. ed., London: Oxford University Press, 1973), 49.

26 "Introductory," DJD 1:6–7.

27 "La Poterie," DJD 1:11.

28 "Post-Scriptum: La cachette des manuscrits hebreux," *Revue Biblique* 56 (1949), 234.

29 "The Linen Textiles," DJD 1:18.

30 "The Linen Textiles," 19.

31 "The Linen Textiles," 24–27.

32 "La grotte des manuscrits hebreux," *Revue Biblique* 56 (1949), 586, n. 2 (translation here by VanderKam).

33 See his essay "Fouille au Khirbet Qumran: Rapport preliminaire," *Revue Biblique 60* (1953), 89.

34 Both fascicles were published by the Mosad Bialik in Jerusalem.

35 See note 8 above. The edition was prepared for publication by N. Avigad. This is an English translation of a Hebrew volume published in 1954.

36 Millar Burrows, ed., with the assistance of John C. Trever and William H. Brownlee, *The Dead Sea Scrolls of St. Mark's Monastery,* vol. 1: *The Isaiah Manuscript and the Habakkuk Commentary* (New Haven, CT: American Schools of Oriental Research, 1950). The frontpiece has a photograph of Mar Athanasius Y. Samuel, and the volume is dedicated to him "in appreciation of the privilege of making these texts available to the world of scholarship."

37 Millar Burrows, ed., with the assistance of John C. Trever and William H. Brownlee, *The Dead Sea Scrolls of St. Mark's Monastery,* vol. 2, fascicle 2: *Plates and Transcription of the Manual of Discipline* (New Haven, CT: American Schools of Oriental Research, 1951). Although this was called fascicle 2, fascicle 1, which was to contain the *Genesis Apocryphon* (see vol. 1, p. x), has never appeared. This manuscript (then called the *Lamech* Scroll) had not been unrolled at that time because of its poor state of preservation.

38 Trever says that in an interview between himself and Sukenik in New York on March 21, 1949, Sukenik reported he was readying a document "to circulate to all libraries and universities which might consider purchasing the scrolls. In it he was warning them that such a purchase would be illegal and subject to antiquities laws, which could be invoked to return the scrolls to the country of their origin" (*The Untold Story,* 126). He was not the only one to challenge the Metropolitan's claim (see pp. 136–38).

39 On the Shrine of the Book, see A. Reitman, "Shrine of the Book," *Encyclopedia of the Dead Sea Scrolls,* ed. L. Schiffman and J. VanderKam (2 vols., New York and Oxford: Oxford University Press, 2000) 2:74–75. N. Avigad and Yadin published much of what could be deciphered on the fourth scroll, the only one of the Metropolitan's texts not issued by the Americans, as *A Genesis Apocryphon* (Jerusalem: Magnes Press and Heikhal ha-Sefer [Shrine of the Book], 1956).

40 "Archeologie," *Les 'petites grottes' de Qumran,* ed. M. Baillet, in T. Milik, and R. de Vaux (DJD 3.1; Oxford: Clarendon Press, 1962), 3. The thirty-three texts from Cave 2 were published in this volume.

41 *Archaeology and the Dead Sea* Scrolls, 51.

42 "Archeologie," *Les 'petites grottes'* DJD 3, 1:4.

43 See: *Les 'petites grottes,'* 94–104. Milik's edition of the Copper Scroll is on pp. 201–302.

44 *Archaeology and the Dead Sea Scrolls,* 52.

45 DeVaux, "Archeologie," in R. de Vaux and T. Milik, eds., *Qumran Grotte 4 II I. Archeologie, II Tefillin, Mezuzot et Targums (4Q/28-4QI57),* (DJD 6; Oxford: Clarendon Press, 1977) 3.

46 "Archeologie," *Qumran Grotte 4 II,* 4 (translation here by J. VanderKam).

47 DeVaux, *Archaeology and the Dead Sea Scrolls,* 52.

48 Harding, *The Antiquities of Jordan* (London: Lutterworth Press, 1959) 201–2.

49 Allegro, *The Dead Sea* Scrolls (Harmondsworth, UK: Penguin, 1956) 37–38. While this was happening, there were reports in the

press of fabulous sums—like $1 million—that Metropolitan Samuel was asking for his four scrolls.

50 He published the texts in *Les 'petites grottes,'* 167–97.

51 They were published by M. Baillet in *Les 'petites grottes,'* 105–41.

52 Baillet published the material in *Les 'petites grottes,'* 142–64.

53 The Psalms scroll was published by J. Sanders, *The Psalms Scroll of Qumron Cave II (11QPsa),* (DJD) 4; Oxford: Clarendon Press, 1965). For the *Temple Scroll,* see Y. Yadin, *The Temple Scroll* (3 vols., Jerusalem: Israel Exploration Society, Institute of Archaeology of the Hebrew University of Jerusalem, and the Shrine of the Book, 1977 [Hebrew]. The English edition appeared in 1983. The remaining texts from Cave 11 appeared officially in F. Garcia Martinez, E. J. C. Tigchelaar, and A. S. van der Woude, eds., *Qumran Cave 11 II: 11Q2–18, 11Q20–31* (DJD 23; Oxford: Clarendon Press, 1998).

Lesson

2

MASADA VERSUS YAVNEH
DIVERGENT JEWISH RESPONSES TO ROMAN TYRANNY

Last Hours of Brave Zealots on Masada, Alex Levin.
(www.ArtLevin.com)

The last stand of Masada's defenders in the year 73 CE has resonated strongly with many modern Israelis, but at the time there were Jews who believed the revolt against Rome was imprudent. What lay behind the clamoring for revolt and why did others oppose it? Why did the people at Masada continue fighting even after Jerusalem was destroyed? By judicious use of the sources, we hope to paint a non-caricatural picture of this great debate that had grave consequences for the rest of Jewish history.

TEXT 1

JOSEPHUS, *THE JEWISH WAR* 7:8*

It is clear that we will be captured at the break of day, but it is still possible for us to die in a glorious manner, together with our dearest friends. Our enemies cannot by any means hinder this, although they very much desire to take us alive. . . .

Let our wives die before they are abused and our children before they taste slavery. And after we have slain them, let us mutually confer this benefit upon each other, preserving our liberty as a noble shroud.

But first let us destroy our belongings and the fortress by fire. I am sure it will cause great grief to the Romans that they will not be able to capture us alive and that they will be deprived of our belongings. Let us spare nothing but our provisions. They will be a testimonial when we are dead that we were not subdued for want of necessities, but that in keeping with our initial resolve, we had preferred death over slavery.

**JOSEPHUS
CA. 37–100**

Jewish historian. Born Yosef ben Matityahu Hakohen, he changed his name to Titus Flavius Josephus upon becoming a Roman citizen. His two principal works, *The Jewish War* and *Antiquities of the Jews,* are considered primary sources in documenting Jewish history during the Second Temple period. Despite surrendering his garrison to the Romans during the great revolt and later accepting Roman patronage, Josephus viewed himself as a faithful Jew.

---

* All quotes from Josephus in this lesson have been taken from William Whiston's eighteenth-century translation (*The Works of Josephus,* [Peabody, MA: Hendrickson, 1987]), revised and updated by JLI to reflect a more modern English, and consulting Henry S. J. Thackeray's translation (Cambridge MA: Harvard University Press, 1927) to ensure accuracy.

TEXT **2**

JOSEPHUS, *THE JEWISH WAR* 2:17

At this time, some of those who encouraged the people to go to war made an assault upon a certain fortress called Masada. They took it by treachery, slew the Romans that were there, and put their own garrison there.

At the same time, another incident occurred at the Temple. Elazar, son of Ananias the High Priest, a very bold youth who was the Temple captain, persuaded those that officiated in the Temple to receive no gift or sacrifice from a foreigner. This was the true beginning of our war with the Romans, for they rejected the sacrifice on behalf of Caesar and Rome on this account. When many of the chief priests and notables besought them not to omit the sacrifice, which it was customary for them to offer for the ruler, they would not be prevailed upon.

Masada, *Edward Lear, 1858.*
(Fine Arts Museum of San Francisco)

TEXT 3

DAVID M. RHOADS, *ISRAEL IN REVOLUTION* (PHILADELPHIA: FORTRESS, 1979), P. 31

Although the principles of the provincial arrangement were tolerable to most Jews, what took place in practice was often less than satisfactory. It is not hard to imagine how the Roman officers in Palestine did not always comprehend or appreciate the religious practices of the Jews. It must have seemed strange to them that the Jews reacted so stubbornly and belligerently to matters which seemed to them so common and so inconsequential such as the placing of image-bearing banners in Jerusalem. The difficulty of understanding Jewish peculiarities sometimes led the procurators to side with the Hellenistic part of the population in Palestine. At other times, as we shall see, matters of religious concern to Jews were treated with indifference or disdain. Related disruptions were frequently handled by military suppression. Such an absence of diplomacy on the part of the procurators simply served to escalate Jewish indignation.

DAVID M. RHOADS, PhD

Professor emeritus, Lutheran School of Theology at Chicago. His *Israel in Revolution 6–74 CE*, critically evaluates the writings of Josephus—the major source for our knowledge of political events leading up to the revolt against Rome in 66 CE—to shed light on important questions about the causes and events of the revolt.

TEXT 4

WILLIAM SHAKESPEARE, *THE MERCHANT OF VENICE,* ACT 3, SCENE 1

If it will feed nothing else, it will feed my revenge. He hath disgraced me and hindered me half a million, laughed at my losses, mocked at my gains, scorned my nation, thwarted my bargains, cooled my friends, heated mine enemies—and what's his reason? I am a Jew. Hath not a Jew eyes? Hath not a Jew hands, organs, dimensions, senses, affections, passions? Fed with the same food, hurt with the same weapons, subject to the same diseases, healed by the same means, warmed and cooled by the same winter and summer as a Christian is? If you prick us, do we not bleed? If you tickle us, do we not laugh? If you poison us, do we not die? And if you wrong us, shall we not revenge?

THE MERCHANT OF VENICE

A play written by William Shakespeare (1564–1616). In the play, Shylock is represented as making a wager with Antonio, a merchant of Venice, setting the return of a loan against a pound of flesh to be forfeited by Antonio if he fails to repay. Antonio fails to meet his bond, and Shylock, who in the meantime had lost his daughter Jessica because of her elopement with a Christian, insists on the forfeit. Numerous commentators have discussed the extent to which this play was influenced by the antisemitic sentiments of its day.

Depiction of the Roman siege of Gamla, a rebel stronghold in the Golan Heights, which fell in 67 CE.

TEXT 5

DAVID M. RHOADS, *ISRAEL IN REVOLUTION* (PHILADELPHIA: FORTRESS, 1979), P. 151

It may have been that some . . . were convinced at the beginning of the war that the Jews could defend their homeland. They might have thought they could depend upon the support of the Jews throughout the empire. Letters were sent to the large and influential Jewish communities in the Parthian Empire to the east, encouraging them to persuade the Parthians to wage war against the Romans. And there was dissatisfaction with the Emperor Nero on the part of nations within the empire. Perhaps . . . other revolts against Roman domination might follow their own.

Coins minted during the Hasmonean Period, when Jews had political sovereignty under the Maccabees. These coins are dated to the 1st century BCE.
(Photo Credit: Meidad Suchowolski)

TEXT 6

THANKSGIVING LITURGY FOR CHANUKAH

בִּימֵי מַתִּתְיָהוּ בֶּן יוֹחָנָן כֹּהֵן גָּדוֹל, חַשְׁמוֹנָאִי וּבָנָיו, כְּשֶׁעָמְדָה מַלְכוּת יָוָן
הָרְשָׁעָה, עַל עַמְּךָ יִשְׂרָאֵל, לְהַשְׁכִּיחָם תּוֹרָתֶךָ וּלְהַעֲבִירָם מֵחֻקֵּי רְצוֹנֶךָ,
וְאַתָּה בְּרַחֲמֶיךָ הָרַבִּים, עָמַדְתָּ לָהֶם בְּעֵת צָרָתָם. רַבְתָּ אֶת רִיבָם, דַּנְתָּ אֶת
דִּינָם, נָקַמְתָּ אֶת נִקְמָתָם. מָסַרְתָּ גִבּוֹרִים בְּיַד חַלָּשִׁים, וְרַבִּים בְּיַד מְעַטִּים,
וּטְמֵאִים בְּיַד טְהוֹרִים, וּרְשָׁעִים בְּיַד צַדִּיקִים, וְזֵדִים בְּיַד עוֹסְקֵי תוֹרָתֶךָ...

In the days of Matityahu, the son of Yochanan the High Priest, the Hasmonean and his sons, when the wicked Hellenic government rose up against Your people Israel to make them forget Your Torah and violate the decrees of Your will: but You, in Your abounding mercies, stood by them in the time of their distress. You waged their battles, defended their rights, and avenged the wrong done to them. You delivered the mighty into the hands of the weak, the many into the hands of the few, the impure into the hands of the pure, the wicked into the hands of the righteous, and the wanton sinners into the hands of those who occupy themselves with Your Torah. . . .

THANKSGIVING LITURGY FOR CHANUKAH

The Thanksgiving liturgy for Chanukah, which begins with the words, *Ve'al hanisim* ("for the miracles"), is recited on the Chanukah festival during the *Amidah* prayer and during Grace after Meals. The *Tosefta* (a work from the same generation as the Mishnah) calls for the recitation of this prayer, which recaps the miraculous triumph of the Maccabees over the Syrian-Greeks in the 2nd century BCE.

TEXT 7

SPEECH OF AGRIPPA II, JOSEPHUS, *THE JEWISH WAR* 2:16

The same procurator will not remain forever, and it is probable that his successors will come with more moderate inclinations. But as for war, if it is started, it is not easily terminated or executed without calamity. . . .

What sort of troops and armor do you rely on? Where is your fleet that will sweep the Roman seas? Where is your treasury needed for your undertaking? . . . Hasn't our army been beaten often even by the neighboring nations, while the power of the Romans is invincible in all parts of the habitable earth? . . . Are you richer than the Gauls, stronger than the Germans, wiser than the Greeks, more numerous than all the peoples of the world? Why are you confident that you can oppose the Romans?

Perhaps you will answer that it is hard to endure servitude. This is true, but how much harder is this to the Greeks, who were esteemed as the noblest of all people under the sun! And nevertheless, although they inhabit a large territory, they are subservient to Rome. . . . When almost all people under the sun submit to the Roman arms, will you be the only people that wages war against them? . . .

AGRIPPA II
CA. 28–100 CE

Son of Agrippa I, who was king of Judea between 41–44 CE and was the grandson of King Herod. After his father's death in 44 CE, Judea was again ruled by Roman procurators. A few years later, Agrippa II was appointed ruler over considerable areas of the Galilee and the eastern side of the Jordan River and was also appointed superintendent over the Temple in Jerusalem. Unlike his father, he did little to mitigate the unhappy lot of the Jews, and once the revolt erupted, he stood unreservedly on the side of the Romans.

Have pity, therefore, if not on your children and wives, then upon this city and its sacred precincts. Spare the Temple and preserve for yourselves the holy house and all of its holy treasures. Because once the Romans conquer you, they will no longer abstain from these, seeing that their former forbearance had been met so ungratefully.

Capture of Jerusalem, Flemish school, ca. 1468. (Museum of Fine Arts, Ghent, Belgium)

TEXT 8

DAVID M. RHOADS, *ISRAEL IN REVOLUTION* (PHILADELPHIA: FORTRESS, 1979), PP. 30–31

The Romans generally guaranteed the local customs of the people in the empire. As a result of the enlightened policies of Augustus, the Jews had been granted special considerations by the Romans regarding their religious freedom. Those privileges, which were the most extensive given to any subject people in the empire, continued under the provincial relationship. The Romans did not require emperor worship from the Jews. They accepted Jewish allegiance in the form of two daily sacrifices in the temple on behalf of the emperor's welfare. They permitted the Jews to accumulate sacred monies for the temple treasury without interference. The Romans did not conscript Jewish men into the Roman army, since such service would have conflicted with the observance of the Sabbath and other Jewish festivals. Also, they did not require that Jews appear in court on the Sabbath. In addition, Rome was committed to respect such local customs as the prohibition against images in Jerusalem. In principle, the Jewish religion had the protection of the Roman Empire.

TEXT 9

RABBI OVADIAH SEFORNO, GENESIS 33:4

> "וַיָּרָץ עֵשָׂו" (בְּרֵאשִׁית לג, ד). נֶהְפַּךְ לִבּוֹ כְּמוֹ רֶגַע בְּהַכְנָעוֹתָיו שֶׁל יַעֲקֹב.
> כְּאָמְרָם זִכְרוֹנָם לִבְרָכָה (תַּעֲנִית כ, א) שֶׁאֲחִיָּהוּ הַשִּׁילוֹנִי קִלֵּל אֶת יִשְׂרָאֵל
> בְּקָנֶה הַנִּכְנַע לְכָל הָרוּחוֹת. הֵן לֹא עָשׂוּ כֵן בִּרְיוֹנֵי בַּיִת שֵׁנִי - לֹא הָיָה נֶחְרַב
> בֵּית מִקְדָּשֵׁנוּ.

RABBI OVADIAH SEFORNO
1475–1550

Biblical exegete, philosopher, and physician. Seforno was born in Cesena, Italy. After gaining a thorough knowledge of Talmud and the sciences, he moved to Rome where he studied medicine and taught Hebrew to the German scholar Johannes Reuchlin. Seforno eventually settled in Bologna where he founded and directed a yeshivah until his death. His magnum opus is a biblical commentary focused on the simple interpretation of text, with an emphasis on philology and philosophy.

"Esau ran [to meet Jacob and embraced him; he threw his arms around his neck and kissed him; and they wept]" (GENESIS 33:4). Esau had a sudden change of heart upon observing Jacob's non-defying posture. Indeed, our sages taught (TALMUD, TA'ANIT 20A) that when Ahijah cursed the Jews to be "like a reed swaying in the water" (I KINGS 14:15), [the curse was laced with hidden blessing in that] a reed submits to all winds [and therefore never breaks, unlike a cedar that withstands most winds, but is broken by the gale]. If only the rebels during the Second Temple would have adopted a non-defying posture, our Temple would not have been destroyed.

TEXT 10a

JOSEPHUS, *THE JEWISH WAR* 2:8

A Galilean, whose name was Judas, pressed his country-men to revolt. He said they were cowards if they would pay a tax to the Romans and submit to mortal masters in addition to their subservience to God. This man was a teacher of a peculiar sect of his own.

TEXT 10b

JOSEPHUS, *ANTIQUITIES* 18:1

These men agree in all other things with the Pharisaic teachings, but they have an uninfringeable attachment to liberty, and say that God is to be their only ruler and master. They also are not afraid of any kind of death, nor are they weakened by the deaths of their relatives and friends, nor can any such fear make them refer to any human as their lord.

TEXT 11

LEVITICUS 25:55 ⊞

▌ כִּי לִי בְנֵי יִשְׂרָאֵל עֲבָדִים, עֲבָדַי הֵם אֲשֶׁר הוֹצֵאתִי אוֹתָם מֵאֶרֶץ מִצְרָיִם. ▐

For the Children of Israel are servants to Me; they are My servants, whom I took out of the land of Egypt.

TEXT 12

JOSEPHUS, *THE JEWISH WAR* 2:17

Meanwhile, one Menachem, the son of Judas the Galilean . . . took his friends with him and went to Masada. He broke open King Herod's armory and gave arms to his own people and to other brigands. With these men as his guards, he returned as a king to Jerusalem to become the leader of the revolt.

Ostracons (fragments) from pottery found on Masada, inscribed with Jewish names, dated to ca. 70 CE.

TEXT 13

AVOT DERABBI NATAN, CH. 4 ⚙

וּכְשֶׁבָּא אַסְפַּסְיָינוּס לְהַחֲרִיב אֶת יְרוּשָׁלַיִם, אָמַר לָהֶם שׁוֹטִים, מִפְּנֵי מָה אַתֶּם מְבַקְשִׁים לְהַחֲרִיב אֶת הָעִיר הַזֹּאת, וְאַתֶּם מְבַקְשִׁים לִשְׂרוֹף אֶת בֵּית הַמִּקְדָּשׁ, וְכִי מַה אֲנִי מְבַקֵּשׁ מִכֶּם אֶלָּא שֶׁתְּשַׁגְּרוּ לִי קֶשֶׁת אַחַת אוֹ חֵץ אַחַת וְאֵלֵךְ לִי מִכֶּם.

אָמְרוּ לוֹ: כְּשֵׁם שֶׁיָּצָאנוּ עַל שְׁנַיִם רִאשׁוֹנִים שֶׁהֵם לְפָנֶיךָ וַהֲרַגְנוּם, כָּךְ נֵצֵא לְפָנֶיךָ וְנַהַרְגֶךָ.

כֵּיוָן שֶׁשָּׁמַע רַבָּן יוֹחָנָן בֶּן זַכַּאי, שָׁלַח וְקָרָא לְאַנְשֵׁי יְרוּשָׁלַיִם וְאָמַר לָהֶם, בָּנַי מִפְּנֵי מָה אַתֶּם מַחֲרִיבִין אֶת הָעִיר הַזֹּאת? וְאַתֶּם מְבַקְשִׁים לִשְׂרוֹף אֶת בֵּית הַמִּקְדָּשׁ? וְכִי מַהוּ מְבַקֵּשׁ מִכֶּם? הָא אֵינוֹ מְבַקֵּשׁ מִכֶּם אֶלָּא קֶשֶׁת אַחַת אוֹ חֵץ אַחַת וְיֵלֵךְ לוֹ מִכֶּם?

אָמְרוּ לוֹ: כְּשֵׁם שֶׁיָּצָאנוּ עַל שְׁנַיִם שֶׁלְּפָנָיו וַהֲרַגְנוּם כָּךְ נֵצֵא עָלָיו וְנַהַרְגֵהוּ.

AVOT DERABBI NATAN

A commentary on, and an elaboration of, the Mishnaic tractate Avot, bearing the name of Rabbi Natan, one of the sages of the Mishnah. The work exists in two very different versions, one of which appears in many editions of the Talmud.

When Vespasian came to subdue Jerusalem, he sent word: "Fools, why do you seek to destroy the city and to burn down the Temple? All I ask is that you send me one bow or one arrow in a show of submission, and I will leave you in peace."

They replied: "Just as we defeated the first two armies that marched against us, so shall we defeat you."

As soon as Rabban Yochanan Ben Zakai heard this, he summoned the people of the city and asked: "My children, why are you destroying this city? Do you wish to burn the Temple? What does Vespasian ask for? All he wants is one bow or one arrow in a show of submission, and he will then leave you in peace!"

They repeated their reply: "Just as we defeated the first two armies, so shall we defeat him."

TEXT 14

TALMUD, GITIN 56A

הֲווֹ בְּהוּ הַנְהוּ בִּרְיוֹנֵי. אָמְרוּ לְהוּ רַבָּנָן: נִיפּוֹק וְנַעֲבִיד שְׁלָמָא בַּהֲדַיְיהוּ.

לֹא שַׁבְקִינְהוּ. אָמְרוּ לְהוּ: נִיפּוֹק וְנַעֲבִיד קְרָבָא בַּהֲדַיְיהוּ.

אָמְרוּ לְהוּ רַבָּנָן: לֹא מִסְתַּיְיעָא מִילְתָא.

קָמוּ קַלְנָהוּ לְהַנְהוּ אַמְבָּרֵי דְחִיטֵי וְשַׂעֲרֵי, וַהֲוָה כַּפְנָא.

BABYLONIAN TALMUD

A literary work of monumental proportions that draws upon the legal, spiritual, intellectual, ethical, and historical traditions of Judaism. The 37 tractates of the Babylonian Talmud contain the teachings of the Jewish sages from the period after the destruction of the 2nd Temple through the 5th century CE. It has served as the primary vehicle for the transmission of the Oral Law and the education of Jews over the centuries; it is the entry point for all subsequent legal, ethical, and theological Jewish scholarship.

There were these hooligans then in the city. The sages said to them, "Let us go out and make peace with them."

But they would not allow it. "On the contrary," they said, "let us go out and fight them."

The sages said: "You will not succeed."

The hooligans rose up and burnt the stores of wheat and barley. A famine ensued.

TEXT 15

MIDRASH, *EICHAH RABAH* 1:31

> יָצָא רַבָּן יוֹחָנָן בֶּן זַכַּאי לְטַיֵּיל בַּשּׁוּק, וְרָאָה אוֹתָם שֶׁשּׁוֹלְקִין תֶּבֶן וְשׁוֹתִין
> מֵימָיו. אָמַר: בְּנֵי אָדָם שֶׁשּׁוֹלְקִין תֶּבֶן וְשׁוֹתִין מֵימָיו יְכוֹלִין לַעֲמוֹד
> בְּחַיְילוֹתָיו שֶׁל אַסְפַּסְיָאנוּס? אָמַר: כָּל סַמָּא דְמִילְתָא נִיפּוֹק לִי מֵהָכָא.

Rabban Yochanan ben Zakai went out to walk in the marketplace. He observed people boiling hay and drinking its water. He said, "People who subsist on hay soup are going to defend against Vespasian's forces?" He said, "The only solution is for me to leave from here."

EICHAH RABAH

A Midrashic text on the Book of Lamentations, produced by the sages of the Talmud in the Land of Israel. Its language closely resembles that of the Jerusalem Talmud. It was first printed in Pesaro, Italy, in 1519 together with four other Midrashic works on the other four *megilot*.

? QUESTION FOR DISCUSSION

What are the arguments for leaving the city? What are the arguments for staying in the city?

TEXT 16a

TALMUD, GITIN 56A

אַבָּא סִקְרָא רֵישׁ בִּרְיוֹנֵי דִירוּשָׁלַיִם בַּר אֲחָתֵיהּ דְּרַבָּן יוֹחָנָן בֶּן זַכַּאי הֲוָה. שָׁלַח לֵיהּ: תָּא בְּצִינְעָא לְגַבָּאי. אָתָא, אָמַר לֵיהּ: עַד אֵימַת עַבְדִיתוּ הָכִי, וְקַטְלִיתוּ לֵיהּ לְעָלְמָא בְּכַפְנָא?

אָמַר לֵיהּ: מַאי אֶיעֱבִיד? דְּאִי אֲמִינָא לְהוּ מִידֵי קַטְלוּ לִי!

אָמַר לֵיהּ: חֲזִי לִי תַּקַנְתָּא לְדִידִי דְּאֵיפּוֹק, אֶפְשָׁר דַּהֲוֵי הַצָּלָה פּוּרְתָּא.

אָמַר לֵיהּ: נְקוֹט נַפְשָׁךְ בִּקְצִירֵי, וְלֵיתֵי כּוּלֵי עָלְמָא וְלִישַׁיְילוּ בָּךְ, וְאַיְיתִי מִידֵי סַרְיָא וְאַגְנִי גַבָּךְ, וְלֵימְרוּ דְּנָח נַפְשָׁךְ, וְלִיעַיְילוּ בָּךְ תַּלְמִידָךְ וְלֹא לֵיעוֹל בָּךְ אִינִישׁ אַחֲרִינָא, דְּלָא לִרְגִּשָׁן בָּךְ דְּקַלִיל אַתְּ, דְּאִינְהוּ יָדְעֵי דְּחַיָּא קַלִיל מִמֵּיתָא.

עֲבִיד הָכִי. נִכְנַס בּוֹ רַבִּי אֱלִיעֶזֶר מִצַּד אֶחָד וְרַבִּי יְהוֹשֻׁעַ מִצַּד אַחַר.

כִּי מָטוּ לְפִיתְחָא בָּעוּ לְמִדְקְרֵיהּ. אָמַר לְהוּ: יֹאמְרוּ רַבָּן דָּקְרוּ! בָּעוּ לְמִדְחֲפֵיהּ, אָמַר לְהוּ: יֹאמְרוּ רַבָּן דָּחֲפוּ! פָּתְחוּ לֵיהּ בָּבָא, נְפַק.

Aba Sikra was the leader of the hooligans of Jerusalem, and he was Rabban Yochanan ben Zakai's nephew. Rabban Yochanan sent him a message asking him to come meet him in secret. When he came, Rabban Yochanan confronted him, "How long will you carry on like this and starve everyone to death?"

Aba Sikra said, "What can I do? If I tell my colleagues anything, they will kill me."

Rabban Yochanan said to him, "Devise a plan that will enable me to leave. Hopefully, I will be able to salvage something."

Aba Sikra said, "Pretend that you are ill, and everyone will come to visit you. Then bring an object with a foul odor and place it next to you, and they'll say that you have died. Have your disciples carry you, but no one else, so that they shall not notice that you are still light, because it is well-known that a living being feels lighter than a corpse."

Rabban Yochanan did so. Rabbi Eliezer took hold of one side of the coffin, and Rabbi Yehoshua took hold of the other side.

When they reached the gate of the city, the guards wanted to stab him to make sure he was dead. He said, "The Romans will say, 'They are stabbing their great rabbi.'"

So they suggested to push him instead. But he said, "The Romans will say, 'They are pushing their great rabbi.'"

So the guards opened the gates, and Rabban Yochanan thus escaped the city.

TEXT 16 b

TALMUD, GITIN 56A–B

כִּי מָטָא לְהָתָם, אָמַר: שְׁלָמָא עֲלָךְ מַלְכָּא, שְׁלָמָא עֲלָךְ מַלְכָּא!

אָמַר לֵיהּ: מִיחַיַּיבְתְּ תְּרֵי קְטָלָא. חֲדָא, דְּלָאו מַלְכָּא אֲנָא וְקָא קָרֵית לִי מַלְכָּא! וְתוּ, אִי מַלְכָּא אֲנָא, עַד הָאִידְנָא אַמַּאי לֹא אָתֵית לְגַבַּאי?

אָמַר לֵיהּ: דְּקָאָמְרַתְּ לָאו מַלְכָּא אֲנָא, אִיבְּרָא מַלְכָּא אַתְּ, דְּאִי לָאו מַלְכָּא אַתְּ לֹא מִימְסְרָא יְרוּשְׁלַיִם בְּיָדָךְ, דִּכְתִיב: (יְשַׁעְיָהוּ י, לד) "וְהַלְּבָנוֹן בְּאַדִּיר יִפּוֹל"... וּדְקָאָמְרַתְּ אִי מַלְכָּא אֲנָא אַמַּאי לֹא קָאָתֵית לְגַבַּאי עַד הָאִידְנָא? בִּרְיוֹנֵי דְּאִית בָּן לֹא שַׁבְקִינָן...

אַדְהָכִי אָתֵי פְּרִיסְתְּקָא עֲלֵיהּ מֵרוֹמִי, אָמַר לֵיהּ: קוּם, דְּמִית לֵיהּ קֵיסָר, וְאָמְרֵי הַנְהוּ חֲשִׁיבֵי דְּרוֹמִי לְאוֹתִיבָךְ בְּרֵישָׁא...

אָמַר לֵיהּ: מֵיזַל אֲזֵילְנָא וְאִינַשׁ אַחֲרִינָא מְשַׁדַּרְנָא, אֶלָּא בְּעֵי מִינַּאי מִידֵי דְּאֶתֵּן לָךְ.

When he reached Vespasian, Rabban Yochanan said to him, "Peace be unto you, King! Peace be unto you, King!"

Vespasian replied, "You deserve the death penalty on two counts of treason. First, I am not king, and you have called me king. Second, if I am king, why have you not come to me until now?"

Said Rabban Yochanan, "The truth is that you are a king. Were you not, Jerusalem would not be given into your hands, for it says (ISAIAH 10:34), 'The Lebanon will fall to the mighty one.' . . . As to why I have yet to come, this is because the hooligans have not allowed this." . . .

In the meantime, a messenger arrived from Rome and said to Vespasian, "Arise! Caesar has died, and the great men of Rome have decided to appoint you at the head." . . .

He then said to Rabban Yochanan, "I am leaving, and another person will be sent in my place. Ask me for something, and I will award it to you."

TEXT 16c

TALMUD, GITIN 56B

אָמַר לֵיהּ: תֵּן לִי יַבְנֶה וַחֲכָמֶיהָ, וְשׁוּשִׁילְתָּא דְרַבָּן גַמְלִיאֵל, וְאַסְוָותָא דְמַסְיָין לֵיהּ לְרַבִּי צָדוֹק.

קָרֵי עֲלֵיהּ רַב יוֹסֵף, וְאִיתֵּימָא רַבִּי עֲקִיבָא: "מֵשִׁיב חֲכָמִים אָחוֹר וְדַעְתָּם יְסַכֵּל" (יְשַׁעְיָהוּ מד, כה). אִיבָּעֵי לְמֵימַר לֵיהּ לִשְׁבְּקִינְהוּ הָדָא זִימְנָא.

וְהוּא סָבַר, דְלְמָא כּוּלֵי הַאי לֹא עָבִיד, וְהַצָלָה פּוּרְתָּא נַמִי לֹא הֲוֵי.

He said to him: "Give me Yavneh and its sages, the family chain of Rabban Gamaliel, and physicians to heal Rabbi Tsadok."

Rabbi Yosef, and some say Rabbi Akiva, said of this, "'God turns wise men backward and makes their knowledge foolish' (ISAIAH 44:25). He ought to have asked Vespasian to leave all together this time."

Rabban Yochanan, however, thought that Vespasian would not grant that much, and then even something minor would not be salvaged.

TEXT **17**

JOSEPHUS, *THE JEWISH WAR* 7:8

My loyal followers, long ago we resolved to serve neither the Romans nor anyone else but God, because He alone is the true and righteous Lord. And now the time has come that bids of us to prove our determination in deed.

At this moment, we must not disgrace ourselves. Until today, we have never submitted to servitude, even when it brought no danger with it. We must not choose servitude now, and with it the penalties awaiting us if we fall alive into the hands of the Romans.

We were the very first that revolted against them, and we are the last that fight against them. I cannot but regard it as a favor that God has granted us that it is still in our power to die nobly, and in a state of freedom, which has not been the case of others.

The storerooms at Masada. (Photo Credit: Samuel Magal)

TEXT 18

SIMON SCHAMA, "THE BEGINNING," *THE STORY OF THE JEWS,* PART I (OXFORD FILM AND TELEVISION PRODUCTION, 2013)

Given the hammer blows of the Roman legions, and coming as they did after century upon century of blows from Egyptians, Syrians, and Babylonians, there would have been scant reason to suppose that the Jews would survive as a people—and yet, two thousand years later the Jews are still here. How?

Well, one answer could be found back at the Arch of Titus—not something that's here, but something that's not. When Josephus describes the procession of loot and prisoners paraded through the streets of Rome, he says, "And last of all of the spoils was carried the Laws of the Jews." But, where are the laws [on the Arch of Titus]? Where are the Torah scrolls? Conspicuously, tellingly, they are absent.

What were scrolls of law anyway? Just many words on parchment, not really worth the time of a sculptor or the cost of the marble.

But words copied, memorized, internalized, made un-forgettable, will beat swords anytime. You can't hold words captive.

SIMON MICHAEL SCHAMA
1945–

British historian. Schama was born in London, the son of Jewish parents with roots in Lithuania, Romania, and Turkey. He is professor of history and art history at Columbia University. He is perhaps best known for writing and hosting the 15-part BBC documentary series *A History of Britain*. His book, *Two Rothschilds and the Land of Israel,* is a study of the Zionist aims of Edmond James de Rothschild and James Armand de Rothschild.

The Roman Empire has come and gone, but go into a synagogue any Saturday and you'll still hear those words.

In September 1913, Dr. Sigmund Freud, the "godless" Jew, was in Rome, and he sent a post card of the Arch of Titus to a friend. On it he wrote, *Der Jude übersteht's*, the Jew survives it.

Dr. Sigmund Freud sent this postcard from Rome. Under the depiction of the Arch of Titus, Freud wrote (September 13, 1913), "Der Jude übersteht's [the Jew survives it]." (Library of Congress)

KEY POINTS

1 Some Jews advocated for a revolt against Rome, because the procurators occasionally disrespected the religious sensibilities of Jews, they governed corruptly, and their policies wrought economic hardship on the people. These Jews hoped that other provinces would rise up in revolt as well, and they trusted that they would be triumphant, despite the daunting odds, just as the legendary Maccabees had achieved miraculous victories against their foes.

2 The Sicarii lent an ideological bent to the revolt. For them, God's statement about the Jews, that "they are My servants whom I took out of the land of Egypt" negated the permissibility of recognizing the Roman emperor as their ruler. The rebels at Masada clung to this belief.

3 The Sages opposed the revolt and advocated for a non-defiant posture. In principle, Rome allowed the Jews to manage their religious affairs without intervention, which rendered their cause dissimilar to that of the Maccabees. Given the odds of success, it was ill advised to revolt as it is forbidden to rely on a miracle.

4 The Sages disagreed with the notion that accepting Roman rule was disloyal to God. In fact, God's statement,

"They are My servants whom I took out of the land of Egypt" indicates that when God took the Jews out of Egypt, He set out for them an immutable purpose that was to be executed whilst living under any political reality. The Jew forever remains loyal to God by remaining loyal to this purpose.

5 Rabban Yochanan ben Zakai sensed the seismic shifts that lay ahead. The upheavals he observed caused other great civilizations to disappear, and he needed to act to save the Jewish future. He maintained that with an attachment to Torah, Jewish identity and civilization can endure, even as Jewish independence is lost, even as the Jews are dispersed, and even as there is no Temple.

6 The sculptor who created the Arch of Titus did not depict the Torah scroll as one of the spoils at the victory parade. The scroll was not valuable in his eyes, but it was the most treasured asset for Rabban Yochanan ben Zakai. His request to Vespasian to be granted "Yavneh and its sages" ensured that the Torah would not be taken captive but be allowed to flourish. This has safeguarded the survival of Jewish life.

Visit
facebook.com/myJLI
to vote on the following question:

Why did the revolt against Rome fail?

1 Rome's military superiority
2 Intra-Jewish civil war
3 No other provinces joined the rebellion.
4 The rebels did not have the support of the sages.

Appendix

Figure 2.1

Timeline of the Revolt (66–73 CE)

DATE	EVENT
Summer 66 CE	Roman garrison at Masada is captured by Judean rebels. The sacrifice for the emperor is halted.
Summer 66 CE	Agrippa II sends three thousand men to put down the revolt, but Judean fighters defeat his force.
Fall 66 CE	The Twelfth Legion under Cestius Gallus is destroyed by Judean fighters.
Fall 66 CE	Independent Judean government is formed in Jerusalem.
Winter 67 CE	Vespasian begins conquering the Galilee.
Winter 68 CE	The Galilee is defeated. War effort moves to Judea.
Summer 69 CE	Vespasian is proclaimed emperor. Titus assumes command of the Roman forces.
Summer 70 CE	Jerusalem walls are breached, the city is conquered, and the Temple is destroyed.
Summer 71 CE	Victory parade is held in Rome.
Spring 73 CE	Masada is captured.

TEXT **19**

TALMUD, MENACHOT 64B

כְּשֶׁצָּרוּ מַלְכֵי בֵּית חַשְׁמוֹנַאי זֶה עַל זֶה, וְהָיָה הוֹרְקְנוֹס מִבַּחוּץ וְאַרִיסְטוֹבּלוּס מִבִּפְנִים. בְּכָל יוֹם וָיוֹם הָיוּ מְשַׁלְשְׁלִין לָהֶן דִּינָרִין בְּקוּפָּה וּמַעֲלִין לָהֶן תְּמִידִין.

הָיָה שָׁם זָקֵן אֶחָד שֶׁהָיָה מַכִּיר בְּחָכְמַת יְוָנִית, לָעַז לָהֶם בְּחָכְמַת יְוָנִית, אָמַר לָהֶן: כָּל זְמַן שֶׁעֲסוּקִין בָּעֲבוֹדָה אֵין נִמְסָרִין בְּיֶדְכֶם.

לְמָחָר שִׁלְשְׁלוּ לָהֶן דִּינָרִין בַּקוּפָּה וְהֶעֱלוּ לָהֶן חֲזִיר. כֵּיוָן שֶׁהִגִּיעַ לַחֲצִי חוֹמָה נָעַץ צִפָּרְנָיו בַּחוֹמָה, וְנִזְדַּעְזְעָה אֶרֶץ יִשְׂרָאֵל אַרְבַּע מֵאוֹת פַּרְסָה עַל אַרְבַּע מֵאוֹת פַּרְסָה.

When the Hasmonean kings fought one another, Hyrcanus was outside [the walls of Jerusalem] and Aristobulus was inside. Each day, those on the inside would lower a basketful of dinars to the party on the outside, and raise in return an animal for the daily sacrifice.

An old man, learned in code language, signaled [from inside the following message] to the group on the outside: "As long as they carry on the Temple service, they will never be delivered into your hands."

The next day, they lowered a basket of dinars, but in return they discovered [that rather than a kosher animal fit for a sacrifice, those on the outside had sent up] a pig. When it reached halfway up the wall, it stuck its claws into it, and the Land of Israel trembled across a span of four hundred *parsa* by four hundred *parsa*.

Figure 2.2

Noteworthy Events, 63 BCE–4 CE

DATE	EVENT
63 BCE	Pompey invades Judea to install Hyrcanus as king. Thousands of Jews are killed. Aristobulus is defeated and imprisoned.
57 BCE	Gabinus, proconsul to Syria, divides Judea into five provinces, abolishes the Sanhedrin, and transfers control of coastal cities to their Greek inhabitants.
56 BCE	Aristobulus escapes captivity and leads a losing war against Rome. Many Jews are killed in these battles.
54 BCE	Crassus, proconsul of Syria, robs all of the gold in the Temple treasury to fund his expedition against the Parthians.
48 BCE	Alexander, son of Aristobulus, who has led a war against Rome to claim the throne, is defeated. Many Jews are killed in these battles.
47/46 BCE	Herod, governor of the Galilee, commits mass murder to enforce his tax collection.
44 BCE	Antipater, advisor to King Hyrcanus and father of Herod, collects exorbitant taxes to fund Cassius's war against Marc Antony.
44 BCE	Cassius, proconsul of Syria, sells inhabitants of four Jewish towns as slaves. The residents of these towns had not paid the steep taxes imposed on the residents of Judea to fund Cassius's war.

DATE	EVENT
42 BCE	Marc Antony, new Roman ruler over the eastern provinces, installs Herod as king. Antony kills the Jewish delegates who came to him to protest Herod's appointment.
40 BCE	Antigonus, son of Aristobulus, deposes Herod to become king.
37 BCE	Herod returns with a massive Roman army and retakes the kingdom, perpetrating a bloodbath across the land.
29 BCE	Herod executes his wife, mother-in-law, and other Maccabean descendants. He fears they might assert claims of Hasmonean royalty.
29 BCE	Herod impoverishes the populace through enormous taxes to fund the building of lavish palaces, fortresses, Greek temples, and new cities.
29 BCE	Herod populates his new cities with non-Jews, tipping the country's demographics. He also introduces Greek culture and practices in Israel.
22 BCE	Herod begins construction of Caesarea on the Mediterranean coast.
4 BCE	Herod had placed a Roman eagle (a prominent symbol of ancient Rome) on the newly renovated Temple. When two sages and forty of their students remove it, Herod has them killed.

TEXT 20

JOSEPHUS, *THE JEWISH WAR* 2:6

They said that Herod was not a king, but the most barbarous of all tyrants. A great number had been slain by him, and those who survived had endured such miseries that they envied the fate of the dead. . . . He had sunk the nation into poverty and great iniquity. . . . The Jews had borne more calamities from Herod in a few years than their forefathers suffered during all that time that had passed since they had come out of Babylon and returned home. . . . This Archelaus, lest he should be in danger of not being thought of as the genuine son of Herod, began his reign with the murder of three thousand citizens, as if he wished to offer so many bloody sacrifices to God for his government. . . .

They prayed that the Romans would have compassion upon the poor remnants of Judea and not expose them to be barbarously torn to pieces. They asked that their country be joined to Syria, and to entrust the administration to governors from among themselves. This would demonstrate that those who are being defamed as rebellious and lovers of war know how to bear equitable governors.

Figure 2.3

Noteworthy Events, 15 CE–66 CE

DATE	EVENT
15 CE	Procurator Gratus imposes heavy taxes. He appoints four high priests during a short period of time, which suggests that he was taking bribes for this office.
26–36 CE	Procurator Pontius Pilate orders his soldiers in Jerusalem to carry the Roman standards with the image of the emperor. Jews risk their lives to protest this offense to their faith.
26–36 CE	Pilate loots the Temple treasury to build an aqueduct. Jews attempt to stop him and are struck down brutally. Many are killed.
37–41 CE	Emperor Caligula orders that a statue of himself be erected in the Temple and dispatches troops to enforce the order. Caligula dies before it is enforced.
41–44 CE	Emperor Claudius declares Agrippa, Herod's grandson, as king over Judea, and he rules (instead of a Roman procurator) until his death in 44 CE. He was a pious king and favorable toward the Jews, and his reign was a period of calm amidst this tumultuous time.
48–52 CE	Jews complain to Procurator Cumanus of lewd and offensive behavior by soldiers stationed at the Temple during the festival. Cumanus dismisses the complaint. When the angry crowds protest, Cumanus orders the soldiers to attack, and thousands are killed.
48–52 CE	Samarians kill Jewish pilgrims, but Cumanus refuses to act. Jewish brigands retaliate, and Cumanus crucifies them.
48–66 CE	Bands of brigands terrorize the countryside. Some suggest that they hail from the poor classes who are crushed by the tax burden and who had lost their land. They aim acts of violence against Romans and against Jews they deemed as collaborating with the Romans.

TEXT 21

JOSEPHUS, *THE JEWISH WAR* 2:14

At this time, the Greeks at Caesarea had won their case. They obtained from Nero the government of the city and brought the text of this determination to the city. . . .

The Jews of Caesarea had a synagogue near the property of a Greek resident, and they frequently endeavored to purchase the property by offering to pay a price that greatly exceeded its true value. But the owner ignored their offers. In fact, in order to affront them, he built workshops on the property, and left the Jews a narrow and difficult passageway to their synagogue. . . .

The Jewish leaders . . . persuaded Florus, with the offer of eight talents of silver, to hinder the work. With his eye only on the money, he promised to do for them anything that they desired, but then left Caesarea for Samaria. . . .

The next day was Saturday. When the Jews were gathered in their synagogue, a mischief maker of Caesarea took an earthen vessel, set it upside down at the entrance of the synagogue, and slaughtered birds upon it. This desecration of the place . . . provoked the Jews beyond endurance. The peaceful and moderate Jews thought it proper to turn to the authorities again, but those inclined to rebel and the passionate young people were inflamed to fight. The Gentiles of Caesarea also stood ready to fight, for they had agreed beforehand to send the man to perform the mock sacrifice. They soon came to blows. . . .

John and twelve leaders went to Florus at Samaria to complain about their case. They besought him to help them, and with all possible decency, reminded him of the eight talents of silver they had given him. But he seized the men and put them in prison. . . .

Jerusalem, Besieged by Titus, *Jan Luyken, 1682.*
(Rijksmuseum, Amsterdam)

TEXT 22

JOSEPHUS, *THE JEWISH WAR* 2:14

This news roused indignation in Jerusalem, yet its citizens restrained themselves.

However, Florus . . . sent to the Temple treasury to take seventeen talents of silver, claiming that these were owed to the imperial service. Immediately, the people were in confusion and ran together to the Temple. They called upon Caesar with piercing cries and besought him to free them from the tyranny of Florus.

Some of the malcontents railed against Florus and cast the greatest rebukes upon him. They carried a basket about and begged for some copper for him, as one does when one is destitute and miserable. . . .

Florus hastily marched with an army of cavalry and infantry against Jerusalem. . . . He commanded the leaders to deliver to him those that had reproached him and told them that they will feel his vengeance if they did not produce the criminals. But the leaders demonstrated that the people were peaceably disposed and begged forgiveness for those who had spoken amiss. It was no wonder, they said, that in so great a multitude there should be some reckless people and foolish youth. And, they said, it was impossible to distinguish the offenders from the rest. . . .

Florus was more provoked by this and called out to the soldiers to plunder the Upper Market and to slay anyone they met. The soldiers . . . did not only plunder the place they were sent to, but forced themselves into every house and slew its inhabitants. The citizens fled along the narrow streets, and the soldiers slew those that they caught. No method of plunder was omitted. They also captured many peaceful people and brought them before Florus. He had them beaten and then crucified. The number of those killed on that day—including women and children, for they did not spare even the infants—was about three thousand six hundred. . . .

TEXT **23**

JOSEPHUS, *THE JEWISH WAR* 2:15

Florus . . . sent for the high priests and the other leaders. He said that the only way to prove that the people would not engage in any other revolutionary acts would be for them to go out and meet the two cohorts of soldiers that were coming from Caesarea.

While the leaders were exhorting the multitude to do so, Florus sent and gave directions to the centurions of the cohorts that they should give notice to those that were under them not to return the Jews' salutations. And if the Jews made any disparaging statement about him, they should make use of their weapons. . . .

The Jewish leaders led the delegation in a peaceful and composed manner. When they approached the troops, they saluted them. But when the troops did not answer, rebels clamored against Florus, which was the signal for falling upon the Jews. The soldiers surrounded them and struck them with their clubs. As they fled, the cavalry trampled them. Many fell dead by the Roman swords, and even more by crushing one another. . . .

TEXT 24

JOSEPHUS, *THE JEWISH WAR* 2:15

The soldiers . . . tried to force their way to occupy the Temple and the fortress of Antonia. . . . But this attempt failed, for the people turned back upon Florus and stopped his attempt. As they stood upon the roofs of their houses, they threw their darts at the Romans. The Romans were very overwhelmed by this, because those weapons came from above, and they were not able to pass the multitude, who blocked the narrow passages. So the Romans retreated. . . .

The rebels were afraid that Florus might come again to take possession of the Temple through Antonia. They therefore attacked the structures that joined the Temple to Antonia and cut them off from the Temple. This cooled Florus's avarice. He was eager to obtain the treasures of God, and on that account was desirous of getting into Antonia. But as soon as the connecting structures were broken, he relinquished his attempt.

He sent for the high priests and the Sanhedrin and told them that he was leaving the city but would grant them as large a garrison as they desired. In reply, the leaders committed to maintain order and prevent any revolution if he would leave them one cohort, but the soldiers could not be those who had fought with the Jews. . . .

With the rest of his forces, Florus returned to Caesarea.

TEXT 25

JERUSALEM TALMUD, KIDUSHIN 1:2

שָׁאֲלוּ הַתַּלְמִידִים אֶת רַבָּן יוֹחָנָן בֶּן זַכַּאי: מַה רָאָה הָעֶבֶד הַזֶּה לִירָצַע
בְּאָזְנוֹ יוֹתֵר מִכָּל אֵיבָרָיו?

אָמַר לָהֶן: אֹזֶן שֶׁשָּׁמְעָה מֵהַר סִינַי "לֹא יִהְיֶה לְךָ אֱלֹהִים אֲחֵרִים עַל פָּנַי"
(שְׁמוֹת כ, ג) וּפֵירְקָה מֵעָלֶיהָ עוֹל מַלְכוּת שָׁמַיִם וְקִיבְּלָה עָלֶיהָ עוֹל בָּשָׂר
וָדָם, אֹזֶן שֶׁשָּׁמְעָה לִפְנֵי הַר סִינַי: "כִּי לִי בְנֵי יִשְׂרָאֵל עֲבָדִים" (וַיִּקְרָא כה,
נה) וְהָלַךְ זֶה וְקָנָה אָדוֹן אַחֵר, לְפִיכָךְ תָּבוֹא הָאֹזֶן וְתִירָצַע, לְפִי שֶׁלֹּא שָׁמַר
מַה שֶּׁשָּׁמְעָה אָזְנוֹ.

JERUSALEM TALMUD

A commentary to the Mishnah, compiled during the 4th and 5th centuries. The Jerusalem Talmud predates its Babylonian counterpart by 100 years and is written in both Hebrew and Aramaic. While the Babylonian Talmud is the most authoritative source for Jewish law, the Jerusalem Talmud remains an invaluable source for the spiritual, intellectual, ethical, historical, and legal traditions of Judaism.

The students asked Rabban Yochanan Ben Zakai: Why is the ear of the indentured servant pierced as opposed to any other part of his body?

Rabban Yochanan answered: The ear heard God say at Sinai, "You shall have no other gods in my presence" (EXODUS 20:3), and yet this person rejected the yoke of heaven for the yoke of a human being. The ear heard God say at Sinai "The children of Israel are servants to Me" (LEVITICUS 25:55), and yet this person went and acquired a different master. Therefore, let his ear be pierced for he failed to obey what his ear heard.

TEXT 26

TALMUD, MEGILAH 14A

בִּשְׁלָמָא הָתָם "הַלְלוּ עַבְדֵי ה'" (תְּהִלִּים קיג, א) - וְלֹא עַבְדֵי פַּרְעֹה,
אֶלָּא הָכָא - "הַלְלוּ עַבְדֵי ה'" וְלֹא עַבְדֵי אֲחַשְׁוֵרוֹשׁ? אַכַּתִּי עַבְדֵי
אֲחַשְׁוֵרוֹשׁ אֲנַן!

In the case of the Exodus, we can appropriately say, "Servants of God, sing His praises" (PSALMS 113:1)— because we were no longer the subjects of Pharaoh. But in the case of Purim, can we say that we are servants of God and not the subjects of Ahasuerus? Even after our salvation, we remained the subjects of Ahasuerus.

TEXT 27

YIGAEL YADIN, *MASADA: HEROD'S FORTRESS AND THE ZEALOTS' LAST STAND*
(LONDON: WEIDENFELD & NICOLSON, 1966), PP. 164–167

YIGAEL YADIN
1917–1984

Israeli archaeologist and military leader. Yadin served as operations officer of the Haganah and, later, chief of staff of the Israeli Defense Forces. His vast archeological digs have shed light on various periods of ancient Israel as well as the Bar Kokhba revolt. Among his best-known published works are *Masada* (1968) and *Tefillin from Qumran* (1969).

We were much surprised by what came to light as we uncovered one of the chambers in the southern section of the casemate wall. When we had cleared all the debris from this room, what we saw was a system of three adjacent pools—one large, one medium-sized and one small. Steps had been built in the two larger pools so that one could reach the bottom, and in the wall between them there was a connecting hole through which water could flow from one to the other. Moreover, as may be seen in the picture, there was an open, plastered, water conduit leading into the first—the largest—pool, and this conduit no doubt served to collect and channel rainwater from the roof of the room and its surroundings.

This find immediately suggested to us that what we had discovered was a ritual immersion bath—*mikve* in Hebrew—and this we announced at our routine press conference. The news that we had brought to light a *mikve* from the period of the Second Temple quickly spread throughout the country, arousing particular interest in orthodox religious quarters and Talmudic scholars; for the traditional Jewish laws of the Talmud relating to the ritual bath are quite complex, and no *mikve* has so far been discovered belonging to this very period. . . .

This special interest in the *mikve* led to one of my strangest meetings on the Masada summit, and it indicates, too, how wide was Masada's appeal to our people, and how it spoke to each in his own language. We received information one day, during the excavations, that Rabbi David Muntzberg, specialist in the laws of the *mikve*, and Rabbi Eliezer Alter, were anxious to visit Masada and see for themselves the *mikve* we had discovered. I signaled that I would be pleased to receive them, and one hot day, during the hottest hour of the afternoon, the two Rabbis arrived on the summit. They had climbed the tough "snake path" on the east face under the broiling sun, wearing their characteristic heavy garments, and accompanied by a group of their Hassidic followers. Though they are no longer young, neither agreed to rest when they finally reached the top; nor did they wish to see any of the handsome structures of King Herod. They wanted one thing only: to be led directly to the *mikve*. We took them there, and the aged Rabbi Muntzberg immediately went into one of the pools, a tape-measure in his hand, to examine whether in fact the volume of this *mikve* was the "forty measures" required by the ritual law. I photographed him and his companions in the process. It remains one of my favourite pictures of the Masada dig. Spiritually, these people had been deeply stirred by what apparently was a very humble structure, though, admittedly, dramatically sited within a wall at the edge of a steep escarpment. This *mikve* meant more to them than anything else on Masada.

I confess that during Rabbi Muntzberg's examination I was rather anxious. What would be his finding? His face throughout bore a serious expression and at times he furrowed his brow as if in doubt as to whether the bath was *kosher*. But when he completed his meticulous study, he announced with a beaming face and to the delight of us all that this *mikve* was indeed a ritual bath "among the finest of the finest, seven times seven."

How had this *mikve* been built? According to Jewish religious law, such a bath, without which no orthodox Jew could live, particularly in those days, had to be filled for the most part with rainwater flowing into it directly, and not brought to it with buckets or the like. This of course was not possible in Palestine during most months of the year, when there is simply no rain, and the law therefore prescribes that it is sufficient if part of the water is "pure"; additional water, drawn and brought from elsewhere and not direct-flowing rain-water, becomes "purified" on contact with the pure water. They therefore built two pools. In one—in ours at Masada the one nearest the entrance—water was gathered during the rainy season and stored; the second was the actual bath itself. Before using it, they would open the bung in the connecting pipe allowing some drops of the stored, direct rain-water to flow into the bathing pool and thus purify it. . . .

This device, incidentally, shed interesting light on a number of hitherto obscure passages in the Mishna. It also illustrates, as do the inscriptions about tithes mentioned earlier, that the defenders of Masada were devout Jews, so that even here, on dry Masada, they had gone to the arduous lengths of building these ritual baths in scrupulous conformity with the injunctions of traditional Jewish law.

The ritual bath (mikveh) at Masada.

Additional Readings

THE DESTRUCTION OF JERUSALEM
THREE ACCOUNTS FROM THE SAGES

TALMUD, GITIN 55B–56B

Jerusalem was destroyed on account of Kamtza and Bar Kamtza.

There was a certain man who had a friend named Kamtza and an enemy named Bar Kamtza. He once made a large feast and said to his servant, "Go bring me my friend Kamtza." The servant went and mistakenly brought him his enemy, Bar Kamtza.

The host came and found Bar Kamtza sitting at the feast. He said to Bar Kamtza, "You are my enemy. What then do you want here? Arise and leave."

Bar Kamtza said to him, "Since I have already come, let me stay and I will give you money for whatever I eat and drink. Just do not embarrass me by sending me out."

The host said to him, "No, you must leave."

Bar Kamtza said to him, "I will give you money for half of the feast; just do not send me away."

The host said to him, "No, you must leave."

Bar Kamtza then said to him, "I will give you money for the entire feast; just let me stay."

The host said to him, "No, you must leave." Finally, the host took Bar Kamtza by his hand, stood him up, and took him out.

After having been cast out from the feast, Bar Kamtza said to himself, "Since the sages were sitting there

BABYLONIAN TALMUD

A literary work of monumental proportions that draws upon the legal, spiritual, intellectual, ethical, and historical traditions of Judaism. The 37 tractates of the Babylonian Talmud contain the teachings of the Jewish sages from the period after the destruction of the 2nd Temple through the 5th century CE. It has served as the primary vehicle for the transmission of the Oral Law and the education of Jews over the centuries; it is the entry point for all subsequent legal, ethical, and theological Jewish scholarship.

and did not protest the actions of the host, although they saw how he humiliated me, it is implicit that they were content with what he did. I will therefore go and inform against them to the king."

He went and said to the emperor, "The Jews have rebelled against you."

The emperor said to him, "Who says that this is the case?"

Bar Kamtza said to him, "Go and test them. Send them an offering to be brought in honor of the government, and see whether they will sacrifice it."

The emperor went and sent with him a fine calf. On his way to the Temple with the calf, Bar Kamtza made a blemish on the calf's upper lip, or, as some say, he made the blemish on its eyelid. Either way, he ensured that the blemish was in a place where according to halachah it is a blemish, but according to gentile rules for their offerings, it is not a blemish. Therefore, when Bar Kamtza brought the animal to the Temple, the priests would not sacrifice it on the altar since it was blemished, but they also could not explain this satisfactorily to the gentile authorities, who did not consider it to be blemished.

The blemish notwithstanding, the sages considered sacrificing the animal as an offering due to the imperative to maintain peaceful relations with the government. Rabbi Zecharyah ben Avkolas said to them, "If the priests do that, people will say that blemished animals may be sacrificed as offerings on the altar."

The sages said, "If we do not sacrifice it, then we must prevent Bar Kamtza from reporting this to the emperor." The sages considered killing him so that he would not go and inform on them to the emperor.

Rabbi Zecharyah said to them, "If you kill him, people will say that one who makes a blemish on sacrificial animals is to be killed." As a result, they did nothing, Bar Kamtza's slander was accepted by the authorities, and consequently the war between the Jews and the Romans began.

Rabbi Yochanan says: The excessive tolerance of Rabbi Zecharyah ben Avkolas destroyed our Temple, burned our Sanctuary, and exiled us from our land.

The Roman authorities then sent Nero Caesar against the Jews. When he came to Jerusalem, he wished to test his fate. He shot an arrow to the east and the arrow fell in Jerusalem. He shot another arrow to the west and it also fell in Jerusalem. He shot arrows in all four directions, and each time the arrow fell in Jerusalem.

Nero then conducted another test. He said to a child, "Tell me the verse that you learned today."

The child responded to him as follows: "And I will lay My vengeance upon Edom by the hand of My people Israel" (Ezekiel 25:14).

Nero said, "The Holy One, Blessed be He, wishes to destroy His Temple, and He wishes to wipe his hands with that man, i.e., with me." [The Romans are associated with Edom, the descendants of Esau. If I continue on this mission, I will eventually be punished for having served as God's agent to bring about the destruction.] Nero fled and became a convert, and ultimately Rabbi Meir descended from him.

The Roman authorities then sent Vespasian Caesar against the Jews. He laid siege to Jerusalem for three years. At that time there were three wealthy people in Jerusalem: Nakdimon ben Guryon, ben Kalba Savua, and ben Tsitsit HaKesat.

[The Talmud explains their names:] Nakdimon ben Guryon was called by that name because the sun shined [*nakad*] on his behalf [as related in Ta'anit 19b]. Ben Kalba Savua earned his name because anyone who entered his house hungry as a dog [*kelev*] would leave satiated [*save'a*]. Ben Tzitzit HaKesat was referred to by this name because his *tsitsit* dragged along on blankets [*keset*] [he would not walk in the street with his feet on the ground, but rather blankets would be placed beneath him]. Others say that the reason for his name was that his seat [*kisei*] was among the nobles of Rome.

These three wealthy people offered their assistance. One of them said to the leaders of the city, "I will feed the residents with wheat and barley."

Another said "I will provide wine, salt, and oil."
Another said "I will supply the wood."

The sages gave special praise to the one who gave the wood, since this was an especially valuable gift. This is like the conduct of Rav Chisda, who would give all of the keys to his servant except for the key to his wood storehouse, explaining that one storehouse of wheat requires sixty storehouses of wood for cooking and baking fuel.

Between them, these three wealthy men had enough commodities to sustain the besieged city for twenty-one years.

There were zealots among the people of Jerusalem. The sages said to them, "Let us go and make peace with the Romans."

But the zealots did not allow them to do this. The zealots countered to the sages, "Let us go and wage war against the Romans."

The sages replied to them, "You will not be successful."

The zealots arose and burned down the storehouses of wheat and barley, and a famine ensued.

[A story about this famine:] Marta bat Baitos was one of the wealthy women of Jerusalem. She sent out her agent and said to him, "Go bring me fine flour."

By the time he arrived, the fine flour was already sold out. He came back and said to her, "There is no fine flour left, but there is ordinary flour."

She said to him, "Go then and bring me ordinary flour."

By the time he arrived, the ordinary flour was also sold out. He came back and said to her, "There is no ordinary flour left, but there is coarse flour."

She said to him, "Go then and bring me coarse flour."

By the time he arrived, the coarse flour was also sold out. He came back and said to her, "There is no coarse flour left, but there is barley flour."

She said to him, "Go then and bring me barley flour."

But once again, by the time he arrived, the barley flour was also sold out.

She had just removed her shoes, but she said, "I will go out myself and see if I can find something to eat." She went out, stepped on some dung which stuck to her foot, and, overcome by disgust, she died.

Concerning this incident Rabban Yochanan ben Zakkai quoted the verse, "The tender and delicate woman among you who would not adventure to set the sole of her foot upon the ground" (Deuteronomy 28:56).

Others say that she did not step on dung, but rather she ate a fig of Rabbi Tsadok, and became disgusted and died. The story of these figs is that Rabbi Tsadok observed fasts for forty years, praying that Jerusalem should not be destroyed. He became so emaciated from fasting that when he would eat something it was visible from the outside of his body. After a fast they would bring him figs to eat and he would suck out their liquid and cast the rest away.

It is further related that as she was dying, she took out all of her gold and silver and threw it in the marketplace. She said, "Why do I need this?" This is like the verse that says: "They shall cast their silver in the streets and their gold shall be as an impure thing; their silver and their gold shall not be able to deliver them in the day of the wrath of the Lord; they shall not satisfy their souls, neither fill their bowels" (Ezekiel 7:19).

Abba Sikkara was the leader of the zealots of Jerusalem and the son of the sister of Rabban Yochanan ben Zakkai. Rabban Yochanan sent a message to him, "Come to me in secret."

He came, and Rabban Yochanan said to him, "How long will you carry on like this and starve everyone to death?"

Abba Sikkara said to him, "What can I do? If I say something to them they will kill me."

Rabban Yochanan said to him, "Show me a method through which I will be able to leave the city—hopefully I will be able to salvage something."

Abba Sikkara said to him, "Pretend to be sick, and have everyone come and ask about your welfare. Then bring something putrid and place it near you, so that people will say that you have died and are decomposing. Have your students then enter to bring you to burial, and don't let anyone else in so that no one should notice that you are still light, because they know that a living person is lighter than a dead person."

Rabban Yochanan did this. Rabbi Eliezer entered from one side and Rabbi Yehoshua from the other side to take out his bed. When they arrived at the entrance of the city, the guards wanted to pierce him with their swords in order to make sure that he was actually dead. But Abba Sikkara said to them, "The Romans will say that they have stabbed even their rabbi."

The guards then wanted at least to push him to see if he would cry out. But Abba Sikkara said to them, "The Romans will say that they push even their rabbi." So the guards opened the gate and he was taken out.

When Rabban Yochanan reached the Roman camp, he said to Vespasian, "Peace be unto you, the king! Peace be unto you, the king!"

Vespasian replied, "You are liable for two death penalties: first, because I am not a king and yet you call me king; and second, if I am indeed a king, why didn't you come to me until now?"

Rabban Yochanan answered him: "As for what you said about yourself: 'I am not a king'—in truth, you are a king. For if you were not a king, Jerusalem would not fall into your hands, as it is written: 'And the Lebanon shall fall by a mighty one' (Isaiah 10:34). A 'mighty one' can only mean a king, as it is written: 'And their mighty one shall be of themselves, and their ruler shall proceed from the midst of them' (Jeremiah 30:21). 'Lebanon' means the Temple, as the verse says: 'That good mountain and the Lebanon' (Deuteronomy 3:25). As for your second comment—'If I am indeed a king, why didn't you come to me until now?'—there are zealots among us who did not allow."

Vespasian said to Rabban Yochanan: "If there is a barrel of honey and a snake is wrapped around it, would one not break the barrel in order to kill the snake?" [Likewise, you should have destroyed the walls of Jerusalem so that the zealots could be driven out.]

Rabban Yochanan was silent. Rav Yosef—others say it was Rabbi Akiva—later read the following verse about him: "I am the Lord . . . Who turns wise men backward and makes their thinking foolish" (Isaiah 44:25).

For Rabban Yochanan should have replied to Vespasian: "In such a case, we would take tongs, remove the snake, and kill it, leaving the barrel intact [So too, we were waiting for an opportunity to drive out the zealots without having to destroy the city]."

As they were talking, a messenger arrived from Rome, and said to Vespasian: "Rise, for the emperor has died, and the noblemen of Rome plan to appoint you as their new leader."

At that time Vespasian was wearing only one shoe, and when he tried to put on the other one, it would not go on his foot. He then tried to remove the other shoe that he was already wearing, but it would not come off. He said, "What is this?"

Rabban Yochanan said to him, "Do not be distressed, good tidings have reached you and this is why your shoe doesn't fit. It is written: 'Good tidings make the bone fat' (Proverbs 15:30), and so your feet have grown fatter out of joy and satisfaction.

Vespasian said to him, "What is the remedy?"

Rabban Yochanan replied, "Have someone whom you dislike come and pass before you, as it is written: 'A broken spirit dries the bones' (Proverbs 17:22)." He did this, and his shoe went on his foot.

Vespasian said to him, "Since you are so wise, why didn't you come to see me until now?"

Rabban Yochanan said to him, "Didn't I already tell you?"

Vespasian replied, "I also told you what I had to say."

Vespasian then said to Rabban Yochanan, "I will be going to Rome to accept my new position, and I will send someone else in my place to continue besieging the city and waging war against it. But before I leave, ask of me something that I can give you."

Rabban Yochanan said to him, "Give me Yavne and its sages, spare the dynasty of Rabban Gamliel, and give me doctors to heal Rabbi Tsadok. Rav Yosef—others say it was Rabbi Akiva—later read the following verse about him: "I am the Lord . . . Who turns wise men backward and makes their knowledge foolish (Isaiah 44:25)," as he should have asked Vespasian to spare Jerusalem.

Rabban Yochanan did not make this request because he reasoned that Vespasian might not fulfill so great a request for him, and there would not be even a small measure of salvation.

How did the doctors Rabban Yochanan had asked for heal Rabbi Tsadok? On the first day they gave him water containing bran to drink. The next day they gave him water containing flour mixed with bran. The following day they gave him water containing flour. So they fed him, and slowly his intestines expanded.

The translation is based on the *Koren Talmud* (Jerusalem, Israel: Koren Publishers, 2015), with revisions by Rabbi Yaakov Gershon, Rabbi Shmuel Klatzkin, and Rabbi Shmuel Super.

AVOT DERABBI NATAN, CH. 4

When Vespasian came to destroy Jerusalem, he said to its defenders, "Fools, why do you seek to destroy this city and to burn down the Temple? All I am asking of you is that you send me one bow or one arrow and I will leave you alone."

They said to him, "Just as we came out to fight the two who had come before you and killed them, so, too, we will come out against you and kill you."

When Rabban Yochanan ben Zakkai heard this, he sent out and called the people of Jerusalem and said to them, "My children, why do you seek to destroy this city and to burn down the Temple? What, after all, is he asking of you? Only one bow or one arrow, then he will leave you alone."

They said to him, "Just as we came out to fight the two who had come before them and killed them, so, too, we will come out against him and kill him."

Vespasian had supporters within Jerusalem's walls, and everything that they heard they would write on an arrow and send it outside the walls. They now sent to him a message that Rabban Yochanan ben Zakkai was a supporter of the Roman Caesar.

After Rabban Yochanan repeated his words to the people of Jerusalem three different times and they did not accept it, he sent and called for his students Rabbi Eliezer and Rabbi Yehoshua. He said to them, "My sons, arise and take me out of here. Make a wooden casket for me and I will sleep in it."

Rabbi Eliezer took hold of the head and Rabbi Yehoshua took hold of the foot. As they were taking

AVOT DERABBI NATAN
A commentary on, and an elaboration of, the Mishnaic tractate Avot, bearing the name of Rabbi Natan, one of the sages of the Mishnah. The work exists in two very different versions, one of which appears in many editions of the Talmud.

him out, it was toward sunset when they came to the gates of Jerusalem. The gatekeepers said to them, "Who is this?"

Rabbi Eliezer and Rabbi Yehoshua replied, "He is dead. Do you not know that one may not leave the dead overnight in Jerusalem?"

The gatekeepers said to them, "If he is dead, then take him out."

They took him out and they brought him to Vespasian. They opened the casket and he stood before him.

Vespasian said, "Are you Rabban Yochanan ben Zakkai? Ask what I may give you."

Rabban Yochanan replied, "All I ask for is Yavneh, that I be able to go there and teach my students and have an established place for prayer and for performing all the *mitzvot*."

Vespasian said, "Go and do all that you desire to do."

Rabban Yochanan said to him, "Do you want me to tell you one thing?"

Vespasian said, "Speak."

Rabban Yochanan said, "You are ascending to the throne."

Vespasian said, "From where do you know this?"

Rabban Yochanan replied, "We know by our tradition that the Temple will not be given into the hand of a common person, but only into the hand of a king. For so it is written, "The thickets of the forest shall be chopped down by iron and Lebanon [i.e., the Temple] shall fall by majesty" (Isaiah 10:34).

It is related that within the next three days, a pair of messengers came from his city to inform him that the emperor had died and that he had been appointed to be sovereign. They brought him a wooden catapult, which he set against the walls of Jerusalem. They brought him cedar logs which they put into the catapult, and used them to batter against the wall until they breached it. They brought him a pig's head, which they put into the catapult and hurled it toward the sacrificial limbs that were on the altar.

At the moment Jerusalem was conquered, Rabban Yochanan ben Zakkai was anxiously sitting and trembling, just as Eli the High Priest, in his day, had been anxiously awaiting news; as it says, "And Eli was sitting on a chair near the road, anxiously awaiting news, for his heart trembled for the Ark of God" (I Samuel

4:13). When Rabban Yochanan ben Zakkai heard that Jerusalem had been destroyed and the Temple burnt in flames, he rent his clothing, as did his students, and they wept and cried and lamented.

Translated by Rabbi Yaakov Gershon, Rabbi Shmuel Klatzkin, and Rabbi Shmuel Super

MIDRASH, *EICHAH RABAH* 1:31

"Her foes are now the masters; her enemies are at ease" (Lamentations 1:5). "Her foes are now the masters": this refers to Vespasian; "her enemies are at ease": this refers to Titus.

For three and a half years Vespasian surrounded Jerusalem with a siege. Together with him were four commanders: the commanders of Arabia, Africa, Alexandria, and Palestine. With regard to the duke of Arabia, two sages differ as to his name. One said his name was Kilus, and the other said his name was Pangar.

There were four city councilmen in Jerusalem: Ben Tsitsit, Ben Guryon, Ben Nakdimon, and Ben Kalba Savua. Each of them was capable of supplying food for the city for ten years. There was also a man named Ben Batiach, the son of Rabban Yochanan ben Zakkai's sister. He was appointed in charge of the stores, and he burned them all down. When Rabban Yochanan heard of this he exclaimed, "Woe!"

It was reported to Ben Batiach, "Your uncle exclaimed, 'Woe!'"

Ben Batiach sent a messenger and had Rabban Yochanan brought before him. He asked Rabban Yochanan, "Why did you exclaim, 'Woe!'?"

Rabban Yochanan replied, "I did not exclaim, 'Woe!', but 'Va!'[an exclamation of happiness.]"

Ben Batiach said to him, "You exclaimed 'Va!'? Why did you make that exclamation?"

EICHAH RABAH

A Midrashic text on the Book of Lamentations, produced by the sages of the Talmud in the Land of Israel. Its language closely resembles that of the Jerusalem Talmud. It was first printed in Pesaro, Italy, in 1519 together with four other Midrashic works on the other four *megilot*.

Rabban Yochanan answered, "Because you burned all the stores, and I thought that so long as the stores were intact the people would not expose themselves to the dangers of battle." Through the difference between "Woe" and "Va," Rabban Yochanan escaped death. He applied to himself the verse, "The advantage of knowledge is that wisdom preserves the life of its possessors" (Ecclesiastes 8:12).

Three days later Rabban Yochanan ben Zakkai went out for a walk in the marketplace and saw people boiling straw and drinking its water because of their hunger. He said to himself, "Can men who boil straw and drink its water withstand the armies of Vespasian?" He said to himself, "The main thing that must be done is that I leave the city and try to appease the enemy."

Rabban Yochanan sent a message to Ben Batiach, "Get me out of the city."

Ben Batiach replied, "We have made an agreement among ourselves that nobody shall leave the city except the dead."

Rabban Yochanan said, "Carry me out in the guise of a corpse."

Rabbi Eliezer carried the casket holding Rabban Yochanan at the head, Rabbi Yehoshua by the feet, and Ben Batiach walked in front. When they reached the city gates, the guards wanted to stab him to make sure he was really dead. Ben Batiach said to them, "Do you wish that our enemies should say that they stabbed their rabbi?" Once he said this to them they allowed him to pass.

After going through the gates, they carried him to a cemetery, left him there, and returned to the city. Rabban Yochanan emerged from the casket and strolled among the soldiers of Vespasian. He asked them, "Where is the king?"

The soldiers went and told Vespasian, "A Jew wishes to greet you."

Vespasian said to them, "Let him come."

On his arrival, Rabban Yochanan exclaimed, "Long live the emperor!"

Vespasian said to him, "You have given me a royal greeting, but I am not king. Should the king hear of it he will put me to death."

Rabban Yochanan said to him, "Even if you are not the king now, you are destined to be the king, because the Temple will only be destroyed by a king. As it is said, 'And the Lebanon [a reference to the Temple] shall fall by a mighty one [a reference to a king].' (Isaiah 10:34)."

Vespasian's officers took Rabban Yochanan and placed him in the innermost of seven chambers, where it was completely dark. They asked him what hour of the night it was and he told them. They subsequently asked him what hour of the day it was and he told them. How did Rabban Yochanan know it? From his study.

Three days later Vespasian went to take a bath in the river Gophna. After he had bathed and put on one of his shoes, a message arrived informing him that Nero had died and the Romans had proclaimed him king. He tried to put on the other shoe but it would not fit onto his foot. He sent for Rabban Yochanan and asked, "Can you explain to me why all these days I wore two shoes which fitted me, but now one fits and the other does not?"

Rabban Yochanan answered, "You have been informed of good news, which caused your foot to expand, as it is written, 'Good news fattens the bone' (Proverbs 15:30)."

Vespasian asked, "What must I do to get my shoe on?"

Rabban Yochanan replied, "Is there anybody whom you hate or who has done you wrong? Let him pass in front of you and your flesh will shrink, because it is written, 'A broken spirit dries the bones' (Proverbs 17:22)."

Vespasian's men then began speaking to Rabban Yochanan in parables. "If a snake nested in a cask, what should be done with it?"

Rabban Yochanan answered, "Bring a charmer to charm the snake into going away, and leave the cask intact."

Pangar, however, said, "Kill the snake even if it requires breaking the cask."

Vespasian's men cited a second parable to prove their point. "If a snake nested in a tower, what should be done with it?"

He answered, "Bring a charmer to charm the snake into going away, and leave the tower intact."

Pangar, however, said, "Kill the snake even if it requires burning down the tower."

Rabban Yochanan said to Pangar, "All neighbors that perform evil acts against others generally perform them against their own neighbors. You, the leader of Arabia that borders the Land of Israel, instead of putting in a plea in our defense, argue for the prosecution against us!"

Pangar replied, "In doing so I seek your welfare. For so long as the Temple stands, kingdoms will attack you, but if it is destroyed they will not attack you."

Rabban Yochanan said to him, "The man's heart knows whether his intent was straight or crooked."

Vespasian said to Rabban Yochanan, "Make a request of me and I will grant it."

Rabban Yochanan said, "I beg that you leave this city of Jerusalem alone and depart."

Vespasian said to him, "Did the Romans proclaim me king so that I should leave this city alone? Make another request of me and I will grant it."

Rabban Yochanan said to him, "I beg that you should leave alone the Western Gate which leads to Lod, and everyone who leaves through it up to the fourth hour shall be spared."

After Vespasian had conquered the city he asked Rabban Yochanan, "Do you have any friend or relative there? Send and bring him out before the troops enter."

Rabban Yochanan sent Rabbi Eliezer and Rabbi Yehoshua to bring out Rabbi Tsadok. They went and found him in the city gate and brought him to Rabban Yochanan. When he arrived, Rabban Yochanan stood up before him. Vespasian asked, "You stand up before this emaciated old man?"

Rabban Yochanan answered, "By your life, if there had been one more like him, even if you would have had double the number of soldiers, you would not have been able to conquer Jerusalem."

Vespasian asked, "What is his righteousness that gives him so much power?"

Rabban Yochanan replied, "His merit is that he eats one fig and on the strength of it studies one hundred sessions in the academy."

"Why is he so lean?" Vespasian asked.

Rabban Yochanan answered, "Because of his numerous abstinences and fasts."

Vespasian sent messengers and brought doctors to cure Rabbi Tsadok. The doctors fed him on small portions of food and small doses of liquid until his physical powers returned to him. Rabbi Tsadok's son Eleazar said to him, "Father, give the doctors their reward in this world so that they should have no merit with you in the World to Come." Rabbi Tsadok taught them how to determine measurements with the use of one's fingers, and taught them how to use unconventional scales for measuring weights.

When Vespasian had subdued the city, he assigned the destruction of the four ramparts to the four commanders mentioned above, and the Western Gate was allotted to Pangar. However, Heaven had decreed that the Western Wall should never be destroyed, because the Divine Presence dwells in the west, where the Holy of Holies stood.

The other three commanders destroyed their sections, but Pangar did not destroy his. Vespasian sent for him and asked, "Why did you not destroy your section?"

Pangar replied, "By your life, I acted so for the honor of the kingdom. For had I demolished it, nobody would have known what a powerful city you destroyed. Now, people will see how powerful Jerusalem was, and they will exclaim, 'See the might of Vespasian, what he was able to destroy!'"

Vespasian said to him, "By your life, you have spoken well. But since you disobeyed my command, you shall ascend to the roof and throw yourself down. If you live, you will live; and if you die, you will die."

He ascended, threw himself down and died. Thus the curse of Rabban Yochanan came upon him.

The translation is based on *Soncino Midrash Rabah* (Soncino Press: London, 1983), with revisions by Rabbi Yaakov Gershon, Rabbi Shmuel Klatzkin, and Rabbi Shmuel Super.

THE BIBLE'S ALLUSION TO THE DESTRUCTION OF JERUSALEM

RABBI DON YITSCHAK ABARBANEL, DEUTERONOMY 28:49–69

After having mentioned the prophecies of the misfortunes that would come upon them with the destruction of the First Temple and their being in the Babylonian exile, Moses goes on to mention the destruction of the Second Temple and the coming of the Romans to conquer the Land of Israel and to destroy Jerusalem.

It is regarding the Romans that he says, "God will raise against you a nation from afar, from the ends of the earth," (Deuteronomy 28:49), since Rome is very far from Jerusalem. In addition, many soldiers in the Roman army came from the West: from Brittany, from England, and from Burgundy. Other soldiers also came from the lands of the East, as recounted in *Josippon.* Therefore he says that they are coming "from afar."

Although they are coming from afar, he mentions that nonetheless they will come with great speed and suddenness. That is the meaning of, "as the eagle will swoop" (Deuteronomy 28:49).

Since their language was not usable in the land alien to them, as its roots are distant from our holy tongue, he said, "a nation whose tongue you will not understand" (ibid.).

He also describes them as, "A brazen-faced nation that will show no deference to the old nor mercy to the young" (ibid., 28:50), for the Romans conquered all the regions of the earth and they instilled fear in all the people so they would not revolt.

RABBI DON YITSCHAK ABARBANEL, 1437–1508

Biblical exegete and statesman. Abarbanel was born in Lisbon, Portugal, and served as a minister in the court of King Alfonso V of Portugal. After intrigues at court led to accusations against him, he fled to Spain, where he once again served as a counselor to royalty. It is claimed that Abarbanel offered King Ferdinand and Queen Isabella large sums of money for the revocation of their Edict of Expulsion of 1492, but to no avail. After the expulsion, he eventually settled in Italy where he wrote a commentary on Scripture, as well as other venerated works.

It is fitting that we know details about this nation, whether it was Vespasian and Titus, the son of his wife, and their armies that came on Jerusalem and destroyed it, as our master Rabbi Moshe ben Nachman [Nachmanides] wrote; or whether there were also other princes that came at a different time.

The Three Roman Conquests

You should know that the Romans did not come just once to wage war against Jerusalem, striking Israel down with the sword of murder and destruction. Rather, this happened many times, in particular the three times of which Yosef ben Guryon [the author of *Josippon*] wrote.

The first time was in the days of Hyrkenos and Aristobulus, the sons of King Alexander who quarreled over the royal succession. Aristobulus, the younger son, asserted his claim to rule. In order to enlist the support of Pompeii, the head of the Roman army—who was in Damascus at the time—Aristobulus sent him a delegation bearing a gift of a golden vine whose gold weighed 500 *kikarim,* and which was also adorned with precious stones.

However, Hyrkenos, the older brother, went there together with Antipater, his counselor. They reached an agreement with Pompeii that he would aid Hyrkenos in becoming king on condition that Hyrkenos would accept vassalage to Rome by paying an annual tax in return for its helping him rule, since Hyrkenos was the first-born son of Alexander.

Pompeii came with all Rome's might against Jerusalem, and the men of Aristobulus came out and struck the Romans a great blow. Pompeii was cowed before their might and thought to withdraw from the city, believing he could not conquer it. But since the men of Hyrkenos that were in Jerusalem were battling the men of Aristobulus his brother, Pompeii approached the gates of the city and Hyrkenos's men opened the gate for him. The Romans entered and conquered Jerusalem and the king's palace, "and the daughter of Zion was overwhelmed by mourning and moaning"

(Lamentations 2:5). Only God's Temple was not captured, for the priests closed the gates of God's House and fought them for many days.

In the fourth month—that is, Tammuz—on its seventeenth day, the day of the fast, when the priests were getting ready to make the offering, Pompeii brought the battering ram, attacked the tower of the Temple and toppled it to the ground. The Romans came into the Temple, striking down the priests as they came, and their corpses fell on top of their sacrifices.

When the last of the priests in the Temple died and the Roman chief officers entered the Sanctuary, Pompeii came, saw the Holy of Holies, and had pity. He did not set his hand on its appurtenances as he had done with the appurtenances of the outer areas of the Temple, all of which he had taken. He gave the kingship to Hyrkenos, and arrested his brother Aristobolus and sent him to Rome.

This was the first time the Romans conquered Jerusalem and they spilled blood like water in the city.

The second time was in the days of King Herod. Herod was battling Antigonos, the son of Aristobolus, who held Jerusalem and had the men of Judah on his side. Herod came to Sosius, the captain of the Roman army, whom Antoninus had sent together with a large Roman force to aid him. They all went up and besieged Jerusalem for nearly a year. One night, twenty Jews from among Herod's most valiant warriors set up ladders on the wall. The Roman soldiers scaled the walls and struck down the sleeping guards. They ran quickly and destroyed the city gates, and Jerusalem was captured.

Herod, Sosius, and the entire Roman army came into the city and they struck down Jews mercilessly, young men and young women alike, until Herod became angry and said to Sosius, "If all the people will be devoured by the sword, over whom will I rule?" Sosius then issued a decree that anyone who would kill anyone would himself be put to death.

Sosius's officers ran to the Temple and sought to open it up and see the Holy of Holies. But they could not, for Herod drew his sword and stood with his young men before the gate of the Temple, and the Romans fled. For the Jews said, "Better that we should die than that these aliens should see the hidden things of God."

The third time was during the days of Agrippas, when Vespasian and his [step-]son Titus came from Rome to subdue Jerusalem to Roman rule. Vespasian went back to Rome to be crowned Caesar, and Titus his son remained until he had captured Jerusalem, broken down its walls, and burned down the House of God, as is related in *Josippon*.

It was regarding these three times that they came to destroy Jerusalem that Moses, the Master of the Prophets, said here in this text, "God will raise against you a nation from afar." Therefore, in these verses, "nation" is mentioned three times—"God will raise against you a nation," "a brazen-faced nation," and "a nation whose tongue you will not understand". These three mentions correspond to the three times that I have mentioned. And since in the last time, Titus and his army devoured us and confounded us, it says of him, "A brazen-faced nation that will show no deference to the old nor mercy to the young."

The Eight Evils against Jerusalem

Associated with this terrible war that Titus made against Jerusalem, he mentions eight terrible evils and losses that came upon the people of God in Jerusalem and upon their descendants who went into exile.

The first was the grave, exacerbated famine among them, which was the cause of Judah's exile. Regarding this, the text says, "And he will devour the offspring of your animals and the fruit of your land . . . he will leave nothing of your grain, wine, or oil . . . until he has eliminated you" (Deuteronomy 28:48). There is no doubt that the famine was the cause of their destruction. Had they not been subdued by hunger, the Romans could never have conquered Jerusalem.

The second was the long duration of the continuous siege that caused Jerusalem to be captured. For had the enemy only warred against it a year or two, they would not have overcome the valor of the men of Judah. But since the siege stretched on and on, and because coupled with it came famine and plague, the men of Judah could no longer withstand the onslaught. Regarding this, the text says, "They will besiege you in all your gates until, all over your land, they will raze the tall and mighty walls in which you had trusted" (Deuteronomy 28:52). Then the text says a second time, "They will besiege you in all your gates" (ibid.), to tells us that not only will the enemy besiege the mighty fortified cities but also all the other cities, so that there will be no place to sow a crop and provide food to the fortified cities.

The text further says, "Which the Lord your God gave you" (ibid.) to tell that this great distress is a result of God's providence. For had God not commanded it, the enemy could not have come into the gates of Jerusalem.

It also says, "And you will eat the fruit of your belly, the flesh of your sons and your daughters" (ibid., 28:53). The meaning is that the distress will be so continuously prolonged that they will eat their sons and daughters. "Even the most delicate and indulged men (and women) among you" (ibid., 28:54) will engage in this cruel act, killing their children by their own hands and eating their flesh. They will even be stingily unwilling to share this food with the rest of their children. Here, too, the text says, "Which the Lord your God gave you" (ibid.), saying that this, too, came from God because of their sins.

All of this is as was prophesied here by Moses, the Master of the Prophets. There is no doubt that so it actually happened in Jerusalem during the destruction of the Second Temple, as it is related in *Josippon*.

This indicates the magnitude of the famine and the extraordinary distress, so that no one was spared, and, as it says, "For lacking all things, you will devour them in the great distress which your enemies will bring you in your gates" (Deuteronomy 28:57). This was so extraordinary a punishment that "The ears of all who hear it will tingle" (I Samuel 3:11). He therefore said about this, "If you will not be careful to observe all the words of this Torah that are written in this Book, to fear God" etc. (Deuteronomy 28:58). This means, know that all this will happen to you in its entirety if you do not humble yourselves before God and fear Him.

He had to mention this here [in the middle of enumerating the curses], since what he had said earlier [regarding the curses being a punishment for not listening to God], at the beginning and at the end [ibid., 28:15; 28:45], was about the destruction of the First Temple. And since this later section is about what they suffered during the destruction of the Second Temple and in the extended exile that followed it, there was a need to state this to them separately. For even though the time has drawn on and on, and the duration of this consequence has stretched through the generations, the Torah will still not be changed. Its power then is its power now, just like that of the glorious, awesome, and blessed God, who will always and forever live and endure.

The third loss was the disease that would occur during the siege, from the fevers and the contagions. Regarding this he said, "God will inflict astonishing plagues on you and your offspring," etc. (ibid., 28:59). This mention of "plagues on you and your offspring" is to make known that this curse will happen during the siege of Jerusalem during the time of the Second Temple, for that is when there were so many kinds of deadly and long-lasting diseases, as described in *Josippon*. This curse has also continued on into this exile of ours all these generations, for one continually finds Jews sick with these acute fevers, with the plague, and with hemorrhoids—more so than the other nations.

"He will bring upon you all the illnesses of Egypt and they will cling to you" (Deuteronomy 28:60). I think that this includes all the hardheartedness of Pharaoh and his servants. Its like was present at the destruction of the Second Temple among the rebellious ones of our people, who would not accept the Roman yoke on their neck. For although Titus had approached in peace and assured them that they could remain in their Land and in their inheritance and keep the service in the House of God, they refused and stiffened their necks, in the end causing the destruction and burning of the Temple. The excesses of these extremists brought upon them and us today, "all the illness and all the blows which were not written" (ibid., 28:61), leading to the persecutions and the destruction, "until you have been wiped out" (ibid.).

The fourth loss that transpired then was the destruction of the people and its diminution. For the number of those that died among the inhabitants of Jerusalem was like the sand by the seashore. Some died by hunger, some by the plague that was in the city; very many died by the hand of the extremists and some few by the enemy. Regarding this, he said, "You will be left a remnant few in number after having been as many as the stars in the sky" (ibid., 28:62). The meaning of this is that they will be left small in quantity and in quality; the survivors would be as if dead. For the Hebrew word for "number" here is like the word meaning "dead" in the verse "Dead who will not live" (Isaiah 26:14). Before this, during their good fortune, they had been "as many as the stars in the sky" (Genesis 22:17), meaning to say that they were like the stars in their quality of eternality as well as in their quantity—*many*.

If you question how they could go from one extreme to another, I will answer that this is because "you have not heeded God's voice" (Deuteronomy 28:62). Therefore, "Just as God was delighted," and desirous of "doing them good" (ibid., 28:63) in quality, and in "making them very numerous" (ibid.) in quantity, and that profusion of good was a result of divine providence, so too, "God will cause them to rejoice over you to make you perish and destroy you" (ibid.). For there was providence in the diminution just as there was in the expansion and multiplication.

Josippon has already written that when Titus conquered Jerusalem, he asked the Jews to tell him the true number of their dead, the many that had been taken out from all the gates of Jerusalem to be buried during the hunger they had endured. The number was 800,575, aside from those who had died in the streets and had not been buried, those who had died in the Temple of God, and the affluent ones who had been killed by the wickedness of the extremists who had not let them be buried, and who lay like dung on the face of the earth. Titus was very much astonished at the great number of people who had been in Jerusalem.

The fifth loss that they received was that they lost the good land God had given them, a land flowing with milk and honey. This was an extraordinary and incalculable loss, regarding which he said, "And you will be plucked off of that land which you had come to inherit" (Deuteronomy 28:63). And since captives have a great comfort when they can join together to cry and talk about their troubles, he said that for them it will not be so: "For God will scatter you among all the peoples, from one end of the earth to the other" (ibid., 28:64). For the people of the time of the Second Temple were scattered among all the nations, east and west. As the Romans ruled over all the lands, each soldier would send some captives to the land in which he dwelt. It could be that it was to this that Jeremiah referred when he said, "Judah has been exiled because of misery and harsh oppression; when she settled among the nations, she found no rest" (Lamentations 1:3). His meaning was that when the tribes were exiled and went away to a far place, they remained by themselves there. Even though the surrounding nations oppressed them with levies and taxes, since they were by themselves, they found rest. But the people of Judah who were exiled in the second destruction dwelt among the nations. That is to say, in their midst, in their cities, and therefore they found no rest. All of this was included in his saying, "God will scatter you among all the peoples."

The sixth loss he mentioned in his words, "And there you will serve other gods which neither you nor your ancestors knew, wood and stone," etc. (ibid.). The intent of these words is not that they served those who worshipped these gods, as Onkelos and Rashi explained. Rather, the meaning is that after they went into exile, many left the religion because they could no longer bear the suffering and the persecution.

It says here, "which neither you nor your ancestors knew, wood and stone," something that was not said earlier. For there it had been talking about the destruction of the First Temple, when they had gone to Babylonia and they served the gods of the Babylonians, whom they had already known well and served often. Now, however, it is speaking about the final exile, and therefore he said to them, "Which neither you nor your ancestors knew, wood and stone."

He said further, "Among those peoples you will have no peace and your foot will find no rest" (ibid., 28:65), explaining and clarifying the idea about which the prophet Ezekiel spoke: "Do you imagine that what you have thought, that 'We will be among the nations like the other clans of the lands, serving wood and stone' will come to be? As I live, says God, if not with a strong arm and with outpouring wrath will I reign over you!" (Ezekiel 20:32–33).

The seventh loss was that despite being mighty and courageous men of valor who were famous among the mighty during the days of the Second Temple, the effect of exile brought about that "you will have an anguished heart, eyes that pine and a despondent spirit" (Deuteronomy 28:65). The meaning of "an anguished heart" is that you will be in a continuous state of fear and terror. "Eyes that pine" to leave the exile—when will the end come of the dismay and of the agitation? "A despondent spirit"—about the destruction of the House of God and the exile of the people.

"Their lives will be precarious" (ibid., 28:66), this means they will be endangered by the enemies among whom they will live, to the point that "they will be afraid night and day, with no assurance of their survival" (ibid.), for all day long they will think death will come upon them, through their windows and into their great homes, and therefore "In the morning you will say, 'Who will bring the evening?' and in the evening, 'Who will bring the morning?'" (ibid., 28:67).

He gives a reason for both these things. When they say that their desire and will in the evening is "Would only that morning would come," it is because of "the fear of your heart which makes you afraid" (ibid.). That is to say, that because during the hours of darkness, they yearn for the morning so that it can remove from them the nightmarish imaginations that terrify them on their beds. In the morning, they say "Would only that evening would come, because of what their eyes would see" (ibid.). That is to say, that when the sun is shining, they would say, "Would only that evening would come," to be hidden from those who would attack or kill them. All of this that he mentioned regarding the fear and faint-heartedness and agitation was not about those who remained good Jews, but was said about those who left the boundaries of the religion and served other gods. He points out that even if they would be wealthy, honored, and having stature among the nations of the land, being great people or officers in cities for many years, nonetheless, fear will never depart from them. Their lives will continually be unsure, for those people will be their enemies and continuously, all day long, the sword will be lying on their neck.

The eighth loss is the disgrace and the shame. That is to say that "they will return to Egypt in ships" (ibid., 28:68), and the Egyptians will rejoice in their downfall. They will say, "Why did you have to return to Egypt? Is it not just to plot against us and take advantage of us as it was the first time?" And this that the text says, "By the way that I said to you that you will not see it anymore" (ibid.), comes to give the reason why he had said "in ships." That is to say, I said that you will return to Egypt in ships because of the way that I had said you will not see it anymore. In order to verify My words that you will not see that way again, it is necessary for the return to be by ship, so that they would not follow the way on dry land about which I had spoken.

It mentions the shame of the going to Egypt, to emphasize that even though the land of Egypt was filled with all good things and food was very inexpensive, it would be emotionally as if you will offer yourselves for sale as slaves, so that your masters would give you food to restore your soul, "but there will be no buyer" (ibid.)—not a single Egyptian would buy a single one of you because they were afraid that it would turn out poorly for them in the end. They also would not buy you so that they wouldn't have to give you food. All of this would be so that you would all die by hunger and thirst.

This curse, being the extraordinary punishment that it was, was caused by God so that the people of Israel should not be sold as slaves among their enemies and be made into merchandise, as we see it among the Africans and the Arabs and other peoples, and they would be locked into perpetual servitude. Rather, they should remain in the hands of the masters of the land, the kings of the earth, and they should be slaves of the kings and not slaves to the rest of the people.

And so it was in truth. The Jews through all the days of our exile are set apart for the kings and nobles of the land, and are not slaves of the rest of the people.

The eight losses and great evils that the Jews received during the destruction of Jerusalem at the time of the Second Temple, and all that followed from them in our generations of exile, have now been explained.

Translated by Rabbi Yaakov Gershon, Rabbi Shmuel Klatzkin, and Rabbi Shmuel Super

Lesson

3

Trial by Fire, *Pedro Berruguete, 13th century.*
(Museo Del Prado, Madrid)

THE MAIMONIDEAN CONTROVERSY
THE NEXUS OF FAITH AND REASON IN JUDAISM

In 1232, Dominican priests publicly burned Maimonides's Guide for the Perplexed *in Montpellier, but this display was the result of a controversy within the Jewish community over the legitimacy of this work. How did one of the greatest rabbis of the Middle Ages become a flashpoint in the Jewish community? What was the ideological nature of this controversy? Much of this story hinges on the tensions between faith and reason, and we will gain clarity about this topic by examining the polemical writings on both sides of this debate.*

TEXT 1

RABBI AVRAHAM BEN HARAMBAM, *MILCHAMOT HASHEM* P. 47

מָה בָּעֲרוּ הָאוֹמְרִים כִּי בָּעֲרוּ

סִפְרֵי חֲמוּדוֹת יָקְרוּ מִזָּהָב.

אֵשׁ אוֹכְלָה הֵמָּה, וְאֵיךְ אֵשׁ תֹּאכְלֵם?

בִּינוּ לָזֹאת בּוֹעֲרִים וְעֹזְרֵי רָהַב,

אֵין זֶה, אֲבָל עָלוּ כְּמוֹ תִשְׁבִּי לָאֵל,

בָּאֵשׁ, וּכְמַלְאָךְ בְּתוֹךְ הַלַּהַב.

RABBI AVRAHAM BEN HARAMBAM
1186–1237

Talmudist and philosopher.
Rabbi Avraham, the only son of
Maimonides, was born in Cairo,
Egypt. Rabbi Avraham studied under
his father's tutelage, and succeeded
him as the leader of the Egyptian
Jewish community. Rabbi Avraham
authored a commentary to the Torah
and a book of ethics, only parts of
which are extant. He is best known
for his writings in defense of his
father, including halachic responsa
and *Milchamot Hashem*, a defense
of the *Guide for the Perplexed*.

How foolish are they who believe that with fire,
One can destroy books more precious than gold.
These books are themselves consuming fire;
How then can they perish in flames?
Know, you who burn and your arrogant helpers,
All is not as it appears: they went up like Elijah to God,
And as an angel in the flame.

Guide for the Perplexed *in the original Arabic and Hebrew
characters, Mardin, 1292. (Bodleian Library, University of Oxford)*

TEXT 2

MAIMONIDES, *GUIDE FOR THE PERPLEXED*, INTRODUCTION

מַטְּרַת הַמַּאֲמָר הַזֶּה לְהָעִיר לְאָדָם דָתִי, שֶׁכְּבָר נִקְבַּע בְּלִבּוֹ וְהוּשַׂג בְּדַעְתּוֹ
אֲמִיתַּת תּוֹרָתֵנוּ, וְהוּא שָׁלֵם בְּדָתוֹ וּמִידוֹתָיו, וְעִיֵּן בְּמַדָּעֵי הַפִילוֹסוֹפִים
וְיָדַע עִנְיָנֵיהֶם, וּמְשָׁכוֹ הַשֵּׂכֶל הָאֱנוֹשִׁי וְהִדְרִיכוֹ לְהַעֲמִידוֹ בִּמְעוֹנוֹ, וְעָמְדוּ
בְּפָנָיו פְּשָׁטֵי הַתּוֹרָה, וּמַה שֶּׁלֹּא הִצְלִיחַ לְהָבִינוֹ, אוֹ שֶׁהֵבִין אוֹתוֹ מֵעִנְיָנֵי
הַשֵּׁמוֹת הַמְשֻׁתָּפִים אוֹ הַמּוּשְׁאָלִים אוֹ הַמְסֻפָּקִים, וְיִשָׁאֵר בִּמְבוּכָה
וְהֵיסוּס.

אוֹ שֶׁיִּימָשֵׁךְ אַחַר שִׂכְלוֹ וְיַעֲזוֹב מַה שֶּׁיָּדַע מֵאוֹתָם הַשֵּׁמוֹת, וְיַחְשׁוֹב
שֶׁעָזַב יְסוֹדוֹת הַתּוֹרָה.

אוֹ שֶׁיַּעֲמוֹד כְּפִי מַה שֶּׁהֵבִין מֵהֶם וְלֹא יִמָשֵׁךְ אַחַר שִׂכְלוֹ, וְנִמְצָא שֶׁפָּנָה
אָחוֹר מִשִׂכְלוֹ וּפִירֵשׁ מִמֶּנּוּ. וְיַחְשׁוֹב עִם זֹאת שֶׁהוּא הֵבִיא עַל עַצְמוֹ נֶזֶק
וְהֶפְסֵד בְּדָתוֹ, וְיִשָׁאֵר עִם אוֹתָם הַדֵעוֹת הַדִּמְיוֹנִיּוֹת תּוֹךְ הַרְגָּשַׁת צַעַר
וּמְצוּקָה, וְלֹא חָדַל לִהְיוֹת בְּכְאֵב לֵב וּמְבוּכָה גְדוֹלָה . . . וּלְפִיכָךְ קָרָאתִי
מַאֲמָר זֶה מוֹרֵה הַנְבוּכִים.

**RABBI MOSHE BEN MAIMON
(MAIMONIDES, RAMBAM), 1135–1204**

Halachist, philosopher, author, and
physician. Maimonides was born in
Cordoba, Spain. After the conquest
of Cordoba by the Almohads, he
fled Spain and eventually settled
in Cairo, Egypt. There, he became
the leader of the Jewish community
and served as court physician to the
vizier of Egypt. He is most noted
for authoring the *Mishneh Torah*, an
encyclopedic arrangement of Jewish
law, and for his philosophical work,
Guide for the Perplexed. His rulings
on Jewish law are integral to the
formation of halachic consensus.

The object of this book is to enlighten a religious man
who believes in and has intellectually grasped the truth
of our holy Law, who conscientiously fulfills his moral
and religious duties, and at the same time has studied
philosophy and understood it. Human reason has attracted him to abide in its sphere; and when he considers the literal interpretation of the Torah, and those
parts that he has not succeeded in understanding, or
misunderstood because of ambiguous terms used in the
Torah, he is lost in perplexity and anxiety.

If he follows his intellect alone, and renounces his previous views that are based on those misunderstandings,

he would consider that he had rejected the fundamental principles of the Law.

If he retains the opinions that were derived from those terms, and abandons the guidance of his reason entirely, his religious convictions would still suffer loss and injury. For he would then be left with those errors that cause him pain and anxiety, and would be in a constant state of grief and great perplexity. . . . For this reason I have called this book *Guide for the Perplexed*.

Plato and Aristotle in Discussion, *Luca Della Robbia, ca. 1437.* *(Opera di S. Maria del Fiore, Florence)*

Figure 3.1

Thirteenth-Century Western Europe

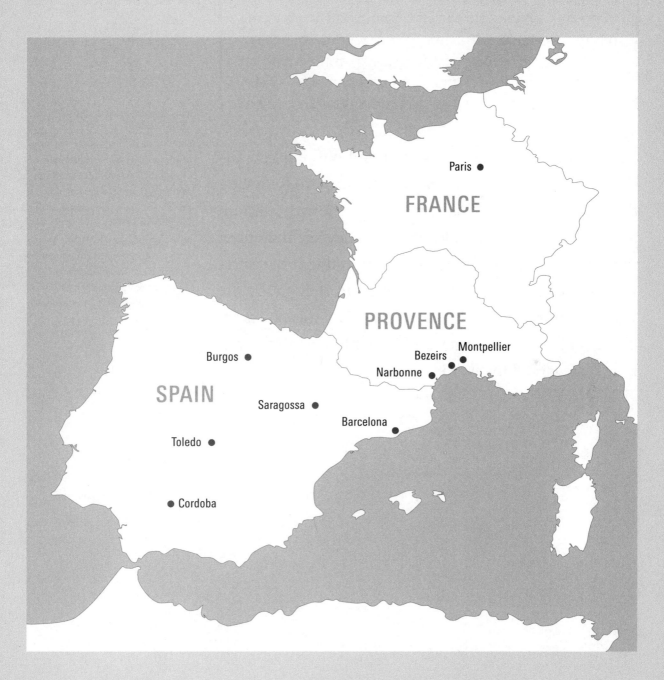

TEXT 3

RABBI SHLOMO OF MONTPELLIER, IN *GINZEI NISTAROT* 3:12

שָׁמַעְנוּ מִקְצָתָם, זְקֵנִים וּנְעָרִים, מְפַרְסְמִים דְּבָרִים, חֲדָשִׁים מִקָּרוֹב
בָּאוּ לֹא שְׂעָרוּם אֲבוֹתָם, הוֹלְכִים בְּדֶרֶךְ לֹא טוֹב אַחַר מַחְשְׁבוֹתָם, לַהֲרוֹס
הַקַּבָּלוֹת, וְלִמְשׁוֹל מְשָׁלִים בְּדִבְרֵי הַתּוֹרוֹת . . . כָּל הַסִּפּוּרִים מְשָׁלִים
וְכָל הַמִּצְוֹת הַנְהָגוֹת, וְכָאֵלֶּה עַצְמוּ מִסְפֵּר, שָׁמַעְתִּי מַלְעִיגִים עַל דִּבְרֵי
רַבּוֹתֵינוּ. וּכְשָׁמְעִי הַדְּבָרִים הָאֵלֶּה נִבְהַלְתִּי, וְנָפְלוּ פָנַי אָרְצָה וְחָרַדְתִּי
וְהִתְוַוכַּחְתִּי עִמָּהֶם פְּעָמִים רַבּוֹת וְהָיִיתִי בְּעֵינֵיהֶם כִּמְתַעְתֵּעַ.

I heard a few people, both young and old, publicly insisting on nontraditional teachings. They are following their intellect down a bad path, to tear down tradition, to reduce the Torah to allegory. . . . They say that all of the stories of the Torah are allegories and that the *mitzvot* are merely traditional customs, and they mock the words of our sages. When I heard this I was shocked, upset, and worried. I argued with them many times, but they disregarded my words.

**RABBI SHLOMO OF MONTPELLIER
13TH CENTURY**

Talmudist. Rabbi Shlomo was born in Barcelona, and lived primarily in Montpellier, Provence (now in southern France), where he was a prominent Talmudic scholar. Only fragments of Rabbi Shlomo's writings have survived, and he is best known as the instigator of the Maimonidean controversy. One of his prime students was Rabeinu Yonah of Gerona, author of *Sha'arei Teshuvah*.

TEXT 4

LEVITICUS 14:9

וְרָחַץ אֶת בְּשָׂרוֹ בַּמַּיִם וְטָהֵר.

He [the ritually impure individual] should immerse himself in water, thereby becoming pure.

Montpellier (where the Maimonidean controversy began), Franz Hogenberg, ca. 1572. (National Library of Israel, Hebrew University)

TEXT 5

EXODUS 30:7–8, 34–35 👥

וְהִקְטִיר עָלָיו אַהֲרֹן קְטֹרֶת סַמִּים בַּבֹּקֶר בַּבֹּקֶר, בְּהֵיטִיבוֹ אֶת הַנֵּרֹת
יַקְטִירֶנָּה. וּבְהַעֲלֹת אַהֲרֹן אֶת הַנֵּרֹת בֵּין הָעַרְבַּיִם יַקְטִירֶנָּה, קְטֹרֶת תָּמִיד
לִפְנֵי ה' לְדֹרֹתֵיכֶם . . .

וַיֹּאמֶר ה' אֶל מֹשֶׁה קַח לְךָ סַמִּים, נָטָף וּשְׁחֵלֶת וְחֶלְבְּנָה סַמִּים וּלְבֹנָה זַכָּה
בַּד בְּבַד יִהְיֶה. וְעָשִׂיתָ אֹתָהּ קְטֹרֶת, רֹקַח מַעֲשֵׂה רוֹקֵחַ, מְמֻלָּח טָהוֹר קֹדֶשׁ.

Aaron shall burn fragrant incense on the altar every
morning when he tends the lamps. He shall burn incense again when he lights the lamps in the afternoon,
a continual incense before God for your future generations. . . .

God said to Moses: "Take the following aromatics: bal-
sam sap, onycha, and galbanum; aromatics and pure
frankincense: they shall be of equal weight. You shall
make them into incense, a compound according to the
art of the perfumer, well blended, pure, and holy."

Figure 3.2

Two Categories of *Mitzvot*

חֹק / חֻקִּים	מִשְׁפָּט/מִשְׁפָּטִים
Chok / Chukim	*Mishpat / Mishpatim*
Decrees	Laws
Mitzvot without obvious reasons	*Mitzvot* with obvious reasons

TEXT 6

MAIMONIDES, *GUIDE FOR THE PERPLEXED* 3:26

כְּמוֹ שֶׁנֶּחְלְקוּ אַנְשֵׁי הָעִיּוּן מִבַּעֲלֵי הַדָּת הַאִם מַעֲשָׂיו יִתְעַלֶּה תּוֹצָאָה שֶׁל
חָכְמָה אוֹ סְתָם רָצוֹן לֹא לְבַקָּשַׁת תַּכְלִית כְּלָל, כָּךְ נֶחְלְקוּ מַחֲלוֹקֶת זוּ
עַצְמָהּ בַּצִּיוּוּיִם אֲשֶׁר צִיוָּה לָנוּ . . .

אֵין הֲמוֹן הַחֲכָמִים סוֹבְרִים שֶׁהֵם דְּבָרִים שֶׁאֵין לָהֶם טַעַם כְּלָל, וְלֹא
נִדְרְשָׁה בָּהֶן תַּכְלִיּוֹת, לְפִי שֶׁזֶּה מֵבִיא לְמַעֲשֵׂי הַהֶבֶל כְּפִי שֶׁהִזְכַּרְנוּ. אֶלָּא
סוֹבְרִים הֲמוֹן הַחֲכָמִים שֶׁיֵּשׁ לָהֶן טַעַם, כְּלוֹמַר: תַּכְלִית מוֹעִילָה בְּהֶחְלֵט,
אֶלָּא שֶׁהִיא נֶעֱלֶמֶת מִמֶּנּוּ, אִם מַחֲמַת קוֹצֶר שִׂכְלֵנוּ אוֹ לְחוֹסֶר יְדִיעָתֵנוּ.

There is disagreement among religious philosophers about whether God's actions are consequences of wisdom or are purely an expression of His will, without having any intended purpose. The same disagreement exists regarding the *mitzvot* that He has commanded us. . . .

Most of the sages do not believe that *mitzvot* are matters for which there is no reason at all and for which one must not seek any purpose. This would lead, according to what we have explained, to the *mitzvot* being considered frivolous actions. Rather, the majority opinion is that they all have a reason, a useful purpose, but that it is hidden from us. This is due to either the incapacity of our intellect or the deficiency of our knowledge.

TEXT 7

MAIMONIDES, *MISHNEH TORAH*, LAWS OF SUBSTITUTING SACRIFICES 4:13 ⊕

אַף עַל פִּי שֶׁכָּל חֻקֵּי הַתּוֹרָה גְּזֵרוֹת הֵם, כְּמוֹ שֶׁבֵּיאַרְנוּ בְּסוֹף הִלְכוֹת
מְעִילָה, רָאוּי לְהִתְבּוֹנֵן בָּהֶן וְכָל מַה שֶׁאַתָּה יָכוֹל לִיתֵּן לוֹ טַעַם תֵּן לוֹ
טַעַם . . . וְרוֹב דִּינֵי הַתּוֹרָה אֵינָן אֶלָא עֵצוֹת מֵרָחוֹק מִגְּדוֹל הָעֵצָה לְתַקֵּן
הַדֵּעוֹת וּלְיַישֵׁר כָּל הַמַּעֲשִׂים.

Although all of the suprarational *mitzvot* in the Torah are decrees, as I have explained elsewhere, it is appropriate to meditate upon them, and, wherever possible, provide a rationale. . . . Most of the Torah's laws contain deep advice from God, the greatest Adviser, to improve our character and conduct.

A 16th-century edition of Maimonides's Mishneh Torah, Venice, 1574. (Library Of Agudas Chassidei Chabad)

TEXT 8

RABBI YESHAYAH HOROWITZ, *SHENEI LUCHOT HABERIT,*
ASARAH MA'AMAROT, MA'AMAR 1

כְּשֶׁ"זֶה אֵ-לִי", שֶׁהוּא אֵ-לִי מִצַּד הַשָּׂגָתִי וִידִיעָתִי, אָז "וְאַנְוֵהוּ", מִלְּשׁוֹן "אֲנִי וָהוּ", רֹצֶה לוֹמַר, אֲנִי וָהוּא דְּבֵקִים בְּיַחַד כִּבְיָכוֹל, כִּי הַיְדִיעָה נִתְפֶּסֶת בְּלֵב. אָמְנָם כְּשֶׁאֵין לִי הַיְדִיעָה מִצַּד הַהַשָּׂגָה, רַק מִצַּד הַקַּבָּלָה שֶׁהוּא "אֱלֹקֵי אָבִי", אָז "וַאֲרֹמְמֶנְהוּ", כִּי הוּא רָם וְנִשְׂגָּב מִמֶּנִּי, וַאֲנִי מְרֻחָק מֵאִתּוֹ בְּמַצְפּוּן הַלֵּב.

RABBI YESHAYAH HALEVI HOROWITZ (*SHELAH*), 1565–1630

Kabbalist and author. Rabbi Horowitz was born in Prague and served as rabbi in several prominent Jewish communities, including Frankfurt am Main and his native Prague. After the passing of his wife in 1620, he moved to Israel. In Tiberias, he completed his *Shenei Luchot Haberit*, an encyclopedic compilation of kabbalistic ideas. He is buried in Tiberias, next to Maimonides.

When my relationship with God is a product of my own comprehension and knowledge, then I and He are united [in a meaningful relationship], for my understanding of Him permeates the emotions of my heart. If, however, I do not comprehend the Divine through my own mind and I depend only on the faith of tradition ("the God of my father"), then God remains exalted and beyond me, and my heart remains emotionally distant from Him.

Maimonides's signature.
(Huntington Manuscript 80, Bodleian Library at Oxford)

TEXT 9

RASHI, EXODUS 15:26 ⚥

> כָּל חֻקָּיו: דְּבָרִים שֶׁאֵינָן אֶלָּא גְזֵירַת מֶלֶךְ בְּלֹא שׁוּם טַעַם.

There are no reasons for God's decrees. They are purely decrees of the King.

RABBI SHLOMO YITSCHAKI (RASHI), 1040–1105

Most noted biblical and Talmudic commentator. Born in Troyes, France, Rashi studied in the famed *yeshivot* of Mainz and Worms. His commentaries on the Pentateuch and the Talmud, which focus on the straightforward meaning of the text, appear in virtually every edition of the Talmud and Bible.

TEXT 10

RASHI, PROVERBS 25:2 ⚥

> כְּשֶׁתִּדְרוֹשׁ . . . בְּחוּקִים הַכְּתוּבִים בַּתּוֹרָה כְּגוֹן חוּקִים וּדְבָרִים שֶׁהַשָּׂטָן מְקַטְרֵג עֲלֵיהֶם וּמֵשִׁיב עֲלֵיהֶם, כַּאֲכִילַת חֲזִיר וְכִלְאֵי כֶּרֶם וְשַׁעַטְנֵז, אֵין לְךָ לַחֲקוֹר רַק לְהַסְתִּיר וְלוֹמַר גְּזֵרַת מֶלֶךְ הוּא.

When you study . . . the decrees given in the Torah that the evil inclination challenges, such as the prohibition on the consumption of pork, sowing a mixture of seeds in the vineyard, and wearing clothes containing a mixture of wool and linen, you should not attempt to offer reasons for them. Rather, you should leave the matter concealed, and consider them decrees of the King.

TEXT 11

RASHI, TALMUD, BERACHOT 33B

לְהַטִּיל עַל יִשְׂרָאֵל חֻקֵּי גְזֵרוֹתָיו לְהוֹדִיעַ שֶׁהֵם עֲבָדָיו וְשׁוֹמְרֵי מִצְוֹתָיו
וּגְזֵרוֹת חֻקּוֹתָיו אַף בִּדְבָרִים שֶׁיֵּשׁ לְשָׂטָן וְלָעַכּוּ"ם לְהָשִׁיב עֲלֵיהֶם וְלוֹמַר
מַה צוֹרֶךְ בְּמִצְוָה זג.

God gave us these decrees in order to show that we are
His loyal servants who observe His commandments and
decrees, even those that our evil inclination and other
nations challenge us about, saying, "Why is this commandment necessary?"

Book of Knowledge (Sefer Hamada) *from Maimonides's* Mishneh Torah, *Italy, 15th
century. (The Israel Museum, Jerusalem; The Metropolitan Museum of Art, New York)*

TEXT 12

RABBI YEHUDAH HALEVI, *KUZARI* 1:98–99, 2:26

אֵין הָאָדָם מַגִּיעַ אֶל הָעִנְיָן הָאֱלֹקִי אֶלָּא בְּדָבָר אֱלֹקִי, רְצוֹנִי לוֹמַר:
בְּמַעֲשִׂים שֶׁיְּצַוֵּם הָאֱלֹקִים . . . וְאֵין בַּעֲבוֹדַת הָאֵ-ל סְבָרָא וְלֹא הַקָּשָׁה וְלֹא
הִתְחַכְּמוּת, וְאִלּוּ הָיָה כֵן, הָיוּ הַפִּילוֹסוֹפִים מַגִּיעִים בְּרֹב חָכְמָתָם וְשִׂכְלָם
לְכְפֵל מַה שֶׁהִגִּיעוּ בְּנֵי יִשְׂרָאֵל . . . מַה שֶׁהוּא יוֹתֵר נִפְלָא וְנַעֲלֶה וְשֶׁהִיא
תוֹרָה מֵאֵת הָאֱלֹקִים יִתְבָּרֵךְ, וּמִי שֶׁקִּבְּלָהּ קִבּוּל שָׁלֵם מִבְּלִי שֶׁיִּתְחַכֵּם בָּהּ
בְּשִׂכְלוֹ, הוּא מְעוּלֶּה מִמִּי שֶׁיִּתְחַכֵּם בָּהּ וְחָקַר.

RABBI YEHUDAH HALEVI
CA. 1075–1141

Noted author, physician, and poet. Rabbi Yehudah Halevi is best known as the author of the *Kuzari*, a philosophical work, written in the form of a discussion between a Jew, a Christian, and a Muslim before the King of the Khazars. In addition to the *Kuzari*, he wrote thousands of poems, of which only a few hundred survive today.

Man can only merit to achieve closeness to God through Godly matters, namely, by performing the actions commanded by God. . . . God is not served through human reason, logical deduction, or intellectual inquiry. Were this to be the way to serve Him, philosophers would attain greater closeness to God through their wisdom and intellectual inquiry than the Jewish people do [through performance of the *mitzvot*]. . . . The greatest and most exalted way to perform the commandments is to do so because they are God's Torah. One who accepts this completely without intellectual speculation is greater than one who speculates and ponders them.

TEXT **13**

RABBI YEHUDAH HALEVI, IBID., 3:65

> וְהַשְּׁלִישִׁי הִפְסִיד הַמַּעֲשִׂים, מִפְּנֵי שֶׁהִשְׁקִיף עַל הַשְׂכָלִים. אָמַר: אֵלֶּה
> הַמַּעֲשִׂים הֵם כֵּלִים וּמִשְׁתַּמְּשִׁים מַגִּיעִים אֶל הַמַּדְרֵגָה הַזֹּאת הָרוּחָנִית,
> וַאֲנִי כְּבַר הִגַּעְתִּי אֵלֶיהָ וְלֹא אַרְגִּישׁ עַל מַעֲשֵׂה הַתּוֹרָה.

Elisha ben Avuyah abandoned the observance of *mitzvot* because he contemplated their reasons intellectually and said, "These actions are means to achieve certain spiritual levels. I have already reached these levels; therefore, I need not observe the *mitzvot*."

QUESTIONS FOR DISCUSSION

Based on Texts 6–13:

1 Do "decrees" such as *ketoret* (incense) and immersion in a *mikveh* have any reason?

2 Should we attempt to rationalize such *mitzvot* to the best of our ability?

3 What is the optimal way to achieve closeness with God: through striving to understand Him or through fulfilling His commandments with acceptance alone?

TEXT **14**

RABBI MENACHEM ME'IRI, *BEIT HABECHIRAH, ETHICS OF THE FATHERS* 3:11 ⊕

אֶפְשָׁר לְכָל חָכָם לַחְשׁוֹב בְּעַצְמוֹ הַטַּעַם, וְלֹא שֶׁיִּסְמוֹךְ עַל סְבָרָתוֹ לִגְזוֹר
עָלָיו כִּי כֵן הוּא, אֲבָל שֶׁדַּעְתּוֹ נוֹטָה לְכָךְ. וַאֲפִלּוּ בְּדֶרֶךְ זֶה אֵין רָאוּי לְפַרְסֵם
הָעִנְיָן, אוּלַי יִכָּשֵׁל בְּנִשְׁעָן אֶל בִּינָתוֹ לוֹמַר אֲנִי אֲקַיֵּם הַמּוּבָן מִבְּלִי קִיּוּם
הַמִּצְווֹת . . .

כָּל שֶׁכֵּן שֶׁיֵּשׁ לָחוּשׁ שֶׁמָּא לֹא יַעֲלֶה בְּיָדֵינוּ בְּכִיּוּון הַטַּעַם לְגַמְרֵי וְיֵשׁ
בָּהּ טַעַם אַחֵר. אֲבָל שֶׁיֹּאמַר דֶּרֶךְ כְּלָל, בְּכָל מִצְוָה יֵשׁ בָּהּ טַעַם וְסִיבָּה
בִּנְתִינָתָהּ, וְלֹא נוֹדַע לָנוּ בְּבֵירוּר אֶלָּא שֶׁאֲנַחְנוּ מְדַמִּים וְסוֹבְרִים עֲלֵיהֶם
סְבָרוֹת, יִהְיֶה, כֵּן אוֹ לֹא יִהְיֶה וְאָז יִישָׁמֵר הָאָדָם מִמִּכְשׁוֹל.

Every scholar may consider a mitzvah and offer a reason for it. However, he should not rely on his own logic and definitely state that this is the reason; rather, he should say that he personally considers this a logical explanation. It is improper to teach these reasons publically, because some may make the mistake of relying on their own understanding and say, "I will observe the underlying reason for the mitzvah, but not fulfill the mitzvah itself." . . .

One must be very cautious about offering reasons for *mitzvot*, because it is possible that they will not be successful in discovering the true reason. The mitzvah may, in fact, have a different reason. The correct way to approach this is to say that, in general, every *mitzvah* was given for a reason and purpose, and we don't know for

RABBI MENACHEM ME'IRI
1249–1310

Talmudist and author. Me'iri was born in Provence (now in southern France). His monumental work, *Beit Habechirah*, summarizes in a lucid style the discussions of the Talmud along with the commentaries of the major subsequent rabbis. Despite its stature, the work was largely unknown for many generations, and thus has had less influence on subsequent halachic development.

sure what they are. However, we attempt to speculate about them and offer possible reasons that may or may not be correct. When we offer reasons for mitzvot in this manner, we will be guarded from reaching erroneous conclusions.

The Greek philosopher Secundus the Silent, Michel Wolgemut, 1493.
(Rijks Museum, Amsterdam)

TEXT 15

RABBI YOSEF ABULAFIA, IN *GINZEI NISTAROT* 3:164–165

הֻגַּד לָנוּ זֶה כַּמָּה שָׁנִים כִּי רַבֵּנוּ הַמְחַבְּרוֹ בִּקֵּשׁ לִגְנוֹז מִמֶּנּוּ הַחֵלֶק הַשְּׁלִישִׁי
הַמּוֹרֶה טַעֲמֵי מִצְוֹת וְחֻקִּים, וְלֹא יָכוֹל לְגָנְזוֹ כִּי יָצָא בְּקַצְוֵי אִיִּים הָרְחוֹקִים.
מִפְּנֵי שֶׁחָשַׁב כִּי יָצָא מִן הַשּׁוּרָה, בִּתְלוּתוֹ הֲדָרִים בִּשְׂעָרָה. וְאֵיךְ יַחְשֹׁב
אָדָם בְּסוֹדֵי טַעֲמֵי מִצְוֹת לְהַשִּׂיגָם, לָתֵת בָּהֶם טְעָמִים לִפְגַּם . . .

וְיָצָא הָעֵגֶל הַזֶּה, כִּי גַם עֵרֶב רַב וְאֶת הָאסַפְסוּף, כָּל אֶחָד בְּעֵינָיו
פִילוֹסוֹף . . . לִנְהֹג בִּדְבָרִים שֶׁל קֹדֶשׁ מִנְהַג חֻלִּין, וּפְטוּרִין מִן הַתְּפִלָּה
וּמִן הַתְּפִלִּין, וּמוֹרִידִין בַּקֹּדֶשׁ וְלֹא מַעֲלִין.

**RABBI YOSEF ABULAFIA
13TH CENTURY**

Rabbi Yosef was a member of the Abulafia family, an illustrious Spanish rabbinic family in the Middle Ages. Rabbi Yosef served as a rabbi in Burgos, Spain, and is known for his participation in the Maimonidean controversy, in which he took a moderate anti-Maimonidean position and attempted to calm the conflict.

I heard a few years ago that our master, the author [of *Guide for the Perplexed*], wished to retract and conceal the third part of the book that gives reasons for *mitzvot*. But he was unable to do so because it had already reached distant lands. He wished to conceal this part because he thought that he had acted improperly, basing important matters on weak foundations. Indeed, how did he think that he had grasped the secret reasons for *mitzvot*? The reasons he gave for them are damaging. . . .

This inadvertently caused the "golden calf" to emerge, because the masses of common people think they are all philosophers. . . . They treat holy matters [*mitzvot*] like ordinary pursuits and consider themselves exempt from prayer and *tefilin*. Their commitment to matters of holiness is in steady decline.

TEXT **16**

MAIMONIDES, *GUIDE FOR THE PERPLEXED* 3:45

כֵּיוָן שֶׁהַמָּקוֹם הַמִּקְדָּשׁ נִשְׁחָטִין בּוֹ זְבָחִים רַבִּים בְּכָל יוֹם, וּמְחַתְּכִין בּוֹ בָּשָׂר, וְנִקְטָר, וְנִרְחָצִין בּוֹ הַקְּרָבַיִם, אֵין סָפֵק שֶׁאִלּוּ הִנִּיחוּהוּ כְּפִי הַמַּצָּב הַזֶּה בִּלְבַד הָיָה רֵיחוֹ כְּרֵיחַ בָּתֵּי הַמִּטְבָּחַיִם. וּלְפִיכָךְ צִיּוָה בּוֹ בְּהַקְטָרַת הַקְּטוֹרֶת פַּעֲמַיִם בְּכָל יוֹם בַּבֹּקֶר וּבֵין הָעַרְבַּיִם, כְּדֵי לְבַשֵּׂם רֵיחוֹ וְרֵיחַ בִּגְדֵי כָּל הָעוֹבְדִים שָׁם.

Many animals were slaughtered every day in the Holy Temple. The flesh of the animals was then cut into pieces and burned as a sacrifice, and the intestines were washed out. If nothing were done to counteract it, the Temple would undoubtedly have had a foul odor like that of a slaughterhouse. They were therefore commanded to burn incense there twice a day, in the morning and in the evening, in order to give the place and the garments of those who officiated there a pleasant odor.

Portrait of Maimonides, from Ugolinus's Thesaurus Antiquitatum Sacrarum, *Venice, 1744.*

TEXT 17

SEFER HACHINUCH, MITZVOT 173, 175

וּבְטַעַם הַמַּיִם שֶׁיְּטַהֲרוּ כָּל טָמֵא, אֶחְשׁוֹב עַל צַד הַפְּשָׁט כִּי הָעִנְיָן הוּא כְּדֵי שֶׁיִּרְאֶה הָאָדָם אֶת עַצְמוֹ אַחַר הַטְּבִילָה כְּאִלּוּ נִבְרָא בְּאוֹתָהּ שָׁעָה, כְּמוֹ שֶׁהָיָה הָעוֹלָם כֻּלּוֹ מַיִם טֶרֶם הֱיוֹת בּוֹ אָדָם, וּכְמוֹ שֶׁכָּתוּב (בְּרֵאשִׁית א, ב) וְרוּחַ אֱלֹקִים מְרַחֶפֶת עַל פְּנֵי הַמָּיִם. וְיִתֵּן אֶל לִבּוֹ בְּדִמְיוֹן כִּי כְּמוֹ שֶׁנִּתְחַדֵּשׁ בְּגוּפוֹ יְחַדֵּשׁ גַּם כֵּן פְּעֻלּוֹתָיו לְטוֹב, וְיַכְשִׁיר מַעֲשָׂיו וִידַקְדֵּק בְּדַרְכֵי ה' בָּרוּךְ הוּא . . .

וְעוֹד נֹאמַר בָּעִנְיָן, שֶׁיֵּשׁ בִּטְבִילָה רֶמֶז אֶל הַטּוֹבֵל שֶׁיְּנַקֶּה נַפְשׁוֹ מִכָּל חֵטְא, כְּמוֹ שֶׁטֶּבַע הַמַּיִם לְנַקּוֹת כָּל דָּבָר הַמִּתְכַּבֵּס בָּהֶן.

SEFER HACHINUCH

A work on the biblical commandments. Four aspects of every mitzvah are discussed in this work: the definition of the mitzvah; ethical lessons that can be deduced from the mitzvah; basic laws pertaining to the observance of the mitzvah; and who is obligated to perform the mitzvah, and when. The work was composed in the 13th century by an anonymous author who refers to himself as "the Levite of Barcelona." It has been widely thought that this referred to Rabbi Aharon Halevi of Barcelona (Re'ah); however, this view has been contested.

Regarding the reason for water effecting purification of all ritually impure people, I think the simple reason for this is in order that we should regard ourselves after immersion as if we were created anew at that moment. For with immersion, we return to the primordial state, when existence was enveloped by water, as it says (GENESIS 1:2), "And the spirit of God was hovering over the face of the water." When we immerse, we should contemplate this and consider that just as our body has been renewed, so too must we renew our actions for the better. We should correct our ways and carefully follow the path of God. . . .

An additional reason for immersion in a *mikveh* is that this process intimates to us that we must cleanse our soul from any sins, just as water naturally cleanses anything washed in it.

TEXT **18**

ZOHAR 2:218B

כָּל מַאן דְּאָרַח בְּהַהוּא תְּנָנָא, כַּד סָלִיק הַהוּא עַמוּדָא מֵהַהוּא מַעֲלֶה עָשָׁן,
הֲוָה מְבָרֵר לִבֵּיה, בִּבְרִירוּ בִּנְהִירוּ בְּחֶדְוָה לְמִפְלַח לְמָארֵיה, וְאַעְבָּר מִנֵּיה
זוּהֲמָא דְּיֵצֶר הָרָע, וְלָא הֲוָה לֵיה אֶלָא לִבָּא חֲדָא לָקֳבֵל אֲבוּהּ דְּבִשְׁמַיָא.
בְּגִין דִּקְטֹרֶת, תְּבִירוּ דְּיֵצֶר הָרָע אִיהוּ וַדַּאי בְּכָל סִטְרִין. . . . .

וְקַיְימָא לְבַטְּלָא חַרְשִׁין, וּמִלִּין בִּישִׁין מִבֵּיתָא. רֵיחָא וַעֲשָׁנָא דִּקְטֹרֶת
דְּעָבְדֵי בְּנֵי נָשָׁא, בְּהַהוּא עוּבְדָא אִיהוּ מְבַטֵּל, כָּל שֶׁכֵּן קְטֹרֶת.

ZOHAR

The seminal work of kabbalah, Jewish mysticism. The *Zohar* is a mystical commentary on the Torah, written in Aramaic and Hebrew. According to Arizal, the *Zohar* contains the teachings of Rabbi Shimon bar Yocha'i, who lived in the Land of Israel during the second century. The *Zohar* has become one of the indispensable texts of traditional Judaism, alongside and nearly equal in stature to the Mishnah and Talmud.

Whoever smelled the smoke that ascended from the incense had their heart completely cleansed to serve their Master with radiance and joy. The foul stench of the evil spirit was removed from them, enabling them to serve God with a complete heart. The incense thus possessed the potency to completely break man's evil spirit. . . .

The incense is able to banish all negative spiritual forces from the Temple. If perfumes prepared by man possess the ability to dispel foul odors and fumes, how much more so does the Temple incense—prepared according to divine instructions—have a similar spiritual effect.

Learning Exercise 1

In Text 14, Meiri raised the concern that offering reasons for *mitzvot* may lead one to say, "I will observe the underlying reason for the mitzvah, but not fulfill the mitzvah itself."

On a scale of 1–5, grade the degree to which the reasons offered in Texts 16–18 are susceptible to Meiri's concern. (1 = not at all susceptible, 5 = very susceptible)

TEXT 16

1 2 3 4 5

TEXT 17

1 2 3 4 5

TEXT 18

1 2 3 4 5

TEXT 19

THE LUBAVITCHER REBBE, RABBI MENACHEM MENDEL SCHNEERSON,
LIKUTEI SICHOT 32:178, FN. 34 AND MARGINAL NOTE

וּמַה שֶׁהָרַמְבַּ"ם שׁוֹלֵל דִּבְרֵי הָאוֹמְרִים שֶׁ"כָּל הַמִּצְוֹת תּוֹצָאַת הָרָצוֹן
הַמּוּחְלָט" - יֵשׁ לוֹמַר כַּוָּנָתוֹ שֶׁאֵין לוֹמַר שֶׁהַצִּיוּוּיִים אֵינָם אֶלָּא רַק רָצוֹן
בִּלְבַד בְּלִי שׁוּם טַעַם כְּלָל, אֲבָל גַּם לְהָרַמְבַּ"ם שֹׁרֶשׁ עִנְיַן הַמִּצְוָה הוּא
רְצוֹנוֹ יִתְבָּרֵךְ אֶלָּא שֶׁאַחַר כַּךְ נִתְלַבֵּשׁ בְּטַעַם ...

בְּמוֹרֶה נְבוּכִים נָחִית לְבָאֵר טַעֲמֵי הַמִּצְוֹת כְּפִי שֶׁהַטְּעָמִים נִתְלַבְּשׁוּ
בְּשֵׂכֶל אֱנוֹשִׁי דְעוֹלָם הַזֶּה. כְּיָדוּעַ שֶׁבְּטַעֲמֵי הַמִּצְוֹת יֵשׁ כַּמָּה דַרְגוֹת:
הַטְּעָמִים כְּפִי שֶׁהֵם מִצַּד חָכְמָתוֹ יִתְבָּרֵךְ - שֶׁטְּעָמִים אֵלּוּ אֵינָם בְּגֶדֶר
הַשָּׂגָה כֵּיוָן שֶׁחָכְמָתוֹ יִתְבָּרֵךְ הִיא לְמַעֲלָה מִשֵּׂכֶל הַנִּבְרָאִים ... וְהַטְּעָמִים
מִצַּד חָכְמָתוֹ יִתְבָּרֵךְ כְּפִי שֶׁנִּתְלַבְּשָׁה בְּשֵׂכֶל נִבְרָאִים ... עַד לְשֵׂכֶל הָאָדָם.

RABBI MENACHEM MENDEL SCHNEERSON
1902–1994

The towering Jewish leader of
the 20th century, known as "the
Lubavitcher Rebbe," or simply as "the
Rebbe." Born in southern Ukraine,
the Rebbe escaped Nazi-occupied
Europe, arriving in the U.S. in June
1941. The Rebbe inspired and guided
the revival of traditional Judaism
after the European devastation,
impacting virtually every Jewish
community the world over. The
Rebbe often emphasized that the
performance of just one additional
good deed could usher in the era
of Mashiach. The Rebbe's scholarly
talks and writings have been printed
in more than 200 volumes.

Maimonides rejected the opinion that *mitzvot* are an
expression of God's will. However, it can be argued
that Maimonides does agree that the original source of
mitzvot is in God's will, above reason. He only intended
to reject the possibility that *mitzvot* are **exclusively** an
expression of will, without any reason at all.

In *Guide for the Perplexed*, Maimonides explains the
reasons for *mitzvot* as they can be understood by the
most basic level of human reason. There are a number
of levels of reasons for *mitzvot*. There are the reasons of
God's wisdom, which are beyond the grasp of human
understanding, and then there are reasons that have
descended into lower forms of wisdom, the lowest of
which is basic human intellect.

KEY POINTS

1 Some Jews in the Middle Ages felt that their beliefs were challenged by the rise of Greco-Islamic philosophy. Maimonides wrote the *Guide for the Perplexed* to answer their questions and to present Judaism in a philosophical framework.

2 The *Guide for the Perplexed* became controversial when some Jews used its ideas to justify the abandonment of Jewish beliefs and practices. The ensuing controversy culminated in the burning of Maimonides's philosophical works by the Christian Inquisition.

3 Some *mitzvot* possess obvious rationales while others do not. These two categories are referred to as "laws" and "decrees," respectively.

4 One approach, favored by some Jews, finds no value in endeavoring to offer reasons for the "decrees," and feared that logical speculation could weaken their observance.

5 A second, more widely accepted approach advocates that we attempt to offer reasons for the "decrees," considering that this will infuse the ritual experiences with meaning and generate passion in their performance.

6 Within this second approach there were some variations: In the *Guide for the Perplexed*, Maimonides explained many "decrees" with a method that some considered highly technical. They felt that this cheapened the importance of these *mitzvot* and could lead to a weakening of observance.

7 An alternative school of thought attempts to explain "decrees" as practices geared toward generating meditative processes of moral and spiritual development. The kabbalistic school explains the "decrees" as physical acts that effect various spiritual achievements. These models imbue the physical performance of the mitzvah with more inherent value.

8 Chabad philosophy teaches that there are multiple layers of meaning with respect to *mitzvot*. At the point of its lofty supernal origin, a mitzvah is the will of God that transcends the realm of reason. However, God's will then enclothes itself within the parameters of reason, and thereby obtains various degrees of rationale. Our performance of *mitzvot* ought to reflect this duality.

Visit
facebook.com/myJLI
to vote on the following question:

Which of the following statements is true?

1 There is too much faith in Judaism.

2 There is too much reasoning and rationalizing in Judaism.

Appendix

TEXT 20

NACHMANIDES, *KITVEI RAMBAN*, VOL. I, PP. 338-340

כָּל אֶרֶץ צָרְפַת רַבָּנֶיהָ וְשָׂרֶיהָ פְּנֵי שְׁבָטֶיהָ, כֻּלָּם הִסְכִּימוּ לְנַדּוֹת וּלְהַחְרִים, עַל כָּל אִישׁ אֲשֶׁר יָדוֹ יָרִים, לַהֲגוֹת בְּסֵפֶר מוֹרֵה הַנְּבוּכִים וּבְסֵפֶר הַמַּדָּע, קַרְנוֹ יִגְדַע, גַּם הַמְקַיְּימָם אַחַת דָּתוֹ לְהָמִית, עַד אֲשֶׁר יִגָּנְזוּ גְּנִיזָה עוֹלָמִית.

זֶה תּוֹפֶס דִּבְרֵיכֶם מְעַט מֵהַרְבֵּה, נִיצוֹץ מֵהַמְּדוּרָה הַגְּדוֹלָה אֲשֶׁר לֹא תִכְבֶּה.

וְלָמָה קְדִישֵׁי עֶלְיוֹנִין פְּרַשְׁתֶּם לְרֹב הַקְּהִלּוֹת רֶשֶׁת הַחֵרֶם, לֹא שְׁלַחְתֶּם לְכַלּוֹת קוֹצִים מִן הַכֶּרֶם, רַק לִקְטֹף עוֹלְלוֹת וְאֶשְׁכּוֹל, לְהַשְׁחִית אֶת הַכֹּל. כִּי תִתְּנוּ הָאֶרֶץ הַלָּזוּ לְבַז וּלְשַׁמָּה, רְכוּשָׁם לִשְׁאוֹל בְּאָלָה נַפְשָׁם.

וְלֹא נְתַתֶּם כָּבוֹד לְהָרַב הַגָּדוֹל, אֲשֶׁר בָּנָה בַּתַּלְמוּד מִגְדָּל, מִגְדָּל עֹז לְשֵׁם ה', וּמִקְדָּשׁ לַהֲמוֹנֵי עַמֵּי הָאֲרָצוֹת הָעוֹלִים בַּפְּרָצוֹת, וּבֵית תַּלְמוּדֵנוּ הַשָּׁמֵם שְׁמָמוֹת עוֹלָם יְקוֹמֵם.

בְּכָל גָּלוּת הַחֵל הַזֶּה בִּסְפָרַד וּבְאֶרֶץ הַמַּעֲרָב, וְאֶל הַמִּזְרָח וְאֶל הַצְּבִי הָיָה מוֹשִׁיעַ וָרָב.

כַּמָּה נִדְחֵי אֱמוּנָה קִבֵּץ, כַּמָּה בָּתֵּי מִקְדָּשׁוֹת רִבֵּץ, לְכַמָּה רְעֵבֵי תוּשִׁיָּה לַחְמוֹ נָתַן מֵימָיו נֶאֱמָנִים, וְכַמָּה אֶפִּיקוֹרְסִים וּמְגַלֵּי כְּנֶגֶד תַּלְמוּדֵנוּ פָּנִים הֵשִׁיב בִּדְבָרָיו הַנְּכוֹנִים.

וְאִם אַתֶּם בְּחֵיק אֱמוּנָה אֲמוּנִים, שְׁתוּלִים בְּחַצְרוֹת הַקַּבָּלָה דְּשֵׁנִים וְרַעֲנַנִּים, הֲלֹא תָּשִׂימוּ לֵב לְיוֹשְׁבֵי הַקְּצָווֹת.

כִּי הֵשִׁיב לְבִצָּרוֹן אֲסִירֵי הַתִּקְוָה, וּמִכַּרְחֵי הַתַּאֲווֹת הַשְּׁבִיעָם בֶּאֱמוּנָתֵנוּ וּבְקַבָּלָתֵינוּ נַפְשׁוֹתָם רְוָה, תַּחַת אֲשֶׁר מִלְאוּ כְּרֵיסָם מֵהַבְלֵי הַיְּוָנִים, וְהֶאֱכִילוּ בְּטָנָם הַוֹּת, וְעָלֵינוּ בְּפִיהֶם הָיָה חֹטֶר גַּאֲווֹת, יַלְעִיגוּ בְּשָׂפָה לַנְּפָשׁוֹת הַבּוֹטְחוֹת וְלַנְּשָׁמוֹת הַמְקַוּוֹת, יָנִיעוּ רֹאשׁ לַתּוֹרָה, כִּי אֵין טַעַם לַעֲבֵירָה וְאֵין רֵיחַ לַמִּצְווֹת, בְּדַרְכֵי תוֹרָתֵינוּ לֹא יַעֲמִיקוּ, וּבְיַלְדֵי נָכְרִים יַשְׂפִּיקוּ.

וְלוּלֵי מִדִּבְרֵי הָרַב וּמִפִּי סְפָרָיו חָיוּ, וְנַפְשָׁם מֵחַדֵּשׁ חָכְמָתוֹ יִרְוָיוּ, וּבְאָהֳלֵי תְעוּדָה יִשְׁלָיוּ, כִּמְעַט רַגְלֵיהֶם נָטִיוּ . . .

**RABBI MOSHE BEN NACHMAN
(NACHMANIDES, RAMBAN) 1194–1270**

Scholar, philosopher, author and physician. Nachmanides was born in Spain and served as leader of Iberian Jewry. In 1263, he was summoned by King James of Aragon to a public disputation with Pablo Cristiani, a Jewish apostate. Though Nachmanides was the clear victor of the debate, he had to flee Spain because of the resulting persecution. He moved to Israel and helped reestablish communal life in Jerusalem. He authored a classic commentary on the Pentateuch and a commentary on the Talmud.

כִּי אֲמַרְתֶּם בְּאֲזְנֵינוּ בְּגַאֲוָה וָבוּז מִילִין דְּלָא נִשְׁמָע, לָהֶם עַיִן קְהִלָּתֵנוּ דָמוֹעַ תִּדְמַע, הוֹצֵאתֶם עָתָק מִפִּיכֶם, דְּבָרִים הַנּוֹרָאִים לְקִנְאָה וּלְשִׂנְאָה נֶאֱמָרִין, אָסוּר לְשָׁמְעָם אַף כִּי לְאָמְרָם, וּמִכָּל שֶׁכֵּן לְכוֹתְבָם . . .

הִנֵּה זֹאת לֹא צָדַקְתֶּם מַעֲנֵכֶם, לֹא דִבַּרְתֶּם נְכוֹנָה בְּעֶבֶד ה' וְאוֹכִיחֲכֶם, וְאֶעֶרְכָה לְעֵינֵיכֶם כִּי לֹא אֶשָּׂא פְּנֵי אִישׁ, לְהָשִׁיב עַל זֶה אַמַהֵר וְאָחִישׁ, וְאֶל אָדָם לֹא אֲכַנֶּה, אֶל הַגָּאוֹן וּמוֹרָאוֹ אֲקַנֶּא.

מַדּוּעַ אֶת הָרַב מִמַּעֲשֵׂהוּ תַּפְרִיעוּ, וְצַדִּיק כַּבִּיר תַּרְשִׁיעוּ, הֲלֹא שְׁאַלְתֶּם עוֹבְרֵי דֶרֶךְ, הַמַּאֲרִיכִים לָשׁוֹן, הַמַּפְלִיגִים מְלִיצָה, הַנּוֹשְׂאִים מָשָׁל בְּעֶרֶךְ, בִּתְהִלַּת הָרַב הַגָּדוֹל, בְּמַעֲלַת חֲסִידוּתוֹ, בְּתוֹקֶף אֱמוּנָתוֹ, בְּעֹצֶם עַנְוְתָנוּתוֹ, בִּגְדוּלַת יִחוּסוֹ, בְּנִדְבַת כִּיסוֹ, בְּמַעֲשָׂיו הַנִּפְלָאִים, בְּמִלָּיו הַנּוֹרָאִים, בִּהְיוֹתוֹ בְּיִרְאַת אֱלֹקָיו דָּבֵק וְחוֹשֵׁק, וּבְתַלְמוּדֵנוּ נוֹשֵׁק, אוֹהֵב דִּבְרֵי חֲכָמִים וּמְחַבְּקָן, הֵם מַחְמַד עֵינָיו וּמַחְמַד לְנַפְשׁוֹ, עֲטָרוֹת לְרֹאשׁוֹ.

The entire country of France, her rabbis and princes, the heads of her communities, have all agreed to ban and to excommunicate every man who will raise his hand to study in the *Guide for the Perplexed* and in the *Book of Knowledge*. All who keep these books are to be condemned, until the books will be permanently concealed.

This is a brief summary of your words, a spark from the great fire that cannot be extinguished.

Why did you, most holy saints, spread out the net of excommunication over most of the communities of Israel? You have not issued your decree to uproot the thorns from the vineyard, but rather to cut down the bunches and clusters of grapes—thus destroying everything. You have given this land for plunder and have made their wealth a desolation by wishing a curse on their life.

You have not shown honor to the great Rabbi [Maimonides], who built a tower in the field of Talmudic scholarship, "a strong tower for the Name of God" (PROVERBS 18:10), and a sanctuary for the unlearned masses, who would otherwise transgress [due to their ignorance]. He restored the desolate house of our Talmud, which had been in a perpetual state of desolation.

For all of the Jewish exiles residing in Spain, in the land of the west and toward the east and the Holy Land, he was a savior and a defender.

How many dispersed of faith has he gathered! How many desolate sanctuaries has he dusted off! How many people hungry for wisdom did he provide with bread and water! How many nonbelievers has he returned with his correct teachings!

Even if you in France are in the bosom of faith, soundly rooted in the courtyards of tradition, "full of sap and richness" (PSALMS 92:15), will you not pay heed to the residents of distant lands?

He [Maimonides] "returned the hopeful prisoners to the stronghold" (ZECHARIAH 9:12), and those who felt forced to follow their lusts he has satisfied with our faith. Now they satiate their souls in our traditions, instead of filling themselves with the vanities of the Greek philosophers.

Previously, there was a "rod of haughtiness against us in their mouths" (PROVERBS 14:3). Previously, they mocked the trusting souls and hoping spirits. They would shake their heads insultingly against the Torah, saying that there is no reason to refrain from its prohibitions, and no purpose in the performance of its commandments. They did not delve into the ways of our Torah; they pastured in foreign fields.

Were it not that they now live by the words of the Rabbi [Maimonides] and by his books, satiate their souls with the substance of his wisdom, and prosper in the tents of Torah, their feet might well have slipped. . . .

We have heard you speak haughtily, uttering disgraceful words, which the eyes of our community sorely weep upon. You have let arrogance come out of your mouth, words which seem to have been said to arouse jealousy and hatred. It is forbidden to hear them, certainly to utter them, and all the more to write them! . . .

You have not responded appropriately. You have spoken improperly of God's servant [Maimonides]. I will reprove you for this, and set the case before your eyes. "I shall not defer to any man" (JOB 32:21), I will hasten to speedily respond to this, "and I will not give flattery to any man" (ibid.).

I shall be zealous for the great scholar [Maimonides] and his honor. Why do you disturb the Rabbi from his work? Why do you condemn the righteous?

Have you not asked visiting travelers about him? They speak at length, stream forth with metaphors, and take up the parable in recounting the great Rabbi's praise. [They speak of] the high degree of his piety, the strength of his faith, the might of his humility, the greatness of his ancestry, the magnanimity of his purse, his wondrous deeds, his awe-inspiring words, his cleaving to the fear and love of God, and his reverence for our Talmud.

He loves the words of the sages and embraces them. They are the desire of his eyes, the yearning of his soul, and the crown of his head.

TEXT 21

NACHMANIDES, IBID., VOL. I, P. 349

לָכֵן רַבּוֹתֵינוּ חוּשׁוּ לְמִנְיַנְכֶם וְהֱווּ מְתוּנִים בְּדִינְכֶם. הַחֵרֶם יוּתַּר, וְהָאָלָה הַיּוֹצֵאת תּוּפָר בִּתְרוּעַת שׁוֹפָר, הַשַּׁמְתָּא בְּמִנְיָן אַחֵר תְּבֻטַל, וְהַנְדוּי לְכָל רוּחַ יְזֹרֶה, טוּט אָסַר טוּט שָׁרִי.

Therefore, our rabbis, consider your decision and be deliberate in your judgment. The ban should be lifted, and the curse you pronounced should be publicly revoked. The ban should be revoked at another rabbinic convention, and scattered to the wind. Just as a ban is invoked by a proclamation, so too is it revoked by a second proclamation.

Additional Readings

CONSIDERING RATIONALES FOR *MITZVOT*

MAIMONIDES, *GUIDE FOR THE PERPLEXED*, PART III

Chapter 26

There is disagreement among religious philosophers about whether God's actions are consequences of wisdom or are purely an expression of His will, without having any intended purpose. The same disagreement exists regarding the *mitzvot* which He has commanded us.

Some philosophers do not seek any reason at all for *mitzvot*, saying that they are all consequent upon God's will alone. Others say that every positive commandment and prohibition of these laws is consequent upon wisdom and each aim at a particular goal. According to this opinion there are reasons for all of the *mitzvot* and they were given for a particular beneficial purpose.

The doctrine of all of us—both the common people and the scholars—is that all the laws have a reason. However, we do not know the reasons for some of them, and the divine wisdom in them is not known to us. Scripture is clear about this: "just decrees [*chukim*] and laws [*mishpatim*]" (Deuteronomy 4:8); "The judgments of God are true, altogether just" (Psalms 19:10).

Regarding the "decrees" [*chukim*]—such as those forbidding the mixture of wool and linen, mixing milk and meat, and the banishing of the goat [on Yom Kippur]—the sages, of blessed memory, said that these are "the matters that I have decreed for you,

RABBI MOSHE BEN MAIMON (MAIMONIDES, RAMBAM), 1135–1204

Halachist, philosopher, author, and physician. Maimonides was born in Cordoba, Spain. After the conquest of Cordoba by the Almohads, he fled Spain and eventually settled in Cairo, Egypt. There, he became the leader of the Jewish community and served as court physician to the vizier of Egypt. He is most noted for authoring the *Mishneh Torah*, an encyclopedic arrangement of Jewish law, and for his philosophical work, *Guide for the Perplexed*. His rulings on Jewish law are integral to the formation of halachic consensus.

about which you do not have permission to think, that the evil inclination and the nations of the world challenge" (Yoma 67b).

Most of the sages do not believe that these *mitzvot* are matters for which there is no reason at all and for which one must not seek any purpose. For this would lead, according to what we have explained, to them being considered frivolous actions. Rather, the majority opinion is that they all have a reason, a useful purpose, but that it is hidden from us. This is due to either the incapacity of our intellect or the deficiency of our knowledge.

This means that every positive commandment and prohibition has a beneficial purpose: In the case of some of them, their purpose is clear to us, such as the prohibition of murdering and stealing. In the case of others, their utility is not clear—such as the prohibition on using the fruits that grow during a tree's first three years [*orlah*], and the prohibition on sowing mixtures of seeds in the vineyard [*kil'ei hakerem*].

Those commandments whose utility is clear to all are called *mishpatim*, "laws," and those whose utility is not clear to all are called *chukim*, "decrees."

The sages always say—regarding the verse, "For it is no vain thing" (Deuteronomy 32:47)—"If it is vain, it is because of you" (Jerusalem Talmud, Pe'ah 1:1). This means that the commandments are not vain matters without a useful purpose, and if it seems to you that this is the case with regard to some of the commandments, the deficiency resides in your comprehension.

We have a well-known tradition that King Solomon knew the reasons for all of the *mitzvot*, with the exception of the mitzvah of the red heifer. The sages also taught that God concealed the reasons for the *mitzvot* so that people should not treat them lightly, as King Solomon came to do regarding three of the *mitzvot* for which the Torah gave explicit reasons. All of the sages' teachings on this matter are along these lines, and Scripture also indicates so.

However, I found in *Bereshit Rabah* a text of the sages, their memory be blessed, from which it appears at first glance that some of the commandments are solely commands, with no intended purpose or any real utility.

This is the passage I am referring to (*Bereishit Rabah* 44:1): "Why would it matter to God if animals are slaughtered by cutting their neck in front or in the back? It must be that the commandments were only given in order to purify the people, as it is written, "the word of God is purified.""

This dictum is very peculiar, and has no parallel in other teachings of the sages. However, I have interpreted it, as you shall hear, in such a manner that it should not contradict the view of all their teachings and not disagree with the universally accepted principle that one should search after a practical beneficial purpose for all of the *mitzvot*. As Scripture states, "For it is no vain thing" (Deuteronomy 32:47) and, "It was not purposeless that I said to the children of seed of Jacob "seek Me." I am the Lord who speaks righteousness, I declare things that are right" (Isaiah 45:19).

Everyone endowed with a sound intellect ought to believe that which I shall set forth to you: Each commandment in general has a reason, and they have all been given because of a certain utility. But regarding their particular details, it is taught that they were given merely for the sake of commanding something.

For example, the killing of animals because of the necessity of having good food is clearly useful, as we shall make clear. But the prescribed details of slaughter, where and how the neck should be cut, these and all similar details are mandated "in order to purifying the people." This is the meaning of the sages' example, "slaughtered by cutting their neck in front or in the back."

I have mentioned this example to you because this is the one the sages gave. However, if one studies the truth of the matter, the reason for this detail can be explained: Since consumption of animals is necessary, the intent of the commandment was to make their slaughter as easy as possible. For beheading would only be possible with the help of a sword or something similar, whereas a throat can be cut with anything. In order that death should come about more easily, the condition was imposed that the knife should be sharp.

The best example of the true reality of details of commandments is illustrated by the sacrifices. The offering of sacrifices in general has a great and manifest utility, as I shall explain later. But no cause can ever be given for the fact that one particular sacrifice must be of a lamb and another of a ram, and that for some sacrifices there must be a particular number.

In my opinion, those who occupy themselves with finding reasons for such details are making a great mistake. This does not eliminate the incongruity, but rather increases the number of incongruities. Those who imagine that a reason can be found for such details are far from the truth, just like those that believe that there are no beneficial purposes for the commandments in general.

You must know that Divine Wisdom demanded—or, if you prefer, that circumstances made it necessary—that that there should be details that cannot be explained. It is impossible that a mitzvah should not include some matter of this kind. The necessity of this can be illustrated by the following example: You ask: Why must this sacrifice be of a lamb and not a ram? But the same question would be asked if a ram had been required instead of a lamb. It is necessary that one species be chosen.

So too regarding the question of why seven lambs were required for a particular sacrifice rather than eight. You would have asked the same question if eight, ten, or twenty lambs were required. A particular number must be specified.

This is similar to the nature of a thing that can receive different forms, and has actually received one of them. We cannot ask why it has received this particular form and not another one of the possibilities, because we would have the same question had it indeed received the alternative possible form. Note this, and understand it.

The repeated assertion of our sages, that there are reasons for all commandments, and the tradition that King Solomon knew them, refer to the general purpose of the commandments, and not to the object of every detail.

This being the case, I find it convenient to divide the six hundred and thirteen precepts into a number of categories. Each category will include many *mitzvot* of the same kind, or related to each other by their character. I will first explain the general reason of each category, showing its clear and unarguable purpose, and then I shall discuss each individual commandment of the category, and explain its reason. There are only a few *mitzvot* for which I have not been able to discover their reason, and they will remain unexplained.

In many cases I have also been able to comprehend reasons for some of the details of the commandments. I will explain these later on.

In order to fully explain these reasons I must premise several chapters, in which I will discuss the underlying principles that form the basis of my theory. I will now begin these chapters.

Chapter 27

The overall object of the Torah is twofold: that we obtain the well-being of the soul and the well-being of the body.

The well-being of the soul is promoted by correct opinions communicated to people according to their capacity. Some of these opinions are therefore imparted in plain form, others allegorically, because certain opinions in their plain form are too strong for the capacity of the common people.

The well-being of the body is established by a proper management of human relations. This is obtained through two things: first by removing all violence from our midst. That is to say, that we disallow an environment where people do as they please, as they desire, and as they are able to do. Rather, we promote a society in which everyone contributes toward the common welfare. Secondly, by teaching us good morals that are necessary to produce a good social state.

Of these two goals, the well-being of the soul—the communication of correct opinions—comes undoubtedly first in rank. But the well-being of the body, the government of the state, and the establishment of the best possible relations among people, is anterior in nature and time. The latter object is required first; it is also treated in the Torah most carefully and most minutely, because the well-being of the soul can

only be obtained after the well-being of the body has been secured.

For it has been found that humans require two perfections: the first perfection is that of the body, and the second perfection is that of the soul. The first requires that we be healthy with regard to our material life, and this is only possible when all of our needs are supplied—if we have our food and other things necessary for the body, e.g., shelter, hygiene, and the like. But a person cannot procure all this alone. It is only possible to achieve this through a society, since humans, as is well known, are by nature social creatures.

The second perfection of the human being is to become an intelligent being; i.e., to know everything possible to know about all things in existence. This second perfection certainly does not include any action or good conduct, but only knowledge, which is arrived at by speculation and research.

It is clear that the second and superior kind of perfection can only be attained when the first perfection has been acquired; for people that are suffering from great hunger, thirst, heat, or cold, cannot grasp an idea even if explained by others, much less can they come to them by their own reasoning. But when people are in possession of the first perfection, they may possibly acquire the second perfection, which is undoubtedly of a superior kind, and is alone the source of eternal life.[1]

The true Torah of Moses, aside from which there is no other Torah, has come to give us this twofold perfection. It aims first at the establishment of good mutual relations among people by removing injustice and creating the noblest feelings, so that the people in every land live with stability and acquire the first perfection. Secondly, it seeks to train us in faith, and to impart correct and true opinions when the intellect is sufficiently developed.

Scripture clearly mentions both of these perfections and tells us that their acquisition is the object of all the divine commandments. "God commanded us to obey all these decrees and to be in awe of Him, for our good always, so that He will preserve us as is the case today" (Deuteronomy 6:24). Here the second perfection is mentioned first because it is of greater importance, being, as we have shown, the ultimate aim of our existence.

This perfection is expressed in the phrase, "For our good, always." The sages (Kidushin 39b) interpreted a different verse—"So that things may go well with you and you may have a long life" (Deuteronomy 22:7)—as referring to the eternal life of the World to Come, the world that is "all well" and "all eternal." In the same sense, I explain the words, "for our good, always," to mean that we will come to the state that is all good and eternal, where we live permanently, and this can happen through the second form of perfection. And I explain the words, "so that He will preserve us as is the case today" as referring to our first and temporal existence, to that of our body, which cannot be in a perfect and good condition except by the cooperation of society, as we have shown.

Chapter 31

There are people who find it difficult to give a reason for any of the commandments, and consider it correct to assume that the commandments and prohibitions have no rational basis whatsoever. They are led to adopt this theory by a certain flawed thinking that they are unable to express or describe. For they imagine that these precepts, if they were useful in any respect, and were commanded because of their usefulness, would have had to originate in the thought and reason of an intellectual human being. But things that are not objects of reason and serve no purpose, they must undoubtedly be attributed to God, because no thought of man could have produced them.

According to the theory of these weak-minded people, the human being is more perfect than the Creator. For what the human being says or does has a certain purpose, whilst the actions of God do not; He commands us to do that which is of no use to us, and forbids us to do that which is harmless.

The truth is that on the contrary, the sole purpose of the Torah is to benefit us. As we have explained the Scriptural passage, "[God commanded us to obey all these decrees and to be in awe of Him,] for our good always, so that He will preserve us as is the case today" (Deuteronomy 6:24). The verse also states, "[adhering to the *mitzvot* will show your wisdom and understanding to the nations,] who will hear about all these decrees [*chukim*], and say, 'Only this great nation is such a wise and understanding people'" (ibid. 4:6).

The verse is saying that even the "decrees" convince the nations of the wisdom and understanding it includes. But if no reason could be found for these commandments, if they produced no advantage and removed no evil, why then should those who believe in them and follow them be considered wise, reasonable, and so excellent as to merit the admiration of all nations?

Rather, the truth is undoubtedly as we have explained, that each of the six hundred and thirteen commandments exists either to communicate a correct opinion, or to dismiss an unhealthy opinion; to communicate a rule of justice, or to ward off an injustice; to endow people with a noble moral quality, or to warn them against a negative moral quality.

The translation is based on the translations by Michael Friedländer (London: George Routledge and Sons, 1904), and Shlomo Pines (Chicago: University of Chicago Press, 1963), revised and updated by Rabbi Shmuel Super.

Endotes

[1] In other places in his writings (see, for example, *Mishneh Torah*, Laws of the Foundations of the Torah 4:13 and Laws of Repentance 9:1), Maimonides also stresses that it is the performance of *mitzvot* that merit one to experience eternal life in the World to Come. In Maimonides's view, as presented here in *Guide for the Perplexed*, Chapter 27 (and chapter 28), one of the purposes of *mitzvot* is to impart "correct and true opinions." Thus, observance of the *mitzvot* and "becoming an intellectual being" are interdependent, and can only be achieved together. See Rabbi Yitschak Shilat, *Hakdamot HaRambam Lamishnah*, pp. 161–163, for further sources and elaboration.

NACHMANIDES, DEUTERONOMY 22:6

The verse reads, "If you come across a bird's nest [beside the road, either in a tree or on the ground, and the mother is sitting on the young or on the eggs, do not take the mother with the young. You may take the young, but be sure to let the mother go, so that things may go well with you and you may have a long life]" (Deuteronomy 22:6–7).

This rationale of this commandment is the same as the rationale behind the commandment, "Do not slaughter the animal and its child on the same day" (Leviticus 22:28). The idea is that we should not have a cruel heart and lack mercy. Another reason is that we are not to be destructive and destroy a species, even though the Torah allowed slaughter within a species. One who kills an animal and its child on one day or takes the mother bird and its young is considered to have cut off that entire species.

Maimonides (*Guide for the Perplexed* 3:48) wrote that the reason for sending the mother away from the nest and for not slaughtering an animal and its child on the same day is to prohibit killing the child in front of the mother, as animals have great pain from this. His point is that there is no difference between the concerns of human beings for their children and the concerns of animals for their children, for the love of a mother toward her children does not stem from the intellect and the faculty of speech, but rather from faculties that are found in animals just as in humans.

If the reason is as Maimonides claims, the main prohibition of killing a mother and child on the same day applies if they are slaughtered in the sequence of child and then parent, and the reverse is only forbidden in order to distance us from the primary prohibition. However, in my opinion, it is more correct to explain that the reason for the commandment is so we do not become cruel.

Maimonides continued: Don't question me from the statement of the sages "We silence the one who says, 'Your mercy reaches as far as the nest of the bird'" (Berachot 33b), which implies that this commandment has nothing do with mercy. This is no

RABBI MOSHE BEN NACHMAN (NACHMANIDES, RAMBAN), 1194–1270
Scholar, philosopher, author and physician. Nachmanides was born in Spain and served as leader of Iberian Jewry. In 1263, he was summoned by King James of Aragon to a public disputation with Pablo Cristiani, a Jewish apostate. Though Nachmanides was the clear victor of the debate, he had to flee Spain because of the resulting persecution. He moved to Israel and helped reestablish communal life in Jerusalem. He authored a classic commentary on the Pentateuch and a commentary on the Talmud.

question for it is one of two opinions among the sages. This statement reflects the view that there is no reason for the commandments except for the fact that it is the will of the Creator. However, we abide by the second opinion, according to which there should be an explanation for each of the commandments.

A further challenge considered by Maimonides (*Guide for the Perplexed* 3:26) is that which we find in the Midrash (*Bereshit Rabah* 44:1), "Does God care whether one slaughters an animal from the front of the neck or from the back? Rather, the *mitzvot* were solely given to refine human beings, as it is stated (Proverbs 30:5), 'Every word of God is purified.'"

Despite this teaching, Maimonides's view, that all of the commandments have a reason, is logical and correct. Each mitzvah has a reason and purpose for the refinement of human beings, in addition to the reward given by their Commander for its observance.

Indeed, the sages have said, "Why were the reasons of the Torah not revealed?" (Sanhedrin 21b). They also expounded upon the verse (Isaiah 23:18), "Ancient covering," and explained, "This is one who reveals things that were covered by the One of Ancient Days. What are they? The reasons of the Torah" (Pesachim 119a). They also expounded about the red heifer, that Solomon said, "I have mastered it all, but about the topic of the red heifer, I have investigated, I have asked, I have searched—'I said I will become wise, but it is far from me' (Ecclesiastes 7:23)" (*Bamidbar Rabah* 19:3–4). Furthermore, Rabbi Yose the son of Rabbi Chanina said (*Tanchuma*, Bamidbar 19:8), "God said to Moses, 'To you do I reveal the reason of the red heifer, but to others it is a decree (without explanation).' . . . That which is covered from you in this world, will be visible in the World to Come, like a blind person who finally sees. As it is written, 'And I will guide the blind ones in the path they did not know' (Isaiah 42:16). And it is written (there), 'I have done these things and not forsaken them'—which means, 'as I have already done them for Rabbi Akiva and his colleagues.'"

What one learns from these sources is that the impediment to understanding the reasons for the commandments is not from His end but rather from the blindness of our intellects, and that the reason of the most difficult mitzvah was revealed to the sages of Israel. There are many other statements like this and many things in Torah and Scripture that indicate this idea.

The statement from the Midrash that was challenging to Maimonides is, in my view, about a different matter. The sages meant to say that the *mitzvot* are not to benefit God. Their purpose is to benefit humankind—to keep us safe from harm; shield us from negative beliefs and base character traits; remind us of the miracles and wonders of the Creator; and help us know God.

The Midrash says that *mitzvot* are intended to "refine" human beings, as we would refer to refining silver. The act of refining silver is not senseless; it removes all impurities. So too, the *mitzvot* remove from our hearts every harmful belief, inform us of the truth, and help us remember God continuously.

The teaching from *Bereishit Rabah* is also found, with variations, in *Tanchuma* (Vayikra 3:8): "Does it matter to God whether one slaughters an animal and eats it, or stabs it and eats it? Do you benefit Him at all or damage Him at all? What does He care whether one eats pure things or eats impure things? 'If you have become wise, you have become wise for yourself' (Proverbs 9:12). Rather, the commandments were only given to refine us, as it says, 'The words of God are pure' (Psalms 12:7), and 'Every word of God is purified' (Proverbs 30:5). Why? Because they protect you."

It is explicit in this version that the sages' intention was to say that the gain is not for Him, that He does not require the light—as might be thought—from the menorah [the candelabra in the Temple], and that He does not require the sacrifices for food and the smell of the incense, as it would appear from the simple meaning of the verses. Even the commandments that He commanded us to do in commemoration of the Exodus from Egypt and of Creation are not for His gain, but for us, so that we will know the truth and merit through it that we will be fit that He should protect us. Our speech and memory of His wonders are considered nothing and void for Him.

The Midrash brought a proof from the case of slaughtering from the front of the neck versus the back, to say that all *mitzvot* are for us and not for God, as it is not logical to say that the Creator should have any gain when it is from the neck as opposed to the back of the neck, or whether it is from traditional slaughter versus a stab. Rather, these commandments guide us in the paths of mercy, even at the time of slaughtering. The Midrash brought another proof from the case of eating kosher food versus nonkosher food, about which the Torah says, "They are impure for you" (Leviticus 11:28). The implication is that the reason for this prohibition is so we can have clean characters that are wise and that contemplate the truth. This is the meaning of the saying, "If you have become wise, you have become wise for yourself."

Thus, active commandments—for example, kosher slaughter of animals—teach us good character traits. The commandments that tell us to refrain from something—like the animals we must not consume—are to purify our souls from negativity, as the Torah states, "You shall not make your souls disgusting with the animal and with the bird and with all that crawls on the ground, which I have separated for you as impure" (Leviticus 20:25). If so, all *mitzvot* are for our benefit alone.

This is like what Elihu said, "If you sin, will this affect Him? If your transgressions are numerous, will you do something to Him?" (Job 35:6). He also said, "What will He take from your hand?" (ibid. 35:7). This matter is unanimous in all of the teachings of our sages.

Translated by Rabbi Shmuel Klatzkin and Rabbi Shmuel Super

REASONING THE STONE

RABBI YANKI TAUBER

And Moses turned and went down from the mountain, and the two tablets of the Testimony were in his hand: tablets inscribed from end to end, on the one side and on the other were they written.

And the tablets were the work of G-d, and the writing was the writing of G-d, engraved upon the tablets.

—Exodus 32:15–16

The Torah refers to its 613 divine commandments by an array of synonyms: *mitzvah* (commandment), *dibbur* (word), *mishpat* (law), *ed* (testimonial), and *chok* (decree), among others.

Chok implies a suprarational decree—a law observed in submission to an authority which we have neither the right nor the capacity to question. Thus, *chok* is also the name of a certain class of *mitzvot*—the *chukim*—which the human mind cannot rationalize: *mitzvot* such as the prohibition to mix meat with milk and the laws of ritual purity, which exemplify our innate inability to fathom the divine will.

The literal meaning of *chok* is engraving. Indeed, explains Chassidic master Rabbi Schneur Zalman of Liadi, the difference between the suprarational *chok* and rational law or testimonial, is the difference between engraved letters and written letters.

The Torah was given to us in writing: by divine command and dictation, Moses wrote it in physical ink on physical parchment, giving us the *Chumash* (the five books of Moses), also referred to as *Torah SheBichtav*, The Written Torah. Even in its spiritual incarnation, before G-d willed that it be translated into a guide to physical life, the Torah is described by

RABBI YANKI TAUBER, 1965–

Chasidic scholar and author. A native of Brooklyn, NY, Rabbi Tauber is an internationally renowned author who specializes in adapting the teachings of the Lubavitcher Rebbe. He is a member of the JLI curriculum development team, and has written numerous articles and books, including *Once Upon a Chassid* and *Beyond the Letter of the Law*.

the Midrash as written in black fire on white fire—the supernal equivalent of ink on parchment.

But there is also a more basic state of Torah—Torah not as written law but as engraved law. The Zohar speaks of a level on which the Torah exists as the genesis of the divine will, engraved in the supernal purity. In its transmission to man, the written Torah was also preceded by an engraved Torah: the entirety of the divine law was first given to us encapsulated in the Ten Commandments, which were etched by the hand of G-d in two tablets of stone.

When something is written, the substance of the letters that express it (the ink) remains a separate entity from the substance upon which they have been set (the parchment). True, the two have bonded to form a single entity—the document—but this remains an entity that consists of two things: the ink and the parchment, the message and the medium, the definitive forms and the abstract background. On the other hand, letters engraved in stone are not added to their medium but are forged in it: the words are stone and the stone is words.

A person's understanding and feelings are inked upon his soul. These are things he has acquired and has come to identify with, to the point that they comprise his personality; nevertheless, they remain an *addition* to his quintessential self. He distinguishes between his I and his intellect and emotions: the former is set and unalterable, while the latter are in a state of flux, developing and changing as he progresses through life.

Thus, the rational *mitzvot*, which we observe with an understanding and appreciation of their positive function—as they indeed should be observed, for it is to this end that they were garbed in garments of reason—are as ink written upon the parchment of our souls. Something has been added to our self, appended to our psyche with the adhesive of reason and emotion. I am doing the mitzvah only to the extent that our intellect and feelings are "me"—to the extent that ink and parchment become one in the document.

The *chok*, however, is an engraved decree. We do it for no reason other than our innate obedience to G-d. And our obedience to G-d is not something we acquire or develop (though there might, at times, exist the need to waken it, when it is silenced and suppressed by the dross of material life). It is something that is of our very essence, something impressed in the spark of G-dliness at the core of every soul.

The Veneer of Reason

Chok, however, is not only a certain type of mitzvah; it is also a general name for all of G-d's commandments.

This is expressed in the opening words of the Torah section that bears the name of the engraved mitzvah—the section of *Chukat* (Numbers 19–21). *Chukat* begins with the law of *parah adumah* (the red heifer), which is prefaced with the statement *Zot chukat haTorah*—"This is the *chok* of Torah." The simple meaning of these words is that this mitzvah is *the chok* of Torah, the ultimate suprarational law. Indeed, the law of the red heifer is often cited as the prototypic *chok*—the law of which King Solomon, the wisest of men, said: I sought to be wise to it, but it is distant from me. There are other *mitzvot* that defy rationalization; but the law of the red heifer is also counter-rational, replete with paradoxes and logical inconsistencies.

But the words "This is the *chok* of Torah" have another meaning as well. As Rabbi Schneur Zalman of Liadi reads it, the verse is telling us: This is the mitzvah that expresses the *chok* of Torah, the most poignant example of the suprarationality of the entirety of divine law. All of Torah is *chok*, the unfathomable will of G-d. Thus, the very quality that distinguishes *parah adumah* from all other *mitzvot* is the quality that makes it the essence of all of the *mitzvot*.

For each and every mitzvah is an expression of the divine will. Obviously, no reason or function—and certainly no reason or function that the human mind can conceive or understand—can possibly explain or describe a divine desire. So it is wrong to think of Torah as consisting of two parts—rationally inked laws on the one hand, and suprarational *chukim* on the other. Rather, these are two dimensions of Torah as a whole, with each mitzvah possessing a written element in addition to its engraved essence.

If the human mind agrees with the mitzvah "Do not murder," if it appreciates the profound impact the weekly observance of Shabbat has on our lives, it is only grasping at an auxiliary garment in which G-d chose to clothe His expressed will. On the other hand, even the most mystifying *chok* can be studied and analyzed, and profound lessons derived from them to guide and inspire our lives.

Indeed, the engraved Ten Commandments (which, incidentally, are all rational *mitzvot*) embody the entire Torah, while also the most suprarational *chukim* were inked by Moses upon parchment. Every mitzvah can, and ought to, be related to as the unfathomable will of G-d, driven by the obedience to G-d etched in the core of our souls. And every mitzvah can, and ought to, be appreciated intellectually and emotionally, and thereby appended to our thinking and feeling selves.

The only reason we classify *mitzvot* into logical laws, rational testimonials, and suprarational decrees is because certain *mitzvot* have been heavily garbed in reason, so that our natural and initial reaction to them is a rational-emotional one, while others come to us as less veiled expressions of the divine will, with the immediate effect of stimulating our innate obedience to their commander. This is not to say, however, that we are to confine our observance and experience of a mitzvah to the most obvious face it presents to us. In the case of the ostensibly rational *mitzvot*, we must strive to nevertheless observe them with a simple, self-negating obedience to the divine will. Regarding the *chukim*, the challenge is to study and ponder their significance (including the significance and function of their non-rationality as stimulators of our unequivocal obedience to G-d) to the point that we observe them with the passion and intellectual involvement that characterize the most profoundly appreciated law or testimonial.

End to End

But why bother with such externalities? If the *mitzvot*, in essence, are the unfathomable will of G-d—if every soul, in essence, possesses an innate obedience to the divine will—why not keep our *mitzvot* pure? Why not strive only to awaken our intrinsic loyalty to G-d and observe His commandments, without the extraneous ink of intellectual inquiry and emotional empathy?

Because G-d commanded otherwise. *G-d* clothed His unqualifiable will in the patent logic of the mitzvah of charity, in the genius of the Torah's judicial code, in the emotional experience of Shabbat, in the subtle insights we glean from the most esoteric *chok*. G-d instructed us to not only implement His will but also to study it, analyze it, debate it and expound upon it. Why think and feel when it comes to G-d's decrees? Because this, too, is a divine decree.

This is the ultimate meaning of the statement, "This is the *chok* of Torah." *All* of Torah is *chok*: not only is every law and testimonial essentially a suprarational decree, but also their written surface, also our intellectual-emotional quest to comprehend and appreciate them, is to be undertaken in suprarational obedience to the divine will.

For this, too, we have a metaphor in the two engraved tablets Moses brought down from Mount Sinai. If the difference between rational appreciation and suprarational obedience is the difference between writing and engraving, the difference between obedience *sans* reason and obedient reasoning is the difference between two types of engraving.

Usually, engraved letters penetrate below the surface of the stone but do not cut through it from end to end. In other words, while the letters form an integral part of the stone, not every part of the stone is of the defining substance of the letters. If the letters are carved one inch deep in a two-inch-thick tablet, then only the front inch of stone is engraved.

This is comparable to a mindless obedience to the divine will. The person's performance of the mitzvah is engraved in his soul's essence, but it does not cut through it from end to end. Certain aspects of his being—his intellect and emotions—remain untouched. True, these are the more external, appended aspects of his being—the reverse of his stone, if you will—but they are part of it nonetheless.

However, regarding the two tablets that embodied the Ten Commandments, we are told that they were inscribed from end to end. Each letter was a complete hollow, bored front to back; every inch of stone was both the medium and the substance of the letters. This represents a state of being in which also the externalities of the soul—the elements of self usually associated with writing—are part and parcel of the engraving of the divine desire in the human essence.

Reprinted with permission of the Judaism website—Chabad.org

The Sanhedrin, People's Cyclopedia of Universal
Knowledge, *1883.*

Lesson

4

IN THE WAKE
OF EXPULSION
WAS THE TIME RIPE TO
REESTABLISH THE SANHEDRIN?

*In 1538, the rabbis of Safed announced
that they had decided to reinstitute the
practice of ordination, which had fallen
into disuse centuries earlier. But soon
thereafter, word came from the rabbis in
Jerusalem that they were opposed to this
initiative. Why did the rabbis of Safed
want to reinstitute ordination, and why
did the rabbis of Jerusalem oppose this?
Dissecting the halachic polemics, we will
learn how this debate was a product
of the unique historical circumstances
of sixteenth-century Jewry still reeling
from the Spanish Expulsion, and we will
see how this story is relevant to modern
attempts to reinstitute the Sanhedrin.*

TEXT 1

"ISRAEL MINISTER OF RELIGION INSISTS ON REVIVAL OF SANHEDRIN; ISSUES CALL TO RABBINATE," *JEWISH TELEGRAPHIC AGENCY,* JANUARY 17, 1950

Israel's Minister of Religion Rabbi Judah Maimon today issued a moving appeal to all chief rabbis in Israel to summon a national conference of practicing rabbis to discuss the possibility of reestablishing the Sanhedrin. (The Sanhedrin was the ancient Jewish tribunal which interpreted Jewish law and enacted decrees for religious observance.)

"I insist on a renewal of the Sanhedrin because I believe it is necessary for the needs of the hour and for our duty towards the future," the Minister of Religion said, speaking at a celebration here dedicated to the ideals of the Sanhedrin.

RABBI YEHUDAH LEIB MAIMON
1875–1962

Israel's first minister of religion. Rabbi Yehudah Maimon was born in Bessarabia and received his rabbinical ordination from Rabbi Yechiel Michel Epstein, author of the *Aruch Hashulchan.* He was one of the founders of the Mizrachi movement, and in 1919 he moved to Israel, where he became the head of the movement. He worked alongside Rabbi Kook in establishing the chief rabbinate, and he also founded the notable publishing house Mosad Harav Kook.

QUESTION FOR DISCUSSION

What are the advantages in reestablishing the Sanhedrin?
What are the disadvantages?

The Alhambra Decree, ordering the expulsion of all Jews from the Kingdoms of Castile and Aragon and their territories, issued by King Ferdinand and Queen Isabella, March 31, 1492. (Museum of the Jewish Diaspora, Tel Aviv)

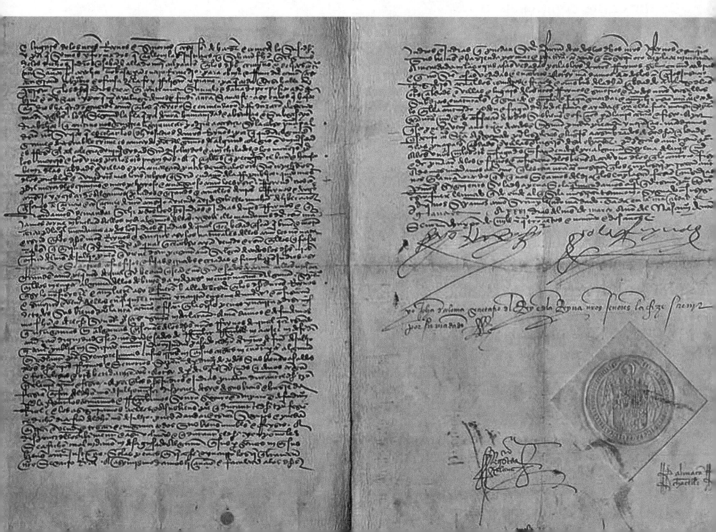

TEXT 2a

NUMBERS 27:18, 22–23 ⊞

וַיֹּאמֶר ה' אֶל מֹשֶׁה, קַח לְךָ אֶת יְהוֹשֻׁעַ בֶּן נוּן, אִישׁ אֲשֶׁר רוּחַ בּוֹ, וְסָמַכְתָּ
אֶת יָדְךָ עָלָיו . . .

וַיַּעַשׂ מֹשֶׁה כַּאֲשֶׁר צִוָּה ה' אֹתוֹ, וַיִּקַּח אֶת יְהוֹשֻׁעַ, וַיַּעֲמִדֵהוּ לִפְנֵי אֶלְעָזָר
הַכֹּהֵן וְלִפְנֵי כָּל הָעֵדָה.

וַיִּסְמֹךְ אֶת יָדָיו עָלָיו וַיְצַוֵּהוּ, כַּאֲשֶׁר דִּבֶּר ה' בְּיַד מֹשֶׁה.

God said to Moses, "Take Joshua son of Nun, a man of spirit, and lay your hand upon him." . . .

Moses did as God commanded him. He took Joshua and presented him before Elazar the Kohen and before the entire congregation.

He laid his hands upon him and commanded him, in accordance with what God had spoken to Moses.

TEXT 2b

MAIMONIDES, *MISHNEH TORAH,* LAWS OF THE SANHEDRIN 4:1–2

אֶחָד בֵּית דִּין הַגָּדוֹל, וְאֶחָד סַנְהֶדְרִין קְטַנָּה, אוֹ בֵּית דִּין שֶׁל שְׁלֹשָׁה, צָרִיךְ שֶׁיִּהְיֶה כָּל אֶחָד מֵהֶן סָמוּךְ מִפִּי הַסָּמוּךְ.

וּמֹשֶׁה רַבֵּנוּ סָמַךְ יְהוֹשֻׁעַ בְּיָד, שֶׁנֶּאֱמַר, "וַיִּסְמֹךְ אֶת יָדָיו עָלָיו וַיְצַוֵּהוּ". וְכֵן הַשִּׁבְעִים זְקֵנִים מֹשֶׁה רַבֵּנוּ סְמָכָם . . . וְאוֹתָן הַזְּקֵנִים סָמְכוּ לַאֲחֵרִים, וַאֲחֵרִים לַאֲחֵרִים. וְנִמְצְאוּ הַסְּמוּכִין אִישׁ מִפִּי אִישׁ עַד בֵּית דִּינוֹ שֶׁל יְהוֹשֻׁעַ, וְעַד בֵּית דִּינוֹ שֶׁל מֹשֶׁה רַבֵּנוּ . . .

וְכֵיצַד הִיא הַסְּמִיכָה לְדוֹרוֹת? לֹא שֶׁיִּסְמְכוּ יְדֵיהֶן עַל רֹאשׁ הַזָּקֵן, אֶלָּא שֶׁקּוֹרִין לוֹ "רַבִּי", וְאוֹמְרִים לוֹ "הֲרֵי אַתָּה סָמוּךְ, וְיֵשׁ לְךָ רְשׁוּת לָדוּן אֲפִילוּ דִּינֵי קְנָסוֹת".

RABBI MOSHE BEN MAIMON (MAIMONIDES, RAMBAM), 1135–1204

Halachist, philosopher, author, and physician. Maimonides was born in Cordoba, Spain. After the conquest of Cordoba by the Almohads, he fled Spain and eventually settled in Cairo, Egypt. There, he became the leader of the Jewish community and served as court physician to the vizier of Egypt. He is most noted for authoring the *Mishneh Torah,* an encyclopedic arrangement of Jewish law, and for his philosophical work, *Guide for the Perplexed.* His rulings on Jewish law are integral to the formation of halachic consensus.

All members of the Supreme Sanhedrin, a minor sanhedrin, and a *beit din* of three judges must be ordained by someone who was himself ordained.

Moses ordained Joshua by placing his hands upon him, as it says, "He laid his hands upon him and commanded him." Similarly, Moses ordained the seventy elders . . . who ordained others, who in turn ordained others. Thus, the sages in later generations were ordained in an unbroken chain all the way back to Joshua's court and Moses's court. . . .

How is the ordination bestowed? The person conveying ordination does not rest his hands on the sage's head. Instead, the sage is addressed by the title Rebbi and is told, "You are ordained; you have the authority to render judgment, even in cases involving penalties."

TEXT 3

TALMUD, SANHEDRIN 13B–14A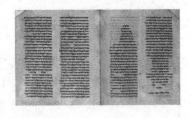

זָכוּר אוֹתוֹ הָאִישׁ לְטוֹב, וְרַבִּי יְהוּדָה בֶּן בָּבָא שְׁמוֹ, שֶׁאִילְמָלֵא הוּא . . . בָּטְלוּ דִינֵי קְנָסוֹת מִיִּשְׂרָאֵל.

שֶׁפַּעַם אַחַת גָּזְרָה מַלְכוּת הָרְשָׁעָה שְׁמַד עַל יִשְׂרָאֵל, שֶׁכָּל הַסוֹמֵךְ - יֵהָרֵג, וְכָל הַנִּסְמָךְ - יֵהָרֵג, וְעִיר שֶׁסוֹמְכִין בָּהּ - תֵּיחָרֵב, וּתְחוּמִין שֶׁסוֹמְכִין בָּהֶן - יֵעָקְרוּ.

מָה עָשָׂה יְהוּדָה בֶּן בָּבָא? הָלַךְ וְיָשַׁב לוֹ בֵּין שְׁנֵי הָרִים גְּדוֹלִים, וּבֵין שְׁתֵּי עֲיָירוֹת גְּדוֹלוֹת, וּבֵין שְׁנֵי תְּחוּמֵי שַׁבָּת, בֵּין אוּשָׁא לְשַׁפַּרְעָם. וְסָמַךְ שָׁם חֲמִשָּׁה זְקֵנִים, וְאֵלּוּ הֵן: רַבִּי מֵאִיר, וְרַבִּי יְהוּדָה, וְרַבִּי שִׁמְעוֹן, וְרַבִּי יוֹסֵי, וְרַבִּי אֶלְעָזָר בֶּן שַׁמּוּעַ. רַב אַוְיָא מוֹסִיף: אַף רַבִּי נְחֶמְיָה.

כֵּיוָן שֶׁהִכִּירוּ אוֹיְבֵיהֶם בָּהֶן, אָמַר לָהֶן: בָּנַיי, רוּצוּ! אָמְרוּ לוֹ: רַבִּי, מָה תְּהֵא עָלֶיךָ?

אָמַר לָהֶן: הֲרֵינִי מוּטָל לִפְנֵיהֶם כְּאֶבֶן שֶׁאֵין לָהּ הוֹפְכִים.

אָמְרוּ: לֹא זָזוּ מִשָּׁם עַד שֶׁנָּעֲצוּ בּוֹ שְׁלֹשׁ מֵאוֹת לוֹנְבִּיאוֹת שֶׁל בַּרְזֶל, וַעֲשָׂאוּהוּ כִּכְבָרָה.

BABYLONIAN TALMUD

A literary work of monumental proportions that draws upon the legal, spiritual, intellectual, ethical, and historical traditions of Judaism. The 37 tractates of the Babylonian Talmud contain the teachings of the Jewish sages from the period after the destruction of the 2nd Temple through the 5th century CE. It has served as the primary vehicle for the transmission of the Oral Law and the education of Jews over the centuries; it is the entry point for all subsequent legal, ethical, and theological Jewish scholarship.

That man, Rabbi Yehudah ben Bava, should be remembered positively. Were it not for him . . . penalty judgments would have ceased from the Jews.

It happened that the evil empire [of Rome] enacted an oppressive decree against the Jewish people: "Whoever confers ordination will be killed; anyone who accepts ordination will be killed; and any town in which ordination is conferred will be destroyed, as will its surrounding areas."

What did Rabbi Yehudah ben Bava do? He went and sat between two large mountains situated between two large cities—Usha and Shfaram—and beyond their surrounding areas. He ordained there five sages: Rabbi Meir, Rabbi Yehudah, Rabbi Shimon, Rabbi Yosei, and Rabbi Elazar ben Shamua. Rav Avya said that Rabbi Nechemiah was ordained there as well.

When the Romans discovered them, Rabbi Yehudah ben Bava said to them, "My children, flee!"

They said to him, "Our Teacher, but what will be of you?"

He said to them, "I am before them like a rock that no one will overturn."

It was reported that the Roman soldiers did not leave the spot where they found Rabbi Yehudah ben Bava until they pierced him with three hundred spears, rendering his body like a sieve.

QUESTION FOR DISCUSSION

Given what we have learned about *semichah*, can you offer any arguments in support of or against the plan to reinstitute it?

The Ordination of Joshua, *Marc Chagall, 1966. (The Jewish Museum, New York)*

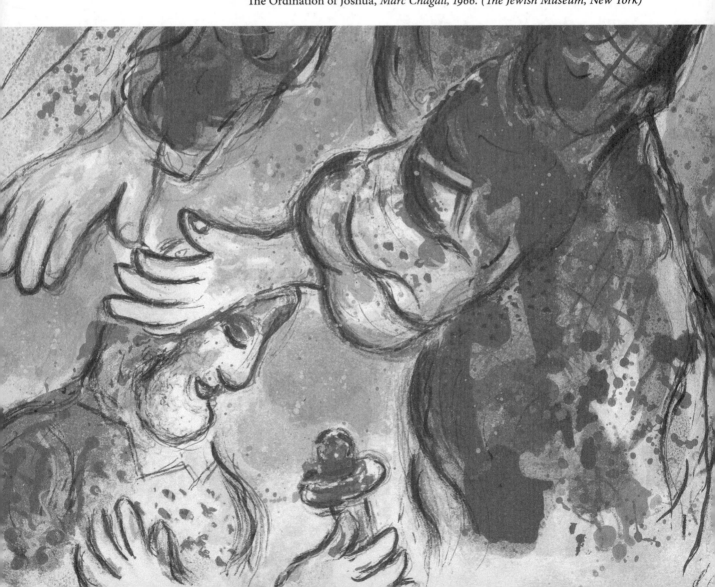

TEXT 4

MAIMONIDES, *MISHNEH TORAH,* LAWS OF KINGS AND THEIR WARS 12:1–5 🕎

אַל יַעֲלֶה עַל הַלֵּב שֶׁבִּימוֹת הַמָּשִׁיחַ יְבֻטַּל דָּבָר מִמִּנְהָגוֹ שֶׁל עוֹלָם, אוֹ יִהְיֶה שָׁם חִידוּשׁ בְּמַעֲשֵׂה בְרֵאשִׁית, אֶלָּא עוֹלָם כְּמִנְהָגוֹ נוֹהֵג.

וְזֶה שֶׁנֶּאֱמַר בִּישַׁעְיָה (יא, ו) "וְגָר זְאֵב עִם כֶּבֶשׂ וְנָמֵר עִם גְּדִי יִרְבָּץ" - מָשָׁל וְחִידָה, עִנְיַן הַדָּבָר שֶׁיִּהְיוּ יִשְׂרָאֵל יוֹשְׁבִין לָבֶטַח עִם רִשְׁעֵי עַכּוּ"ם... וְכֵן כָּל כַּיּוֹצֵא בְאֵלּוּ הַדְּבָרִים בְּעִנְיַן הַמָּשִׁיחַ הֵם מְשָׁלִים...

וְכָל אֵלּוּ הַדְּבָרִים וְכַיּוֹצֵא בָּהֶן לֹא יֵדַע אָדָם אֵיךְ יִהְיוּ עַד שֶׁיִּהְיוּ, שֶׁדְּבָרִים סְתוּמִין הֵן אֵצֶל הַנְּבִיאִים...

וּבְאוֹתוֹ הַזְּמַן לֹא יִהְיֶה שָׁם לֹא רָעָב, וְלֹא מִלְחָמָה, וְלֹא קִנְאָה, וְתַחֲרוּת, שֶׁהַטּוֹבָה תִּהְיֶה מֻשְׁפַּעַת הַרְבֵּה, וְכָל הַמַּעֲדַנִּים מְצוּיִּין כֶּעָפָר, וְלֹא יִהְיֶה עֵסֶק כָּל הָעוֹלָם אֶלָּא לָדַעַת אֶת ה' בִּלְבַד.

Do not presume that in the era of Redemption any facet of the world's nature will change. Rather, the world will continue according to its pattern.

Although Isaiah states (11:6): "A wolf shall live with a lamb, and a leopard shall lie with a young goat"—these words are a metaphor and a parable. The interpretation of the prophecy is that the Jewish people will dwell securely with those who had theretofore sought their destruction. . . . Other similar prophecies about this era are also metaphors. . . .

With respect to all of these matters [about the exact order that will lead into this era]—no one knows what will happen until it actually happens. For these matters are not clearly defined in the words of the prophets. . . .

In that era, there will be neither famine nor war, neither envy nor [destructive] competition, for there will be abundance, and all delights will be freely available as dust. The occupation of the entire world will be solely to know God.

TEXT 5

ISAIAH 1:1, 26–27 ⊕

חֲזוֹן יְשַׁעְיָהוּ בֶן אָמוֹץ אֲשֶׁר חָזָה עַל יְהוּדָה וִירוּשָׁלָם . . .
וְאָשִׁיבָה שׁפְטַיִךְ כְּבָרִאשׁוֹנָה וְיֹעֲצַיִךְ כְּבַתְּחִלָּה, אַחֲרֵי כֵן יִקָּרֵא לָךְ עִיר הַצֶּדֶק קִרְיָה נֶאֱמָנָה.
צִיּוֹן בְּמִשְׁפָּט תִּפָּדֶה, וְשָׁבֶיהָ בִּצְדָקָה.

The vision of Isaiah the son of Amoz, which he saw concerning Judah and Jerusalem. . . .

I will restore your judges as in the days of old, and your counselors as in the beginning. Afterward you shall be called the City of Righteousness, Faithful City.

Zion shall be redeemed through justice, and her returnees will be redeemed through righteousness.

TEXT 6a

MAIMONIDES, *COMMENTARY TO THE MISHNAH*, SANHEDRIN 1:3 ⊕

וַאֲנִי סָבוּר שֶׁאִם תִּהְיֶה הַסְכָּמָה מִכָּל הַתַּלְמִידִים וְהַחֲכָמִים לִמְנוֹת אִישׁ
בַּיְשִׁיבָה, כְּלוֹמַר שֶׁיַּעֲשׂוּהוּ רֹאשׁ, וּבִתְנַאי שֶׁיְּהֵא זֶה בְּאֶרֶץ יִשְׂרָאֵל כְּמוֹ
שֶׁהִקְדַּמְנוּ, הֲרֵי אוֹתוֹ הָאִישׁ תִּתְקַיֵּים לוֹ הַיְשִׁיבָה, וְיִהְיֶה סָמוּךְ, וְיִסְמֹךְ
הוּא אַחַר כַּךְ אֶת מִי שֶׁיִּרְצֶה.

לְפִי שֶׁאִם לֹא תֹאמַר כֵּן, לֹא תְהֵא אֶפְשָׁרִית מְצִיאוּת בֵּית דִּין הַגָּדוֹל
לְעוֹלָם, לְפִי שֶׁצָּרִיךְ כָּל אֶחָד מֵהֶם שֶׁיְּהֵא סָמוּךְ בְּלִי סָפֵק, וַהֲרֵי כְּבָר
הִבְטִיחַ ה' בְּשֵׁיבָתָם, בְּאָמְרוֹ "וְאָשִׁיבָה שׁוֹפְטַיִךְ כְּבָרִאשֹׁנָה".

I think that if all of the sages and their students agree to nominate one person to serve as their head, he will thereby be ordained and he could ordain whomever he wishes.

If you do not accept this, the Sanhedrin will never be able to return—because each member must, without a doubt, be ordained. But God already promised that it will return, as it says, "I will restore your judges as in the days of old."

TEXT 6b

MAIMONIDES, IBID. 👥

וַאֲנִי סָבוּר שֶׁהַסַנְהֶדְרִין תָּשׁוּב לִפְנֵי הִתְגַּלּוּת הַמָּשִׁיחַ, וְזֶה יִהְיֶה מִסִּימָנָיו. אָמַר: "וְאָשִׁיבָה שׁוֹפְטַיִךְ כְּבָרִאשׁוֹנָה וְיוֹעֲצַיִךְ כְּבַתְּחִלָּה וְאַחֲרֵי כֵן יִקָּרֵא לָךְ עִיר הַצֶּדֶק".

וְזֶה יִהְיֶה בְּלִי סָפֵק כַּאֲשֶׁר יַכְשִׁיר ה' לִבּוֹת בְּנֵי אָדָם, וְיִרְבּוּ בְּמַעֲשֶׂה הַטּוֹב, וְתִגְדַּל תְּשׁוּקָתָם לַה' וּלְתוֹרָתוֹ, וְיִתְרַבֶּה יָשְׁרָם לִפְנֵי בּוֹא הַמָּשִׁיחַ, כְּמוֹ שֶׁנִּתְבָּאֵר בִּפְסוּקֵי הַמִּקְרָא.

I think that the Sanhedrin will return before Mashiach's arrival, and that this restoration will be one of Mashiach's harbingers. Indeed, it says, "I will restore your judges as in the days of old, and your counselors as in the beginning. Afterward you shall be called the City of Righteousness, Faithful City."

The restoration of the judiciary will surely occur when, as mentioned in the Bible, God will inspire the human heart to perform an abundance of positive deeds, to have a strengthened desire for God and His Torah, and to increase in virtue. This will transpire before Mashiach's arrival.

QUESTION FOR DISCUSSION

Why did Maimonides's reading of Text 5 lead him to suggest that the restoration of the Sanhedrin would occur before Mashiach's arrival?

Pilgrimage to the Second Jerusalem Temple, *Alex Levin. (www.ArtLevin.com)*

TEXT 7

LETTER FROM SAFED RABBIS, IN *SEMICHAT ZEKENIM* (JERUSALEM, 2005), P. 5 ⊕

וְלָכֵן בֵּרַרְנוּ לְגָדוֹל שֶׁבָּנוּ בְּחָכְמָה וּבְמִנְיָן, הֶחָכָם הַשָּׁלֵם הָרַב הַגָּדוֹל מהר"ר בֵּירַב נר"ו, שֶׁיִּהְיֶה סָמוּךְ וְרֹאשׁ יְשִׁיבָה . . . וְהוּא יוֹשִׁיב מֵהַיּוֹתֵר חֲכָמִים שֶׁבָּנוּ אֶצְלוֹ . . . וְיִהְיוּ סְמוּכִים לָעַד לְעוֹלָם . . .

וְהָיָה מַעֲשֵׂה הַצְּדָקָה וְהַשָּׁלוֹם הַזֶּה תְּחִלָּה וְרֹאשׁ לְפִדְיוֹן נַפְשֵׁנוּ, וְלִהְיוֹתֵנוּ "עֲטֶרֶת תִּפְאֶרֶת בְּיַד ה', וּצְנִיף מְלוּכָה בְּיַד אֱלֹקֵינוּ" (יְשַׁעְיָהוּ סב, ג).

הוּא בְּרַחֲמָיו יַשְׁרֶה שְׁכִינָתוֹ בְּמַעֲשֵׂה יָדֵינוּ, וְיָקִים דְּבַר עַבְדּוֹ, "וְאָשִׁיבָה שׁוֹפְטַיִךְ כְּבָרִאשׁוֹנָה וְיוֹעֲצַיִךְ כְּבַתְּחִלָּה אַחֲרֵי כֵן יִקָּרֵא לָךְ עִיר הַצֶּדֶק קִרְיָה נֶאֱמָנָה", אָמֵן וְאָמֵן.

We have therefore chosen the greatest one in wisdom and years from among us, Rabbi Ya'akov Beirav, to be ordained as our leader . . . . He will nominate other sages from among us . . . and they shall be ordained forever. . . .

This righteous and peaceful act should be the dawn and beginning of our salvation and of our becoming "a crown of splendor in God's hand, and a royal diadem in the hand of our God" (ISAIAH 62:3).

May God in His mercy grace our action with His presence. Let the word of His prophet materialize: "I will restore your judges as in the days of old, and your counselors as in the beginning. Afterward you shall be called the City of Righteousness, Faithful City." Amen. Amen.

TEXT **8**

RABBI YA'AKOV BEIRAV, IN *SEMICHAT ZEKENIM* (JERUSALEM, 2005), P. 92

וְאִם תֹּאמַר שֶׁהָיָה לָהֶם לַחֲשׁוֹב שֶׁמָּא לֹא יַחְתְּמוּ . . . מִי יַעֲלֶה עַל דַּעְתּוֹ
שֶׁהַדָּבָר שֶׁיֵּשׁ בּוֹ עִכּוּב גְּאוּלָתֵינוּ - כְּפִי סְבָרַת הָאֵשֶׁל הַגָּדוֹל הָרַמְבַּ"ם -
שֶׁכָּל הַשּׁוֹמֵעַ לֹא יָבֹא מִמְּקוֹמוֹ לַחֲתוֹם בְּתֻפִּים וּבִמְחוֹלוֹת?

RABBI YA'AKOV BEIRAV
CA. 1474–1546

You claim that the rabbis of Safed should have considered that perhaps the rabbis of Jerusalem would not agree to sign the document. . . . Actually, given that per the teaching of Maimonides, this is a matter that is withholding our Redemption, who would have thought that anyone could respond in any other way than coming from his place to sign the document with timbrels and dances?

Leading rabbinic figure in 16th-century Safed. Rabbi Beirav was born in Moqueda, near Toledo, Spain. When he was about 18 years old, he and his family were among the thousands who were expelled from Spain in 1492. He first went to Morocco, where he was appointed rabbi in Fez; but a few years later, he traveled to Egypt and then to Israel, settling in Safed. He is known for his failed attempt to reintroduce the conferring of *semichah*, a practice that had long fallen into disuse.

Depiction of the holy sites in the Land of Israel. Safed is on the upper left corner and Jerusalem on the bottom right. Moshe Ganbash, Turkey, 1838. (The Jewish Museum, New York)

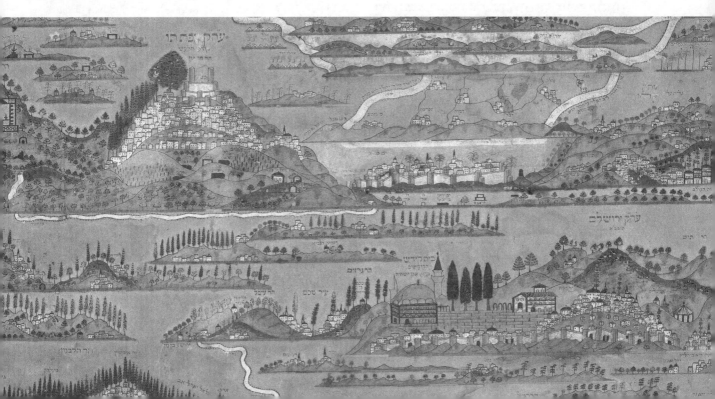

TEXT 9

RABBI LEVI CHABIB, IN *SEMICHAT ZEKENIM* (JERUSALEM, 2005), PP. 32–33

וְטֶרֶם שֶׁאַפְסִיק הַדִּבּוּר רָאִיתִי לְהוֹדִיעַ לַכֹּל, שֶׁגַּם שֶׁכָּתַבְתִּי כָּל זֹאת, אֵינִי תּוֹקֵעַ עַצְמִי לִדְבַר הֲלָכָה. וְכָל זְמַן שֶׁאֶשְׁמַע תְּשׁוּבָה הֲגוּנָה לְכָל רְאָיוֹתַי שֶׁכָּתַבְתִּי, אִם אֶפְשָׁר, עִם רְאָיָה מַסְפֶּקֶת, לְקִיּוּם הַסְּמִיכָה הַנִּזְכָּר, אֲנִי אֶחֱזוֹר בִּי, וְאוֹדֶה בָּהּ בְּשִׂמְחָה וּבְשִׁירִים. כִּי אֲפִילוּ שֶׁהָיָה נוֹשֵׂא אַחֵר הָיִיתִי חוֹזֵר בִּי לְאַהֲבַת הָאֱמֶת וַעֲבוֹדַת שָׁמַיִם, כָּל שֶׁכֵּן בְּנוֹשֵׂא הַזֶּה שֶׁלְּפָנֵינוּ.

שֶׁהִנְנִי מֵצֵר וּמִצְטַעֵר וְעָלַי לִבִּי דַוָּי, עַל שֶׁלֹּא זָכִיתִי לִהְיוֹת נִמְנֶה בְּמִצְוָה כָּזֹאת - מִצְוַת מִינּוּיֵי דַיָּנִים כְּשֵׁרִים בְּאֶרֶץ הַקְּדוֹשָׁה, וְשֶׁתִּתְקַיֵּם עַל יָדִי בְּחֶבְרַת כָּל רַבּוֹתַי יִשְׁמְרֵם צוּרָם, כִּי שְׂכָרָהּ גָּדוֹל מְאֹד. כְּמוֹ שֶׁדָּרְשׁוּ עַ"ה בְּסִפְרֵי (שׁוֹפְטִים קמד) עַל פָּסוּק (דְּבָרִים טז, יח-כ) "שׁוֹפְטִים וְשׁוֹטְרִים תִּתֶּן לְךָ" וְגוֹמֵר "לְמַעַן תִּחְיֶה וְיָרַשְׁתָּ אֶת הָאָרֶץ" - כְּדַאי הוּא מִנּוּי הַדַּיָּנִים הַכְּשֵׁרִים לְהַחֲיוֹת אֶת יִשְׂרָאֵל וּלְהוֹשִׁיבָם עַל אַדְמָתָם ...

וְלָכֵן אֲנִי אוֹמֵר, שֶׁאִם יִרְאֶה עֲדַיִן בְּעֵינֵי רַבְּנֵי צְפַת יצ"ו שֶׁיֵּשׁ רְאָיוֹת לְקִיּוּם הַסְּכָמָתָם, וְשֶׁנִּתְקַבֵּץ אֶל מָקוֹם אֶחָד ... וְשָׁם נִשָּׂא וְנִתָּן בַּדִּין ... גַּם בְּעֵינַי נִרְאֶה דָּבָר יָפֶה וְהָגוּן. וְהִנְנִי יָדַעְתִּי שֶׁגַּם אַלּוּפֵי וּגְבוֹרֵי הַחֲכָמִים הַשְּׁלֵמִים יצ"ו שֶׁבָּעִיר הַקְּדוֹשָׁה הַזֹּאת יַסְכִּימוּ בָּךְ. וְאִם בְּאוּלַי אַחַר הַמַּשָּׂא וּמַתָּן יַעֲלֶה בְּיָדֵינוּ שֶׁיֵּשׁ בָּנוּ כֹּחַ לַעֲשׂוֹת הַמִּצְוָה הַזֹּאת וּלְקַיְּמָהּ בַּכֹּל, אַשְׁרֵינוּ שֶׁזָּכִינוּ לְכָךְ וְשָׁמַעְנוּ וְעָשִׂינוּ.

וַאֲפִילוּ אִם לֹא תַעֲלֶה בְּיָדֵינוּ, וְכֵן הוּא הַנִּרְאֶה וּכְמוֹ שֶׁכָּתַבְתִּי, עִם כָּל זֶה רָאוּי לָנוּ לֶאֱחוֹז בָּהּ בְּחֶזְקַת הַיָּד לְפִי הָעֵת וְהַשָּׁעָה, וְנִמְנֶה דַיָּנִים הֲגוּנִים וּכְשֵׁרִים בְּכָל אֶרֶץ הַקְּדוֹשָׁה, לָדוּן בְּכָל מָה שֶׁהָיוּ יְכוֹלִין לָדוּן עַד עַתָּה. וְאוּלַי בִּשְׂכַר זֶה אֵ-ל חַי חֶלְקֵנוּ יִגְמוֹר בַּעֲדֵנוּ, וְנִזְכֶּה לִהְיוֹת נִמְנִים בְּזֹאת הַמִּצְוָה מְהֵרָה, בְּשׁוּב שׁוֹפְטֵינוּ וְסַנְהֶדְרִינוּ אֶל לִשְׁכַּת הַגָּזִית.

RABBI LEVI CHABIB
CA. 1483–1541

Leading rabbinic figure in 16th-century Jerusalem. Rabbi Chabib was born in Zamora, Spain, but when he was about 9 years old, his family was expelled from Spain in 1492 and settled in nearby Portugal. In 1497, his family, along with all Jews in Portugal, were forcibly converted to Catholicism. He eventually escaped to Salonika, then part of the Ottoman Empire, and then to Israel. He opposed Rabbi Beirav's attempt to renew ordination; at the end of his volume of responsa, he published many of the treatises that he and Rabbi Beirav wrote about their dispute.

Before I sign off, I wish to make it known to all, that despite everything that I have written, I am not riveting myself to my interpretation of the law. I will change my mind and happily submit whenever I hear a cogent response to all the arguments that I wrote and sufficient proof that supports the prospect of reinstituting *semichah.* My love of truth and my being in the service of God would impel me to behave this way even if the matter of dispute were a different subject; how much more so for this matter that is before us.

For I am distressed and pained, and my heart feels faint within me that I, along with my colleagues, have not merited to take part in this mitzvah to nominate fitting judges in the Holy Land. For its reward is very great, as it says, "Appoint judges and officials," etc., "so that you may live and possess the Land" (DEUTERONOMY 16:18–20). And our sages commented (SIFREI, SHOF-TIM 144), "The appointment of fitting judges is meritorious enough to give life to Israel and for them to take possession of the Land." . . .

I therefore say that if the rabbis of Safed believe that they still have proof to support their decision, and they wish to hold a conference . . . to discuss the issue thoroughly . . . then I too support this idea. And I know that my esteemed colleagues of this Holy City will agree. If, after our discussions, we conclude that we have the power to perform this mitzvah, then how happy will be our lot that we have merited to do this!

If we do not conclude that we can reinstitute ordination—and this is my view, as I have written—nevertheless, we should not let this opportunity slip away, but use it to respond to a contemporary need. We should appoint respectable and fitting judges throughout the Holy Land to adjudicate all matters of the law for which non-ordained judges have the authority to act. And perhaps God will soon reward us for this act that we should merit to take part in this mitzvah when the judges of the Sanhedrin will return to their place in the Holy Temple.

QUESTION FOR DISCUSSION

Compare how Rabbi Chabib discusses the reinstitution of *semichah* and the future Redemption (in Text 9) with how the rabbis of Safed (in Text 7) and Rabbi Beirav (in Text 8) discuss these matters. How would you articulate the differences?

TEXT 10

RABBI CHAIM YOSEF DAVID AZULAI, *BIRKEI YOSEF, CHOSHEN MISHPAT* 1:7

וַאֲנִי רָאִיתִי מְטַהֲרַת יַד הַקֹּדֶשׁ מוֹרֵנוּ הָרַב מֹשֶׁה אַלְשִׁיךְ זלה"ה כָּתַב
סְמִיכָה שֶׁהִסְמִיךְ לְהָרַב הַקָּדוֹשׁ מוֹרֵנוּ הָרַב חַיִּים וִיטַאל זלה"ה, וּכְתִיב
בְּגַוֵּוהּ שֶׁהוּא נִסְמָךְ מִמָּרָן מוֹרֵנוּ הָרַב יוֹסֵף קָארוֹ זלה"ה, וּבְכֹחַ זֶה סָמַךְ
לְמוֹרֵנוּ הָרַב חַיִּים וִיטַאל זלה"ה.

I have seen a note in the handwriting of Rabbi Moshe Alshich that he conferred *semichah* on Rabbi Chaim Vital. It specified that he himself had received *semichah* from Rabbi Yosef Caro, and that with this authority he conferred *semichah* on Rabbi Chaim Vital.

RABBI CHAYIM YOSEF DAVID AZULAI (CHIDA), 1724–1806

Talmudist and noted bibliophile. Born in Jerusalem, scion to a prominent rabbinic family, he studied under Rabbi Chaim ibn Atar. A prolific writer on various Jewish topics, his *Shem Hagedolim* is particularly famous, chronicling short biographies of Jewish authors with overviews of their works. He traveled extensively in Europe to raise funds on behalf of the Jewish community in the Land of Israel, and died in Italy.

RABBI YOSEF CARO (MARAN, *BEIT YOSEF*) 1488–1575

Rabbi Caro was born in Spain, but was forced to flee during the expulsion in 1492. His magnum opus, the Shulchan Aruch (Code of Jewish Law), has been universally accepted as the basis for modern Jewish law.

RABBI MOSHE ALSHICH 1508–1593

Student of Rabbi Yosef Caro. His biblical, homiletical, and ethical teachings remain popular to this day, including *Torat Moshe*, a commentary on the Torah.

RABBI CHAIM VITAL CA. 1542–1620

Rabbi Vital was authorized by his teacher, Rabbi Yitschak Luria, the Arizal, to record his teachings. His many works constitute the foundation of the Lurianic school of Jewish mysticism.

KEY POINTS

1 The judges of the Sanhedrin and other Jewish courts used to receive an official nomination, called *semichah*, from someone who himself had received this nomination, in a chain going back to Moses. This highlighted the continuous link of the Jewish tradition and ensured that only competent and fitting judges would occupy the seats of justice.

2 The Roman government forced the Sanhedrin to disband during the fourth century and also disallowed the bestowal of *semichah*. If the bestowal of *semichah* continued thereafter, it was conferred on very few sages and soon ceased to be conferred altogether.

3 There have been a few attempts throughout Jewish history to reestablish *semichah* and to renew the Sanhedrin. These attempts have been controversial and have not been successful.

4 The Torah teaches that there is nothing eternal or immutable about the way we construct societies and live our lives. Time is heading toward an almost unimaginable era of global Redemption, where peace, truth, and goodness will prevail.

5 The era of Redemption will introduce numerous changes for the Jewish people. For example, the prophets spoke of the restoration of the judiciary and the Redemption of Jerusalem.

6 Maimonides suggested that the restoration of the judiciary will occur before the Redemption and will serve as its harbinger. He formulated a strategy whereby *semichah* could be reinstituted by mass rabbinic consensus in order to nominate judges to serve on the Sanhedrin.

7 Many Jews regarded the aftermath of the Spanish Expulsion in 1492, and the forced conversion of Jews in Portugal in 1497, as a period that carried the potential to develop into the era of Redemption. A debate then ensued as to whether Jews should engage in extraordinary endeavors to trigger the materialization of the Redemption.

8 The rabbis of Safed wished to adopt Maimonides's plan to reinstitute *semichah*, and one of their stated goals was to trigger the emergence of the Redemption. The rabbis of Jerusalem, in addition to the various legal concerns they had with this plan, disagreed that Jews should trigger the emergence of the Redemption by reinstituting *semichah*. They advocated for a stronger commitment in all areas of Torah and *mitzvot* to prepare the world for Redemption.

Visit
facebook.com/myJLI
to vote on the following question:

Would it have been a good idea if Jews in Israel had established the Sanhedrin soon after the State of Israel was founded?

1 Yes. It would have generated more Jewish unity.
2 Yes. A Sanhedrin would have been able to tackle complex halachic issues.
3 Yes. It would have inspired more Jewish prestige.
4 No. It would have caused more harm than good.

Appendix

TEXT **11a**

RABBI ELIYAHU CAPSALI, *SEDER ELIYAHU ZUTA* 1:83 (JERUSALEM, 1976), P. 239 📖

אַחֵינוּ בְּנֵי עֵשָׂו גֵּרְשׁוּנוּ וַיְכַלּוּנוּ וַיַּשְׁמִידוּנוּ . . . סְפָרַד מִקֶּדֶם וּפוּרְטוּגָאל
מֵאָחוֹר, וַיֹּאכְלוּ אֶת יִשְׂרָאֵל בְּכָל פֶּה. בְּכָל זֹאת לֹא שָׁב אַפָּם וְעוֹד יָדָם
נְטוּיָה, וְשִׁחֲתוּ רַחֲמֵיהֶם וְעֶבְרָתָם שָׁמְרָה נֶצַח.

וַיַּעַמְדוּ עַל אֵם הַדְּרָכִים לִשְׁלוֹל שָׁלָל וְלָבוֹז בַּז, עֵרוֹם הָלִינוּ מִבְּלִי לְבוּשׁ
וְאֵין כְּסוּת בַּקָּרָה, בַּיּוֹם הַקֶּרַח הַנּוֹרָא.

וְאֵלּוּ לַעֲבָדִים וְלִשְׁפָחוֹת נִמְכַּרְנוּ הֶחָרַשְׁתִּי נֶאֱלַמְתִּי דוּמִיָּה. אֲבָל
מָה אֶעֱשֶׂה לָאֵלֶּה הַיּוֹם כִּי עָשׂוּ בָם יִסּוּרִין וְצָרוֹת, אִשָּׁה אֶל אֲחוֹתָהּ
חוֹבְרוֹת . . . מֵהֶם הָרְגוּ בַחֶרֶב, וּמֵהֶם הֵבִיאוּ בָאֵשׁ, וּמֵהֶם הֵבִיאוּ בַמַּיִם . . .
וּמֵהֶם הֵמִיתוּ בְּרָעָב, הַשּׁוֹד וְהַשֶּׁבֶר וְהָרָעָב וְהַדֶּבֶר . . .

וְהָאַחֲרוֹן הִכְבִּיד עַד מְאֹד, בְּחוֹטְפָם יוֹנְקֵי שָׁדַיִם מִשְּׁדֵי אִמּוֹתֵיהֶם, וַיֹּאמְרוּ
לַאֲבוֹתֵיהֶם: לָמָה לָכֶם בָּנִים? שֶׁלָּנוּ הֵם! וְרָעָה עוֹד מִזֹּאת כִּי שֻׁמְּדוּ בַּעַל
כָּרְחָם אֲלָפִים וּרְבָבוֹת מִיִּשְׂרָאֵל . . .

וְהָיָה כַּאֲשֶׁר יָנוּס אִישׁ מִפְּנֵי הָאֲרִי וּפְגָעוֹ הַדֹּב, וּבָא הַבַּיִת, וְסָמַךְ יָדוֹ עַל
הַקִּיר וּנְשָׁכוֹ הַנָּחָשׁ, כֵּן הַדָּבָר הַזֶּה . . .

לוּלֵי ה' צְבָאוֹת הוֹתִיר לָנוּ שָׂרִיד כִּמְעַט, וּנְתָנָנוּ לְחֵן בְּעֵינֵי שׁוּלְטָן
בֵּייְזִיט מֶלֶךְ תּוּגַרְמָה, וְקִבֵּל הַיְּהוּדִים בְּמַלְכוּתוֹ בְּסֵבֶר פָּנִים יָפוֹת, וְשָׁלַח
וְהֶעֱבִיר קוֹל בְּכָל מַלְכוּתוֹ וְגַם בְּמִכְתָּב לֵאמֹר: "כָּל הָרוֹצֶה לָדוּר בְּמַלְכוּתִי
וּבִחוּמוֹתַי בֹּא יָבֹא בְּרִנָּה לֹא יֵאָחֵר" . . .

RABBI ELIYAHU CAPSALI
(*SEDER ELIYAHU ZUTA*) 1483–1555

Jewish historiographer. Rabbi
Eliyahu was born in Crete. His
father was the rabbi of the Jewish
community, and directed relief work
for the Spanish and Portuguese
refugees who came to settle on the
island. When Eliyahu grew older, he
became rabbi of Crete. He authored
an impressive work of history titled
Seder Eliyahu Zuta. It is mostly a
history of the Ottoman Empire with
special reference to how this history
affected the Jews. It also includes
accounts of the sufferings of the Jews
of Spain and Portugal at the time of
the expulsion and forced conversion.

Our Christian brothers expelled us, consumed us, and
destroyed us. . . . First Spain and then Portugal devoured
Israel with every mouth. And yet, their antagonism has
not subsided, and their persecuting arm is still operative.

They have suppressed any sense of pity and have kept their fury unchecked.

They stood by the crossroads in order to plunder the Jews [who had been expelled and were making their way out of the country]. Our people spent the nights naked with no clothes, and they had no cover against the cold on very frosty days.

Had we merely been sold as slaves, I would have remained silent; however, I must intervene on behalf of my people because they have caused them continuous suffering and pain. . . . Some have been killed by sword, some by fire, some by water . . . some by hunger, and some by the plague. . . .

But the most grievous is what I now mention last. They grabbed infants from their mothers, telling the parents, "Why are these children yours? These are our children!" In fact, they forcibly converted tens of thousands of Jews. . . .

We were like someone who runs from a lion but is attacked by a bear, so he runs indoors looking for a place to hide only to be bitten by a snake. This is what happened to us. . . .

But God ensured that we were left with some survivors and granted us favor in the eyes of the Ottoman

Emperor Bayezid II, who accepted the Jews with open arms. He sent messengers throughout his kingdom to let it be known, and he issued a written declaration, saying, "Whoever wishes to live in my country and my cities can happily come without delay."

TEXT **11b**

RABBI ELIYAHU CAPSALI, IBID., PP. 240–241

וּמִי יוֹדֵעַ אִם לְעֵת כָּזֹאת הִגַּעְנוּ לַמַּלְכוּת, וְהֵחֵלָּה הַתְּשׁוּעָה **בָּרָן** . . . כִּי קִבְּצָנוּ הַמְקַבֵּץ נִדְחֵי יִשְׂרָאֵל לִהְיוֹתֵנוּ מוּכָנִים לְקִבּוּץ גָּלֻיּוֹת . . .

וְהַגֵּרוּשׁ הַנִּרְאֶה לָעַיִן, הָעִנְיָן רָעָה חוֹלָה מְעֻף צוּקָה וַאֲפֵלָה מְנֻדָּה תַּחְתָּיו יַעֲמוֹד צֶמַח יְשׁוּעָה. וּמִן הַיּוֹם הַהוּא וָהָלְאָה הֵחֵל ה' לְקַבֵּץ נִדְחֵי עַמּוֹ לְמַעַן יִהְיוּ מוּכָנִים וּמְעוּתָּדִים אֶל מָקוֹם אֶחָד בְּבִיאַת הַגּוֹאֵל.

וְהַצָּרוֹת שֶׁעָבְרוּ עַל הַיְּהוּדִים בָּעֵתִּים הָהֵם הוּא מַאֲמַר הַנָּבִיא ע"ה: "וְהָיְתָה עֵת צָרָה אֲשֶׁר לֹא נִהְיְתָה מִהְיוֹת גּוֹי עַד הָעֵת הַהִיא כוּ'" (דָּנִיאֵל יב, א). "אַשְׁרֵי הַמְחַכֶּה וְיַגִּיעַ" (יב, יב) "עַד עֵת קֵץ" (יב, ט). "קֵץ בָּא, בָּא הַקֵּץ" (יְחֶזְקֵאל ז, ו), "וְקָרוֹב לָבֹא" הַגּוֹאֵל "וְיָמָיו לֹא יִמָּשֵׁכוּ" (יְשַׁעְיָהוּ יג, כב).

Perhaps this whole affair occurred at that time for another aim—for our salvation to begin in 1492. . . . For the Gatherer of the Jewish exiles has assembled us to be prepared for the ingathering of the exiles. . . . The Expulsion that we all witnessed as a grievous evil, fearful gloom, and utter darkness—from it will sprout salvation. Indeed, since that day, God has started to gather the exiles of His people, that they should all be prepared in one place for the coming of the Redeemer.

These persecutions that the Jews have suffered are to be understood per the words of the prophet (DANIEL 12:1), "There will be a time of distress such as has not happened from the beginning of nations until then, [and at that time your people will be delivered]." "Blessed is the one who waits for and reaches" "the time of the end" (IBID. 12:12, 9). "The end has come! The end has come!" (EZEKIEL 7:6). The Redeemer "is at hand, and his days will not be prolonged" (ISAIAH 13:22).

Elijah the Prophet heralds Mashiach's arrival, illustrated Haggadah, *Munich, 15th century.* (The Jewish Encyclopedia)

TEXT 12

RABBI YOSEF OF ROSHEIM, MEMOIR, NO. 17, IN *REVUE DES ÉTUDES JUIVES* (PARIS: SOCIÉTÉ DES ÉTUDES JUIVES, 1888), P. 91

בִּשְׁנַת רצ"ב לִפְרָט קָטָן הוּצְרַכְתִּי לַחֲזוֹר וְלָבוֹא אֶל הַקֵּסָר יָרוֹם הוֹדוֹ בְּיוֹם הַוַעַד בְּעִיר רֶעגִין'שפּוּרְק לַעֲמוֹד עַל מִשְׁמֶרֶת יִשְׂרָאֵל. וַיְהִי ה' אִתָּנוּ וְהִצִּילָנוּ גַם בְּאוֹתָן הַיָּמִים מִקַּטְגוֹרִים שֶׁל הַשָּׂרִים וְהַפַּרְתְּמִים לָתֵת לָנוּ מִחְיָה בַּגּוֹיִם עַל דְּבַר הָרִבִּית וְכוּ'.

וּבְאוֹתָן הַיָּמִים בָּא הָאִישׁ לוֹעֵז גֵּר צֶדֶק הַמְכוּנֶּה רַבִּי שְׁלֹמֹה מוֹלְקָא נִשְׁמָתוֹ עֵדֶן בְּדֵעוֹת חִיצוֹנִיּוֹת לְעוֹרֵר הַקֵּסָר, בְּאָמְרוֹ שֶׁבָּא לִקְרוֹא כָּל הַיְּהוּדִים לָצֵאת לְמִלְחָמָה נֶגֶד הַתַּגָּר.

וּכְשׁוֹמְעִי מַה שֶּׁעָלְתָה בְּרוּחוֹ כָּתַבְתִּי אִגֶּרֶת לְפָנָיו לְהַזְהִירוֹ שֶׁלֹּא לְעוֹרֵר לֵב הַקֵּסָר פֶּן יֹאכְלֵנוּ הָאֵשׁ הַגְּדוֹלָה.

וְסַלַקְתִּי מִן הָעִיר רֶעגִין'שפּוּרְק כְּדֵי שֶׁלֹּא יֹאמַר הַקֵּסָר יָדִי אִתּוֹ בִּמְלַאכְתּוֹ דֵעוֹת חִיצוֹנִיּוֹת.

וּכְבוֹאוֹ אֶל הַקֵּסָר נִתְפַּס בְּחֶבְלֵי בַּרְזָלוֹת וְהוֹלִיכוּ עַד עִיר בָּלוּנְיָיא. שָׁמָּה נִשְׂרָף עַל קִדּוּשׁ הַשֵּׁם דָּתוֹת יִשְׂרָאֵל. וְרַבִּים הֵסִיר מֵעָוֹן, נִשְׁמָתוֹ צְרוּרָה בְּגַן עֵדֶן.

RABBI YOSEF OF ROSHEIM, 1480–1554

Jewish advocate at the courts of Maximilian I and Charles V. Rabbi Rosheim was a scholar and kabbalist, but he is primarily known as the skillful intermediary on behalf of German and Polish Jews. One of his famous achievements was saving the Talmud from the flames in 1510. He wrote several religious and ethical works, and his brief memoir was published in 1888.

In 1532, I had to return to His Highness the Emperor at the general assembly in the city of Regensburg to protect Jewish interests. God was with us, and then too He saved us from the accusations of the nobles, granting us the ability to earn a livelihood by lending on interest, and so forth.

At that time, there came along a foreigner, a righteous convert, called Rabbi Shlomo Molcho, whose soul now dwells on high. He wanted to persuade the emperor with foreign ideas, namely, to gather all of the Jews to go to war with the Ottomans.

When I heard of this, I wrote to him and warned him not to provoke the emperor's heart, lest the great fire consume him. I left the city of Regensburg so that the emperor would not think that I collaborated with this foreign idea.

When he came before the emperor, he was detained in metal chains and was taken to Bologna. He was burned there, sanctifying God's name and the Jewish faith. He caused many to repent, and his soul is surely bound in the Garden of Eden.

RABBI SHLOMO MOLCHO
1500–1532

Rabbi Shlomo Molcho was born in Portugal to a Jewish family that had been forcibly converted along with all of the Jews in Portugal in 1497. As a child, he was not circumcised and he was not taught Torah, but when he grew older, he was inspired to circumcise himself, fled to Italy, and lived there as a Jew. Very charismatic and intelligent, he became acquainted with some of the aristocrats and rulers in Italy, and he engaged them in religious disputations, arguing the merits of Judaism. While in Italy, he studied and taught kabbalah, which generated a following of admirers. He taught that Mashiach's arrival was imminent and actively sought to hasten his arrival.

Discussion #1

The rabbis of Safed acted under the assumption that . . .	Rambam's proposal to reinstitute *semichah* is compelling and should be adopted.
Rabbi Chabib objected:	Why did Rabbi Yehudah ben Bava give his life to keep the chain of ordination alive? Couldn't it have been restarted with Rambam's idea? Quite evidently, he did not consider that to be a valid option. Thus, we should not adopt Rambam's proposal.
Rabbi Beirav responded:	He gave his life because at the time, there was a decree against *semichah*. Had he not acted, no conference would have taken place for some time, and for that duration, there would be no one with *semichah,* and *dinei kenasot* (penalties) would have ceased for a while — even if one day it could be reinstituted. That's why he gave his life.
Rabbi Chabib responded:	Even if we accept these arguments, the Talmud (Text 3) only praised Rabbi Yehudah for keeping *dinei kenasot* alive. They did not mention that he also kept the Sanhedrin alive. The implication is that we do not need the Sanhedrin before Mashiach's arrival.

Discussion #2

The rabbis of Safed acted under the assumption that . . .	The order of the Redemption, as indicated in the verses (Text 5), is that first the Sanhedrin will be restored, and only afterward will Mashiach arrive and the Temple will be rebuilt.
Rabbi Chabib objected:	Mashiach will arrive not after but before the restoration of the judiciary. The verse is saying that even after Mashiach arrives, Jerusalem cannot be deemed a "city of righteousness" until the Sanhedrin is restored. And the next verse, which discusses the Redemption of Zion through justice, never intended to say that this refers to the justice administered by the Sanhedrin; it refers to the acts of justice that we should be doing today. Accordingly, there is no reason to reestablish ordination before Mashiach arrives.
Rabbi Beirav responded:	Rambam, in his commentary to the Mishnah (Text 6b), could not have been clearer about the meaning of the verses: first the Sanhedrin must be restored, and only afterward can the Temple be rebuilt and Mashiach can arrive.
Rabbi Chabib responded:	While Rambam, in his commentary to the Mishnah (Text 6b), does say this, in *Mishneh Torah* (Text 4), which he authored later, and which is most authoritative, Rambam rules that we do not know the order of his coming. This indicates that Rambam was no longer sure whether the judiciary will be restored before Mashiach's arrival. So why bother?

Discussion #3

The rabbis of Safed acted under the assumption that . . .	If we do not reinstitute *semichah* using Rambam's method, there is no way the Sanhedrin could ever be reestablished.
Rabbi Chabib objected:	We have other options. Elijah the prophet, who will come along with Mashiach, was ordained and can confer *semichah* on others. Mashiach himself, given his high stature, can confer ordination as well.
Rabbi Beirav responded:	The Talmud (Eiruvin 43b) says that Elijah will announce Mashiach's arrival to the Supreme Sanhedrin in Tiberias. This indicates that this court will be in existence before his and Mashiach's arrival. In addition, once someone passes away, he can no longer confer *semichah*, and this applies to Elijah as well. And how can we say that Mashiach will confer *semichah* if he never received it?
Rabbi Chabib responded:	This Talmudic passage need not mean that the actual Sanhedrin will be in existence; it has been interpreted to mean that Elijah will go to the place where the Sanhedrin last convened to make his announcement.

Discussion #4

The rabbis of Safed acted under the assumption that . . .	Their actions were consistent with Rambam's formula.
Rabbi Chabib objected:	Rambam (in Text 6a) required the consent of *all* scholars of Israel. Even if we assert that a majority suffices, a vote must occur after deliberations with *all* sages present. This didn't occur, and so the action taken by the rabbis of Safed is ineffective.
Rabbi Beirav responded:	"All" surely means "most." And we did not have to deliberate with all rabbis present because Rambam does not mention anything about deliberation; he just says "agreement." In addition, we sent a messenger to discuss the matter with you, and that counts as having included all rabbis in the deliberation.
Rabbi Chabib responded:	On the contrary, given the huge implications of this project, a majority does not suffice and unanimity is required. Besides, sending a messenger after having taken action is too late, for you will not be open to hearing alternative points of view.

TEXT 13

THE LUBAVITCHER REBBE, RABBI MENACHEM MENDEL SCHNEERSON,
IGROT KODESH 25:253–256

RABBI MENACHEM MENDEL SCHNEERSON
1902–1994

The towering Jewish leader of the 20th century, known as "the Lubavitcher Rebbe," or simply as "the Rebbe." Born in southern Ukraine, the Rebbe escaped Nazi-occupied Europe, arriving in the U.S. in June 1941. The Rebbe inspired and guided the revival of traditional Judaism after the European devastation, impacting virtually every Jewish community the world over. The Rebbe often emphasized that the performance of just one additional good deed could usher in the era of Mashiach. The Rebbe's scholarly talks and writings have been printed in more than 200 volumes.

הִנְנִי לְאַשֵׁר קַבָּלַת מִכְתָּבוֹ מִיוֹם ו' אֱלוּל וְתָכְנוֹ מִשְׁאָל עַל נוֹשֵׂא חֲדוּשָׁה שֶׁל הַסַנְהֶדְרִין . . .

וְהִנֵּה עֶצֶם הַמִשְׁאָל בְּנוֹגֵעַ חֲדוּשָׁה שֶׁל הַסַנְהֶדְרִין . . . מְיוּסָד כָּאָמוּר עַל הַהֲנָחָה שֶׁהַמַּצָב בְּאֶרֶץ הַקֹדֶשׁ תִּבָּנֶה וְתִכּוֹנֵן וּבְגָלֶה מְעוֹרֵר אֶת בְּעָיַת הַסַמְכוּת הַדָתִית, וַאֲשֶׁר חִדוּשׁ הַסַנְהֶדְרִין כְּאִלוּ הַתְרוּפָה לְהַמַּצָב. וַאֲנִי שׁוֹאֵל אֶת כְּבוֹדוֹ מֵאַיִן לוֹ זֶה? הַאִם אֱמֶת נָכוֹן הַדָבָר אֲשֶׁר חִדוּשׁ הַסַנְהֶדְרִין הוּא תְרוּפָה, וְלֹא עוֹד, אֶלָּא הַתְרוּפָה הַיְחִידָה, לְהַמַצָב הַשׁוֹרֵר בְּחַיֵי הָרוּחַ וְהַדָת שֶׁל עַמֵנוּ כְּהַיוֹם הַזֶה?

אֵלוּ בֶּאֱמֶת הָיָה מַחֲלֹקֶת וּבְלִי סֵדֶר בְּכַמָּה וְכַמָּה עִנְיָנִים בִּשְׁטַח הַהֲלָכָה, שֶׁנָפְלוּ אֵיזוֹ סְפֵיקוֹת בְּבֵרוּר הַהֲלָכָה וְנֶחְלְקוּ בָּהֶם גְדוֹלֵי יִשְׂרָאֵל, הַלָלוּ אוֹמְרִים כָּךְ וְהַלָלוּ אוֹמְרִים כָּךְ, וְעַל פִּי הַהֲלָכָה עַצְמָהּ אִי אֶפְשָׁר שֶׁיִתְבָּרֵר הַדָבָר לַהֲלָכָה לְמַעֲשֶׂה אֶלָּא אַךְ וְרַק עַל פִּי סַנְהֶדְרִין . . . אֵלוּ כָּךְ הָיָה הַמַצָב, הָיָה מוּבָן גוֹדֶל הַשְׁאִיפָה שֶׁל אוֹתָם הַחֲגִים הָרוֹצִים בְּחִדוּשׁ הַסַנְהֶדְרִין . . .

הֲרֵי יָדוּעַ לְכָל בַּר בֵּי רַב אֲשֶׁר גַם בְּהֶעְדֵר הַסַנְהֶדְרִין לֹא אַלְמָן יִשְׂרָאֵל, וְהַהֲלָכָה קוֹבַעַת אֵיךְ לְהִתְנַהֵג אֲפִלוּ בְּמָקוֹם שֶׁיֵשׁ סְפֵיקוֹת . . . שֶׁלָכֵן דַוְקָא בַּחֲגִים הַחֲרֵדִים לִדְבַר ה' וְהַמְקַיְמִים אֶת מִצְוֹת הַתּוֹרָה בְּפוֹעַל וּבְדַיְקָנוּת, לַמְרוֹת גוֹדֶל שְׁאִיפָתָם לִזְכּוֹת לִרְאוֹת בְּחִדוּשׁ הַסַנְהֶדְרִין בַּזְמַן הַמְיוּעָד לָזֶה בְּתוֹרָתֵנוּ הַקְדוֹשָׁה וּבְאֹפֶן הָרָאוּי, הִנֵּה דַוְקָא בַּחֲגִים חֲרֵדִים אֵלוּ לֹא נִרְאֵית מְבוּכָה לְרֶגֶל הֶעְדֵר הַסַנְהֶדְרִין, וְאֵין נִרְגֶשֶׁת בָּהֶם הַעֲפָלָה לְחִדוּשׁ הַסַנְהֶדְרִין . . .

וְאֵלוּ מֵהַדוֹרְשִׁים חִדוּשׁ הַסַנְהֶדְרִין אֲשֶׁר אֵינָם מְסוּרִים וּנְתוּנִים לַתּוֹרָה וּלְמִצְוֹתֶיהָ, הֲרֵי בָּרוּר הַדָבָר שֶׁאֵין מַכִּירִים בְּמַהוּת הַסַנְהֶדְרִין . . . שֶׁהֲרֵי בָּרוּר הַדָבָר שֶׁאֵין בְּכֹחַ הַסַנְהֶדְרִין לַהֲתֵר עַל קוּצוֹ שֶׁל יוֹד מֵהַתּוֹרָה, וְעִנְיָנָהּ אַךְ וְרַק לְהוֹרוֹת עַל פִּי הַתּוֹרָה וְלַעֲמוֹד עַל הַמִשְׁמָר שֶׁמִשְׁפָּטֶיהָ יֵצְאוּ מֵהַכֹּחַ אֶל הַפֹּעַל . . . וּמִמֵּילָא טוֹעִים אֵלוּ הַחוֹשְׁבִים שֶׁעַל יְדֵי חִדוּשׁ הַסַנְהֶדְרִין יִסְרוּ כַּמָּה חוּמְרוֹת וְיִתְרוּ כַּמָּה אִסוּרִים בְּחַיֵי הַפְּרָט וְהַצִבּוּר, שֶׁמִלְבַד עֶצֶם הַטָעוּת שֶׁבַּשְׁאִיפָה לְקוּלוֹת הַנוֹבַעַת מִשְׁרִירוּת הַלֵב וּפְרִיקַת עֹל הַמוּסָר וְכֵלֵי, הִנֵּה אֵין מָקוֹם בִּכְלָל לְשִׁנּוּיִים הַמְקוּוִים הָאֵלֶה.

וְכֵן טוֹעִים אֵלוּ שֶׁחוֹשְׁבִים שֶׁעַל יְדֵי חִדּוּשׁ הַסַּנְהֶדְרִין יִתְאַחֶה הַקֶּרַע בֵּין שׁוֹמְרֵי הַתּוֹרָה וּמִצְוֹוֹתֶיהָ וּבֵין אֵלֶּה שֶׁלְּעֵת עַתָּה מְנֻגָּדִים לַתּוֹרָה וּלְמִצְוֹוֹתֶיהָ, שֶׁהֲרֵי בָּרוּר שֶׁגַּם בְּהִתְחַדֵּשׁ הַסַּנְהֶדְרִין לֹא יִפְחַת מִמִּסְפַּר הַל"ט מְלָאכוֹת הָאֲסוּרוֹת בַּשַּׁבָּת, וְלֹא יָקֵל דָּבָר בְּעִנְיְנֵי אִישׁוּת וּצְנִיעוּת, וְלֹא תִּהְיֶינָה פְּשָׁרוֹת בְּחִנּוּךְ כָּשֵׁר עַל טַהֲרַת הַקֹּדֶשׁ וְכֵלֵי וְכֵלֵי.

הַמּוּרָם מֵהָאָמוּר הוּא אֲשֶׁר סִבַּת הַקֶּרַע הַנִּזְכָּר אֵינָה בְּהֶעְדֵּר הַסַּנְהֶדְרִין, וּבְמֵילָא אֵין הַתְּרוּפָה בְּחִדּוּשָׁהּ . . .

וַאֲשֶׁר לְעֶצֶם חִדּוּשׁ הַסַּנְהֶדְרִין . . . כָּל הַמְעַיֵּן בְּהִלְכוֹת מִנּוּי סַנְהֶדְרִין, וְיוֹדֵעַ מִי הוּא הָרָאוּי עַל פִּי הַהֲלָכָה לִמְנוֹת סַנְהֶדְרִין, וּמִי הוּא הָרָאוּי לִהְיוֹת חֲבֵר הַסַּנְהֶדְרִין וְכֵלֵי, בָּרוּר יִהְיֶה לוֹ אֲשֶׁר כְּמוֹ שֶׁאִי אֶפְשָׁר הָיָה שֶׁיִּתְחַדֵּשׁ הַסַּנְהֶדְרִין מִיּוֹם שֶׁבָּטְלָה עַד עַתָּה, כָּךְ לֹא בָּטְלוּ הַמְּנִיעוֹת וְהָעִכּוּבִים לְחִדּוּשָׁהּ עַל פִּי הַהֲלָכָה גַּם עַכְשָׁו. וְכָל אִרְגּוּן שֶׁבְּשֵׁם סַנְהֶדְרִין יְכֻנֶּה מִבְּלִי הִתְחַשֵּׁב עִם הַהֲלָכָה, הֲרֵי מוּבָן שֶׁאֵין זוֹ אֶלָּא רַמָּאוּת גְּדוֹלָה, וּבְשׁוּם פָּנִים לֹא תֵחָשֵׁב לְסַנְהֶדְרִין . . .

אֲבָל הַהֲכָנָה הָאֲמִתִּית לְחִדּוּשׁ הַסַּנְהֶדְרִין הִיא, כָּאָמוּר, עַל יְדֵי כָּךְ שֶׁכָּל אֲשֶׁר בְּיָדוֹ לְהַשְׁפִּיעַ לְהָשִׁיב עֲטֶרֶת הַתּוֹרָה לְיוֹשְׁנָהּ וּלְהַחֲזִיק וּלְהָפִיץ שְׁמִירַת הַתּוֹרָה וְהַמִּצְווֹת בְּחַיֵּי יוֹם יוֹם, יַעֲשֶׂה כֵן בְּאֹמֶץ, וְלֹא יֵבוֹשׁ מִפְּנֵי הַמַּלְעִיגִים. וְכָל אֶחָד וְאֶחָד בְּיָדוֹ לַעֲשׂוֹת, כָּל אֶחָד כְּפִי מַעֲמָדוֹ וּמַצָּבוֹ, לְהָסִיר אֶת הַסִּבּוֹת שֶׁבִּשְׁבִילָן בָּטְלָה הַסַּנְהֶדְרִין, וּלְקָרֵב אֶת הַגְּאֻלָּה הָאֲמִתִּית עַל יְדֵי מָשִׁיחַ צִדְקֵנוּ, שֶׁאָז יְקֻיַּים הַיִּעוּד, "וְאָשִׁיבָה שֹׁפְטַיִךְ כְּבָרִאשֹׁנָה וְיֹעֲצַיִךְ כְּבַתְּחִלָּה".

I acknowledge the receipt of your letter, dated the sixth of Elul [1968], which included a survey about reinstating the Sanhedrin. . . .

This survey is based on the assumption that there is a problem of religious authority in the Holy Land and in the Diaspora, and that reinstating the Sanhedrin is the remedy for this situation. But why do you think that reinstating the Sanhedrin is in fact the remedy, and the only remedy, for the situation that plagues the spiritual and religious life of our nation today?

If there were indeed disorder and doubt regarding halachic issues because there were areas where rabbinic leaders were in dispute—one side saying this and the other saying that—and there were no halachic method to clarify the law without a Sanhedrin . . . if that were the case, I would understand the strong desire to reinstate the Sanhedrin. . . .

In reality, even without a Sanhedrin, the Jewish people are not "widowed," because halachah determines how we are to behave even in scenarios of halachic uncertainty. . . . Therefore, the lack of the Sanhedrin is not a source of confusion among God-fearing Jews who meticulously observe the Torah's commandments, nor do we see in such communities the drive to reinstate the Sanhedrin, despite their strong desire to see it reinstated—at the right time, as determined by our holy Torah. . . .

With respect to those who demand that the Sanhedrin be reinstated but who are not committed to a life of Torah—it is obvious that they do not understand what the Sanhedrin is. . . . For it is not within the Sanhedrin's mandate to revoke even the slightest detail of the Torah; its purpose is merely to issue rulings based on Torah principles and to ensure that their rulings are implemented. . . . Consequently, these Jews are misguided in their presumption that by reinstating the Sanhedrin certain halachic stringencies will be revoked and several prohibitions will be removed. Aside from the inappropriate desire for leniencies—which stems from a disobedient and undisciplined outlook—these sought-after leniencies will never materialize.

There are those who believe that reinstating the Sanhedrin will cure the rift between those who observe the Torah and those who do not. But they too are mistaken because even were the Sanhedrin to be reinstated, the number of Shabbat primary labors will remain thirty-nine; the laws of relationships and modesty will not be more permissive; and there will be no compromises with respect to providing children with a proper Jewish education, and so forth.

The upshot of all this is that the rift among Jews is not a result of the lack of a Sanhedrin, and so reinstating it will not be the remedy. . . .

Returning to the original survey regarding reinstating the Sanhedrin: . . . If one studies the laws of the Sanhedrin and is aware of who is eligible to make appointments to this body and who is eligible to serve on it, etc., it will become evident that the hurdles that made it impossible to renew the Sanhedrin in the past are still very much in place. Therefore, any institution that refers to itself as a Sanhedrin, without consideration of halachic requirements, is clearly perpetuating a fraud, and can in no way be considered a Sanhedrin. . . .

Rather, the appropriate preparation for the eventual return of the Sanhedrin is for all those in positions of influence to do all that they can to return the crown of Torah to its former glory, promoting the observance of Torah and *mitzvot* in daily life, and doing so proudly without being ashamed of detractors. All of us can act in this regard according to our unique abilities. And this will do away with the cause of the Sanhedrin's abolishment and bring the true Redemption that will be initiated by Mashiach. That is when we will see the fulfilment of the promise, "I will restore your judges as in the days of old and your counselors as in the beginning."

Additional Readings

THE *SEMICHAH* CONTROVERSY
PRIMARY SOURCES

MAIMONIDES, *COMMENTARY TO THE MISHNAH*, SANHEDRIN 1:3

There is some doubt as to whether three ordained judges are required before it is possible to ordain others, or one ordained judge is sufficient to confer *semichah*. The Talmud seems to say that only the greatest of the three needs to be ordained, and that he can recruit two others—whomever he wishes—to facilitate ordination.

I think that if all of the sages and their students agree to nominate one person to serve as their head, he will thereby be ordained and he could ordain whomever he wishes.

If you do not accept this, the Sanhedrin will never be able to return—because each member must, without a doubt, be ordained. But God already promised that it will return, as it says, "I will restore your judges as in the days of old" (Isaiah 1:26).

We cannot say that Mashiach will nominate those who have no ordination to the Sanhedrin. For as I have explained in my introduction to this commentary, Mashiach will not add to nor detract from the Torah—not the Written Torah and not the Oral Torah.

I think that the Sanhedrin will return before Mashiach's arrival, and that this restoration will be one of Mashiach's harbingers. Indeed, it says, "I will restore your judges as in the days of old and your counselors as in the beginning. Afterward you shall be called City of Righteousness, Faithful City" (ibid.).

The restoration of the judiciary will surely occur when, as mentioned in the Bible, God will inspire the human heart to perform an abundance of positive deeds, to have a strengthened desire for God and His Torah, and to add in virtue. This will be before Mashiach's arrival.

MAIMONIDES, *MISHNEH TORAH*, LAWS OF THE SANHEDRIN 4:11

It appears to me that if all the all the wise men in *Eretz Yisrael* agree to appoint judges and convey *semichah* upon them, the *semichah* is binding and these judges may adjudicate cases involving financial penalties and convey *semichah* upon others.

If so, why did the sages suffer anguish over the institution of *semichah* [that it not be lost], so that the judgment of cases involving financial penalties would not be nullified among the Jewish people? Because the Jewish people were dispersed, and it is impossible that all could agree. If, by contrast, there was a person who had received *semichah* from a person who had received *semichah*, he does not require the consent of all others. Instead, he may adjudicate cases involving financial penalties for everyone, for he received *semichah* from a court.

This matter requires resolution.

RABBI MOSHE BEN MAIMON (MAIMONIDES, RAMBAM), 1135–1204
Halachist, philosopher, author, and physician. Maimonides was born in Cordoba, Spain. After the conquest of Cordoba by the Almohads, he fled Spain and eventually settled in Cairo, Egypt. There, he became the leader of the Jewish community and served as court physician to the vizier of Egypt. He is most noted for authoring the *Mishneh Torah*, an encyclopedic arrangement of Jewish law, and for his philosophical work, *Guide for the Perplexed*. His rulings on Jewish law are integral to the formation of halachic consensus.

SEMICHAH PROCLAMATION (SEMICHAT ZEKENIM [JERUSALEM, 2005], PP. 4–5)

The *semichah* accord from the rabbis of Safed has been sent to us, the rabbis of Jerusalem, signed in their names. Because of their great refinement and humility, they gave us the (veto) power to confirm this accord with our names and signatures.

Semichah Accord

We are one people, the people of God, a nation of priests and a holy nation, formed from the beginning of the world. Nations will seek God out. From Him come rulers and governors, judges and officers, who govern the people with glory, renown, and splendor. But now, the Jewish nation transgressed the rulings and violated the laws. God became angry at His people who made breaches upon breaches in the Torah. There is no king, no prince; there are no Torah scholars or wise men due to our many sins. The people of God are now scattered and isolated. All of us have strayed like sheep, each person turning his own way. Our sins increase daily, and the crown of our head has fallen and been profaned. We no longer have a prophet teaching righteousness. No longer can anyone apply the laws of fines. We do not reprove the wicked with his blemish, stirring him from within to return to God. He says in his heart: "Why should I work futilely? What benefit is there if I fast or receive the thirty-nine lashes? Nothing will be accomplished because there is no power to release me from my punishment of *karet* (premature death and spiritual excision of the soul). I am continuously confronted by my sin; my disgrace is not wiped away."

This has been a stumbling block for our people, causing them not to return to God, but rather to hold on to their foolishness and their straying way, locking the doors of return. Who is the person who, called by the name of Israel and putting his trust in the God of Israel, proclaims, "I am for God!"? If one takes pause over this matter, will one's eyes not pour out tears? For the people of God have descended greatly.

And now in a flash there has been mercy before God to sustain us and to take us up from the pit of destruction, from the exiles and the persecutions which have entwined around our necks in the gentile lands, and to bring us to the place He has chosen, and to the city which is called by His name, and to give us permanence in this place.

Therefore, in all the words of this letter, we, the young sheep of the Holy Land, have arisen and stirred ourselves to be zealots for God's glory. For how can it be that no one calls to establish the judicial system? To return to God wholeheartedly? Let each say to his brother: Be strong! And we will all be strong for our people's sake and for the sake of the cities of God. We shall raise the banner of the Torah which has been thrown to the ground and trampled for so long.

We have therefore chosen the greatest one in wisdom and years from among us, Rabbi Ya'akov Beirav, to be ordained as our leader, to be the head of the yeshivah, and to be called Rav. He will nominate other sages from among us, and they will be ordained forever, setting into action the laws of the Torah in truth and uprightness. When they judge the people, if an individual deserves punishment they will administer the Torah's punishment of lashes as they are able to do. In that way, the wrongdoer will escape the punishment of *karet* and will return to eternal life. The entire nation will then be whole and complete.

This righteous and peaceful act should be the dawn and beginning of our salvation and of our becoming "a crown of splendor in God's hand, and a royal diadem in the hand of our God" (Isaiah 62:3).

May God in His mercy grace our action with His presence. Let the word of His prophet materialize: "I will restore your judges as in the days of old and your counselors as in the beginning. Afterward you shall be called City of Righteousness, Faithful City." Amen. Amen.

TREATISE ONE—RABBI LEVI BEN CHABIB (EXCERPTS FROM SEMICHAT ZEKENIM, PP. 24–27)

I will not hold back from the rabbis of the generation what I have discovered about this matter. I will first clarify the intent of Maimonides's words in his *Commentary to the Mishnah* and his *Mishneh Torah*.

All Torah scholars know that if there is no known source for Maimonides's writings, in our holy Talmud, in a *beraita,* or the Tosefta, they are words in a sealed book. We are unable to completely understand them, neither their essential meaning as law nor the reasoning behind them. And so it is in our case. Furthermore, nobody else cites these ideas in their works, and therefore I have no source by which to verify their true intent aside from the words Maimonides himself wrote in his *Commentary to the Mishnah* and in his *Mishneh Torah.*

What seems evident is that Maimonides in his *Mishneh Torah* retracted the position he wrote during his youth in his *Commentary to the Mishnah.* He reconsidered two things. The first is the broad scheme about first seating a head of the yeshivah. It seems his intent is to setup a Supreme Sanhedrin. Whereas in *Mishneh Torah* he omits this language and just talks about ordaining judges and courts of law. . . . The second point is the rationale and proof, from the verses in Isaiah, to renew ordination. In his *Mishneh Torah* he concludes that this idea needs further deliberation.

Although Maimonides provides a pathway in Mishnah to establish the Supreme Sanhedrin, there is no need for it in exile. For truthfully, before the rebuilding of the Holy Temple, they have neither the power nor the stature of a Sanhedrin, since the majority—if not almost all—of their work is dependent on the existence of the Holy Temple. . . . Thus, during the time the Holy Temple is in ruins, we do not need the Supreme Sanhedrin; rather, just a court of three ordained rabbis.

Accordingly, when Maimonides wrote in his Mishnah and hinted that a corrective action could be taken

RABBI LEVI IBN CHAVIV (MAHRLBACH, RALBACH), CA. 1480–1545

Born in Zamora, Spain; died in Jerusalem. His family settled in Portugal after being forced from Spain during the 1492 expulsion. A few years later, he fled the Portuguese inquisition and moved to Salonika, Greece. In 1525 he settled in Jerusalem, where he was appointed chief rabbi. He vehemently opposed Rabbi Ya'akov Beirav's plan to reestablish the Sanhedrin and the practice of *semichah.* Among his works are a collection of responsa and a commentary on the laws governing the calendar. He also completed his father's work, the *Ein Ya'akov,* which excerpts ethical and inspirational teachings from the Talmud.

to set up a Sanhedrin court with a Supreme leader, this was because he quoted the prophecies about renewing the judicial system. The prophecy discusses the complete renewal of the judicial system with the Supreme Sanhedrin at the helm. However, this is not enough of a basis for a legal ruling, and when Maimonides does make a ruling later in *Mishneh Torah*, his concise ruling does not mention a Supreme leader. Implicit is that there would not be a Sanhedrin, either, in our days.

I will also add a nice inference, which explains why Maimonides reconsidered the prophecies as proof to renew the Sanhedrin before the coming of Mashiach.

Maimonides's proof is built on the prophetic promise that the judges of Israel would be brought back before the coming of Mashiach. And thus Maimonides wrote in his commentary: "This will undoubtedly come to be when the blessed Creator prepares the hearts of humanity before the coming of Mashiach" (Maimonides, *Commentary to the Mishnah,* Sanhedrin 1:3). The need for Maimonides to say as a starting point that that prophecy refers to the time before Mashiach's coming is that apparently, were it maintained that it would come afterward, there would be no need to assure us about it, for the prophets promised much more about those times.

This point seemed to him to be made by the prophetic verses as well. The second half of the verse says, "Afterward you shall be called City of Righteousness" (Isaiah 1:26), and this seems to be saying that before the city and Holy Temple are rebuilt, the Sanhedrin and judges will return to Israel. However, if the rebuilding of the city were to be before the return of the judges, the prophet should have instead prophesied about rebuilding the city and the Temple, for that is a greater thing. We must rather conclude that the prophet means the Sanhedrin and the judges will return first.

Also, the understanding of the next verse, "Zion will be redeemed by justice," (Isaiah 1:27), is that this justice will be rendered by the judges. This verse also indicates that the return of the judges will be prior to the Redemption and will herald the rebuilding of Zion.

It seems that Maimonides also relies on the subsequent verse as evidence to his premise that the

Sanhedrin will be established first. The next verse states that: "The rebellious and the sinners will be crushed together" (Isaiah 1:28), and this will also occur before the coming of Mashiach and the building of the Temple, because afterward, when Mashiach comes, there will be tranquility and peace amongst Israel.

I have explained this topic at length to show why Maimonides originally thought the prophecy about the return of the judicial system will be fulfilled before the coming of Mashiach. At any rate, it is indisputable that Maimonides in his *Commentary to the Mishnah* adopts the position that this prophecy will precede Mashiach's arrival.

However, in his later years, Maimonides retracted this position while authoring his *Mishneh Torah*. He saw that, in truth, this time sequence upon which he built his proof does not necessarily follow from that text, and the prophecy may occur after the arrival of Mashiach. Although a gathering of all the sages does not have the power to ordain, Elijah the prophet—who is coming with Mashiach—is ordained already, and existing as a body and soul, he could ordain all the courts of Israel, thereby setting up a Sanhedrin. Mashiach himself could also ordain, because the verse says "He is greater than Moses." If Moses was able to ordain the seventy elders, Mashiach can as well.

TREATISE ONE—RABBI YA'AKOV BEIRAV (EXCERPTS FROM *SEMICHAT ZEKENIM*, PP. 40–42)

Although from the Talmud it seems that the one who ordains must be ordained himself, if the ordination is with the agreement of all or at least the majority of the sages of Israel, then they may ordain others de-

RABBI YA'AKOV BEIRAV (MAHARI BEIRAV), 1475–1546
Born near Toledo, Spain; died in Safed, Israel; talmudist and rabbi. After fleeing Spain, he settled in Safed. Rabbi Beirav is noted for his effort to reestablish the Sanhedrin as a central legal authority. In 1538, his colleague, Rabbi Levi ibn Chaviv, the chief rabbi of Jerusalem, came out in opposition to him. Among the students he did successfully ordain were Rabbi Yosef Caro—the author of the Shulchan Aruch—and Rabbi Moshe di Trani.

spite not having ordination themselves. Maimonides explained this ruling in his *Commentary to the Mishnah*. See his commentary cited above.

If the requirement to grant ordination is only reserved for a person who had been previously ordained, in a chain leading back to our teacher Moses, then ordination is forever lost. This is true even when Mashiach comes, for Mashiach—or anyone else—may not add anything to either the Written or Oral Torahs.

However, God promised Israel that when they return to their Land, He will bring back their judges and their counselors. This can then only happen through ordination by the agreement of the sages in the Land of Israel, even if they do not have ordination themselves.

It now becomes clear that Maimonides's conclusion, "This matter requires resolution" (*Mishneh Torah*, Laws of the Sanhedrin 4:11), refers to a different halachah. In the same section, he discusses whether all three members of a court need ordination in order to grant *semichah* to others, or perhaps one member is sufficient. If the law follows that all three court members require *semichah*, we would then say, if only one member of the court possesses *semichah*, all three members must consent to his decisions and *semichah* granting. Without this consent *semichah* is not effective even when the ordainee on the court so desires. This reverts back to the idea that the consent of all the sages is necessary when there is no operating judicial court.

Maimonides rules that one *semichah* member is enough for a court of three to grant *semichah* upon others, and for this reason we do not need the agreement of all the members of the court even if only one ordainee is a member of this court.

This is because a properly ordained person received ordination from the Supreme Sanhedrin court, and the court gives him the power to adjudicate all cases including those involving fines. Everybody in the Land of Israel is subject to the Supreme Sanhedrin court; they must accept all that the Great Court decrees; and the Court decreed this person whom they ordained may ordain whom he chooses to have the same coercive power to judge the inhabitants of Israel. For this reason, he does not need the consent of others, for he possesses official legal power of adjudication.

But when the *semichah* chain stopped and we need to renew ordination, then no one has these powers to force others to obey him. Therefore, all or a majority of sages need to agree to ordain in order to grant these powers to someone. Furthermore, the same follows if we adopted the position that all three members of a court require ordination and only one such person is found. It then follows that this person does not possess legal coercive powers to force his judgment on others. For he is only one person and not a court.

Maimonides rules that only one of three court members needs ordination to possess coercive powers but then immediately concludes: "This matter requires resolution." In other words, Maimonides says here that although he just ruled that one ordainee, accompanied by any two other rabbis not necessarily ordained, is enough to ordain others, this still needs a final ruling.

He also wrote about this in his *Commentary to the Mishnah*, on the first chapter of Sanhedrin. "There is some doubt as to whether three ordained judges are required before it is possible to ordain others, or one ordained judge is sufficient to confer *semichah*. The Talmud seems to say that only the greatest of the three needs to be ordained, and that he can recruit two others—whomever he wishes—to facilitate ordination (Maimonides, *Commentary to the Mishnah*, Sanhedrin 1:3).

Two other references also necessitate this idea that Maimonides is only unsure concerning this latter ruling.

Firstly, he brings decisive arguments in his Mishnah commentary that the Sanhedrin will return before Mashiach's coming. The verse says: "I will restore your judges as in the days of old," and if we cannot renew *semichah* as Maimonides outlines, this verse cannot be fulfilled. For Mashiach himself cannot ordain, as Maimonides writes that he cannot add or detract anything from what is written in the Torah. . . .

Furthermore, when introducing the idea to renew *semichah* in his *Mishneh Torah* Maimonides says, "It appears to me" (Maimonides, *Mishneh Torah*, Laws of the Sanhedrin 4:11), which indicates that he already deliberated and determined a final ruling that seems right to him. So his final words, "This matter requires resolution" (ibid.), which indicates an incisiveness, must refer to a different law altogether.

TREATISE TWO—RABBI LEVI BEN CHABIB
(EXCERPTS FROM *SEMICHAT ZEKENIM*, PP. 67–69)

Rabbi Beirav again cites Maimonides in Arabic, who in his *Commentary to the Mishnah*, went on at great length about how the consent of all the rabbis of Israel results in an effective *semichah*: were this not so, there could never be *semichah* again, even with the coming of Mashiach.

Regarding this, I say that, not being a prophet, I understand Maimonides's words as they are translated into the Hebrew differently, and I tried to explain his intent at first and the reason for his reconsideration in his *Mishneh Torah*. Now too, even according to the original Arabic, he has a strong reason to reconsider what he had written.

In truth, the idea of *semichah* in the era of Mashiach, granted by Mashiach and the prophet Elijah, is not considered a new religious law. According to our received tradition, Elijah is still alive and he is ordained by someone himself ordained, linking back to Moses. Mashiach as well could ordain, since, as stated by the rabbis, he is greater than Moses, as he will be ordained by our blessed God Himself.

Accordingly, it would not be outside the law for Mashiach too to ordain others. For this would not be making a forbidden change in the religion, since the mitzvah from the Torah is that no one can adjudicate cases involving fines without ordination; but that ordination only needs to be from someone who is himself ordained, and how much the better then if he is ordained by the Holy One Himself, just like Moses. This is not making up a new mitzvah, but rather a new level in that person who would be ordained.

He further wrote that Maimonides's conclusion, "This matter requires resolution," refers to a different law and not the idea to renew *semichah*. This is imperative to confirm his new *semichah* accord.

But I bitterly lament these words and I say: Where is the Holy Land? Where is the cornerstone? Where are the elder scholars who sit and study Torah from youth until old age?

Rabbi Beirav is certainly influenced by his great desire and love to be ordained and crowned with a crown of gold to give such an interpretation of Maimonides's words. Saying that what Maimonides's writes—that the matter needs to be resolved—refers to a law which is just parenthetically mentioned here, while in five other places he codes this clear halachah. . . . This matter is clear even to school children; there is no need to be a scholar, a sage, or a rabbi to deduce this. The language clearly refers to the premise of renewing *semichah.*

What Maimonides's writes in his *Commentary to the Mishnah* is also irrelevant, because there are many things that that he later reconsidered and ruled differently in his *Mishneh Torah.* How much more so is this true in our case. In his Mishnah commentary, when discussing whether all three members of a court require *semichah,* at first he writes that he is unsure about this law but then he concludes that the Talmud makes it clear that one *semichah* member is sufficient. If that is what the Talmud makes clear, what doubt can remain? How can one come afterward with a decision saying that the matter needs resolution?

TREATISE TWO—RABBI YA'AKOV BEIRAV (EXCERPTS FROM *SEMICHAT ZEKENIM,* PP. 89–110)

One might well be astonished at the author of this second scroll, the honorable Rabbi Levi, who writes in his conclusion: "Thus says the young man of Jerusalem, who groans with his loins broken for he sees the ruins of the Temple all around." He tells of his state of pain over the ruin of the Temple as if it were just now destroyed again. . . .

The astonishment is that, in Maimonides's opinion, the Holy Temple cannot be rebuilt until ordination is renewed. As he writes in his *Commentary to the Mishnah* about the judicial prophecy, "I will restore your judges as in the days of old and your counselors as in the beginning. Afterward you shall be called City of Righteousness, Faithful City," the meaning of this is

that first will come the restoration of the judges and afterward the salvation.

Although Rabbi Levi thinks he's a great rabbi, as is evident from his words, and he understands a different way to interpret this prophecy, still, he should give some thought to Maimonides's interpretation, and not put such effort into destroying what rabbis, great in both number and quality, built with their *semichah* accord. After all, he worries so much over the destruction. . . .

In great length, and with poor but exacting arguments, he turns an explanation that should be elementary even for young schoolchildren into a complicated matter. Something that could have been written on a thumbnail, he draws out through several folio pages. All this because he craves to nullify the great holy work that fulfills the words of the prophets and is the pathway to our Redemption.

This writer revealed his envy and his hatred for this accord. If I merit, I wish to meet with him face-to-face and I will debate him on this and other issues, but I don't want to reveal everything in writing.

In his Mishnah commentary, Maimonides set down reasoning that is true and correct, following sources from our holy Torah, saying that if it is true that we have no power to ordain at the present time, then even when Mashiach comes, we have no power to ordain and appoint judges. Even Mashiach and Elijah do not have the power to add or subtract a single mitzvah.

If you argue that Elijah is already ordained and it's not a new mitzvah, we could answer that Elijah is like the other righteous people who died, and when they are resurrected, the ordination they had had previously in this world is no longer effective. . . .

This, together with the judicial prophecies, is the premise for Maimonides's idea that all the sages of the Land of Israel [together], who are called the whole of the congregation, have the power to ordain. If not, even Elijah and Mashiach would not be able to do so, for they cannot add or subtract even one mitzvah from the Torah.

Furthermore, the verse says that the renewal of ordained judges will occur before Mashiach's arrival, as it says, "Afterward you shall be called City of Righteousness, Faithful City."

Rabbi Levi writes two lines of reasoning supporting his ruling. Had he written them in the time of the sages who trained me, I am certain they would have compelled him never to issue another legal ruling all his life. The first is when he writes that the mitzvah of ordination is a new mitzvah that the Safed rabbis wanted to innovate, and for that reason, it needs unanimous consent from all the scholars in Israel. The second is the dialect regarding a court of three . . . "All three are considered one". I swear that these arguments are Trinitarian, who believe that a prophet after Moses can invent a new mitzvah, and that the three are one. . . .

But it is a waste of time to spend much energy writing about insubstantial matters; rather, I want to meet with him face-to-face, to prove that he did not deliberate with his colleagues before he issued these legal rulings. I did not see in any of the details something that was different from what is written in the first treatise. Rather, again the same error is made about a fundamental Torah principle, claiming that ordination today is a new mitzvah and therefore needs unanimous consent.

By the Temple service! If one were to ordain on that basis, he would incur a great punishment. His friend would call him a false prophet, for he prophesied that the Holy One wanted to add a new mitzvah. Maimonides writes of such a person that he is to be put to death by the sword.

TREATISE THREE—RABBI LEVI BEN CHABIB (EXCERPTS FROM *SEMICHAT ZEKENIM,* PP. 117–197)

Rabbi Beirav wrote of his astonishment: "The astonishment is that, in Maimonides's opinion, the Holy Temple cannot be rebuilt until ordination is renewed. . . . and afterward the salvation [will come]."

However, this is not true and nothing like this can be found in the words of Maimonides. Quite to the contrary, a close reading yields the opposite understanding. . . .

If it is true that, according to Maimonides, Mashiach cannot come and the Temple will not be rebuilt until after the judges return, then, why did he not give this reason earlier when he suggested that perhaps Mashiach can appoint the new judges? In response to this proposal, he should have added another reason (in addition to the reason asserting that Mashiach does not possess the legal power to appoint judges): that this is not a viable option because the judges need to return before Mashiach's coming. He did not write this because it's not necessarily clear to him; it's just that the verses seem to give this implication.

This is the reason why, in his *Commentary to the Mishnah,* Maimonides simply writes, "It appears to me." In his later years, in his *Mishneh Torah,* he retracted this, interpreting the verses differently. The prophet's words, "Afterward you shall be called City of Righteousness," are not necessarily prophesying the building of the Temple, for it will already be built before the return of the judges. But these words are, rather, solely a prophecy that the judges will act righteously and therefore Jerusalem is called a "Righteous City".

All this follows the way of this sage who treats distant things as near and who erases distinctions, for in his mind, the building of the Temple and the coming of Mashiach are the same thing.

I, too, was confused about this when I wrote my first treatise and explained Maimonides's earlier and later rulings. Since the verse does not mention Mashiach's coming and just the rebuilding of Jerusalem and the Temple, it seems that the return of the judges will precede both the arrival of Mashiach and the rebuilding of Jerusalem and Temple.

But in truth, it is not so. Firstly, this interpretation is difficult, for if the prophecy, "Afterward you shall be called City of Righteousness," is about rebuilding the city and the Temple, what then is the source that teaches us about the coming of Mashiach?

Another strong proof that this is not so is because, according to Maimonides's opinion, all the actions of a Supreme Sanhedrin are dependent on the existence of an actual Temple. The legitimacy of the Sanhedrin to operate on all laws, including laws involving capital punishment, requires the Holy Temple.

And one cannot say that the return of the judges, which the prophet promises, means judges who are empowered by ordination and fit to judge, but not actually judging. Since he specifically said that their return would be "as in the days of old and . . . as in the beginning," it is certain that his intent was that they should be actually judging all the kinds of cases that come before the Sanhedrin, as they were at first.

It is also impossible to say that the return of the judges means they will judge in the required area for the Sanhedrin even though the Temple is not yet built. Since the verse says "as in the days of old" it is clear that this means they will operate in the physical Temple. . . .

What I must then say is that the coming of Mashiach will precede the return of the judges, and that is the very thing that this text is telling us. Even though when Mashiach comes it is already proper to call Jerusalem the City of Righteousness, nonetheless, that will only happen after the judges return later (after the Temple is built). This is how it appears in my humble judgment. . . .

But because of another reason, it appears, I cannot say this. The rabbis explicitly said in the Talmud (Eiruvin 43b) that Elijah the prophet will announce the coming of Mashiach before the Supreme Sanhedrin. So it is clear that the Great Court will be reestablished before the coming of Elijah and Mashiach. This indicates that the return of the judges will precede the coming of Mashiach.

However, I saw that Rabbi Yom Tov Asevilli explained this passage to mean "the place of the Great Court." This seems to be the correct interpretation, that Elijah will simply "come to the Great Court" but not necessarily address a functioning Great Court. Although there will be many great sages in Israel, they do not yet have the legal status of a court until they will be ordained by Elijah or Mashiach. This interpretation was also the position of Maimonides in his later years; he recanted his youthful interpretation that the meaning of this passage means the actual Great Court.

But I fear that this will not soothe the mind of the one who is using this Talmudic passage as proof to renew ordination. For the simple reading of this passage indicates that the Talmudic rabbis agreed with what Maimonides wrote in his Mishnah commentary, that the return of the judges and Sanhedrin will precede the coming of Mashiach.

However, I can propose two alternative ways to explain this passage.

If we were still to adopt the position that, according to Maimonides, Mashiach is unable to ordain by himself, nonetheless, he together with all the sages of his generation can ordain, or even before his coming, with the ingathering of all the sages from the entire world, they would be able to ordain. Since this affects all the Jewish people, even those who live outside the Land—for they too are judged in cases involving fines and penalties—therefore, all the sages of the generation must agree to this ordination, something which the sages of Israel today cannot do alone when the majority of the Jewish people are in exile. In addition, this will affect those living in exile more upon their return to the Land of Israel. Perhaps this is the reason Maimonides writes in *Mishneh Torah*, "This matter requires resolution" (*Mishneh Torah*, Laws of the Sanhedrin 4:11). This is one thing I could say.

I could also say that the reason Maimonides recanted in his later years what he wrote in his youth in his *Commentary to the Mishnah* —even though we must admit that the simple meaning of the Talmud and the verses follow his youthful understanding—is because the order of the messianic era is hidden from us all, even from the sages, as Maimonides writes at the end of his *Mishneh Torah*. This is why he concludes, about his idea to renew the Sanhedrin, "this matter requires resolution."

Furthermore, Maimonides's position on these matters appears to differ from the position of our sages. Of particular importance is the story of Rabbi Akiva and Bar Kochba, whom Rabbi Akiva thought to be Mashiach, although this occurred before the building of the Temple. For Maimonides wrote several times that Mashiach will rebuild the Temple and gather Israel from its dispersion. If, according to his position, the coming of Mashiach will precede the building of the Temple, how much more so that it will precede the return of the judges, for there cannot be a Sanhedrin without the Temple. So here, Maimonides clearly recanted all he had written in his Mishnah commentary about the order of the messianic era.

With these words, I have completely uprooted the words of this rabbi; it is he who is "astonishing." With all the great wisdom he reputes himself to have, he should have remembered all these things, considered them well, and through them made the truth clear.

Regarding what he writes about me, that I crave to nullify this *semichah* accord which is the fulfillment of a prophecy and a pathway to our Redemption, these are the words he used to blandish the other rabbis of Safed, and caused them to exaggerate beyond measure so that they appointed him the head of the academy to proceed to appoint the Sanhedrin. For without a Sanhedrin this act is no longer a pathway to Redemption.

But after he recanted and agreed several times in his treatise that his intent is just to establish a court of three and not a Sanhedrin, due to fear of ruining the unanimity of our calendar and holidays, I don't understand why he still claims that I am forestalling a pathway to Redemption. For without reestablishing the Sanhedrin there is no longer a pathway. What's really happening is that he cannot conceal his true intentions.

Regarding that which he writes, that Elijah cannot ordain because he is not among the living and that this is also Maimonides's position in his Mishnah commentary: Perhaps this was Maimonides's earlier position, which he later reconsidered when he wrote his *Mishneh Torah*. For Elijah is different than other great sages who passed away, because he did not die a natural death and ascended, body and spirit together. He will therefore surely be able to ordain.

Even concerning the other sages who died, it is possible to say that they will be able to ordain others when they are resurrected with all their wisdom and with the very degree of elevation they had when they died. The reason we need Elijah for ordination is because we do not know when the resurrection of the dead will occur. Some say the resurrection will be a long time after the coming of Mashiach, and we need judges before then.

Hopefully, this rabbi will retract his position, and no longer stand by the responses in his pamphlet, with which he led astray and blandished the foolish by saying that the ordination he proposed is necessary and that it is greatly effective in speeding the building of the Temple and the coming of Mashiach. . . .

He also wrote that this matter is clear to all, and continuously repeats that it's agreed upon by all. However, the contrary is true! Even someone as small as me caught him in the numberless errors he writes in his articles, mistakes which even a simple student would not make. . . .

To summarize: From all that he wrote on this, he merited to become the chief of damages and their causes in all their most important forms. Included in this are the two descriptions I wrote of him in my article earlier, which he then confirmed in this letter of his.

May God give us a new heart and a new spirit in our midst. May he remove the heart of stone from our flesh with the rebuilding of our Holy House speedily in our days, amen!

Translated by Rabbi Shmuel Klatzkin, Rabbi Eli Raksin, and Rabbi Shmuel Super

Lesson

5

Two Rabbis, *Jankel Adler, 1842.*
(Museum of Modern Art, New York)

CHASIDIC RENAISSANCE
POWER AND CONTROVERSY IN THE TEACHINGS OF THE CHASIDIC MASTERS

In the aftermath of the devastation wrought by the Khmelnytsky pogroms of 1648–1649, Rabbi Yisrael Ba'al Shem Tov initiated a movement that breathed new life into the hearts of the Jewish masses. But the teachings of Chasidism were soon regarded with suspicion by other Jews, and this led to some bitter controversies. Our lesson will examine the writings of one of the central figures who lived through this unfortunate saga, Rabbi Shne'ur Zalman of Liadi. We will explore how he understood the causes and nature of this controversy, and how he guided his followers through it, until he finally saw the day when peace and reconciliation prevailed.

TEXT 1

RABBI SHNE'UR ZALMAN OF LIADI, *IGROT KODESH* (NEW YORK: KEHOT, 2012), PP. 235–237 🕮

הִנֵּה מוּדַעַת זֹאת חוֹמֶר עֲוֹן הַמַּחֲלֹקֶת וְשִׂנְאַת חִנָּם, אֲשֶׁר עַל כֵּן רָאוּי לְכָל הֶחָיִל אֲשֶׁר נָגַע יִרְאַת ה' בְּלִבּוֹ וְחָרֵד לִדְבָרוֹ, לִיזָּהֵר מְאֹד מִהְיוֹת גּוֹרֵם אוֹ גּוֹרֵם דְּגוֹרֵם בְּנִזְקִין חַס וְשָׁלוֹם בְּתַכְלִית הַזְּהִירוּת עַד קְצֵה הָאַחֲרוֹן.

אֲשֶׁר נִלְאֵיתִי נְשׂוֹא לְהַעֲלוֹת בְּמִכְתָּב נְקוּדַת לְבָבִי הָאֲמִתִּית, לְעוֹרֵר בְּלֵב כָּל סִיעַת מְרַחֲמֵינוּ אַהֲבָה גַּם לַאֲנָשִׁים אֲשֶׁר לֹא מִסִּיעָתֵנוּ, בִּכְלַל אַהֲבַת כָּל בְּנֵי יִשְׂרָאֵל כְּמִצְוָה עָלֵינוּ.

אֲשֶׁר לָזֹאת גַּם בַּשָּׁנָה דְּאֶשְׁתָּקַד, אַחַר פְּטִירַת כְּבוֹד הַגָּאוֹן הֶחָסִיד זִכְרוֹנוֹ לִבְרָכָה מֵוִולְנָא, כָּתַבְתִּי אַזְהָרָה נוֹרָאָה לְכָל סִיעַת מְרַחֲמֵינוּ שֶׁלֹּא לְסַפֵּר אַחַר מִטָּתוֹ שֶׁל תַּלְמִיד חָכָם שׁוּם שֶׁמֶץ דְּבַר דֹּפִי וְשִׂמְצָה, בְּלִי שׁוּם הוֹרָאַת הֶיתֵּר בָּעוֹלָם.

אַךְ עַתָּה הַפַּעַם בְּצוֹק הָעִתִּים שֶׁעָבְרוּ עָלֵינוּ, לְמֵחַשׁ מִבָּעְיָא אוּלַי הֻגְּתָּרָה הָרְצוּעָה חַס וְשָׁלוֹם מֵחֲמַת שֶׁאַנְשֵׁי רִיבֵנוּ נִתְלִים בְּאִילָן גָּדוֹל, הֶחָסִיד הַמָּנוֹחַ זִכְרוֹנוֹ לִבְרָכָה.

עַל כֵּן בָּאתִי לְהַזְהִיר שֵׁנִית בְּאַזְהָרָה כְּפוּלָה וּמְכֻפֶּלֶת לְכָל סִיעַת מְרַחֲמֵינוּ, הַקְּרוֹבִים וְהָרְחוֹקִים בְּכָל מְקוֹמוֹת מוֹשְׁבוֹתָם, בַּל יוֹרוּ הֶיתֵּר לְעַצְמָם לִפְתֹּחַ פֶּה וְלָשׁוֹן עַל כָּבוֹד הַתּוֹרָה, כְּבוֹד הַגָּאוֹן הֶחָסִיד הַנִּזְכָּר לְעֵיל זִכְרוֹנוֹ לִבְרָכָה לְחַיֵּי הָעוֹלָם הַבָּא, כִּי יָדוּעַ לָנוּ בְּבֵרוּר שֶׁלֹּא מֵאִתּוֹ יָצְאוּ הַדְּבָרִים כְּבוּשִׁים חַס וְשָׁלוֹם וְיֵלֶךְ לֵילֵךְ עִמָּנוּ בִּגְדוֹלוֹת, וְכָל יְמֵי חַיָּיו לֹא יָצָא הַמַּכְשֵׁלָה וְהַשְּׁגָגָה מִלְּפְנֵי הַשַּׁלִּיט חַס וְשָׁלוֹם . . .

עוֹד זֹאת אֶדְרֹשׁ וַאֲבַקֵּשׁ מֵאִתָּם, לְהַרְגִּיל אֶת לִבָּם לֶאֱהֹב אֶת כָּל אֶחָד מִבְּנֵי יִשְׂרָאֵל, אַף אִם אֵינוֹ מִסִּיעַת מְרַחֲמֵינוּ, וְלָדוּנָם לְכַף זְכוּת, כִּי בֶּאֱמֶת לַאֲמִיתּוֹ כָּל יִשְׂרָאֵל כְּאַחִים מַמָּשׁ. וְעַל כֻּלָּם נֶאֱמַר "בָּנִים אַתֶּם לַה' אֱלֹקֵיכֶם" (דְּבָרִים יד, א), "וּבֵין כַּךְ וּבֵין כַּךְ קְרוּאִים בָּנִים" (קִדּוּשִׁין לו, א). וּבְוַדַּאי כְּשֶׁהֵם נוֹטְרִים שִׂנְאָה בְּלֵב כָּל אֶחָד וְאֶחָד עַל שֶׁכְּנֶגְדּוֹ, הוּא לְמוֹרַת וְעִצְּבוֹן לְרוּחַ קָדְשׁוֹ אֲבִיהֶן שֶׁבַּשָּׁמַיִם.

בְּכֵן מִי שֶׁנָּגַע יִרְאַת שָׁמַיִם בְּלִבּוֹ לְקַיֵּם מַה שֶּׁכָּתוּב (זְכַרְיָה ח, יז) "וְאִישׁ אֶת רָעַת רֵעֵהוּ אַל תַּחְשְׁבוּ בִּלְבַבְכֶם", "כַּמַּיִם הַפָּנִים אֶל הַפָּנִים" (קֹהֶלֶת כז, יט), בְּוַדַּאי גַּם מֵהֶם יִפּוֹל הַקִּנְאָה וְהַהִתְחָרוּת מִלִּבָּם.

RABBI SHNE'UR ZALMAN OF LIADI (ALTER REBBE), 1745–1812

Chasidic rebbe, halachic authority, and founder of the Chabad movement. The Alter Rebbe was born in Liozna, Belarus, and was among the principal students of the Magid of Mezeritch. His numerous works include the *Tanya*, an early classic containing the fundamentals of Chabad Chasidism, and *Shulchan Aruch HaRav*, an expanded and reworked code of Jewish law.

It is well-known that the sin of divisiveness and baseless hatred is very severe. It is therefore fitting for all upstanding and God-fearing people to be cautious to an extreme degree not to cause—even indirectly—any detriment in this regard.

It is difficult to pen in a letter a true and deep feeling of my heart, which is to awaken in the hearts of our community a love for all Jews, even to those who are not inclined to help us, because this is part of the mitzvah to love all Jewish people.

It was for this reason that last year, after the passing of the pious Ga'on of Vilna—may his memory be for a blessing—I wrote a stern warning to all members of our community not to utter even a trace of negative speech about this Torah scholar in the wake of his passing, with no exceptions.

RABBI ELIYAHU OF VILNA (VILNA GA'ON, GRA), 1720–1797

Talmudist, halachist, and kabbalist. The Vilna Ga'on was one of the greatest scholars of his day. In addition to Talmud, he excelled in all aspects of Torah study, including kabbalah, and was proficient in secular subjects as well. He left a tremendous legacy, both from his vast writings on the Tanach, Talmud, and Shulchan Aruch, and from the many students that he inspired to Torah and scholarship.

But now, because of the distressing times that we have just experienced, I am concerned that some may think that this prohibition has been lifted, God forbid—given that the perpetrators of our suffering relied on the late pious great sage, may his memory be for a blessing.

Therefore, I have come to warn everyone once again, whether they reside near or far, with a double and redoubled warning: Do not permit yourself to open your mouth and tongue against the honor of the Torah, the honorable and righteous Ga'on, of blessed memory. For it is known to us with certainty that this oppression did not originate with him, God forbid, and that he did not advocate aggressive measures against us. Indeed, such an error did not come from the master for as long as he lived. . . .

Additionally, I demand and request of you all to accustom your hearts to love every Jew and to judge them favorably, even those who do not support us. For the real truth is that all Jews are literally like siblings, and about us all it is written "You are children of God" (DEUTERONOMY 14:1), and [the Talmud teaches that] we are called God's children regardless of our behavior (KIDUSHIN 36A). Thus, God is surely saddened and grieved when we harbor hatred in our hearts toward those who oppose us.

Therefore, one whose heart is touched with the awe of Heaven must fulfill that which is written, "Do not harbor evil in your heart against another" (ZECHARIAH 8:17). And then, "as water reflects the image of the face looking into it" (PROVERBS 27:19), so will the jealousy and rivalry dissipate from their hearts.

TEXT 2

RABBI SHNE'UR ZALMAN OF LIADI, IBID., P. 383

הִנֵּה בְּרֹבוֹת הַשָּׁנִים אַחַר פְּטִירָתוֹ שֶׁל הַגָּאוֹן הֶחָסִיד הַמָּנוֹחַ זִכְרוֹנוֹ
לִבְרָכָה, זְכוּת תּוֹרָתוֹ עָמְדָה לוֹ וּלְכָל הַמִּסְתּוֹפְפִים בְּצִלּוֹ שֶׁלֹּא לִשְׁפּוֹךְ
עוֹד דָּמִים חִנָּם, בְּהִגָּלוֹת נִגְלוֹת לְעֵינֵי כֹל, וְנוֹדַע הָאֱמֶת, וְנִרְאָה בַּעֲלִיל
שֶׁאֵין בָּנוּ שֶׁמֶץ מִינוּת חַס וְשָׁלוֹם, וְלֹא שִׁמְצָא דְשִׁמְצָא. וְאִי לָזֹאת הוּתְּרוּ
הַשְּׁבָטִים לָבֹא זֶה בָּזֶה וּמִתְחַתְּנִים עִמָּנוּ תָּמִיד. וּכְמוֹ כֵן נִתְבַּטְּלוּ שְׁאָר
הַרְחָקוֹת וּגְזֵרוֹת קַלּוֹת וַחֲמוּרוֹת דִּשְׁנַת תקל"ב, שֶׁהָיוּ בִּשְׁגָגָה וְהֶעְלֵם
דָּבָר מֵעֵינֵי הָעֵדָה.

וְעַל זֶה נֶאֱמַר "שְׁגִיאוֹת מִי יָבִין מִנִּסְתָּרוֹת נַקֵּנִי" (תְּהִלִים יט, יג) ...וּגְדוֹלָה
מִזּוֹ מָצִינוּ שִׁגְגַת הוֹרָאָה אֲפִילוּ בְּסַנְהֶדְרֵי גְדוֹלָה שֶׁבְּלִשְׁכַּת הַגָּזִית...

Now that many years have elapsed since the passing of the late pious Ga'on of Vilna—may his memory be for a blessing—the merit of his Torah has stood for him and for all of his students and the useless persecutions have stopped. The truth has become known, and it is clearly apparent to all that there is not even a trace of heresy with us, God forbid—not even a trace of a trace. Therefore, our communities have been allowed to intermingle, and there are many instances in which members of our communities have married each other. Similarly, all the other decrees that were instituted in 1772 have been nullified, both the minor ones and the severe ones—all of which were issued erroneously by the communal leaders.

Regarding this it is written (PSALMS 19:13), "Who can contemplate errors? Cleanse me of my mistaken misdeeds." . . . In fact, greater examples of errors in judgment exist, for Jewish law recognizes the possibility that the Supreme Sanhedrin sitting in the Temple could issue an erroneous ruling. . . .

TEXT 3

RABBI SHNE'UR ZALMAN OF LIADI, IBID., P. 197 ⊕

וְגַם שֶׁלֹּא לְעוֹרֵר שִׂנְאָה בַּלֵּב וְלִיטוֹר אֵיבָה חַס וְשָׁלוֹם לְאַנְשֵׁי עִירְכֶם, כִּי לְכָל הָעָם בִּשְׁגָגָה, שֶׁנִּתְלִין בְּאִילָן גָדוֹל, אֲשֶׁר סָמוּךְ רֹאשׁוֹ וְרוּבּוֹ עַל גְּבִיַּת עֵדוּת שַׁקְרָנִים שֶׁגָּנְבוּ לְבָבוֹ וּלְבַב בֵּית דִּין, וכו'. וְכַאֲשֶׁר הֶאֱרַכְתִּי בְּמִכְתָּבִי אֶשְׁתָּקַד.

Do not arouse hatred or anger in your hearts toward the Jews of your city, God forbid. For they have done wrong only inadvertently, having relied upon the great rabbi who himself was misled by false witnesses who stole his heart and the heart of the *beit din*, as I have written at length last year.

TEXT 4

RABBI YISRAEL BA'AL SHEM TOV, CITED IN *LIKUTEI YEKARIM* (JERUSALEM, 1974), NO. 120, P. 57

כְּשֶׁאָדָם הוֹלֵךְ בַּדֶּרֶךְ וְאֵינוֹ יָכוֹל לְהִתְפַּלֵּל וְלִלְמוֹד כְּדַרְכּוֹ, וְצָרִיךְ לְעוֹבְדוֹ בְּאוֹפַנִּים אֲחֵרִים, אַל יִצַּעֵר אֶת עַצְמוֹ בָּזֶה, כִּי הַשֵּׁם יִתְבָּרַךְ צָרִיךְ שֶׁיַּעַבְדוּהוּ בְּכָל הָאוֹפַנִּים, פְּעָמִים בְּאוֹפֶן זֶה וּפְעָמִים בְּאוֹפֶן זֶה. לָכֵן הִזְדַּמֵּן לְפָנָיו לֵילֵךְ לַדֶּרֶךְ אוֹ לְדַבֵּר עִם בְּנֵי אָדָם בִּכְדֵי לַעֲבֹד אוֹתוֹ בָּאוֹפֶן הַשֵּׁנִי.

RABBI YISRAEL BA'AL SHEM TOV (BESHT), 1698–1760

Founder of the Chasidic movement. Born in Slutsk, Belarus, the Ba'al Shem Tov was orphaned as a child. He served as a teacher's assistant and clay digger before founding the Chasidic movement and revolutionizing the Jewish world with his emphasis on prayer, joy, and love for every Jew, regardless of his or her level of Torah knowledge.

When people travel and cannot pray or study as they normally do but are forced to serve God in other ways, they should not be pained by this. God needs us to serve Him in many different ways, sometimes in one manner and sometimes in another manner. This is the real reason that the opportunity to travel or to converse with others presents itself to us, so that we can serve God in these alternative ways.

En Route, *Marc Chagall, 1924–5. (Petit Palais, Geneva)*

TEXT **5**

RABBI YISRAEL BA'AL SHEM TOV, *TSAVA'AT HARIVASH* (NEW YORK: KEHOT, 1998), NO. 45, P. 20

הַבְּכִיָּה הוּא רַע מְאֹד, שֶׁהָאָדָם צָרִיךְ לַעֲבוֹד בְּשִׂמְחָה. רַק אִם הַבְּכִיָּה הִיא מֵחֲמַת שִׂמְחָה אָז טוֹבָה הִיא מְאֹד.

Crying is extremely detrimental, because we need to serve God with joy. But if the tears are tears of joy, they are very good.

TEXT **6**

RABBI YISRAEL BA'AL SHEM TOV, CITED BY RABBI YOSEF YITSCHAK SCHNEERSOHN, *IGROT KODESH* 3:325

כַּאֲשֶׁר תִּסְתַּכֵּל בְּעִנְיַן טוֹב בְּהַחוֹמֶר שֶׁלְּךָ שֶׁהוּא הַגּוּף . . . "וְחָדַלְתָּ מֵעֲזֹב לוֹ" - שֶׁיּוּכַל לְקַיֵּים שְׁלִיחוּתוֹ, כִּי אִם תַּתְחִיל בְּסִגּוּפִים לְשַׁבֵּר אֶת הַחוּמְרִיּוּת. הִנֵּה לֹא בְּזוֹ הַדֶּרֶךְ יִשְׁכּוֹן אוֹר הַתּוֹרָה, כִּי אִם "עָזֹב תַּעֲזֹב עִמּוֹ" - לְבָרֵר אֶת הַגּוּף וּלְזַכְּכוֹ וְלֹא לְשַׁבְּרוֹ בְּסִגּוּפִים.

RABBI YOSEF YITSCHAK SCHNEERSOHN (RAYATS, FRIERDIKER REBBE, PREVIOUS REBBE), 1880–1950

Chasidic rebbe, prolific writer, and Jewish activist. Rabbi Yosef Yitschak, the 6th leader of the Chabad movement, actively promoted Jewish religious practice in Soviet Russia and was arrested for these activities. After his release from prison and exile, he settled in Warsaw, Poland, from where he fled Nazi occupation, and arrived in New York in 1940. Settling in Brooklyn, Rabbi Schneersohn worked to revitalize American Jewish life. His son-in law, Rabbi Menachem Mendel Schneerson, succeeded him as the leader of the Chabad movement.

When you carefully examine the corporeality of your body . . . you may be tempted to refrain from helping it fulfill its mission, and to instead set out to afflict it in order to break its crass materiality. However, this is not the approach of the Torah. Rather, you must aid it. You must purify the body and refine it, but do not break it through affliction.

TEXT 7

RABBI YISRAEL BA'AL SHEM TOV, CITED BY RABBI YA'AKOV YOSEF OF POLNOYE,
TOLDOT YA'AKOV YOSEF, VAYIGASH 1 🔢

"תְּפִלָּה לְעָנִי כִי יַעֲטֹף וְלִפְנֵי ה' יִשְׁפֹּךְ שִׂיחוֹ" (תְּהִלִים קב, א) - עַל
פִּי מָשָׁל:

שֶׁהִכְרִיז הַמֶּלֶךְ בְּיוֹם שִׂמְחָתוֹ, כָּל מִי שֶׁיְּבַקֵּשׁ דָּבָר מִן הַמֶּלֶךְ יְמַלְאוּ
מְבֻקָּשׁוֹ. וְיֵשׁ מִי שֶׁבִּקֵּשׁ שְׂרָרָה וְכָבוֹד, וְיֵשׁ שֶׁבִּקֵּשׁ עוֹשֶׁר, וְנָתְנוּ לְכָל
אֶחָד מְבֻקָּשׁוֹ.

וְהָיָה אֶחָד חָכָם שֶׁאָמַר שֶׁשְּׁאֵלָתוֹ וּמְבֻקָּשׁוֹ שֶׁיְּדַבֵּר הַמֶּלֶךְ עִמּוֹ ג'
פְּעָמִים בְּיוֹם. וְהוּטַב מְאֹד בְּעֵינֵי הַמֶּלֶךְ, מֵאַחַר שֶׁדִּיבּוּרוֹ חָבִיב עָלָיו מִן
עוֹשֶׁר וְכָבוֹד. לָכֵן יְמוּלָא בַּקָּשָׁתוֹ שֶׁיִּתְּנוּ לוֹ רְשׁוּת לִיכָּנֵס בְּהֵיכָלוֹ לְדַבֵּר
עִמּוֹ, וְשָׁם יִפְתְּחוּ לוֹ הָאוֹצָרוֹת שֶׁיִּקַּח מִן עוֹשֶׁר וְכָבוֹד גַּם כֵּן.

וְזֶהוּ שֶׁכָּתוּב "תְּפִלָּה לְעָנִי וְגו', לִפְנֵי ה' יִשְׁפֹּךְ שִׂיחוֹ" - שֶׁזֶּה מְבֻקָּשׁוֹ.

**RABBI YA'AKOV YOSEF OF POLNOYE
CA. 1710–1784**

Chasidic pioneer and author. Rabbi Ya'akov Yosef was a dedicated disciple of the Ba'al Shem Tov, the founder of the Chasidic movement, and is credited with taking a leading role in the dissemination of the philosophy of Chasidism in its nascent years. He authored *Toldot Ya'akov Yosef,* the first printed work of Chasidic philosophy. This work is cherished in Chasidic circles.

"A prayer from a poor person who is pained; he pours out his speech before God" (PSALMS 102:1). [The plain meaning of this verse is that the poor person beseeches God to relieve him of his poverty. But the following parable will explain the deeper meaning of the verse:]

Once there was a king who announced on the day of his rejoicing that all requests would be granted. Some people asked for offices and honors, some people asked for wealth, and the king granted every wish.

But there was one wise person who requested that the king agree to talk to him three times a day. This request was very pleasing to the king, because it demonstrated that conversing with the king was more precious to this man than riches and honors. The king granted his request that he be allowed into the king's chamber for a conversation. Once there, the king opened for him all of the treasures so that this person could also benefit from wealth and honor.

This is the meaning of the verse, "A prayer from a poor person." His prayer and request is that he be allowed to be one who "pours out his speech before God."

TEXT 8

RABBI YISRAEL BA'AL SHEM TOV, *TSAVA'AT HARIVASH* (NEW YORK: KEHOT, 1998), NO. 137, P. 66

יַחְשֹׁב שֶׁהַבּוֹרֵא מְלֹא כָל הָאָרֶץ כְּבוֹדוֹ, וּשְׁכִינָתוֹ תָּמִיד אֶצְלוֹ . . . וְיִהְיֶה תָּמִיד בְּשִׂמְחָה, וְיַחֲשׁוֹב וְיַאֲמִין בֶּאֱמוּנָה שְׁלֵימָה שֶׁהַשְּׁכִינָה אֶצְלוֹ וְשׁוֹמֶרֶת אוֹתוֹ.

Consider that the Creator is present everywhere and therefore God is always with you. . . . Always be happy, thinking and believing that God is with you and watching over you.

Learning Exercise 1

Consider how each of these teachings could have been particularly meaningful to Jews in eighteenth-century Poland. Indicate below which idea resonated with which aspect of the Jews' situation at the time.

THE JEWS' SITUATION

1	Sadness
2	Divide between scholars and non-scholars
3	Feeling distant and rejected by God
4	Asceticism
5	Lack of a meaningful relationship with God

TEACHINGS

Text 4: There are multiple ways to serve God.	1	2	3	4	5
Text 5: Serve God with joy.	1	2	3	4	5
Text 6: Don't forsake the body.	1	2	3	4	5
Text 7: To pray is to connect.	1	2	3	4	5
Text 8: God is always with us.	1	2	3	4	5

QUESTION FOR DISCUSSION

Can you identify a philosophical principle that ties some or all of these teachings together?

TEXT 9

RABBI CHAIM VITAL, *ETS CHAYIM, SHA'AR* 1:2

דַּע כִּי טֶרֶם שֶׁנֶּאֱצְלוּ הַנֶּאֱצָלִים וְנִבְרְאוּ הַנִּבְרָאִים, הָיָה אוֹר עֶלְיוֹן פָּשׁוּט
מְמַלֵּא כָּל הַמְּצִיאוּת... וְכַאֲשֶׁר עָלָה בִּרְצוֹנוֹ הַפָּשׁוּט לִבְרֹא הָעוֹלָמוֹת...
אָז צִמְצֵם אֶת עַצְמוֹ... וְאָז נִשְׁאַר מָקוֹם פָּנוּי וַאֲוִיר וְחָלָל רֵקָנִי.

RABBI CHAIM VITAL
CA. 1542–1620

Before Creation, God's supernal and undefined light was the only existence. . . . When it arose in His undefined will to create . . . He condensed Himself . . . and an empty space emerged.

Lurianic kabbalist. Rabbi Vital was born in Israel and lived in Safed and Jerusalem, and later in Damascus. He was authorized by his teacher, Rabbi Yitschak Luria, the Arizal, to record his teachings. Acting on this mandate, Vital began arranging his master's teachings in written form, and his many works constitute the foundation of the Lurianic school of Jewish mysticism. His most famous work is *Ets Chayim*.

QUESTION FOR DISCUSSION

What question does Text 9 seek to answer?

TEXT 10

RABBI SHNE'UR ZALMAN OF LIADI, *IGROT KODESH* (NEW YORK: KEHOT, 2012), PP. 184–185

לְפִי הַנִּשְׁמָע בִּמְדִינוֹתֵינוּ מִתַּלְמִידָיו, אֲשֶׁר זֹאת הִיא תְּפִיסַת הַגָּאוֹן הֶחָסִיד עַל סֵפֶר לִקּוּטֵי אֲמָרִים וְדוֹמָיו, אֲשֶׁר מְפֹרָשׁ בָּהֶם פֵּרוּשׁ "מְמַלֵּא כָּל עַלְמִין" (זֹהַר ג, רכה, א) וְ"לֵית אֲתָר פְּנוּי מִינֵיהּ" (תִּקּוּנֵי זֹהַר צא, ב) כִּפְשׁוּטוֹ מַמָּשׁ . . . וּבְפֵירוּשׁ מַאֲמָרִים הַנִּזְכָּרִים יֵשׁ לָהֶם דֶּרֶךְ נִסְתָּרָה וְנִפְלָאָה. וּ"מְלֹא כָל הָאָרֶץ כְּבוֹדוֹ" (יְשַׁעְיָהוּ, ג) הַיְינוּ הַשְׁגָּחָה וכו'.

וּמִי יִתֵּן יָדַעְתִּיו וְאֶמְצָאֵהוּ וְאֶעֶרְכָה לְפָנָיו מִשְׁפָּטֵינוּ לְהָסִיר מֵעָלֵינוּ כָּל תְּלוּנוֹתָיו.

According to reports from his disciples who live in our area, the reason that the pious Ga'on takes issue with the work *Likutei Amarim,* and other similar works, is because these works interpret the statements, "He pervades all worlds" (*ZOHAR* 3:225A) and "There is no place devoid of Him" (*TIKUNEI ZOHAR* 91B), literally. . . . But the Ga'on and his students interpret these passages in obscure ways. And the verse, "His glory fills the whole earth" (*ISAIAH* 6:3), they interpret figuratively, as pertaining to divine providence.

TEXT 11

THE LUBAVITCHER REBBE, RABBI MENACHEM MENDEL SCHNEERSON, *LIKUTEI SICHOT* 30:174

הַחִדּוּשׁ בְּאֹפֶן גִּלּוּי הַחֲסִידוּת עַל יְדֵי רַבֵּינוּ הַזָּקֵן לְגַבֵּי הַבַּעַל שֵׁם טוֹב וְהַמַּגִּיד וְתַלְמִידֵיהֶם - יֵשׁ לִרְאוֹת בְּפַשְׁטוּת כְּשֶׁלּוֹמְדִים תּוֹרַת הַחֲסִידוּת שֶׁנִּתְגַּלְתָה לָנוּ, שֶׁעִנְיָנֵי חֲסִידוּת שֶׁנִּתְגַּלּוּ עַל יְדֵי הַבַּעַל שֵׁם טוֹב וְהַמַּגִּיד וְתַלְמִידֵיהֶם הֵם בְּאֹפֶן שֶׁל "נְקֻדּוֹת" וּבְקִצּוּר, עַל דֶּרֶךְ לָשׁוֹן הַמִּשְׁנָה שֶׁהִיא דָּבָר קָצָר.

מַה שֶׁאֵין כֵּן בְּבִאוּר הָעִנְיָנִים שֶׁבְּתוֹרַת חֲסִידוּת חַבַּ"ד שֶׁנִּתְגַּלָּה עַל יְדֵי רַבֵּינוּ הַזָּקֵן הוּא בְּאֹפֶן שֶׁל "הַרְחָבָה" וְשַׁקְלָא וְטַרְיָא, שֶׁבְּמַאַמְרֵי וְתוֹרַת חֲסִידוּת שֶׁלּוֹ (הָחֵל מִסֵּפֶר הַתַּנְיָא) בִּיאֵר עִנְיָנֵי תּוֹרַת הַחֲסִידוּת בְּאֹפֶן שֶׁל הַבָּנָה וְהַשָּׂגָה, וּכְשִׁמְהּ חֲסִידוּת חַבַּ"ד.

וְשִׁינּוּי זֶה בְּאֹפֶן גִּלּוּי תּוֹרַת הַחֲסִידוּת יֵשׁ לוֹמַר שֶׁהוּא שֶׁגָּרַם לַקִּטְרוּג הֶחָדָשׁ עַל רַבֵּינוּ הַזָּקֵן.

RABBI MENACHEM MENDEL SCHNEERSON
1902–1994

The towering Jewish leader of the 20th century, known as "the Lubavitcher Rebbe," or simply as "the Rebbe." Born in southern Ukraine, the Rebbe escaped Nazi-occupied Europe, arriving in the U.S. in June 1941. The Rebbe inspired and guided the revival of traditional Judaism after the European devastation, impacting virtually every Jewish community the world over. The Rebbe often emphasized that the performance of just one additional good deed could usher in the era of Mashiach. The Rebbe's scholarly talks and writings have been printed in more than 200 volumes.

The novelty of the Alter Rebbe's teachings is readily observable when we study his works, and those of the Ba'al Shem Tov, the Magid of Mezeritch, and their students. The teachings of the latter are expressed tersely, similar to the language of the Mishnah, where the writing is concise.

On the other hand, the teachings of the Alter Rebbe are more elaborate and contain broader discussion. Thereby, his discourses and works (starting with *Tanya*) explain Chasidism in ways that can be comprehended, as the name Chabad indicates. [Chabad is an acronym for *chochmah, binah,* and *da'at,* three faculties of the mind.]

One can therefore suggest that this novel way of teaching Chasidic concepts provoked a heavenly complaint against the Alter Rebbe.

Affidavit written by Rabbi Shne'ur Zalman of Liadi for the Russian authorities upon his arrest in 1798. (Russian government archives)

KEY POINTS

1 By the beginning of the eighteenth century, Polish Jewry was in decline. There were widening social rifts, a weakening of spirituality, poor economic conditions, and an overall depressed morale. Some Jews responded to this state of depletion by turning to ascetic ways, but this only exacerbated the communal difficulties.

2 The Ba'al Shem Tov taught that there are multiple ways to serve God and that one always ought to do so with joy. The ascetic lifestyle, he argued, was counterproductive. He underscored that prayer is primarily about fostering a relationship with God, and he encouraged his fellow Jews to consider that God is omnipresent and always with them. Each of these teachings addressed a contemporary challenge confronting Polish Jewry.

3 Many of the Ba'al Shem Tov's teachings are premised on the notion that God is present everywhere and in everything, which was, in fact, a matter of debate in kabbalah. The Torah teaches that God should not be confused with nature because He transcends it, and that God should not be removed from nature because He controls it. But kabbalists debated whether God can be said to be present in everything that He created.

4 Rabbi Yitschak Luria (Arizal) taught that God removed Himself to allow for Creation, and some kabbalists understood this literally. In their view, although Providence extends over all of existence, it cannot be said that God is present within existence. Rabbi Eliyahu, the Ga'on of Vilna, adopted this approach. But other kabbalists explained that Rabbi Yitschak Luria's language was merely a metaphor for the idea that God concealed His presence to allow existence to sense its own identity. This approach is a foundational idea of Chasidic philosophy.

5 This theological debate was insufficient to drive a bitter dispute. Rather, unscrupulous actors offered false testimony against Chasidim that led to the unfortunate events of this dispute, culminating in the arrest of Rabbi Shne'ur Zalman of Liadi, the founder of Chabad Chasidism. Nevertheless, upon his release, Rabbi Shne'ur Zalman wrote to his students that they should accustom their hearts to love every Jew and to judge them favorably, including those who did not support their cause, because all Jews are like siblings.

6 Toward the end of his life, Rabbi Shne'ur Zalman wrote that the senseless persecutions against Chasidim had ceased because it has become widely apparent that they were driven by falsehoods. Peace and mutual respect returned to the Jewish community.

Visit
facebook.com/myJLI
to vote on the following question:

Which teaching of the Ba'al Shem Tov resonates most with you today?

1 There are multiple ways to serve God.

2 We ought to serve God with joy.

3 One should not mortify his/her body.

4 Prayer is primarily about a connection with God.

5 God is always with each of us.

Appendix

TEXT **12a**

RABBI SHNE'UR ZALMAN OF LIADI, *IGROT KODESH* (NEW YORK: KEHOT, 2012), P. 194

פָּתַח דְּבָרַי לְהָאִיר אוֹר הַסְּלִיחָה עַל אִיחוּר תְּשׁוּבָתִי עַד הֵנָּה. כִּי לֹא בְּמֶרֶד וְלֹא בְּמַעַל, וְלֹא הִשְׁלַכְתִּי דְּבָרָם אַחַר גֵּיוִי חַס וְשָׁלוֹם. כִּי בְּכָל צָרָתָם לָנוּ צַר מְאֹד מְאֹד. וְהִיא צָרַת הַצִּבּוּר מַמָּשׁ, כְּמַאֲמַר רַבּוֹתֵינוּ זִכְרוֹנָם לִבְרָכָה שֶׁאוֹתוֹ הַיּוֹם "הָיָה קָשֶׁה לְיִשְׂרָאֵל כְּיוֹם שֶׁנַּעֲשָׂה הָעֵגֶל" (שַׁבָּת יז, א) שֶׁ"נַּעֲשֵׂית תּוֹרָה כִּבְ' תּוֹרוֹת" (סוֹטָה מז, ב) חַס וְשָׁלוֹם.

וה' יֹאמַר לְצָרָתָם דַּי, וִיזַכֵּנוּ לִרְאוֹת בְּנֶחָמוֹת צִבּוּר בִּמְהֵרָה בְּיָמֵינוּ אָמֵן.

I open my words with an apology for the delay in my responding until now. This was not in betrayal or breach of faith, nor was I neglecting your words, God forbid. In fact, we are very much troubled by all of your troubles, which are actually the troubles of all Jews. As our sages relate, the day [that disputes abounded between the students of Hillel and Shamai] "was difficult for the Jews like the day on which the golden calf was made" (TAL-MUD, SHABBAT 17A), for "the Torah became like two Torahs" (SOTAH 47B), God forbid.

May God proclaim upon your troubles "enough," and may He give us the merit of seeing the communal comfort speedily in our days. Amen!"

TEXT 12b

RABBI SHNE'UR ZALMAN OF LIADI, IBID., P. 195

אַךְ לִהְיוֹת כִּי הִקְשׁוּ לִשְׁאוֹל בְּמֻפְלָא מִמֶּנִּי לְחַוּוֹת דֵּעִי לְמֵרָחוֹק בְּדָבָר שֶׁלֹּא שָׁמַעְתִּי מִפִּי רַבּוֹתַי נִשְׁמָתָם עֵדֶן כְּשֶׁנַּעֲשָׂה מַעֲשֶׂה רַב וְעָצוּם בִּמְאוֹד מֵהַנַּעֲשָׂה עַתָּה.

דְּהַיְינוּ בִּשְׁנַת תקל"ב קְהִלַּת בְּרָאד, שֶׁהִדְפִּיסוּ הַכָּרוֹז דְּמַחֲנֵכֶם. וְעוֹד נוֹסָף עֲלֵיהֶם דְּבָרִים רַבִּים קָשִׁים כְּגִידִים וּמְרוֹרוֹת פְּתָנִים שְׁקָרִים וְכִיזּוּבִים גְּדוֹלִים וַעֲצוּמִים עַל כַּמָּה נְיָירוֹת, וְנִשְׁלְחוּ הַסְּפָרִים בְּכָל תְּפוּצוֹת הַגּוֹלָה מַמָּשׁ, לֹא יֵאוּמָן כִּי יְסֻפַּר גּוֹדֶל הַבִּזְיוֹנוֹת וְהַיִּסּוּרִין שֶׁנַּעֲשׂוּ אָז לְהַצַּדִּיקִים הַמְפֻרְסָמִים דְּוָואלִין, עַד שֶׁלֹּא יָכְלוּ לָשֶׁבֶת בְּבָתֵּיהֶם. וּבָאוּ כֻּלָּם לַחֲסוֹת בְּצֵל כְּנָפָיו שֶׁל רַבֵּינוּ הַגָּדוֹל הַמָּנוֹחַ זִכְרוֹנוֹ לְחַיֵּי הָעוֹלָם הַבָּא בִּקְהִלַּת רָאוונֶע, וּלְטַכֵּס עֵצָה כְּדַת מַה לַעֲשׂוֹת. וְהָיוּ אָז דְּרָכִים הַרְבֵּה לַעֲשׂוֹת מַעֲשֶׂה לִסְתּוֹר וּלְהָפֵר מַחְשְׁבוֹתָם, וְלִכְתֹּב עֲלֵיהֶם מְרוֹרוֹת בְּכִפְלֵי כִפְלַיִם בִּשְׂפַת אֱמֶת תִּכּוֹן לָעַד, וּלְהַדְפִּיס גַּם כֵּן, וּלְשַׁלְּחָם בְּיַעֲקֹב, וְעוֹד דְּרָכִים אֲחֵרִים.

You have asked me a difficult question, to share from afar my perspective about your plan. But this is a novel plan, and I did not observe my teachers employing this approach in response to a much greater offense to which they were subjected.

In 1772, the community of Brody published the proclamation made in Vilna against us. They also added other notes with many additional words, complete lies and falsehoods, which were harsh as bitter plants and the venom of vipers. The booklets were spread throughout the entire Diaspora. The extent of the disgrace and torments suffered by the renowned holy righteous men of Volhynia was unbelievable. They could no longer reside in their homes, and so they all came to Rovno to take shelter under the wings of our late great Rabbi [Dov Ber of Mezeritch] of blessed memory. They sought to draw up a plan of appropriate response. There were many conceivable ways to destroy and annul the plans of the attackers. We could have written, published, and distributed many more bitter accusations against them than they had written against us. And these would have all been true, and truth endures! There were also other means available to us at the time.

TEXT 12c

RABBI SHNE'UR ZALMAN OF LIADI, IBID. 🕮

אַךְ רַבֵּינוּ הַגָּדוֹל, זֵכֶר צַדִּיק לִבְרָכָה לְחַיֵּי הָעוֹלָם הַבָּא, לֹא בָּחַר בָּהֶן לַעֲשׂוֹת שׁוּם מַעֲשֶׂה לְנֶגְדָּם, רַק כָּל כּוֹחָם שֶׁל יִשְׂרָאֵל בְּפִיהֶם לִזְעוֹק לַה' מֵפֵר מַחְשְׁבוֹת עֲרוּמִים וְלֹא תַעֲשֶׂנָה יְדֵיהֶם תּוּשִׁיָּה.

But our great Rabbi of blessed memory did not choose retaliatory options. He said that the power of Jews is in their tongues, that is, to cry out to God, Who thwarts the plans of schemers so that the work of their hands will not succeed.

TEXT 12d

RABBI SHNE'UR ZALMAN OF LIADI, IBID., P. 196

וְכַאֲשֶׁר פָּתַר לָנוּ כֵּן הָיָה.

וְנִתְקַיֵּים בָּהֶם "עַד אַרְגִּיעָה לְשׁוֹן שָׁקֶר" (מִשְׁלֵי יב, יט). וְנֶעְקְרוּ הַסְּפָרִים הַנִּזְכָּרִים לְעֵיל מִן הָעוֹלָם.

וּבָנוּ נִתְקַיֵּים "לְמַעַן עַנּוֹתְךָ לְהֵיטִבְךָ בְּאַחֲרִיתֶךָ" (דְּבָרִים ח, טז), "וְהָיָה רֵאשִׁיתְךָ מִצְעָר וְאַחֲרִיתְךָ יִשְׂגֶּה מְאֹד" (אִיּוֹב ח, ז) כַּאֲשֶׁר עֵינֵינוּ רָאוּ וְלֹא זָר, אֲשֶׁר אַחֲרֵי זֶה נִתְרַבּוּ לַאֲלָפִים וּרְבָבוֹת אַנְשֵׁי שְׁלוֹמֵנוּ בְּכָל הַמְּדִינוֹת, בִּרְאוֹתָם הַפְּלָגוֹת הַשְּׁקָרִים שֶׁמַּפְלִיגִים שֶׁכְּנֶגְדֵּינוּ עָלֵינוּ, בְּהַעֲצִימָם וְהִרְעִישָׁם כָּל הָעוֹלָם עָלֵינוּ בְּרַעַשׁ גָּדוֹל וְקוֹל תְּרוּעָה, וּבָזֶה הֵם מְעוֹרְרִים אֶת הַיְשֵׁנִים בְּהַבְלֵי הַזְּמָן לְהָקִיץ מִשְּׁנָתָם וְלִרְאוֹת הָאוֹר כִּי טוֹב, וּלְהַבְדִּיל בֵּין הָאֱמֶת לַשֶּׁקֶר שֶׁאֵין לוֹ רַגְלַיִם וְשִׁיקְרָא לָא קָאֵי.

מַה שֶּׁאֵין כֵּן אִם לֹא הָיוּ סוֹבְלִים אָז וּמְקַבְּלִים הַיִּסּוּרִים בְּאַהֲבָה, וְהָיוּ מְעוֹרְרִים מְדָנִים וּמַחֲלוֹקוֹת, בְּוַדַּאי הָיוּ נִדְחִים חַס וְשָׁלוֹם אֲלָפִים וּרְבָבוֹת מִלִּרְאוֹת הָאֱמֶת בַּעֲבוּר הַנִּצְחוֹנוֹת, "דְּהַאי תִּיגְרָא דַּמְיָא לְבִידְקָא דְמַיָּא וְכוּ'" (סַנְהֶדְרִין ז, א).

As he foretold, so it came to be.

With regard to our opponents, the following verse came to fruition: "A lying tongue is for but a moment" (PROVERBS 12:19), for their pamphlets of propaganda have ceased to circulate.

As for us, the following verses came to fruition, "Your affliction was . . . to benefit you in your end" (DEUTERONOMY 8:16), and "Your beginning shall be small, but your end will increase exceedingly" (JOB 8:7). We observed how, soon thereafter, our movement grew to number tens of thousands in many regions. The Jewish masses saw through the extreme lies that our opponents fabricated against us, when they incited the world in opposition to us with a great uproar and tumult. This clamoring aroused those who were in a spiritual slumber to awaken and to see that the light of Chasidism was good. They were able to differentiate between truth and falsehood, the latter of which has no feet and cannot endure.

If, however, we had not suffered quietly, accepting the pain with love, and we had instead initiated quarrels and disputes, it is certain that this would have prevented tens of thousands from seeing the truth. For [the Talmud teaches, Sanhedrin 7a, that] "a quarrel is like a burst of water." [Once water begins to burst through a crack in a structure, the crack will continue to widen, and more and more water will rush through. Similarly, a dispute can start as something minor, but it will soon rage out of control.]

View of the Peter and Paul Fortress and Palace Embankment, *Fyodor Alekseyev, 1799. This is where Rabbi Shne'ur Zalman of Liadi was imprisoned in 1798. (The State Russian Museum)*

TEXT 13a

RABBI SHNE'UR ZALMAN OF LIADI, *IGERET HAKODESH* 2

שֶׁבְּכָל חֶסֶד וָחֶסֶד שֶׁהַקָּדוֹשׁ בָּרוּךְ הוּא עוֹשֶׂה לָאָדָם, צָרִיךְ לִהְיוֹת שְׁפַל
רוּחַ בִּמְאֹד. כִּי "חֶסֶד דְּרוֹעָא יְמִינָא" (תִּיקוּנֵי זֹהַר יז, א). וִימִינוֹ תְּחַבְּקֵנִי.
שֶׁהִיא בְּחִינַת קִרְבַת אֱלֹקִים מַמָּשׁ בְּיֶתֶר שְׂאֵת מִלְּפָנִים. וְכָל הַקָּרוֹב אֶל
ה' בְּיֶתֶר שְׂאֵת וְהַגְבָּהָה לְמַעֲלָה מַעֲלָה, צָרִיךְ לִהְיוֹת יוֹתֵר שְׁפַל רוּחַ לְמַטָּה
מַטָּה... וּכְנוֹדָע דְּכוּלָּא קַמֵּיהּ דַּוְקָא כְּלָא חָשִׁיב, וְאִם כֵּן כָּל שֶׁהוּא קַמֵּיהּ
יוֹתֵר, הוּא יוֹתֵר כְּלָא וְאַיִן וָאֶפֶס.

Every act of kindness that God bestows upon us must render us more humble. For God's kindness is "an embrace of His right arm" (*TIKUNEI ZOHAR 17A*), a metaphor for God's bringing us closer to Himself—far more intensely than before. The closer we are to God, the more humble we need to be. . . . Indeed, it is known that everything that is before Him lacks any sense of independent existence. This implies that the more we are "before Him," the more we ought to sense our nothingness.

TEXT **13b**

RABBI SHNE'UR ZALMAN OF LIADI, IBID.

וְלָזֹאת בָּאתִי מִן הַמּוֹדִיעִים מוֹדָעָה רַבָּה לִכְלָלוּת אַנְשֵׁי שְׁלוֹמֵנוּ עַל רַבֵּי הַחֲסָדִים אֲשֶׁר הִגְדִיל ה' לַעֲשׂוֹת עִמָּנוּ . . . לְבִלְתִּי רוּם לְבָבָם מֵאֲחֵיהֶם כוּ', וְלֹא לְהַרְחִיב עֲלֵיהֶם פֶּה אוֹ לִשְׁרֹק עֲלֵיהֶם חַס וְשָׁלוֹם. הַס מִלְהַזְכִּיר בְּאַזְהָרָה נוֹרָאָה . . . וְכוּלֵי הַאי וְאוּלֵי יִתֵּן ה' בְּלֵב אֲחֵיהֶם כְּמַיִם הַפָּנִים וְגוֹ'.

For this reason I have come to make an announcement of great import to our collective community regarding the many acts of kindness that God has done for us. . . . Do not become haughty in the face of your brethren. Do not open your mouths in mockery at them, God forbid. Refrain from mentioning anything; this is a stern warning. . . . Hopefully, [in response to your peace-loving posture,] God will instill in the hearts of your brethren [a sense of conciliation,] "as water reflects the image of the face looking into it."

The Great Synagogue of Vilna, Lithuania, built 1633–1635, burned by the Germans during World War II. (Museum of the Jewish Diaspora, Tel Aviv)

TEXT 14

RABBI NOSON NOTA HANOVER, *YEVEN METSULAH* (VENICE, 1653), PP. 42–44

עַמּוּד הַתּוֹרָה . . . שֶׁלֹּא הָיָה כָּל כַּךְ הַרְבֵּה תּוֹרָה בְּכָל תְּפוּצוֹת יִשְׂרָאֵל כְּמוֹ בִּמְדִינַת פּוֹלִין. בְּכָל קְהִילָּה וּקְהִילָּה הָיוּ תּוֹפְסִין יְשִׁיבוֹת, וְהָיוּ מַרְבִּין שָׂכָר לְרֹאשׁ יְשִׁיבָה שֶׁלָּהֶם כְּדֵי שֶׁיּוּכַל לִתְפּוֹס יְשִׁיבָה בְּלֹא דְּאָגָה . . . וְכָל קְהִילָּה וּקְהִילָּה הָיוּ מַחְזִיקִים בַּחוּרִים וּמְסַפְּקִים לָהֶם מָמוֹן דָּבָר קָצוּב בְּכָל שָׁבוּעַ שֶׁיִּלְמְדוּ אֵצֶל הָרֹאשׁ יְשִׁיבָה . . . וְכִמְעַט שֶׁלֹּא הָיָה בַּיִת בְּכָל מְדִינוֹת פּוֹלִין שֶׁלֹּא הָיוּ לוֹמְדִים בּוֹ תּוֹרָה אוֹ הַבַּעַל הַבַּיִת בְּעַצְמוֹ הָיָה לַמְדָן, אוֹ בְּנוֹ אוֹ חֲתָנוֹ הָיוּ לוֹמְדִים, אוֹ בָּחוּר אֶחָד מֵאוֹכְלֵי שֻׁלְחָנוֹ. וְלִפְעָמִים הָיָה כֻּלָּם בְּבַיִת אֶחָד . . .

עַמּוּד עֲבוֹדָה . . . בָּרֹאשׁ הָיוּ חֶבְרָה שֶׁמַּשְׁכִּימִין לִפְנֵי עֲלוֹת הַשַּׁחַר לַשּׁוֹמְרִים לַבּוֹקֶר לְהִתְפַּלֵּל וּלְקוֹנֵן עַל חָרְבָּן הַבַּיִת. וְכַעֲלוֹת הַשַּׁחַר הָיוּ מַשְׁכִּימִין בְּנֵי הַחֶבְרָה שֶׁל תְּהִלִּים וְאָמְרוּ תְּהִלִּים כְּמוֹ שָׁעָה אֶחָד לִפְנֵי הַתְּפִלָּה, וְסִיְּימוּ תְּהִלִּים בְּכָל שָׁבוּעַ. וְחָלִילָה שֶׁיַּעֲבוֹר אָדָם בַּבֹּקֶר זְמַן תְּפִלָּה בְּשֵׁינָה וְלֹא יֵלֵךְ לְבֵית הַכְּנֶסֶת, אִם לֹא בְּאוֹנֶס גָּדוֹל. וְאִם הָלַךְ לְבֵית הַכְּנֶסֶת לֹא יָצָא אָדָם מִשָּׁם לְמַשָּׂא וּמַתָּן שֶׁלּוֹ עַד שֶׁשָּׁמַע דִּבְרֵי תּוֹרָה . . .

עַמּוּד גְּמִילוּת חֲסָדִים - הָיָה אֵין שִׁיעוּר לִגְמִילוּת חֲסָדִים שֶׁבִּמְדִינַת פּוֹלִין . . . וְהַרְבֵּה נָשִׁים צִדְקָנִיּוֹת עוֹסְקוֹת בְּמִצְוָה זֹאת . . .

RABBI NOSON NOTA HANOVER
?–1683

Chronicler of the Khmelnytsky massacres. Rabbi Noson was born in Ostroh, then part of the Polish-Lithuanian commonwealth, and lived in the Volhynia region. He fled to Italy when the Khmelnytsky Uprising began in 1648. He wrote a number of scholarly works, but he is most famous for his important account of the Khmelnytsky massacres of Polish Jewry, titled *Yeven Metsulah*, first printed in Venice, in 1653.

With respect to Torah . . . in no country was the study of the Torah so widespread among the Jews as it was in Poland. Every Jewish community maintained a yeshivah, paying its head a large salary to enable him to devote himself to the yeshivah without worry. . . . Every community had young men whom they supported with a weekly stipend so that they could learn with the head of the yeshivah. . . . There was scarcely a house in all of Poland where the Torah was not studied—either by the head of the house, the son, the son-in-law, or the yeshivah student who was boarding there. Frequently, all of them could be found under one roof. . . .

With respect to prayer . . . first was the group that rose before dawn to pray and lament the loss of the Holy Temple. At dawn, a group rose to recite Psalms for about an hour before the prayers, concluding the book each week. No one missed the time of prayer at the synagogue unless there was some great emergency. And when one went to the synagogue, he didn't leave to work before hearing some words of Torah. . . .

With respect to charity—there was no limit to the amounts of charity that were distributed in Poland. . . . Many women were engaged in this mitzvah. . . .

TEXT 15

GLÜCKEL OF HAMELN, *THE MEMOIRS OF GLÜCKEL OF HAMELN* (NEW YORK: SCHOCKEN BOOKS, 1977), P. 45*

About this time people began to talk of Shabetai Zevi [the Messianic pretender]. But woe unto us that we have sinned and did not live to see what we had heard and believed. When I think of the repentance done by

---

* With minor updates to the archaic English.

young and old, my pen fails me, but the whole world knows of it!

O Lord of all worlds, hoping as we did that You were about to show compassion on Israel and redeem us, we were like a woman who sits in labor and suffers mighty pangs, and who thinks that once her suffering is over she shall be blessed with a child, but finds nothing but wind. So, dear God and King, it befell unto us. Throughout the world, Your servants and children rent themselves with repentance, prayer, and charity. For two or three years Your beloved people Israel sat in labor; but there came forth nothing but wind. It was not enough that we were unworthy to behold the child for whom we had labored and in whom our hope was sure; we were left, in the end, abandoned.

Still, my Lord and God, Your people Israel despair not; daily they trust that in Your mercy You will redeem them. Though redemption may be deferred, yet every day I hope upon its coming.

GLÜCKEL OF HAMELN
1646–1724

Jewish businesswoman and diarist. Glückel was born in Hamburg to an affluent family of merchants. She was an active partner in her husband's jewelry and money-lending business, and following his death in 1689, she continued to manage these affairs. Glückel began writing her memoirs in 1691 in order to "stifle and banish her melancholic thoughts," and to convey to her descendants their family history. These memoirs provide a rare and intimate picture of German Jewish life in the late 17th and early 18th centuries.

Shtetl, My Destroyed Home, A Recollection, *Issachar ber Ryback*, 1923. *(The Jewish Museum, New York)*

TEXT 16

RABBI SHNE'UR ZALMAN OF LIADI, *IGROT KODESH* (NEW YORK: KEHOT, 2012), PP. 211–213 (ii)

הַמִּנְהָג הָיָה בְּכָל יִשְׂרָאֵל מִימֵי עוֹלָם, לִהְיוֹת בְּכָל עִיר וָעִיר ב' בָּתִּים גְּדוֹלִים לִתְפִלָּה, בֵּית הַכְּנֶסֶת וּבֵית הַמִּדְרָשׁ. בֵּית הַכְּנֶסֶת לַהֲמוֹן עַם הַטְּרוּדִים בְּעִסְקֵיהֶם כָּל הַיּוֹם, וְרוּבָּם אֵין יוֹדְעֵי סֵפֶר כְּלָל, וְאֵין יְכָלְתָּם לְהִתְפַּלֵּל בְּכַוָּונָה כַּנִּזְכָּר לְעֵיל, רַק לוֹמַר תֵּיבוֹת הַתְּפִלָּה ג' פְּעָמִים בְּכָל יוֹם. וּבֵית הַמִּדְרָשׁ לְיוֹדְעֵי סֵפֶר לְהִתְפַּלֵּל שָׁם בְּכַוָּונַת הַלֵּב בַּאֲרִיכוּת אִישׁ כְּפִי יְכוֹלֶת שִׂכְלוֹ וְלִבּוֹ. וְהִנֵּה בַּסְּפָרִים שֶׁכָּתְבוּ חֲכָמֵינוּ שֶׁלִּפְנֵי מָאתַיִם שָׁנָה מֵהַיּוֹם מְפוֹרָשׁ שָׁם אֵיךְ שֶׁאָז הָיוּ מַאֲרִיכִים בִּתְפִלַּת הַשַּׁחַר בְּכָל יוֹם וָיוֹם עֶרֶךְ ב' שָׁעוֹת וְיוֹתֵר, מֵחֲמַת אֲרִיכוּת כַּוָּונָה שֶׁבַּלֵּב כַּנִּזְכָּר לְעֵיל.

אַךְ אַחַר כָּךְ עָמְדוּ אֶצְלֵנוּ רַבָּנִים שֶׁאֵינָם הֲגוּנִים וְקָנוּ אוֹ שָׂכְרוּ הָרַבָּנוּת מִשַּׂר הָעִיר בְּסַךְ מְסֻיָּם בְּכָל עִיר וָעִיר בְּכָל מַלְכוּת פּוֹלִין. כִּי הַמֶּלֶךְ הֶעְלִים עַיִן, וְהַשָּׂרִים בְּעַד בֶּצַע כֶּסֶף נָתְנוּ מִכְתָּב הַנִּקְרָא קָאנְסֶעשׁ לְהָרַב שֶׁבְּכָל עִיר, לִהְיוֹת מוֹשֵׁל עַל כָּל הַיְּהוּדִים שֶׁבְּעִירוֹ בְּכָל עִנְיַן הַנּוֹגֵעַ לְדָתָם, וְגַם לָדוּן בְּדָבָר שֶׁבְּמָמוֹן בֵּין אִישׁ לְרֵעֵהוּ כְּפִי דַעְתּוֹ, אַף שֶׁאֵינוֹ בָּקִי בַּדִּינִים כָּרָאוּי. וְגַם בְּעִנְיַן הַתְּפִלָּה לֹא הָיָה רְשׁוּת לְהַתְחִיל לְהִתְפַּלֵּל עַד שֶׁיָּבֹא הָרַב לְבֵית הַכְּנֶסֶת אוֹ לְבֵית הַמִּדְרָשׁ אֲפִלּוּ עַד חֲצִי הַיּוֹם. וְאַנְשֵׁי הָעִיר הָיוּ מֻכְרָחִים לִתֵּן לוֹ כֵּן גַּם כֵּן כְּתַב רַבָּנוּת עַל פִּי צִיוּוּי הַשַּׂר שֶׁלָּהֶם.

הָרַבָּנִים הַנִּזְכָּרִים לְעֵיל, אֲשֶׁר עָמְדוּ עַל פִּי הַשַּׂר, לֹא רָצוּ לְהַטְרִיחַ עַצְמָן לְהִתְפַּלֵּל בְּכַוָּונָה כַּנִּזְכָּר לְעֵיל. וּכְדֵי שֶׁלֹּא יִהְיוּ מְבֻזִּים בְּעֵינֵי הָעָם, הִתְחִילוּ לְהַשְׁפִּיל מַעֲלַת הַתְּפִלָּה, וּלְהַגְבִּיהַּ מַעֲלַת הַלִּמּוּד בַּתַּלְמוּד, לִלְמֹד גַּם בְּעֵת וּזְמַן הַתְּפִלָּה. וְהָיוּ מִתְפַּלְלִים בִּמְרוּצָה בְּלִי כַּוָּונָה, וְלוֹמְדִים מִיָּד עִם תַּלְמִידִים עוֹמֶק הַתַּלְמוּד בַּחֲרִיפוּת, כְּדֵי לְהַרְאוֹת חָכְמָתָם וּלְהַגְדִּיל שְׁמָם בָּאָרֶץ. וְאַחֲרֵיהֶם נִמְשְׁכוּ כָּל יוֹדְעֵי סֵפֶר הַמִּתְפַּלְלִים בְּבֵית הַמִּדְרָשׁ לְהִתְפַּלֵּל גַּם כֵּן בִּמְרוּצָה בְּלִי כַּוָּונָה כַּנִּזְכָּר לְעֵיל, מֵחֲמַת יִרְאָתָם אוֹ חֲנִיפוּתָם לְהָרַב, כִּי הוּא הָיָה הַשַּׁלִּיט עַל הָעָם. רַק מִקְצָת יְחִידֵי סְגֻלָּה בְּכָל דּוֹר הָיוּ מִתְפַּלְלִים בַּאֲרִיכוּת בְּכַוָּונָה, וְהָיוּ נִקְרָאִים בְּשֵׁם חֲסִידִים מִימֵי עוֹלָם.

The universal Jewish custom had always been that in every city there were two large houses of worship: the synagogue and the study hall. The synagogue was for the masses who were preoccupied with their work throughout the day. Most of them were not scholars and were not in a position to pray with concentration, so they would just recite the words of prayer thrice daily. The study hall was for the Torah scholars, where they could pray at length with deep concentration, each according to his ability. The books that our sages wrote two centuries ago describe how they would pray in the morning for two hours, sometimes more, because of the level of concentration that they had during their prayers.

But then unworthy rabbis came forth and purchased or rented the title "rabbi" from the local nobles with cash payments. This occurred in each city in Poland, because the king turned a blind eye, which enabled the greedy nobles to grant documents that were called "concessions" to rabbis in each city. This granted the rabbis authority to rule over the Jews in their cities with respect to all matters of religion, and also to issue judgments in civil cases, despite not being sufficiently proficient in the relevant laws. The community could not begin their prayers until this rabbi had arrived at the synagogue or study hall, even if this extended to midday. And the people of the city were forced, per the command of the noble, to give the rabbi a written document appointing him as their rabbi.

These rabbis who were appointed by the nobles were not inclined to bother with the hard work of lengthy prayer and intense concentration described above. To ensure that they would not be disgraced on this account in the eyes of the people, they began to downplay the value of prayer and emphasized the value of studying Talmud. They would study Talmud during the communal prayer, and then pray hastily without concentration. Immediately after the prayer, they would study Talmud with their students in depth, to exhibit their keen analytic abilities, hoping to become widely known. All of the learned people in the study hall were drawn to emulate this behavior, to also pray hurriedly and without concentration, either out of fear of the rabbi or out of a desire to flatter him, for he was akin to their ruler. Only a select few individuals in each generation would pray with concentration and at length, and they were always referred to as Chasidim.

TEXT **17**

RABBI EMANUEL CHAI RICCHI, *SEFER YOSHER LEVAV, BAYIT RISHON, CHEDER RISHON,* CH. 12–13

חָחָס עַל כְּבוֹד קוֹנוֹ צָרִיךְ לְהַעֲלוֹת עַל לִבּוֹ מַחְשֶׁבֶת צִמְצוּם זֶה כִּפְשׁוּטוֹ, לְבַל יִפְגֹּם בִּכְבוֹדוֹ בְּחָשְׁבוֹ שֶׁעַצְמוּתוֹ נִמְצָא גַּם בַּגַּשְׁמִיִּים הַשְּׁפָלִים הַבִּלְתִּי נִכְבָּדִים וְאַף בַּנִּבְזִים, חַס וְשָׁלוֹם.

וּמֵאַחַר שֶׁדְּבָרִים הַנִּסְתָּרִים הָאֵלֶּה אֵין אָנוּ מַשִּׂיגִים אוֹתָם בְּכֹחַ הַחֲקִירָה טִבְעִית, דְּאִי אֶפְשָׁר לַעֲמוֹד עֲלֵיהֶם עַל יָדָהּ אֶלָּא מִפִּי הַתּוֹרָה . . . לָכֵן [אֵין] אֲנִי חוֹשֵׁשׁ כְּלָל וְעִיקָּר לְהָשִׁיב לַאֲשֶׁר רָצוּ לְהוֹכִיחַ בַּחֲקִירָתָם שֶׁהַצִּמְצוּם אֵינוֹ כִּפְשׁוּטוֹ . . .

אַף כִּי לֹא נֶעְדַּר כֹּחַ הַסִּיבָּה רִאשׁוֹנָה לִבְרֹא הָעוֹלָמוֹת אִם הָיָה רוֹצֶה בְּלִי שֶׁיְּצַמְצֵם . . . וְאַף כִּי לֹא יָדַעְתִּי לְצַיֵּיר בְּדַעְתִּי אֵיךְ הָיָה אֶפְשָׁר זֶה . . . הַחִסָּרוֹן תָּלוּי בִּי . . . כִּי מִתְיַשֵּׁב יוֹתֵר עַל לִבִּי לוֹמַר שֶׁהוּא כִּפְשׁוּטוֹ, וְשֶׁהַשְׁגָּחָתוֹ הִיא הַמְמַלֵּאת מְקוֹם הַצִּמְצוּם בְּדִקְדּוּק עָצוּם - וְזֶהוּ מַה שֶּׁאָמְרוּ בַּתִּקּוּנִים "לֵית אֲתַר פָּנוּי מִינֵיהּ בָּעֶלְיוֹנִים וְתַחְתּוֹנִים" - מִשֶּׁנֹּאמַר שֶׁאֵינוֹ כִּפְשׁוּטוֹ, וּנְמַעֵט בִּכְבוֹדוֹ יִתְעַלֶּה בְּאָמְרֵנוּ שֶׁעַצְמוּתוֹ נִמְצָא בֵּינֵינוּ אַף בַּמְּקוֹמוֹת הַבִּלְתִּי רְאוּיִם לוֹ.

וּכְמוֹ שֶׁכָּתַבְתִּי בְּפֶרֶק י"ב, שֶׁאֵינוֹ הֶעְדֵּר כָּבוֹד שֶׁנֹּאמַר שֶׁהַמֶּלֶךְ מַשְׁגִּיחַ מֵחַלּוֹנוֹ דְּבַר לִכְלוּךְ כְּמוֹ שֶׁהוּא הֶעְדֵּר כָּבוֹד שֶׁנֹּאמַר חַס וְשָׁלוֹם שֶׁהַמֶּלֶךְ עַצְמוֹ בְּתוֹכוֹ.

וְכֵן כְּתִיב בֵּיהּ (תְּהִלִּים קי"ג ה'-ו') "הַמַּגְבִּיהִי לָשָׁבֶת הַמַּשְׁפִּילִי לִרְאוֹת".

RABBI EMANUEL CHAI RICCHI
1688–1743

Italian kabbalist. Rabbi Ricchi was born in Ferrara, Italy. At age 30 he immigrated to Safed, Israel, where he devoted himself to the study of kabbalah and the teachings of Rabbi Yitschak Luria (Arizal). He traveled widely and lived in numerous places. He wrote multiple works; most notable is *Mishnat Chasidim*, a restatement and explanation of many of Arizal's teachings. He was killed by bandits during one of his travels.

If we wish to be careful about God's honor, we must think of the *tsimtsum* in a literal sense. Then we will not dishonor God by thinking that He is present in lowly and disgraceful things, God forbid. . . .

We cannot discover the truth of these esoteric matters by our own human investigation. The only way to discover the truth in this regard is through the Torah. . . . Therefore, I see no need to respond to those who wish to prove by the force of logic that the *tsimtsum* is a metaphor. . . .

Surely, the First Cause could have created the world without a literal *tsimtsum*. . . . Although I cannot picture how this is possible . . . that's due to my own shortcomings. . . . But it makes more sense to say that the *tsimtsum* is literal, and that it is only God's ultra-specific providence that controls the realm from which He removed Himself. The *Zohar* is referring to this providence when it says, "There is no place, high or low, that is devoid of Him." This is more reasonable than the claim that the *tsimtsum* is a metaphor, which would diminish God's honor, because it implies that God is present among us, even in places that are inappropriate for Him.

As I have written earlier, there is nothing undignified about a king looking out of his window and seeing waste, but it is quite undignified to say that the king himself is present within it.

Indeed, the verse says (PSALMS 113:5–6), "He dwells on high and lowers His gaze."

TEXT 18

RABBI YOSEF IRGAS, *SHOMER EMUNIM, VIKU'ACH SHEINI* 35–39

כָּל הָרוֹצֶה לְהָבִין עִנְיַן הַצִּמְצוּם כִּפְשׁוּטוֹ מַמָּשׁ, הֲרֵי הוּא נוֹפֵל בְּכַמָּה שִׁבּוּשִׁים וּסְתִירוֹת שֶׁל רוֹב עִיקָרֵי הָאֱמוּנָה . . .

אִיתָא בְּזֹהַר חָדָשׁ דַּף נ"ה ג' וּבְכַמָּה מְקוֹמוֹת מֵהַזֹּהַר וְהַתִּקּוּנִים, "דְּלֵית אֲתַר דְּלָאו אִיהוּ תַּמָּן לְעֵלָּא עַד אֵין סוֹף, וּלְתַתָּא עַד אֵין תַּכְלִית, וּלְכָל סִטְרָא". וְאִם הַצִּמְצוּם הוּא כִּפְשׁוּטוֹ הֲרֵי יֵשׁ מָקוֹם דְּלָאו אִיהוּ תַּמָּן . . .

דָּבָר פָּשׁוּט וּמֻסְכָּם מִכָּל הַמְקֻבָּלִים שֶׁהָאֵין סוֹף הוּא תָּמִיד בִּמְצִיאוּת אֶחָד קַיָּם בִּלְתִּי מִשְׁתַּנֶּה כְּלָל . . . וְאִם אַתָּה אוֹמֵר שֶׁהַצִּמְצוּם הוּא כִּפְשׁוּטוֹ נִמְצָא שֶׁנִּשְׁתַּנָּה . . .

מִלְּבַד הָרְאָיוֹת שֶׁהֵבֵאתִי, מָצָאתִי גַם כֵּן בְּסִפְרֵי כַמָּה רַבָּנִים שֶׁכָּתְבוּ בְּהֶדְיָא כֵּן. כִּי בְּסֵפֶר אוֹצְרוֹת חַיִּים א' רָאִיתִי הַגָּהָה כְּתוּבָה בְּשֵׁם תַּלְמִידֵי הָאֲרִ"י זִכְרוֹנוֹ לְחַיֵּי הָעוֹלָם הַבָּא, שֶׁהַצִּמְצוּם הוּא מָשָׁל וְדִמְיוֹן לְהָבִין מְצִיאוּת בְּרִיאַת הָעוֹלָמוֹת . . . וְזֶהוּ לְשׁוֹן סֵפֶר נוֹבְלוֹת חָכְמָה דַּף מ"ט ב': "וּכְבָר אָמַרְתִּי וְשָׁנִיתִי וְשִׁלַּשְׁתִּי, שֶׁכְּדֵי לְסַבֵּר אֶת הָאֹזֶן אֲנִי מִשְׁתַּמֵּשׁ בְּמִלּוֹת: מָקוֹם, וְרֵיקוּת, וּפְנִיָּה, וַעֲלִיָּה, וְצִמְצוּם, וְדוֹמֵיהֶם - הֲגַם שֶׁכָּל אֵלּוּ הֵם מִמַּשִּׂיגֵי הַגַּשְׁמִיִּים".

RABBI YOSEF IRGAS
1685–1730

Italian kabbalist. Rabbi Irgas was born in Livorno. He established a *yeshivah* in Pisa and later became the rabbi of Livorno. He authored several works, including *Shomer Emunim,* which is considered an important work of kabbalah.

Those who wish to understand the *tsimtsum* literally will err in areas that are fundamental to our faith. . . .

The *Zohar* says numerous times that "there is no place where He is not—from the highest of levels to the lowest of levels, and all directions." But if you say that the *tsimtsum* is literal, then you are saying that there is a place devoid of Him. . . .

In addition, all kabbalists regard it as self-evident that God's infinite light is unchanging. . . . But if you say that the *tsimtsum* is literal, then you are asserting that God's infinite light experienced change. . . .

Beyond the proofs that I have cited, I have also found various rabbinic books that clearly express this same view. In the work *Otsarot Chayim* [authored by Rabbi Chaim Vital], I found a note, quoting the students of the Arizal, that the *tsimtsum* is a metaphor geared toward helping us understand the process of Creation. . . . And [Rabbi Yosef Shlomo Delmedigo writes in his work] *Novelot Chochmah* (49B): "I have already said it once and repeated it multiple times. It is only to help people understand a particular concept that I use such terms as 'place,' 'emptiness,' 'turning,' 'rising,' '*tsimtsum*,' and so forth. Obviously, these physical terms cannot apply to God."

RABBI YOSEF SHLOMO DELMEDIGO
1591–1655

Physician, mathematician, rabbi, and kabbalist. Rabbi Yosef was born in Crete and later moved to Padua, where he became acquainted with the sciences and studied under Galileo. He spent 27 years traveling in the Middle East and Europe and lived out his final years in Prague. He wrote on mathematics, astronomy, medicine, optics, kabbalah, philosophy, chemistry, and mechanics.

Additional Readings

THE PROCESS OF CREATION
TZIMTZUM AND RELATED CONCEPTS

RABBI NOSON GURARY

In chapter 5 we examined the question of how Jewish thinkers reconciled the ineffable *Atzmut* with the finite universe, the Oneness of God and the existence of multiplicity, and so on. Among the solutions that they offered are those called "intermediate agency" and "emanationism"—in other words, that creation came into being by way of a series of intermediate steps, emanated by the Creator, that place a sufficiently great distance between Him and that which He created, so that the corporeality and the multiplicity of the latter are disassociated and set apart from God Himself. In other words, the creation came about by way of a long chain of evolutionary processes, a chain of cause and effect, emanated by the Creator as the First (and very distant) Cause, until eventually the corporeality of this material world came into being.

We also cited the view of R. Moshe Cordovero (Ramak)—that in order to avoid the implication of a direct continuity between the Creator and the created (the classical pantheistic view) there must be a series of intermediate steps—according to his view, these are the ten *sefirot,* including *keter,* which are produced by the Creator and which provide a gradual descent from the transcendent infinity of *Atzmut* to the plane of immanent, finite being. Each succeeding *sefirah* from *keter* downward represents a descending level of spirituality, a series of causes and effects wherein each successive level is emanated by the previous level, until the lowest of the *sefirot, malchut,* eventually

evolves. The actual creation comes about only from the level of *malchut.* Thus, a sufficiently great distance has been placed between Him and that which He created. Corporeality and the multiplicity of creation is disassociated and set apart from God Himself.

However, we pointed out that *Ramak's* solution does not solve the problem, for the question as to how, and at what point, the changeover from infinite to finite takes place has not been answered: As long as there is some causal relationship between the Creator and the created, between the first link in the evolutionary chain and the last, no matter how long the chain might be, there always remains some association between one level and another, and thus between the first link and the last.

Accordingly, the aspect of infinity is never completely nullified. On the contrary, because each successive level emanates from or is produced by the previous level, it "inherits" the infinity of its predecessor, so that finite material matter could never have been created from infinite spiritual being, despite numerous causes and effects interposed between the Creator and the created. Of course, the ultimate result of this is that a unity of substance between the Creator and the created (a classical case of pantheism) is implied. This was the very problem that R. Moshe Cordovero tried to avoid.

The *Tzimtzum*

It was explained that Rabbi Isaac Luria, the *Arizal,* therefore expounded the doctrine of *tzimtzum.* In the *Arizal's* view the process of creation was not an uninterrupted sequence of causes and effects, nor a gradual descent of emanations. Rather, the primary act of creation was to establish a "gap" between the Creator and the created, a "quantum leap" *(dilug)* that

RABBI NOSON GURARY

Rabbi and lecturer. Rabbi Gurary is the executive director of Chabad in Buffalo, NY, servicing the local Jewish community and the University of Buffalo. He is a respected lecturer on Jewish mysticism and Chasidism.

breaks the gradualism and establishes a radical distinction between the First Cause and all subsequent effects. This radical break is called the *tzimtzum*. The doctrine of *tzimtzum* was expounded by the *Arizal* in the following way: Before the universe was created, there was only the Infinite One, Whose infinity filled all of existence. Within this infinity, there was no place for finite existence. But when it arose in God's will to create finite worlds, He withdrew Himself from the place where the finite worlds would exist after the *tzimtzum* in order to create a void *(makom panui* or *chalal)* wherein finite reality could exist. Finite being then came about by means of a reintroduction of finite light into the void.

Although the doctrine of *tzimtzum* places a sufficiently great distance between the Creator and the created, avoiding the problems of pantheism, it seems to place the wholly contingent created world entirely outside of God, as the classic theistic position maintains. In other words, if God withdrew Himself by way of the *tzimtzum,* leaving a *makom panui,* the creation that exists within the *makom panui* is devoid of God's *Atzmut.* Moreover, this also implies a change within God, for prior to the creation He was everywhere and after the creation there is one place where He is not—the *makom panui.* This violates the basic principle that the creation does not bring about any change whatsoever in God—"I, God, have not changed" (Malachi 3:6).

Rabbi Shneur Zalman of Liadi therefore adopts the idea of *tzimtzum* proposed by the *Arizal,* but adds some important qualifications regarding its interpretation. First, the *tzimtzum* is not to be understood literally, that God actually withdrew Himself from the void. Nor did He withdraw the *Or Ein Sof.* Rather, God merely concealed the *Or Ein Sof,* by "raising it up" to a level beyond revelation, much the same way as raising the pitch of audible sound makes it imperceptible to the human ear. Moreover, since the *tzimtzum* took place only in the *Or Ein Sof* and not in God Himself, no change whatsoever is affected in Him by the *tzimtzum,* and the principle of God's immutability is thus upheld. God remains exactly as He was prior to the creation.

In order to explain the actual process of *tzimtzum,* as expressed in Chasidic texts, a number of prefatory remarks must be made.

Levels in the *Or Ein Sof*

The *Or Ein Sof* has an internal and an external aspect *(pnimiut* and *chitzoniyut).* In a general sense, the *pnimiut* of the *Or Ein Sof* is called *etzem ha'or* ("the essence of the Infinite Light," not to be confused with *Atzmut),* whereas the *chitzoniyut* of the *Or Ein Sof* is called *hitpashtut ha'or* ("the diffusion or extension of the Infinite Light"). *Etzem ha'or* is the way the *Or Ein Sof* is within its source, the *Ma'or* ("Luminary"), whereas *hitpashtut ha'or* is the way the *Or Ein Sof* becomes extended and drawn downwards to become revealed.

However, in a more specific way, three descending levels of *Or Ein Sof* are identified:

Etzem ha'Or "The essence of the light." This is the aspect of the *Or Ein Sof* that merges completely with its Source and is thus unidentifiable and set completely apart from the other levels of *Or Ein Sof* that emerge from it.

Ha'Or she'b'gilui l'Atzmo "The light that is revealed only to Himself." Its purpose is to reveal Godliness and bring about a state of total existential nullification, called *bittul b'metzius* in Chasidic terminology. This is also the source of the (post-*tzimtzum) Or Ha-Sovev kol Almin,* the transcendent light that both envelops and pervades all of creation without ever being perceived by creation.

Ha'Or hashayach l'olamot "The light that is relevant to the worlds." This light suffuses each of the worlds and is revealed within each of them, according to the level of each world. This level is the source of the (post-*tzimtzum) Or HaMemalei kol Almin,* the immanent revelation of light that "fills all worlds" and permeates all created beings as their very existence and life-force. In fact, to create and sustain the existence of all the worlds is precisely the purpose of the extension of this level of light. Nevertheless, even this level of light is far too sublime to give rise to material existence without the *tzimtzum.*

Prior to the *tzimtzum,* this level of *Or Ein Sof* is described in the writings of the *Arizal* as follows: "Initially everything was supernal, uncompounded light which filled all of existence . . . It had no beginning and no end, but was uniform in every way . . . When it rose in His will to create worlds . . . He contracted [tzimtzum] Himself in the middle of His light . . . ."

Chasidic texts explain that because the *Or Ein Sof* "had no beginning and no end, but was uniform in every way, when it rose in His will to create worlds," God "measured out within Himself in potential what would exist in the future in actuality." Or, in other words, He "measured out" within Himself how He would bring about a finite existence—prior to actually doing so. This "measuring out" is called in the Zohar *galif galifu b'tehiru ila'ah*—"He engraved letters [or, 'engravings') in the Supernal Purity" (the *Or Ein Sof*). These "letters" signify the structuring and formation of the Divine Will prior to the *tzimtzum*, although (prior to the *tzimtzum*) they cannot yet be regarded as the manifestation of His will. They are therefore called only "the potential for limitation." *Chabad* texts refer to these "letters" as the "letters of the *reshimu* ('traces or imprints') prior to the *tzimtzum*."

Prior to the *tzimtzum* however, these "letters" are flooded with *Or Ein Sof*, so that the attribute of limitation that they constitute is not actualized but remains a mere potential for limitation. It is only after the *tzimtzum* that these "letters" become the root of finite being. One of the functions of the *tzimtzum*, therefore, is to remove the *Or Ein Sof* that floods these letters, so that limitation and finitude can be actualized. From this point of view, the effect of the *tzimtzum* is to prevent the *Or Ein Sof* from illuminating these letters, so that after the *tzimtzum* the letters of the *reshimu* remain as the actualization of the "measuring out" of the Divine Will. According to some views, they are also known as the *esser sefirot hagenuzot beMa'atzilan*—"the ten primordial *sefirot* that are concealed within He-Who-brought-them-forth."

The *tzimtzum* thus achieves two goals:

1. On the one hand, the *tzimtzum* reveals the "wholeness" or "completeness" *(shleimut)* of the Holy One, blessed is He—that God is not limited to infinite revelation (i.e., the *Or Ein Sof*), but has the ability as well of finite revelation, or, the other side of the coin, the ability to limit His infinite revelation. As mentioned in Chapter 4, if we say that God's power is manifested on infinite planes of existence, but not on finite planes of existence, we detract from His perfection and completeness.

2. On the other hand, paradoxically, the act of *tzimtzum* is, in fact, for the purpose of revelation and not for the purpose of the concealment that it initially brings about. This may be explained in two ways: Because of the *tzimtzum*, without which the worlds could not have been created, in the future (in the messianic era and particularly with the subsequent Resurrection of the Dead) the level of *Or Ein Sof* that illuminated all of existence prior to the *tzimtzum* will again be revealed. The only difference is that prior to the *tzimtzum*, this infinite revelation did not allow the existence of finite being, whereas after the *tzimtzum*, as a result of the fulfillment of Torah and *mitzvot* in this physical world in the interim, the level of *Or Ein Sof* that illuminated all of existence prior to the *tzimtzum* will be revealed within the world, which will nevertheless continue to exist as a finite world. Second, not only will the same level of *Or Ein Sof* that illuminated all of existence become revealed, but the inner dimension and essence of the *Or Ein Sof*, which was never before revealed, will become manifested within the material world.

This can be explained by way of an analogy: When a great sage mulls over some concept in his mind, he does not need to simplify the concept for himself, for he understands it perfectly. However, when he wishes to communicate the concept to a student, he is obligated to abridge his own understanding of the concept so that it will be comprehensible to his student. After all, one cannot explain calculus to first-grade students. Nevertheless, the purpose of the abridgement is, in fact, revelation—the teacher's intention is to teach his student as much as the student is ready for, until eventually, with the passage of time, the student will be able to attain his teacher's knowledge. This idea is reflected in a statement of the Talmud: "One should always teach one's students in a concise manner."

According to the latter explanation, the *tzimtzum* is essentially for the sake of creating "vessels" for the

Or Ein Sof— in other words, that which can contain and give outward form and expression to what is essentially infinite *Or Ein Sof.* In this regard, R. Yitzchak Luria states: The *tzimtzum* and reduction of the light enables the formation and revelation of *keilim* ["vessels"], and reveals the root of *din* ["restriction, limitation"]. Therefore, in other words: In order for the unlimited *Or Ein Sof* to also be "internalized," (i.e., revealed in an immanent way within creation, instead of only transcending it), the *tzimtzum* was necessary.

To sum up: Although the process of *tzimtzum* causes a reduction and concealment of the *Or Ein Sof,* nevertheless, this is not its purpose. Rather, the purpose is to create a physical world *sans* revelation of Godliness, so that man, through his activities in Torah and *mitzvot,* can transform this world into a "home" for the Holy One.

Four Views of the *Tzimtzum*

We mentioned previously that the doctrine of *tzimtzum* does not appear at all in the writings of R. Moshe Cordovero. It was first proposed by the *Arizal* in order to explain that the process of creation was not an uninterrupted sequence of causes and effects or a gradual descent of emanations. Rather, a radical distinction, called the *tzimtzum,* was made between the First Cause and all subsequent effects.

The doctrine of *tzimtzum,* however, was formulated very tersely and was apparently never explained by the *Arizal* at great length. Accordingly, it was open to differing interpretations and, in fact, became one of the major bones of contention between Chasidim and their opponents, the *mitnagdim.*

It should be pointed out that according to R. Moshe Cordovero, there is no question that the *Or Ein Sof* pervades all worlds and, at the same time, transcends them, and that "no place is devoid of Him." Moreover, as regards the omnipresence of God, Chasidism adopts R. Moshe Cordovero's view, which, at face value, appears to contradict the doctrine of *tzimtzum* proposed by the *Arizal.* (The former view affirms the omnipresence of God, while the latter seems to imply that God withdrew His presence from the area called the *makom panui*). However, *Chabad* texts interpret the *Arizal's* doctrine of *tzimtzum* in a way that agrees entirely with R. Moshe Cordovero's view.

In order to understand how this is so, we must examine the various interpretations of the doctrine of *tzimtzum.*

Differing interpretations of the *tzimtzum* center around a disagreement regarding two concepts:

1. Whether the *tzimtzum* is to be interpreted literally (as actual withdrawal), or not;
2. Whether the *tzimtzum* took place in the Infinite Light (the *Or Ein Sof)* or in the Luminary (God, or what we referred to earlier as *Atzmut).* Thus, there are four possible interpretations:

***Tzimtzum* is meant literally and takes place in *Atzmut*:** This means that the Holy One, blessed is He, removed His *Atzmut* from the place that was to become the worlds, leaving a *makom panui* or *chalal* that is devoid of God's Essence. God then oversees matters from above the void. This is the view of R. Emmanuel Chai Riki, adopted by R. Elijah of Vilna. One of the proofs adduced for this literal interpretation of the *tzimtzum* is that if the *tzimtzum* was only metaphorical, God's *Atzmut* would be found in unworthy places and lowly things. Accordingly, He removed His Essence from the place where He created a finite world in which impurity is found. Nevertheless, God's *hashgachah* ("providence, overseeing") fills the void that is created by the withdrawal of His *Atzmut.* This is comparable to a king sitting in his palace and gazing upon a garbage heap. The garbage remains at a sufficient distance from him that he cannot be said to be associated with it. Nevertheless, it is not removed completely from his realm of authority, for he has jurisdiction over it from his palace window. Analogously, God's Essence is removed from the *makom panui* and is not affected by what goes on in this material Creation. Nevertheless, this world remains within the realm of His authority and jurisdiction because He provides it with its life force—from a distance, of course. But His Essence is not present in the lowly worlds at all. As for the *Lahar's* statement that "no place is devoid of Him"—this is interpreted as meaning that no place is devoid of His *hashgachah.* The Chasidic response to this interpretation of *hashgachah* will be discussed in chapter 10.

Tzimtzum is meant literally, but takes place in the Or Ein Sof, not in Atzmut: This is the view maintained by R. Yonatan Eibeschutz. He writes that had the Arizal stated explicitly that the tzimtzum took place in Atzmut, we would have been forced to understand it this way. However, the Arizal mentions only the words Or Ein Sof; "the aspect of severity [din];" malchut, and so forth—none of which are Atzmut. He cites R. Yisrael Sarug and R. Menachem deFano, who point out that the entire matter of tzimtzum takes place in God's Will, not in His Atzmut. He discusses the matter at length and absolutely rejects the interpretation of tzimtzum as the withdrawal of Atzmut. R. Y. Eibeschutz then continues with a discussion of whether the tzimtzum itself should be interpreted literally or allegorically.

He writes: Were it not for the fact that the Arizal *clearly implies that the* tzimtzum *means a literal withdrawal, I would have interpreted [the word* tzimtzum*] as a borrowed expression, meaning that God conceals His presence in that place where the worlds exist, so that His presence cannot be comprehended. However, anyone who examines the words of the* Arizal *will see that one cannot interpret them this way since he speaks about actual withdrawal . . .*

He therefore concludes that the tzimtzum is a literal withdrawal. However, it is the withdrawal of Or Ein Sof, not Atzmut, from the makom panui. Thus, the entire tzimtzum takes place only in the Or Ein Sof, not in Atzmut.

Tzimtzum is not meant literally, but takes place in Atzmut: This view is maintained by R. Chaim of Volozhin. He writes: The word tzimtzum in this context does not mean "withdrawal" or removal from one place to another . . . [but] in this context it means "concealment" and "veiling." The intention is that God's Essential Oneness, which fills all worlds absolutely equally, is what we call tzimtzum. This is because God's Essential Oneness, which fills all worlds absolutely equally, is concealed and veiled from our comprehension. . . .

Tzimtzum is not meant literally and takes place only in the Or Ein Sof, not in Atzmut: This is the view maintained by Rabbi Shneur Zalman of Liadi and the Chabad school as the official Chasidic interpretation, since it is a corollary of the Ba'al Shem Tov's commentary on the verse "Forever, O God, Your word stands firm in the heavens" (Psalms 119:89), as will be explained at length below.

Rabbi Shneur Zalman presents several arguments against interpreting the tzimtzum literally:

1. Literal withdrawal, as if from place to place, applies only to material objects.
2. To make a distinction between the king himself and his hashgachah (the metaphor used by R. Emmanuel Chai Riki) can only be posited of a human king, not of God. God's knowledge of things is not something additional to His Essence. On the contrary, "by knowing Himself, He knows all things." Moreover, His knowledge is not merely "overseeing" from a distance, but actually envelops the object He knows, and creates and animates it.
3. A verse states explicitly, "Do I not fill the heavens and earth, says God?" (Jeremaiah 23:24). "I" in this context is to be understood literally—"My Essence"—for we have no reason to interpret it otherwise, as will be explained shortly.
4. God's Omnipresence is a matter of uncomplicated faith and solid tradition among Jews of all generations, and they have not tried to find out by rational inquiry exactly how God, Who transcends all comprehension, fills the worlds.

Rabbi Shneur Zalman's interpretation of the tzimtzum, then, is that the tzimtzum takes place in the Or Ein Sof only, not in Atzmut; and that tzimtzum is not to be taken literally as withdrawal, but merely as concealment. Consequently, the Or Ein Sof is to be found in the makom panui exactly as it was prior to the tzimtzum, although what was previously revealed is now concealed by means of the tzimtzum. Furthermore, even in the area affected by the tzimtzum, the concealment of the Or Ein Sof applies only regarding the world, not regarding God Himself, as will be explained below.

One of the arguments presented by those who maintain that the tzimtzum is meant literally is that it is in God's power to actually remove Himself from the *makom panui*. To this, two answers may be given:

1. It is certainly possible that God could have removed His *Atzmut* from the *makom panui*, but, in fact, He didn't! This is proved by the verse cited above, "Do I not fill the heavens and earth, says God?" The counter argument that the verse should not be interpreted literally may be answered as follows: There is a general exegetical rule that states that "no verse is ever excluded from its literal interpretation" *(Shabbat* 63a; *Yevamot* 24a). Because of this rule, the *tzimtzum* should not be taken literally—for if the *tzimtzum* is interpreted literally, the verse must be interpreted allegorically, contradicting the above rule. Alternatively, if the verse is interpreted literally, preserving the above exegetical rule, the *tzimtzum* must be interpreted figuratively! Now, which is preferable—to interpret the *tzimtzum* literally and the verse allegorically, or vice versa? Rabbi Shneur Zalman explains that his interpretation is also supported by the statement of the *Zohar,* "No place is devoid of Him." He explains that this means that, "His Essence and Being, called *Ein Sof* [i.e., *Atzmut,* and not *Or Ein Sof*] . . . completely fills the whole earth within time and space!" Although R. Elijah of Vilna, the leader of the opposition *mitnagdic* camp, interprets this statement as meaning that no place is devoid of His *hashgachah,* the *Zohar* uses the masculine grammatical form in this expression: *panui Minei* ("no place is devoid of Him"—clearly referring to God) rather than the feminine form *panui Mina* ("no place is devoid of her"), which is the proper form if the intention is to refer to God's *hashgachah.*

2. In addition, the *tzimtzum* cannot be taken as an isolated doctrine. It must be understood in the context of an entire ontological and cosmological system. We explained earlier that Chasidic teachings maintain that only "the blessed Emanator, whose Being is of His Essence, and He is not . . . caused by some other cause preceding Himself . . . only He has it in His power and ability to create something out of absolutely naught

and nothingness. . . . "Furthermore, the Ba'al Shem Tov interpreted the verse "Forever, O God, Your word stands firm in the heavens" (Psalms 119:89)—as follows: "Your word," which You uttered, "There shall be a firmament in the midst of the waters. . . ." (Genesis 1:6), these very words and letters stand firmly forever within the firmament of heaven and are forever clothed within all the heavens to give them life, as it is written, "The word of our God shall stand firm forever" (Isaiah 40:8), and "His words live and stand firm forever . . ." For if the letters were to depart [even] for an instant, God forbid, and return to their source, all the heavens would become naught and absolute nothingness, and it would be as though they had never existed at all, exactly as before the utterance "There shall be a firmament . . ." And so it is with all created things, in all the upper and lower worlds, and even the physical earth . . . if the letters of the Ten Utterances by which the earth was created during the Six Days of Creation were to depart from it for [even] an instant, God forbid, it would revert to naught and absolute nothingness, exactly as before the Six Days of Creation. . . .

With the withdrawal of the power of the Creator from the thing created, God forbid, it would revert to naught and complete nonexistence. Rather, the Activating Force of the Creator must continuously be in the created thing to give it life and existence.

It follows that had God removed His Essence from this world *(tzimtzum,* interpreted literally), the entire creation would not now exist, for it would have reverted to "naught and complete nonexistence." It is therefore obvious that those who understand the *tzimtzum* literally must also disagree with the principle of continuous creation as proposed by the Ba'al Shem Tov.

The Chabad View of *Tzimtzum*

We are now in a position to explain the view of Rabbi Shneur Zalman of Liadi and his successors regarding the *tzimtzum.* As mentioned above, Rabbi Shneur Zalman maintains that the entire *tzimtzum* took place in the *Or Ein Sof* and not in *Atzmut.* The effect of the *tzimtzum* is to conceal the *Or Ein Sof* that pervades all of existence, bringing about a *makom panui* that is devoid of the revelation of *Or Ein Sof,* but not of *Atzmut,* and that introduces a limited revelation by way of what is called the *kav.* The "withdrawal" of the *Or Ein Sof* from the *makom panui* is therefore not to be interpreted literally, but merely as concealment.

The necessity for this concealment was, in a general sense, that a finite, material world could not exist within the infinite revelation of the *Or Ein Sof.* However, more specifically, several explanations of the necessity for the *tzimtzum* are to be found in *Chabad* texts. Some of them are as follows:

Because of the Loftiness of the *Or Ein Sof*: We explained above that there are three levels within the *Or Ein Sof.* Even after the *tzimtzum,* the two higher levels of *Or Ein Sof* transcend the worlds completely, for the *tzimtzum* has no effect on them, as will be explained below. Thus, we are dealing here with only the level of light that is relevant to the worlds. Prior to the *tzimtzum,* even the level of *Or Ein Sof* that is relevant to the worlds is infinite, does not have the qualities of higher and lower, beginning and end, and so forth. Accordingly, it, too, is beyond any of the worlds, for even the highest of the worlds is nevertheless limited. Consequently, in order for the worlds to exist as they are at present, the *tzimtzum* was necessary.

Because of the Status of the *Or Hashayach L'Olamot*: Prior to the *tzimtzum,* the light that is relevant to the worlds did not exist as a separate level. Rather, it was completely merged within its source. For this reason as well, the *tzimtzum* was necessary, for it brought about the "separation" of the higher levels of *Or Ein Sof* from the lower level, so that this level would be relevant to the worlds.

So That the Worlds Would Exist: Prior to the *tzimtzum,* the *Or Ein Sof* filled all of existence. Even though there was already potential for existence, this was actualized only through the *tzimtzum.*

So That the *Sefirot* Could Emerge as Separate Entities: Prior to the *tzimtzum,* the *Or Ein Sof* that filled all of existence was absolutely *pashut*—that is, "noncompound and unformed," and everything was absolutely uniform with no individuating characteristics. Now, even though the potential for individual *sefirot*

had already been measured out prior to the *tzimtzum,* in a type of measuring out in thought called *hash'ara bekoach* ("measuring in potential everything that was to be in actuality," as mentioned above), nevertheless, the way this existed in thought was completely different from the way God wanted this to be in actuality. Accordingly, the *tzimtzum* was necessary.

As yet, we have not described what actually happened to the *Or Ein Sof* when the *tzimtzum* took place. Rabbi Shneur Zalman explains as follows: The Holy One, blessed is He, *tzimtzum* ("withdrew" or "rescinded," in a figurative sense) the *Or Ein Sof,* so that it would merge back into its source, and remain in a state of potentiality—in Rabbi Shneur Zalman's words: *nichlal ha'Or beMa'or.* (It should be noted that in this context, the term *Ma'or* does not signify *Atzmut,* for *Atzmut* cannot be regarded as the source of the *Or Ein Sof* in the same way that the sun, as a luminary, is the source of its rays, as explained in Chapter 4. Rather, the term *Ma'or* here signifies that level from which the *Or Ein Sof* emerges). The *tzimtzum* is therefore the (figurative) elevation of the *Or Ein Sof* to its former level, prior to its state of revelation. That is, it was returned to the potential to illuminate.

When the *Or Ein Sof* was figuratively "withdrawn" back into its source, so that the light was no longer revealed, *Atzmut* then became "revealed." When Rabbi Shneur Zalman says that *Atzmut* is "revealed," he means that it is revealed as the immutable, omnipresent, ineffable *Atzmut,* of which everyone is aware, and which no one comprehends, as explained previously in Chapter 4.

It is therefore precisely by way of the *tzimtzum* that *Atzmut* is revealed. That is to say, the awareness of *Atzmut* becomes actualized by way of the *tzimtzum,* for when the *Or Ein Sof* illuminates all of existence, there is more awareness of *Or Ein Sof,* because of its state of revelation, and less awareness of *Atzmut.* Although at present this "revelation" of *Atzmut* is incomprehensible and remains merely as a feeling of awareness, nevertheless, in the Messianic era and especially in the time of the Resurrection of the Dead, *Atzmut* will be revealed to everyone, without any obstruction or concealment. At that time "Your teacher shall no longer hide Himself" (Isaiah 30:20)—by way of the *tzimtzum*. That is, this world will become the place "where God can be Himself, at home," as was explained in chapter 5. Furthermore, this is not only regarding God Himself, but also regarding man, "Your eyes shall see your Teacher"—so that "the glory of the Lord shall be revealed and all flesh [even physical flesh] shall see together" (Isaiah 40:5).

However, as explained above, the ultimate purpose of the *tzimtzum* is not to bring about a lack of revelation of the *Or Ein Sof*, even though this reveals the *Atzmut*. On the contrary, the ultimate purpose of the *tzimtzum* is to enable a revelation of *Or Ein Sof* that allows the worlds to exist and allows people to internalize the greatest measure of illumination of which they are capable (while the *Atzmut* is simultaneously revealed as *Atzmut*). We may ask, therefore, how this comes about by way of raising the *Or Ein Sof* into a state of non-illumination? How does the situation of *nichlal ha'Or beMa'or* bring about the existence of finite worlds and vessels?

In order to explain this, we must examine the effect of the *tzimtzum* on each of the three levels of *Or Ein Sof*:

Etzem ha'Or—the essence of the light that merges completely with its Source and is thus unidentifiable—was never in a state of revelation to begin with. Accordingly, one cannot speak of it as being concealed by the *tzimtzum* either. This level of light was therefore untouched by the *tzimtzum*.

Ha'Or she'b'gilui l'Atzmo—the light that is revealed only to Himself, and the purpose of which is to reveal Godliness and bring about a state of total existential nullification. When this level of light was revealed, finite beings and worlds could not exist. Furthermore, while this level of light was revealed, the *or hashayach l'olamot* ("light appropriate for creation") was totally flooded by it, and it was consequently of no benefit to the worlds. The *tzimtzum* therefore merely concealed this level of light, by raising it into its source so that it would no longer flood the *makom panui* with the revelation of Godliness. The *tzimtzum* is thus described as merely "touching" (*naga bo*) the *Or she'b'gilui l'Atzmo*.

Ha'Or hashayach l'olamot—This is the level of *Or Ein Sof* that is relevant to the worlds, and suffuses each

of the worlds, and is revealed within each of them as the Creative Force that brings them into existence and sustains them, each according to its level. Nevertheless, in itself, even this level of light is far too sublime to give rise to material existence and must be reduced and transformed by way of the *tzimtzum*. In this case, the *tzimtzum* was not mere concealment of the light but such a drastic reduction of the light that all that remained was a mere residue or impression (*reshimu*) of the original light within the *makom panui*.

The explanation of this is as follows: Prior to the *tzimtzum*, the *Or Ein Sof* did not fill all of existence in a way of *hitpashtut* ("extension"). In this sense, it is unlike the flow of a stream of water. A stream of water, in order to irrigate some distant spot, must extend that far. It cannot irrigate that spot by remaining where it is. The obvious corollary of this is that the stream of water is not to be found at all in any place that it does not reach or that it is prevented from reaching. The *Or Ein Sof*, however, filled (and fills) all of existence in a way of *gilui* ("revelation") rather than *hitpashtut* ("extension"). This means that the *Or Ein Sof* is not found in a different place from *Atzmut* but is in the very place in which the *Atzmut* is found—that is, everywhere, for "there is no place devoid of Him." Accordingly, the *Or Ein Sof* did not go anywhere when it ceased to be revealed in the *makom panui* after the *tzimtzum*. It was merely concealed (although so drastically that only a residue of it remains revealed within the *makom panui*).

(*Chabad* sources point out that the very fact that a residue of the light remained within the *makom panui*—the *reshimu*—also indicates that the *tzimtzum* is not a literal withdrawal of the light.)

The *tzimtzum* is therefore not to be regarded as a cessation of *hitpashtut* of the *Or Ein Sof* but merely as a suspension of its *gilui*. This means that the *Or Ein Sof* remains within the *makom panui* even after the *tzimtzum*, and the only difference between before and after *tzimtzum* is in terms of its revelation.

The term *makom panui* is therefore meant metaphorically, not literally. For this reason, it is also referred to as a *makom kadosh*—"a holy place," for it is precisely within the *makom panui* that God's true unity is to be realized—even within a place that is apparently devoid of God, He is also to be found. This is also the meaning of the midrashic statement explaining the oneness of God:

> Moses placed [located] Him even within chalalo shel olam [the chalal or makom panui], as it says, "The Lord is God in the heavens above, and on the earth below, there is nothing else" (Deuteronomy 39:4). What does "there is nothing else" mean? Even within chalalo shel olam!

Immutability

According to Rabbi Shneur Zalman, the tzimtzum took place only in the Or Ein Sof—and in the lowest level thereof—and not in Atzmut, as explained above. It follows that the tzimtzum does not cause any change within Atzmut, just as the sun itself is unaffected when its rays are blocked by clouds.

In this regard the verse states, "I, God, have not changed" (Malachi 3:6). This refers to Atzmut, in which the tzimtzum causes no innovation and which undergoes no change. Nevertheless, one may ask, since the Or Ein Sof was concealed or withdrawn to a higher, inscrutable level, does this not imply a change of status? The answer again is that the tzimtzum is not a lack of hitpashtut, but only a lack of gilui, as was explained previously. Accordingly, it is self-evident that Atzmut is unaffected thereby, just as a person's intellectual ability is unaffected by the fact that he is not thinking at present, or his power of sight is unaffected by the fact that he presently has his eyes closed.

Furthermore, the tzimtzum brought about no change in the Or Ein Sof either, since it was not removed as such (in the sense of being transferred from one place to another) but was simply concealed. The Or Ein Sof therefore remains just as it was, except for the fact that after the tzimtzum, it is no longer revealed. This is comparable to a person who stops revealing his thoughts in speech, even though he continues to think. The only change here concerns the recipients.

All of the above applies to the Or Ein Sof in general. More specifically, not all the three levels of Or Ein Sof were affected equally by the tzimtzum: The highest level of the Or Ein Sof, Etzem Ha'or, remains absolutely unaffected. Since this level of Or Ein Sof is not in the category of revelation at all, being too sublime to be revealed, it is not appropriate to speak of it as being concealed by the tzimtzum either. The second level of the Or Ein Sof, Ha'or she'b'gilui l'Atzmo, in essence remains unaffected by the tzimtzum. Only the aspect of it that was revealed prior to the tzimtzum became concealed by the tzimtzum. The reason for this is that since this level of light transcends the worlds, the tzimtzum does not have the power to constrict the essence of this level of light. All that the tzimtzum can do is prevent this level of Or Ein Sof from becoming revealed within the makom panui. Nevertheless, as far as God's knowledge is concerned, this level of light remains revealed, just as it was prior to the tzimtzum.

Even the Or Hashayach L'Olamot ("the light that is relevant to the worlds"), which fills the makom panui prior to the tzimtzum, is essentially unaffected by the tzimtzum. The only difference between prior and post-tzimtzum is that before the tzimtzum, the Or Ein Sof illuminated the letters of the reshimu, whereas after the tzimtzum, the Or Ein Sof no longer illuminated the letters of the reshimu, as mentioned previously This is comparable, for example, to a person who knows a certain tractate of the Talmud thoroughly. When he is occupied with studying it and explaining it out loud to himself or to someone else, the depth of meaning of the letters of the text before him becomes revealed. However, when he ceases to study the tractate, although he still knows its entire breadth and depth, this remains in a non-revealed state that is non-revealed within his speech or to another person, although he himself still clearly retains all the depth of meaning of the words and letters. Thus, despite the fact that every world that is brought about by the tzimtzum contains a different level of Divine revelation, this is only regarding the worlds and not regarding their Creator.

Thus, the state of concealment brought about by the tzimtzum only concerns us and doesn't concern God. Just as the Or Ein Sof filled all of existence prior to the tzimtzum, so, too, does it after the tzimtzum, except that now it is concealed so that a finite world can come into existence.

This does not mean to say, however, that the tzimtzum is simply a sleight of hand or an imaginary event, for the Torah states clearly that "In the beginning God created..." (Genesis 1:1). The creation that came about by way of the *tzimtzum* really exists. Furthermore, even if one wished to interpret this verse allegorically, the body of authoritative Jewish law (*halachah*) takes it as axiomatic that the world does indeed exist. The *Mishnah*, in Tractate *Sanhedrin* (67a), states: "Two people were picking vegetables [by means of sorcery]. One of them is liable [for the death sentence], and the other is exempt. The one who actually did the deed is liable [for having violated the prohibition of tinkering with spirits], whereas the one who simply used sleight of hand is exempt." This proves that as far as the *halachah* is concerned, the world clearly exists, for if it was merely a "sleight of hand" no one would be liable for reward or punishment. This obviously has bearing on the question of whether chasidic (and more specifically, *Chabad*) philosophy should be categorized as acosmic or not.

Chasidism in general (and *Chabad* Chasidism in particular) has often been branded as pantheistic or acosmic.

Acosmism, loosely defined, maintains that God is the only reality and all else is simply an illusion. An acosmic conception of the world therefore acknowledges only the existence of God and views all other reality as an illusion totally devoid of substance. This challenges empirical experience and conventional criteria. Its basic assumption maintains that there is only a single essence, the Divine Essence, that fills all of existence. All other reality, which appears to be substantial, is merely an illusion, intellectual nearsightedness, and a lie.

In this context, Rabbi Shneur Zalman's *Sha'ar Ha-Yichud v'haEmunah* might seem to imply an acosmic position:

> . . . *Their existence is nullified in relation to their source, just as the light of the sun is nullified and is considered naught and complete nothingness and is not [even] referred to as "existing" at all when it is in its source; only beneath the heavens, where its source is not present [can it be called "existing"]. In the same manner, the term* YESH *("existence") can be applied to all created things only as they appear to the corporeal eyes, for we do not see nor comprehend at all the source, which is the spirit of God, that brings them into existence. Therefore, it appears to our eyes that the materiality, grossness, and tangibility of the created things actually exist, just as the light of the sun appears to have actual existence when it is not within its source.*

From the above, one can easily conclude that since Godliness, unlike the sun, is everywhere equally, therefore the world is merely an illusion! In other words, the world does not exist as the result of a cosmological act but as the result of a psychological act, in which the universe is brought into existence (by way of the *tzimtzum*) only from the point of view of man. However, the truth of the matter is that Chasidism does not move the process of creation to the realm of psychological sleight-of-hand. The mention of the above quote is merely to show that the creation is absolutely contingent, in contrast to the necessary existence of God. As pointed out above, Chasidism adheres to the doctrine of creation *ex nihilo*, with the important corollary that the creative force is always present within the creation and is continuous: for the fact that they were created during the Six Days of Creation is not sufficient for their continued existence. Accordingly, the creation is an act, and a continuous act at that, not a thing, and it therefore requires the constant input of the Creator in order to exist. Nothing can be more contingent than this.

Furthermore, the persistent reminder throughout *Chabad* literature that the purpose of creation is that "God desired a dwelling place in the lower worlds" clearly refutes any acosmic position.

As for the accusation of pantheism, the entire concept of creation *ex nihilo*, which is a cornerstone of chasidic philosophy, clearly rules out any pantheistic approach. The material world is not a manifestation of His being, for God cannot be consubstantial with a universe that was created from nothingness.

Nevertheless, the apparent tendency toward viewing the universe as an illusion must be explained. This subject will be treated in Chapter 9.

The Finite Worlds

We explained earlier that one of the purposes of the *tzimtzum* is to create "vessels" for the *Or Ein Sof*. In this regard, R. Yitzchak Luria states: The *tzimtzum* and reduction of the light enables the formation and revelation of *keilim* ["vessels"], and reveals the root of *din* ["restriction, limitation"].

The purpose of the *tzimtzum*, from this point of view, is to create a void in which the intensity of the *Or Ein Sof* that filled the void prior to the *tzimtzum* has been dimmed, so that finite worlds can come into being where they could not exist previously.

However, the withdrawal (i.e., concealment) of the *Or Ein Sof* is, in and of itself, insufficient to actually bring about a finite creation. It is merely the prerequisite thereof. In order for finite beings to exist, a second step was needed. This second phase of the creative process is described as the introduction of a thin beam or line of light, called the *kav*, into the *chalal*. This *kav* illuminates the *chalal* and is the source of all subsequent emanations. The *kav* is thus a creative and vivifying force, bringing the worlds into being and maintaining their existence. It signifies the immanent revelation of God, as opposed to the infinite, transcendent revelation of God, that is, the *Or Ein Sof*, which envelops and transcends the void.

The *kav* itself subsequently undergoes a number of contractions and concealments, bringing about various planes of reality, referred to as the "worlds" in kabbalistic and chasidic literature. The word for "world" in Hebrew, *olam*, is derived from the word *he'elem*, meaning "concealment." Only when infinite Godliness has been concealed can finite existence come into being. Because Godliness is concealed in various degrees, the existence of manifold planes of reality is brought about. These are known in kabbalistic literature as the five worlds. The higher the world, the greater is its level of revelation of Godliness. The lower the world, the greater the concealment of Godliness. Of course, "there is no place devoid of Him." The essence of God is found everywhere equally, in the highest worlds as in the lowest. The only difference between them is in terms of the revelation of *Or Ein Sof* in them. The higher worlds receive the radiation of the *Or Ein Sof* in a more revealed way than the lower worlds. Although a detailed description of the various worlds, and the *sefirot* that are their structural form, is beyond the scope of the present work, some

aspects of these concepts will be examined in the following chapter.

Chasidism: Its Development, Theology, and Practice (Northvale, NJ: J. Aronson, 1997), pp. 93–122
Reprinted with permission of the publisher

Glossary of Hebrew Terms

Arizal. Rabbi Yitzchak Luria.

Atzmut. Lit., essence; the essence of G-d.

Bittul b'metzius. A complete surrender and nullification of one's ego.

Chabad. An acronym for *Chochmoh, Binah, Da'at* (wisdom, understanding and knowledge); the name of a Chassidic movement—predicated on the concept of studying and understanding G-d and His relationship with the world—founded by Rabbi Schneur Zalman of Liadi in White Russia in the latter part of the 18th century. This movement is also known as Lubavitch, or Chabad-Lubavitch.

Chalal. Lit., void; a space from where G-d withdrew His light.

Chitzoniyut. The external.

Dilug. Leap.

Din. Restriction, limitation.

Ein Sof. The infinite dimension of G-dliness.

Etzem ha'or. The essence of G-d's light.

Gilui. Revelation.

Ha'Or hashayach l'olamot. The light that is relevant to the worlds.

Ha'Or she'b'gilui l'Atzmo. The light that is revealed only to Himself.

Halachah (Halakhah). Jewish law.

Hashgachah. Divine providence.

He'elem. Concealment.

Hitpashtut ha'or. Diffusion or extension of the Infinite Light.

Kav. Thin beam of G-dly light in the *chalal*.

Keilim. Vessels.

Keter. (Lit., crown) the sublime level of divine emanation that transcends the set of the ten *Sefirot*; in man's spiritual personality it is the source of the corresponding "superconscious" faculties of pleasure and will.

Ma'or. Luminary.

Makom kadosh. A holy place.

Makom panui. An empty space. See *Chalal*.

Malchut. Royalty; the last of the ten *sefirot*.

Mitnaged (plural mitnagdim). Opponent of Chasidism.

Olam., Lit. world; level of G-dly revelation.

Or Ein Sof. G-d's infinite light.

Or hamemalei kol Almin. The light that fills all worlds.

Or hasovev kol Almin. The light that surrounds all worlds.

Pnimiut. The internal.

Ramak. Rabbi Moshe Cordovero.

Reshimu. Remnant.

Sefirah (pl. Sefirot). Divine attributes or emanations that are manifested in each of the Four Worlds and are the source of the corresponding ten faculties of the soul.

Tzimtzum. The process of contraction and withdrawal of G-dly light.

Yesh. Existence.

RELIGIOUS DUTY AND RELIGIOUS EXPERIENCE IN CHASSIDISM

RABBI JACOB IMMANUEL SCHOCHET

I. The Dilemma

Mystical movements invariably stress the mystical experience. It is an experience of all-pervading ecstasy: sensing a reality different from that of our everyday life. It means penetrating beyond the world that appears to our physical senses and being absorbed in a higher, spiritual realm. This spiritual realm is regarded as true and real. The awareness and experience of it is seen as an ultimate goal. Man is to experience, to be aware of, and to be gripped by the true and real, as opposed to being confounded by the transient—and thus misleading—world of appearance.

This goal, however, can be achieved only by transcending the confinements of time and space: by a profound concentration on the Absolute immanent throughout, albeit hidden and concealed. Mysticism thus demands purity of intent (*Kavanah*).

All one's doings must be ordered in such a way that they are not performed by rote, mechanical or habitual. They require an intense devotion that places all actions into the full context of the all-pervasive reality of the Absolute. Perfunctory motions, egocentric-pursuits, self-concern in any shape or manner, have no place in this scheme. Self-effacement (*bitul hayesh*) is the prerequisite major premise, and pure awe and love of the Divine are the means to achieve the ideal.

This poses a serious problem. What is one to do when enjoined to fulfill specific religious duties, when subject to an objective code of laws, as mandated by Torah and *mitzvot*? It would seem that tensions must arise between the legal obligation to perform rituals on the one hand, and the ideal condition of the religious experience on the other. What is one to do if there is a duty (*mitzvah*) to be performed in a set time and place, when one is not in the proper frame of mind to do so in ideal fashion of right intent and devotion? Which of the two takes precedence—the physical act or the mental-emotional consideration?

This problem is quite serious. It would seem to affect Chassidism in a very special way. For Chassidism is emphatic in its insistence to inculcate the principle of the "ideal action." It insists that our life and actions, particularly with respect to Torah and *mitzvot*, be imbued with the right intent and proper devotion: with *ahavah veyirah* (love and awe); *lishmah—leshem Hashem* (for the good deed's own sake—for the sake of G-d).

Paradoxically, this very problem is at the root of the secular-popular stereotype distortion of Chassidism. In this misinterpretation, Chassidism is presented as careless or negligent in matters of *Halachah*, or as an emotional reaction and sentimental rebellion against the formal "rigors" of *Halachah* and "Rabbinic legalism."

In other words, Chassidism is depicted as having surrendered Halachic duties for the sake of the mystical experience. Formal ritual is said to have been sacrificed for the sake of emotive awareness, the objective act yielded for the sake of subjective feeling. This view of Chassidism, however, is based on total ignorance. Those who present it betray their failure to study or understand the teachings and practices of Chassidism. Obviously they did not take the trouble of studying, at the very least, the basic, seminal teachings and practices of the first leaders and guides of Chassidism, namely R. Israel Baal Shem Tov and R. Dov Ber, the Maggid of Mezhirech. Even a cursory glance at their teachings would have shown how totally wrong and distorted these views are.

Chassidism itself was fully aware of the problem. Its leaders dealt with it quite explicitly and in no

RABBI JACOB IMMANUEL SCHOCHET, PHD, 1935–2013

Torah scholar and philosopher. Rabbi Schochet was born in Switzerland. Rabbi Schochet was a renowned authority on Kabbalah and Jewish law and authored more than 30 books on Jewish philosophy and mysticism. He also served as professor of philosophy at Humber College in Toronto, Canada. Rabbi Schochet was a member of the executive committee of the Rabbinical Alliance of America and of the Central Committee of Chabad-Lubavitch Rabbis and served as the halachic guide for the Rohr Jewish Learning Institute.

uncertain terms. Let us examine and see how R. Dov Ber of Mezhirech, disciple and successor of the Baal Shem Tov, dealt with this question.˙

II. Torah and *Mitzvot*: Basis for All

The Midrash defines the purpose of this world's creation with the words, "The Holy One, blessed be He, desired to have an abode in the lower worlds."[2] Thus it is man's task to establish an abode for Divinity in the terrestrial realm.

Man is to manifest G-d's immanence in the physical world. The achievement of this manifestation establishes the ultimate unity of G-d, that is, that G-d is recognized to be the sole true reality. To that end man was given the Torah, the revelation of the Divine precepts which instruct[3] man precisely "the way in which he is to walk and the deed he is to do."[4]

Torah is the intermediary between man and the world and the Divine. Creation comes about through Torah.[5] The world is sustained through Torah: the very existence of the universe and all therein, man's every need, all man has and receives, depend on the Torah.[6] The Torah thus is the direct link between the upper and the lower, between G-d and man, in both directions: it is the channel through which the supernal effusions and emanations flow downward to sustain all beings, and it is the channel through which man attaches himself to the Divine.[7]

"The Torah and the Holy One, blessed be He, are altogether one."[8] On this Zoharic maxim, the Maggid comments: Divinity *per se* is beyond any creature's grasp and endurance.[9] The Almighty, therefore, "condensed" and "concentrated" Himself (*tzimtzum*),[10] as it were, into the letters of the Torah.[11] With these letters He then created the world, as it is said, "The Holy One, blessed be He, created the world by means of the Torah."[12] This refers to the "Ten Fiats of Creation" in the very first chapter of the Torah.[13]

The letters of the Torah dim and conceal the essence of Divinity. Nonetheless, they do not become a separate entity but remain fully unified with G-d. G-d is not separate or distinct from Torah, as it is said, "He and His causations are one."[14] On the other hand, the Torah speaks to man. Thus we are able to relate to it. By virtue of the Torah's identification with G-d,

therefore, the letters of the Torah enable us to absorb and endure G-dliness. Whatever apprehension of, and attachment to, the Divine, that man may achieve, is possible only by means of the Torah and its *mitzvot*.[15]

In this vein, the Maggid interprets the term *Keviyachol*. This term is usually found in context of an anthropomorphic analogy, and is generally translated 'as it were,' or 'if it were possible to say so.'[16] The Maggid reads it as a compound of two words: *Khaf Bet* and *Yachol*. The implication is that G-d concentrated Himself into the *khaf bet*—22—letters of the Torah's alphabet, and thereby *yachol*—*it is possible* for G-d to be in this world.[17]

The Torah is thus "G-d's 'garment,'" which makes it possible for a finite creation to come into being and for the infinite G-d to dwell within it.[18]

Any indwelling of the *Shechinah* and Divine emanations requires a "receptacle," something to have a "hold" on these, something to which they may become attached.[19] For the holiness of a Divine emanation is too bright and intense to be absorbed as it is in itself by man and the world. Thus there is need for a medium through which it may vest itself below.[20] This medium is Torah and *mitzvot*.[21]

Thus, it is said, "The Holy One, blessed be He, desired *lezakot* the people of Israel, and therefore He gave them Torah and *mitzvot* in abundance."[22] The term *lezakot* means to refine and purify. The implication is that there is a refinement and purification of Israel's material reality so that it will be able to become attached and joined to holiness. This is indeed suggested by the term *mitzvah*—*mitzvot*, which is an idiom of *tzavta*—attachment, union.[23] This principle is alluded in the saying of "A *mitzvah* brings about a *mitzvah*":[24] doing a *mitzvah* brings about, and leads to, *tzavta*—attachment and conjunction, while "An *aveirah* (transgression) brings about an *aveirah*,"[25] i.e., overstepping, to pass beyond, and to be separated from the Creator.[26]

By means of Torah and *mitzvot*, therefore, man—the prospective recipient renders himself into a proper receptacle. Thus he becomes like a channel or conduit for the supernal "spring" from which the beneficent abundance flows forth to that individual and to the whole world.[27]

In this context, too, the Torah is said to consist solely of Divine Names.[28] The Divine Names are in effect synonymous with the Divine Attributes.[29] Thus, all the words and aspects of the Torah are, or signify, the Divine Attributes. Hence, as certain parts of the Torah are studied or observed, the corresponding Attributes are aroused to become manifest below. When one is called by name, one leaves everything aside to answer the caller. So, too, G-d, who is "concentrated" in the Torah (His Names—Attributes), and altogether one with His Name, responds to the one that calls Him through His Torah.[30]

III. *Lishmah*

The intimate and inseparable relationship between Torah and the very existence and sustenance of all beings thus appears quite clearly. In this context of the Torah's cosmic significance it is readily seen why the Maggid emphasizes that when learning Torah one must keep in mind the Talmudic saying, "The Holy One, blessed be He, has in His world only the four cubits of *Halachah*."[31] Thus one should say in his heart: "His blessed Being is concentrated, and dwells, here (in Torah); hence it is only fit to study Torah with joy, with awe and with love."[32]

In other words, Torah and *mitzvot* must be studied and fulfilled *lishmah*, which means: (a) For its name, i.e., as its very name indicates, the term "Torah" meaning "instruction, teaching,"[33] for it teaches man the way in which he is to walk and instructs him in the awe and love of G-d.[34] (b) *For its sake*, (*leshem heh*, the letter *heh* being an abbreviation of the word G-d) i.e., for the sake of G-d[35]: to bring about a realization of the Divine purpose, to cause the Divine "delight," as it were, from G-d having commanded and His will having been fulfilled.[36]

In turn, this implies that man learn Torah and practice *mitzvot* with fervor and ardor (*hitlahavut*). For, one could conceivably study Torah as a natural act, simply because of enjoying the study, just as one may indulge in business or other mundane affairs simply because one enjoys doing so. In essence, then, these two actions are not distinguishable from one another! The principal Divine "delight" in man's performance of *mitzvot*, therefore, is not from the very act itself, but from the extent of man's *hitlahavut*, from the devotional involvement, the sense of *lishmah*.[37]

We note here the emphasis on *kavanah* (intention; motivation; devotion), the significance of *lishmah*, the requirement of *ahavah veyirah*, as indispensable ingredients for the religious act. This reiterates the Zoharic maxim that *ahavah* and *yirah* are the wings needed for Torah and *mitzvot* to soar upwards to effect their ultimate purpose.[38]

The Maggid, as do Kabbalah and *Chassidut* in general, never tires of stressing this requirement.[39] Our initial problem thus comes to the fore: what is man to do if and when he lacks this emotive condition, if and when—due to his mundane entanglements—he has difficulty in bringing himself to the ideal state of *ahavah* and *yirah*?

If the state of *hitlahavut* is the ultimate achievement, would it not follow that perhaps man should expend all his efforts to achieve just that, to achieve the inner, spiritual perfection, as opposed to the external, corporeal action of the study of Torah and the practice of *mitzvot*?

IV. Deed and Thought

The Maggid was quite aware of this tension. His essential answer may be put as follows:

Kavanah, *lishmah*, *hitlahavut* are the ideal state. Nonetheless, the study of Torah and the practice of *mitzvot* have an objective validity of their own. Thus they must be followed even if the ideal state has not been attained yet. One cannot possibly achieve *yirah*, the fear and awe of G-d, without a prior absolute and objective fulfillment of Torah and *mitzvot*![40] *Hitlahavut* is not realizable except by way of actions: by way of deeds to which it can attach itself and in which it becomes vested.[41]

Indeed, *hitlahavut* in isolation harbors an element of danger. For he who acts purely out of love, from a sense of immense ardor and ecstasy (*hitlahavut*), may get carried away and fail to be meticulous with his obligations. *Hitlahavut* thus need be tempered and restrained by a sense of fear, submission, and discipline.[42]

When the Maggid states that it is impossible to achieve *devekut* (attachment to G-d) except by means of Torah and *mitzvot*, he is quite explicit in stating that he means the *act* of Torah and *mitzvot*. For *mitzvot* have three aspects: thought, speech, and deed. When the Torah was given at Sinai, it was given by way of *speech* (G-d's words in the proclamation of the commandments). Needless to say that this includes *thought* as well, because speech derives from thought. The Torah was thus given by way of thought and speech, and the *deed* was left to us. Hence, when we actually perform *mitzvot*, in actual deed, we effect the unity of the act of the *mitzvah* with its thought and speech.[43]

Let us take, for example, the *mitzvah* of *tefillin*. The section in the Torah which ordains the *mitzvah* of *tefillin* is the speech of the *mitzvah*. The *kavanah* is the thought. The commandment itself is the deed. That is why our sages said, "He who recites the *Shema* without *tefillin* bears false witness against himself."[44] For how can the thought (the *kavanah*) vest itself in the speech? What will the thought and speech dwell upon if not on the actual deed? If, again, he recites the *Shema* with *tefillin*, the speech becomes a garment unto the thought, and the deed becomes a garment unto the speech.[45]

Thus despite the inestimable importance of *kavanah*, the very act of the *mitzvah* has an objective, independent value and validity of its own. It may not be suspended, therefore, even when the proper *kavanah* is lacking.

The Maggid lays down what he calls "an important rule": When a *mitzvah* comes to man's mind, he should not refrain from doing it because of his apprehensions that its performance may cause in him a feeling of pride or self-satisfaction, or whatever other ulterior motive. One must pursue the *mitzvah* anyway. No doubt but that from the present lack of *lishmah* he will eventually come to a state of *lishmah*.[46] The good deed in and by itself effects a "good instrument" (the "body" of the deed), while the faculty of thought (*kavanah*) effects the *pnimiyut* (inwardness; the "soul") of that instrument.[47]

For all of Torah and the *mitzvot* have an external aspect (*chitzoniyut*) that "guards the fruit," i.e., the inner essence (*pnimiyut*). This is analogous to the sac of the fetus and the placenta, the "external aspects" without which the fetus cannot develop. For example, the *mitzvah* of *teshuvah* (repentance; return to G-d) has an external aspect of being motivated by fear of negative consequences.

We see this in the case of "Pharaoh *hikriv*"[48]— which our sages read to mean not only that "Pharaoh came close" but also that "Pharaoh brought close": he brought Israel close to G-d. Pharaoh's pursuit caused Israel to do *teshuvah*.[49] Now surely Pharaoh did not intend to bring them to *teshuvah*. They did so because they feared him. Their initial motivation, therefore, was one of fear. That fear was like a shell that protects the fruit. Thereafter, however, the Israelites found the "fruit" itself, "ate" it, and did *teshuvah* in proper fashion. Thus from the initial *shelo lishmah* (lack of *lishmah*) will ultimately come about a state of *lishmah*.[50]

V. The Study of Torah

In view of the paramount importance of *ma'aseh hamitzvot* (the actual deed or action of the *mitzvot*), the Maggid stresses the significance of studying *Halachah* in particular: "The *yetzer hara* (inclination to evil) does not seek to entice man to refrain from learning altogether, for man would not normally agree to this. Rather, the *yetzer hara* entices him not to study those subjects which will inspire *yirat Shamayim* (fear and awe of G-d), such as *Mussar* (ethical works), or *Shulchan Aruch* (Code of Jewish Law) from which one gains clear knowledge of the laws!"[51]

This is not to say that one should study only practical *Halachah* and inspirational literature like *Mussar*. Nor, for that matter, does it mean that one should concentrate on *pnimiyut haTorah* (the esoteric, inner meanings as distinguished from *peshat*, the exoteric, outer or plain meaning of the Torah). *Peshat* is no less than the very key necessary to enter and attain the inner part.[52]

In fact, the "Oral Torah" (Talmud; the Rabbinic tradition explicating the "Written Torah") is referred to as *kishutei kalah* (bridal ornaments).[53] This means that the Rabbinic analysis and discussions, in which each one expresses his insight and opinion, is analogous to each one saying, "this or that way is a nicer ornament, this or that way is more fitting and beautiful."[54]

The Maggid offers the following parable:

A king was lost. He wandered about like an ordinary peasant in shabby clothes, and no one recognized him. When his faithful subjects finally did find and recognize him, they decided to make for him beautiful new garments. Then they started to argue among themselves: one says, "*This* will be more fitting and beautiful," while another claims, "No, *this* will be more fitting and beautiful." The king is greatly delighted by these arguments, even by suggestions that are altogether inappropriate, because his subjects sincerely seek to enhance his honor and glory. In that sense, then, *pilpul*, the Oral Torah, is referred to as the "bridal adornments." For G-d takes delight, as it were, even from one who may arrive at a mistaken conclusion, insofar that he seeks to enhance His blessed honor.[55]

The Heavenly interrogation (after man leaves this world), "Did you conduct your business in good faith? Did you set aside times for the study of Torah?,"[56] the Maggid interprets as follows:[57] "When you conducted your business, did you do so in good faith, that is, did you think of G-d at all times, every moment, without separating your thoughts from His blessed Being? If you reply, 'But there is a *yetzer hara*!' then you are asked: Did you set aside times for the study of Torah, for 'I have created the *yetzer hara*, but I have also created the Torah as an antidote to it!'"[58]

The Maggid elaborates on the antidotal quality of the Torah: It is written, "All that are thirsty go to the water,"[59]—that is, go to the Torah which is referred to as water.[60] Elsewhere, though, it is written, "My word is like fire!"[61] There are, however, two forms of *yetzer hara*: one inflames man to commit sin, while the other cools man and casts upon him a sluggishness not to fulfill the commandments. Thus it is said, "I have created the *yetzer hara*, but I have also created the Torah as an antidote to it": with regard to the *yetzer hara* that inflames it is said, "All that are thirsty go to the water;" and with regard to the *yetzer hara* that cools and generates coldness it is said, "My word is like fire."[62]

When at times man's heart becomes "coarse" (lit., "material," that is, insensitive to spirituality), the way to correct this is by attaching oneself to Torah, and thereby one will slay his evil inclination.[63] Likewise, when contrite for having gone astray and committing sins, the study of Torah will rectify man's perverted actions.[64]

The study of Torah is so important in the teachings of the Maggid as an objective act and duty on its own, that he counts the failure to study among the most serious roots of evil. He refers to the Mishnah,[65] which enumerates the four principal categories of culpable harm on the physical level, and reads these as signifying also the four principal categories of culpable harm on the spiritual level. Thus he interprets the second one—*bor*: the term *bor* means a pit, but it means also emptiness, waste, signifying a neglected and uncultivated field that was not plowed or sown.[66] In its inner sense, then, this refers to one who failed to study Torah.[67]

Rather than fasting and mortifying oneself, one should use the energy expended thereon for the study of Torah with all one's might and devotion, and thus one will ascend on the ladder of spirituality.[68] Intense study of Torah, to the point of discovering new insights (*chidushei Torah*) in Talmud and *Halachah*, purifies man for the service of G-d.[69] Moreover, as G-d and the Torah are essentially one, by binding oneself to the letters of Torah one is able to transcend the temporal.[70]

VI. Two Levels

These teachings of the Maggid, essential to—and typical of—authentic Chassidism (as evident from their sources), are merely a sample, a few selected passages. They are supplemented, and vastly elaborated upon, in the wide range of his other teachings available to us.

It follows, then, quite clearly, that Chassidism must be understood to speak of two levels in man's worship of G-d:

a) There is an initial stage, relating to everyone without exception. It impresses upon man his Divinely ordained obligations to study Torah and practice *mitzvot* in accordance with all specifications of *Halachah*—as an *objective and absolute reality in itself.*

Even so, one is not to say that being occupied with G-d's Torah and is in any case adequate and sufficiently holy on its own. The fact of their intrinsic and comprehensive sanctity does not negate the need for proper *kavanah*. On the contrary: the very fact of intrinsic sanctity demands the more adequate *kavanah*, pure thought and perfect speech, so that every word coming from your mouth, every single letter as well as its vowels and accents, be distinct.[71] Thus—

b) on a second, higher level, man must strive to study Torah and practice *mitzvot* in ideal fashion, with proper devotion and intent, with a sense of *ahavah* and *yirah*, *hitlahavut* and *devekut*.

The religious experience, therefore, the very soul and spirit of the *mitzvot*, the mystical involvement, is all-important. Nonetheless, it needs be attached to actual deeds.

The Torah enjoins us to cleave unto G-d (*devekut*). A permanent state of perfect *devekut* or *hitlahavut*, however, is humanly impossible in itself and by itself. The fulfillment of this commandment, therefore, is as our sages interpreted it: "How is it possible to cleave unto the Holy One, blessed be He, when it has been said, 'For G-d, your G-d, is a devouring fire'?[72] But this precept means, 'cleave unto His attributes: as He is compassionate, so you be compassionate.' . . . "[73] In other words, in order to cleave unto G-d one must practice Torah and *mitzvot*.[74]

VII. Primacy of Torah Study

One can read a succinct summary of the above in the following guideline:

When studying Torah [or performing a *mitzvah*] one should pause every so often in order to attach oneself to His blessed Being. At the very time of actual learning, the necessary requirement of full mental involvement and concentration precludes a simultaneous pursuit of *devekut*. Nonetheless, one must still learn, for the Torah itself clears and furbishes the soul and is "A Tree of Life unto those that hold on to it."[75] In fact, if one does not learn, his *devekut* would have to cease [for "a *boor* (a boor; an empty person) cannot be fearful of sin, nor can an *am ha'aretz* (an unlearned person; an ignoramus) be scrupulously pious."[76]]. Thus one must pursue Torah study notwithstanding the fact of the temporary suspension of *devekut* at the time of concentrating on the learning. Even so, every

so often one should pause to dwell on, and reinforce, attachment to the Creator.[77]

In a parallel passage of this teaching,[78] it is expanded and elaborated on with the following words:

"If one were to sit idle, the *yetzer* (*hara*) would lead him to improper thoughts, evil desires and idle talk, and to all the other 'forces and hosts' (of the *yetzer hara*).[79] For the faculty of thought is continuously at work and never rests . . .[80] Would that we, in our generations, could cleave unto the blessed Creator during the daily three prayers and the recitation of the benedictions! Thus if one were to cease studying, one would remain 'bald from here and bald from there' (i.e., forfeiting both the study of Torah and the *devekut*)."

In short, one must submit to the Divine Will expressed in Torah and *mitzvot*. One must obey it to the best of one's abilities without introducing any personal considerations, even if they appear noble and spiritual. Man's concern must be G-d-centered, and not self-centered.

When all actions are geared toward fulfilling the Divine Will and "gratification," they become infused with G-dliness. This will also effect the ultimate goal of a Divine indwelling.[81]

The Mystical Dimension III: Chassidic Dimensions (Brooklyn, NY: Kehot Publication Society, 1990), pp. 155–177
Reprinted with permission of the publisher

Endnotes

* Unless stated otherwise, the quotations are taken from the Maggid's teachings in the following works: *MDL (Maggid Devarav Leya'akov*, also called *Likutei Amarim)*, ed. Kehot: New York 1984; *OrTo (Or Torah)*, ed. Kehot: New York 1984; *LiYek (Likutim Yekarim)*, ed. Toldot Aharon: Jerusalem 1974; *OrEm (Or HaEmet)*, ed. Husziatin: New York 1960; *TzHar (Tzava'at Harivash)*, ed. Kehot: New York 1982. All other sources are spelled out fully.

1 *Tanchuma*, Nasso:16. See there also Bechukotai: 3; and *Bamidbar Rabbah* 13:6. Cf. *MDL*, Hossafot, par. 37.

2 See below, note 32.

3 See Exodus 18:20.

4 *Tanchuma*, Bereishit:1; *Bereishit Rabbah* 1:1; *Zohar* 1:5a, and 47 a. See also below, note 11.

5 *Zohar* 1:47a. See *Pesachim* 68b. *Tanchuma*, Bereishit:1. *Pirkei de R. Eliezer*, ch. 16.

6 *OrTo*, par. 105. *LiYek*, par. 131.

7 See *Zohar* 11:90b. See also *ibid*. 1:24a, and 11:60a.

8 See *Tikunei Zohar* 17a; and *cf. Tanya*, ch. 4.

[9] For a detailed explanation of the concept of *tzimtzum*, see *Mystical Concepts in Chassidism*, ch. II.

[10] For a detailed explanation of the significance of the *aleph-bet*, the letters of the Torah, see my "Gimatriya: The Principle of Numerical Interpretation."

[11] *Zohar* 11:204a. See *Sefer Yetzirah* 2:2; *Berachot* 55a; Rashi on Job 28:23.

[12] *Avot* 5:1. *Rosh Hashanah* 32a.

[13] *Tikunei Zohar* 3b.

[14] MDL, par. 177; *OrTo*, par. 248. See also MDL, par. 164; *OrTo*, par. 200.

[15] See Rashi on *Yoma* 3b, and on *Megilah 21a*, s.v. *kibeyachol*.

[16] *No'am Elimelech*, Vayera, on Genesis 18:1. Cf. *Shenei Luchot Haberit, Torah Shebe'al Peh*, s.v. *kibeyachol*; *Techilat Chochmah* III:1, klal 35; and *Pachad Yitzchak*, s.v. *kibeyachol*.

[17] *OrTo*, par. 167. *TzHar*, par. 111, and see there for further references.

[18] *Zohar* 1:88a. Cf. *OrTo*, par. 491; *LiYek*, par. 111. See also *Zohar* III:187a; and *Tanya*, ch. 35 and end of ch. 53.

[19] MDL, par. 259; *OrTo*, par. 363.

[20] *MDL*, par. 179. *OrTo*, par. 71, 80, and 245.

[21] *Makot* 23b.

[22] See *Sefer Chareidim*, Teshuvah, ch. 7; *Or Hachayim* on Numbers 27:23; R. Shneur Zalman of Liadi, *Likutei Torah*, Bechukotai, p. 45c; *Sefer Halikutim-Dach*, s. v. *mitzvah*, p. *1089ff.*; *Likutei Sichot*, vol. VII, p. *30ff.* *Hayom Yom*, p. 102.

[23] *Avot* 4:2.

[24] *Ibid.*

[25] MDL, par. 259; *OrTo*, par. 363.

[26] *OrTo*, par. 105; *LiYek*, par. 131. See also *MDL*, par. 94, and *OrTo*, par. 243.

[27] *Zohar* 11:90b and 124a. Ramban, lntr. to his Torah Commentary, and *idem, Tarat Hashem Temimah*, (*Kitvei Ramban*, vol. l: p. 167{). Cf. *MDL*, par. 84, 177, 214, and 223; *OrTo*, par. 65, 152, and 248.

[28] See *Zohar* 11:42b, and III:288a. Cf. *Mystical Concepts in Chassidism*, p. 59f. and notes 203 there.

[29] *OrEm*, p. 15a. Cf. *Eliyahu Rabba*, ch. 18; *Yalkut Shimoni*, Eicha, par. 1034.

[30] *Berachot* 8a.

[31] *OrEm*, p. 15a. *TzHar*, par. 119.

[32] *Zohar* III:53b. See also *ibid.*, III:260a. *Netivot Olam*, Netivot Hatorah, ch. 1, and Netiv Ha'emunah, ch. 2.

[33] OrTo, par. 317, and 453; *LiYek*, par. 201. Cf. MDL, par. 122

[34] *OrTo*, par. 317, and 419. Cf. *Sha'ar Hamitzvot*, Va'etchanan and *Sha'ar Ma'amarei Razal*, Avot VI.

[35] *MDL*, par. 134.

[36] *Ibid.*

[37] *Tikunei Zohar* 10:25b.

[38] See MDL, par. 60, 64, 246, and 253. *OrTo*, par. 105, 108, 341, and 498.

[39] *Kedushat Levi*, Lech Lecha, on Genesis 15:8.

[40] *MDL*, par. 134.

[41] *OrTo*, par. 124.

[42] *MDL*, par. 179; *OrTo*, par. 72, and 80.

[43] *Berachot* 14b.

[44] *OrTo*, par. 245.

[45] *Pesachim 50b*.

[46] *MDL*, par. 190. *TzHar*, par. 126, and see the notes there.

[47] Exodus 14:10.

[48] *Shemot Rabba* 21:5.

[49] *MDL*, par. 242; *OrTo*, par. 492.

[50] *OrTo*, par. 22; *LiYek*, par. 237. *TzHar*, par. 117.

[51] *OrTo*, par. 258. Cf. *Zohar* 1:154a.

[52] *Zohar Chadash*, Shir: 64a.

[53] *MDL*, par. 88; *OrTo*, par. 397.

[54] *OrTo*, par. 397.

[55] *Shabbat* 31a.

[56] *MDL*, par. 79; *OrTo*, par. 401.

[57] *Kidushin* 30b.

[58] Isaiah 55:1.

[59] *Baba Kama* 17 a.

[60] Jeremiah 23:29.

[61] *Zichron Zot*, Parshat Zachor.

[62] *OrTo*, par. 84b.

[63] *MDL*, par. 223.

[64] *Baba Kama* 2a.

[65] See *Baba Metzia* 104a.

[66] *OrTo*, par. 460. *TzHar*, par. 121, and see the notes there.

[67] *OrTo*, par. 205d; *LiYek*, par. 178.

[68] *Darkei Tzedek*, V: p. 18a.

[69] *MDL*, par. 122. See there also par. 179; and *OrTo*, par. 72 (80).

[70] *OrTo*, par. 178; *LiYek*, par. 132.

[71] Deuteronomy 4:22.

[72] *Sifre*, Ekev, par. 49; *Ketuvot* 111 b. See *Shabbat* 133b; and *Sotah* 14a.

[73] *OrTo*, par. 167. *TzHar*, par. 111, and see the notes there.

[74] Proverbs 3:18.

[75] *Avot* 2:5.

[76] *OrEm*, p. 99a. *TzHar*, par. 29.

[77] Cited in margin of *TzHar*, par. 29, and see the notes there. See also *TzHar*, par. 30.

[78] Cf. *Ketuvot* 59b. *Midrash Le'olam*, end of ch. 10.

[79] See *MDL*, par. 176, and 252. *OrTo*, par. 118, and 179b.

[80] *MDL*, par. 134.

Lesson

6

Sketch of the U.S Supreme Court during the 2013 term.

THE PUBLIC MENORAH

IS ALL PUBLICITY GOOD PUBLICITY?

In the 1970s, when Chabad began erecting large Chanukah menorahs in public places, a number of Jewish organizations objected to this practice and filed lawsuits against it. This debate brought into sharp relief differing approaches within the Jewish community regarding how to preserve and express Jewish identity in the modern world. This lesson also confronts the question: In light of the Jewish historical experience as a "minority religion," should Jews advocate for a more secular society? Or, does an irreligious society actually pose the greater threat to our Jewishness, and to a civil society in general?

TEXT **1**

UNITED STATES CONSTITUTION, AMENDMENT I

Congress shall make no law respecting an establishment of religion, or prohibiting the free exercise thereof.

TEXT **2**

JUSTICE ANTHONY KENNEDY, COUNTY OF ALLEGHENY V. AMERICAN CIVIL LIBERTIES UNION, 492 U.S. 573 (1989) (THE MENORAH CASE)

If government is to participate in its citizens' celebration of a holiday that contains both a secular and a religious component, enforced recognition of only the secular aspect would signify the callous indifference toward religious faith that our cases and traditions do not require; for by commemorating the holiday only as it is celebrated by nonadherents, the government would be refusing to acknowledge the plain fact, and the historical reality, that many of its citizens celebrate its religious aspects as well. Judicial invalidation of government's attempts to recognize the religious underpinnings of the holiday would signal not neutrality but a pervasive intent to insulate government from all things religious.

JUSTICE ANTHONY KENNEDY
1936–

Senior Associate Justice of the US Supreme Court. Born in California, he graduated from Stanford University with his B.A. and received his LL.B. from Harvard Law School. He took over his father's law practice for 12 years. He was a professor of constitutional law at McGeorge School of Law and at the University of the Pacific, and in 1988, he was nominated by President Reagan as associate justice of the United States Supreme Court.

TEXT 3a

TALMUD, MEGILAH 13A

וְאַמַּאי קָרֵי לֵיהּ יְהוּדִי? עַל שׁוּם שֶׁכָּפַר בַּעֲבוֹדָה זָרָה. שֶׁכָּל הַכּוֹפֵר בַּעֲבוֹדָה
זָרָה נִקְרָא יְהוּדִי, כְּדִכְתִיב (דָנִיֵאל ג, יב): "אִיתַי גֻּבְרִין יְהוּדָאִין וְגוֹ'"

BABYLONIAN TALMUD

Why was [Mordecai] called "the Jew"? Because he repudiated idolatry. For anyone who repudiates idolatry is called *Yehudi* ("Jew"), as it is written (DANIEL 3:12): "There are these Jews [whom you have appointed over the affairs of the province of Babylonia. . . . They serve not your gods, nor worship the golden image that you have erected.]"

A literary work of monumental proportions that draws upon the legal, spiritual, intellectual, ethical, and historical traditions of Judaism. The 37 tractates of the Babylonian Talmud contain the teachings of the Jewish sages from the period after the destruction of the 2nd Temple through the 5th century CE. It has served as the primary vehicle for the transmission of the Oral Law and the education of Jews over the centuries; it is the entry point for all subsequent legal, ethical, and theological Jewish scholarship.

"In God We Trust" first appeared on U.S. currency in 1864 on the two-cent piece.

TEXT **3b**

SIFREI, DEUTERONOMY 11:28

כָּל הַמוֹדֶה בַּעֲבוֹדָה זָרָה כְּכוֹפֵר בְּכָל הַתּוֹרָה כּוּלָהּ. וְכָל הַכּוֹפֵר בַּעֲבוֹדָה זָרָה כְּמוֹדֶה בְּכָל הַתּוֹרָה כּוּלָהּ.

Anyone who accepts idolatry is considered to have repudiated the entire Torah. And one who repudiates idolatry is considered to have accepted the entire Torah.

SIFREI

An early rabbinic Midrash on the biblical books of Numbers and Deuteronomy. *Sifrei* focuses mostly on matters of law, as opposed to narratives and moral principles. According to Maimonides, this halachic Midrash was authored by Rav, a 3rd-century Babylonian Talmudic sage.

The Inquisition Tribunal, *Francisco Goya, ca. 1815.*
(*Real Academia de Bellas Artes de San Fernando, Madrid*)

Figure 6.1

A History of Religiously Motivated Persecutions Experienced by the Jewish People through the Ages

C. 357 BCE Haman persuades King Ahasuerus to issue a decree calling for the annihilation of all the Jews in the Persian Empire by arguing: "There is one people that is scattered and separate among the peoples throughout all the provinces of your kingdom. Their laws differ from those of every people, and they do not keep the king's laws; it is therefore of no value for the king to allow them to exist" (Esther 3:8).

C. 170 BCE Antiochus IV attempts to forcefully Hellenize the Jewish people. "King Antiochus wrote to all his kingdom that all the people should be one, and every one should leave his own law . . . The king sent letters by the hands of messengers to Jerusalem, and to all the cities of Judah; that they should . . . forbid burnt-offerings, sacrifices and atonements to be made in the temple of of God, and should should prohibit the Sabbath and the festival days to be celebrated . . . He commanded altars to be built, and temples, and idols, and swine's flesh to be offered, and unclean beasts; and that they should leave their children uncircumcised . . . They cut in pieces and burnt with fire the books of the law of God . . . Those who would not break the holy law of God were put to death" (*First Book of Maccabees*, Chapter One).

First Century CE Christianity begins as a Jewish sect and then breaks away to form its own religion. The authors of the New Testament place the responsibility for the killing of Jesus on the Jews. As a result, for centuries Christians view Jews as "Christ killers," and as "a people condemned forever to suffer exile and degradation" as punishment for this deed. The Gospel of John in particular contains many verses that refer to Jews in a pejorative manner, fueling hatred and persecution of Jews throughout Christendom for the next 18 centuries.

125–135 CE Roman Emperor Hadrian outlaws the study of Torah and the practice of Judaism on pain of death. Among the tens of thousands of Jews killed for teaching Torah and observing the *mitzvot* are some of the greatest sages of Jewish history, including Rabbi Akiva and Rabbi Haninah ben Teradyon (who was burned alive wrapped in a Torah scroll).

4th to 6th Centuries Christianity becomes the state religion of the Roman Empire, and its rulers proceed to use their power to enforce the "one true faith." Non-Christians are barred from public office, and numerous other restrictions are imposed on them. The Sanhedrin (the high court of Torah law), which had served as the epicenter of Jewish learning and jurisprudence for more than 1,700 years, is forced to disband.

613 The Spanish Visigoth realm, which adopted Christianity as the state religion in 587, issues a decree compelling all Jews to convert to Christianity and expels all who refuse to do so.

7th and 8th Centuries Muhammad, the founder of Islam, initially allies himself with the Jews of Arabia. But when the Jews refuse to convert to the religion he founded, Muhammad turns on them. In 627, Muhammad has six hundred Jews beheaded in Medina, takes their wives and children as slaves, and expels the two other Jewish tribes in the area under his control. In 640 (three years after Muhammad's death), Jews are expelled from the entire Arabian Peninsula, where numerous Jewish tribes had flourished for centuries. Muhammad's inflammatory statements about the Jews, recorded in the Koran, have stoked Islamic hatred and persecution of Jews for fourteen centuries.

Muhammad and his successors embark on a policy of imposing their new religion by the force of the sword, conquering vast territories and forcefully converting millions of people. All Jews and Christians remaining in Moslem-ruled lands are designated "Dhimmi," made to pay special taxes, and subjected to humiliating laws and regulations designed to emphasize their degraded status. At times they are compelled to wear distinctively marked clothing, such as a yellow belt for Jews and a blue belt for Christians.

681 The Twelfth Synod of Toledo orders the burning of the Talmud and other "heretical" books.

694 King Ergica of Visigoth Spain orders that all Jewish children over the age of seven should be taken from their homes and raised as Christians.

722 Emperor Leo III forcibly converts all the Jews in the Byzantine Empire to Christianity.

828 French King Charles the Simple confiscates Jewish-owned property in Narbonne and donates it to the Church.

1016 The ancient Jewish community of Kairouan, Tunisia is forced to choose between conversion and expulsion.

1090 The Moslem Almoravides decimate the Jewish community of Granada, bringing to an end the 400-year golden age of Jewish culture in Spain.

1096 A Crusader army led by Count Emicho passes through the Rhineland and attacks its Jewish communities under the slogan, "Why fight Christ's enemies abroad when they are living among us?" Eight hundred Jews are killed in Worms. Another 1,200 Jews commit suicide in Mainz to escape the mob's attempt to forcibly convert them. Thousands more are killed or forcefully converted in the events surrounding the First Crusade.

1099 The Crusaders conquer Jerusalem and massacre its Moslem and Jewish inhabitants. Jews are barred from living in Jerusalem for the next 90 years, and suffer severe persecution and slaughter throughout the Holy Land.

1150 The Moslem Almohades, who were particularly aggressive in forcefully converting non-Moslem populations, conquer wide stretches of Spain and North Africa and compel Jews to convert or die. Maimonides's family flees Spain, and subsequently Morocco, to avoid forced conversion to Islam.

1165 Forced mass conversions in Yemen.

1171 Thirty-one Jews are burned at the stake in Blois, France after they are accused of murdering Christians and using their blood for ritual purposes. The infamous "blood libel" would claim many Jewish lives throughout the centuries.

1179 The Third Lateran Council bars Jews from being plaintiffs or witnesses against Christians in the courts.

1190 Five hundred Jews of York are massacred after a six-day siege by departing Crusaders.

1215 The Fourth Lateran Council, headed by Pope Innocent III, orders all Jews in Christian lands to be marked by distinctive dress.

1240-1244 Pope Gregory IX puts the Talmud on trial on charges that it contains blasphemy and attacks on the Church. Twenty-four wagonloads of handwritten Talmudic manuscripts are burned in the streets of Paris.

1242 James I of Aragon compels Jews to attend churches and listen to conversion sermons.

1254 Louis IX expels the Jews from France and confiscates their property and synagogues.

1267 The Synod of Breslau orders the Jews to live in ghettoes. The Vienna city council forces Jews to wear a cone-shaped headdress in an addition to the yellow badge Jews are already forced to wear.

1290 Edward I expels all Jews from England.

1298 German knight Rintfleisch claims to have received a mission from heaven to exterminate "the accursed race of the Jews." Under his leadership, a mob goes from town to town massacring Jews, often by mass burning at the stake; 146 Jewish communities are destroyed, and almost 100,000 Jews are killed.

1306 Jews are expelled from France.

1333 Forced mass conversions in Baghdad.

1349 Six hundred Jews are burned at the stake in Basel, 140 children are forcibly baptized, and the city's remaining Jews are expelled. The city synagogue is turned into a church, and the Jewish cemetery is destroyed.

1389 A mob slaughters approximately 3,000 of Prague's Jews, and destroys the city's synagogue and Jewish cemetery. King Wenceslaus IV of Bohemia insists that the responsibility lay with the Jews for going outside during the Christian Holy Week.

1413 Disputation of Tortola, Spain, staged by the Avignon Pope Benedict XIII, is followed by forced mass conversions.

1438 Establishment of *mellahs* (Jewish ghettos) in Morocco.

1478–1834 The Spanish Inquisition is instituted for the purpose of maintaining Catholic orthodoxy throughout the lands under Spanish rule. Similar "Inquisitions" are established by Portugal and Rome, bringing much of Europe (as well as the European colonies in the Americas and throughout the world) under their reign of terror for the next 350 years. Those suspected of practicing Judaism in secret (referred to as *Marranos,* or "pigs") are arrested, cruelly tortured, and burned alive at the stake.

1492 Ferdinand II and Isabella issue a "General Edict on the Expulsion of the Jews from Spain." Some 300,000 Jews leave the country. Many Jews opt to remain and ostensibly covert, while continuing to practice Judaism in secret. These *conversos* are hunted down by the Inquisition, tortured, and put to death.

1493 Sicily's 37,000 Jews are expelled.

1497 Forced conversion of all the Jews in Portugal.

1528 Three "Judaizers" are burned at the stake in Mexico City.

1543 Martin Luther writes "On the Jews and Their Lies," in which he advocates an eight-point plan to get rid of the Jews either by religious conversion or by expulsion: " . . . set fire to their synagogues or schools . . . their houses also be razed and destroyed . . . their prayer books and Talmudic writings . . . be taken from them . . . their rabbis be forbidden to teach henceforth on pain of loss of life and limb . . . safe conduct on the highways be abolished completely for the Jews . . . usury be prohibited to them, and that all cash and treasure of silver and gold be taken from them. . . . If we wish to wash our hands of the Jews' blasphemy and not share in their guilt, we have to part company with them. They must be driven from our country . . . we must drive them out like mad dogs." By 1573, Jews have been expelled from their communities throughout Germany.

1555 In the Papal Bull *Cum nimis absurdum*, Pope Paul IV writes: "It appears utterly absurd and impermissible that the Jews, whom God has condemned to eternal slavery for their guilt, should enjoy our Christian love." He renews anti-Jewish legislation, and installs a ghetto in Rome that was locked every night.

1563 Russian troops take Polotsk from Lithuania, and its Jews are given an ultimatum: embrace the Russian Orthodox Church or die. About 300 Jewish men, women, and children are thrown into ice holes in the Dvina River.

1648–1655 Ukrainian Cossacks, led by Bohdan Chmielnicki, go from town to town massacring Jews, sparing only those who agree to convert to Christianity. About 100,000 Jews are killed, and 300 Jewish communities are destroyed.

1654 Peter Stuyvesant tries to prevent Jews from settling in New Amsterdam (later New York City).

1721 Catherine I expels all the Jews from the Russian Empire.

1762 Rhode Island refuses to grant citizenship to two Jews, Aaron Lopez and Isaac Eliezer, stating, "No person who is not of the Christian religion can be admitted free to this colony."

1776 The State of Maryland requires Christian faith for public office.

1791–1917 After the Russian Empire acquires territories (formerly part of Poland and Lithuania) containing millions of Jews, it decrees that all Jews be confined to a limited "Pale of Settlement" and forbids them to reside outside of its boundaries. (Jews converting to Russian Orthodox Christianity are released from these restrictions.) This creates conditions of severe hardship and poverty for millions of Eastern European Jews for a period of 126 years, until the Pale's abolishment in 1917.

1800 Pope Pius VII rebuilds the walls of the Roman Ghetto (which had been torn down by Napoleon two years earlier) and reconfines the city's Jews in it. Jews are restricted to the ghetto through the end of the Papal States in 1870.

1827 Tsar Nicholas I drafts young Jewish boys for 25 years of military service ("cantonists"), with the purpose of converting them to Christianity.

1840 The Damascus Blood Libel results in arrests, the seizure of Jewish children, and attacks on Jewish communities throughout the Middle East.

Moslem persecution of the Jews worsens during the nineteenth century, with massacres of Jews by Moslems occurring in Baghdad (1828), Meshed (1839), Marrakech (1864), Fez (1864), Barfurush (1867), Tunis (1869), Demnat (1875), and Tripolitania (1897).

1847 Lionel de Rothschild is repeatedly elected to the British Parliament but denied his seat for refusing to swear on a Christian Bible, until the law is amended in 1858.

1905 In Yemen, old laws are revived forbidding Jews from raising their voices in front of Muslims, building their houses higher than Muslims' houses, or engaging in any traditional Muslim trade or occupation.

20th Century The rise of radical Islam produces fundamentalist terrorist groups such as Hamas, Islamic Jihad, Al-Qaeda, the Taliban, and ISIS, who rape, pillage, and slaughter all "infidels" who do not conform with their religious beliefs and practices.

TEXT **4**

SUE ANNE PRESSLEY, "TOUGH LESSONS IN AN ALABAMA TOWN," *THE WASHINGTON POST*, SEPTEMBER 2, 1997

When Paul Herring, 14, was sent to the school office to be disciplined for disrupting class, he was ordered by the vice principal to write an essay on "Why Jesus Loves Me." When David Herring, 13, failed to bow his head during a school assembly prayer, a teacher allegedly reached over and lowered it for him. After Sarah Herring, 11, heard a minister deliver a fire-and-brimstone sermon at her elementary school, she said, she had nightmares for weeks about burning in hell.

The children's parents, Sue and Wayne Willis, said they have complained frequently about the activities, as well as name-calling and other alleged abuse by other students, only to be dismissed as troublemakers and to be told, "This is how we do things in Alabama."

Recently, aided by the state chapter of the American Civil Liberties Union, they filed suit in U.S. District Court against the school system for violating their children's religious freedom and persecuting them for being Jewish. The suit asks that the religious practices and persecution be stopped at once, but does not ask for any specific monetary damages. . . .

Attorneys with the ACLU contend that this is not just a story of one family's ordeal, but is representative of a pattern of institutional intolerance in Alabama toward anyone who is not Christian—and a continued flouting of the separation of church and state. They say the attitude filters down from Gov. Fob James, Jr. (R), who has supported a circuit judge's right to display the Ten Commandments and to open his court sessions with prayer, and a state legislature that has passed school prayer statutes four times in recent years.

A 20th-century public school classroom in the United States.
(Museum of the City of New York)

TEXT 5

JUSTICE HUGO BLACK, EVERSON V. BOARD OF EDUCATION, 330 U.S. 1 (1947)

A large proportion of the early settlers of this country came here from Europe to escape the bondage of laws which compelled them to support and attend government favored churches. The centuries immediately before and contemporaneous with the colonization of America had been filled with turmoil, civil strife, and persecutions, generated in large part by established sects determined to maintain their absolute political and religious supremacy. With the power of government supporting them, at various times and places, Catholics had persecuted Protestants, Protestants had persecuted Catholics, Protestant sects had persecuted other Protestant sects, Catholics of one shade of belief had persecuted Catholics of another shade of belief, and all of these had from time to time persecuted Jews. In efforts to force loyalty to whatever religious group happened to be on top and in league with the government of a particular time and place, men and women had been fined, cast in jail, cruelly tortured, and killed. . . .

These practices of the old world were transplanted to and began to thrive in the soil of the new America. . . . Catholics found themselves hounded and proscribed because of their faith; Quakers who followed their conscience went to jail; Baptists were peculiarly obnoxious to certain dominant Protestant sects; men and women

JUSTICE HUGO BLACK
1886–1971

Justice Black was born in Alabama. In 1926, he was elected to the U.S. Senate as a Democrat from Alabama. In 1937, President Roosevelt nominated Black as a Supreme Court Justice. During his career, he vigorously defended the "plain meaning" of the Constitution, rooted in the ideas of its era. He later became the senior associate justice, a position he held for 25 years.

of varied faiths who happened to be in a minority in a particular locality were persecuted because they steadfastly persisted in worshipping God only as their own consciences dictated. . . .

The people . . . reached the conviction that individual religious liberty could be achieved best under a government which was stripped of all power to tax, to support, or otherwise to assist any or all religions, or to interfere with the beliefs of any religious individual or group.

The movement toward this end reached its dramatic climax in Virginia in 1785–86 when the Virginia legislative body was about to renew Virginia's tax levy for the support of the established church. Thomas Jefferson and James Madison led the fight against this tax. Madison wrote his great "Memorial and Remonstrance" against the law. In it, he eloquently argued that a true religion did not need the support of law; that no person, either believer or non-believer, should be taxed to support a religious institution of any kind; that the best interest of a society required that the minds of men always be wholly free; and that cruel persecutions were the inevitable result of government-established religions. . . .

This Court has previously recognized that the provisions of the First Amendment, in the drafting and adoption of which Madison and Jefferson played such leading roles, had the same objective and were intended to provide the same protection against governmental intrusion on religious liberty. . . . In the words of Jefferson, the clause against establishment of religion by law was intended to erect "a wall of separation between Church and State" . . . That wall must be kept high and impregnable.

TEXT 6a

EXODUS 20:1–3

וַיְדַבֵּר אֱלֹקִים אֵת כָּל הַדְּבָרִים הָאֵלֶּה לֵאמֹר.
אָנֹכִי ה׳ אֱלֹקֶיךָ אֲשֶׁר הוֹצֵאתִיךָ מֵאֶרֶץ מִצְרַיִם מִבֵּית עֲבָדִים.
לֹא יִהְיֶה לְךָ אֱלֹהִים אֲחֵרִים עַל פָּנָי.

God spoke all these words, saying:

I am God, your God, Who took you out of the land of Egypt, out of the house of slavery.

You shall not have other gods in My presence.

TEXT 6b

RABBI AVRAHAM IBN EZRA, EXODUS 20:1

כִּי הַדִּבּוּר הָרִאשׁוֹן הוּא הַיְסוֹד, וְעָלָיו כָּל בִּנְיְנֵי הַמִּצְוֹת, וְאַחֲרָיו כָּתוּב
לֹא יִהְיֶה לָךְ. וּפֶשַׁע מִי שֶׁאֵינוֹ מַאֲמִין בְּשֵׁם גָּדוֹל מִפֶּשַׁע עוֹבֵד עֲבוֹדַת
גִּילוּלִים . . . וְהִנֵּה אֵלֶּה מוֹדִים בַּשֵּׁם, רַק מְשַׁתְּפִים עִמּוֹ אַחֵר.

RABBI AVRAHAM IBN EZRA
1092–1167

Biblical commentator, linguist
and poet. Ibn Ezra was born in
Tudela, Spain and fled the Almohad
regime to other parts of Europe.
It is believed that he was living in
London at the time of his death.
Ibn Ezra is best known for his
literalistic commentary on the
Pentateuch. He also wrote works
of poetry, philosophy, medicine,
astronomy, and other topics.

The First Commandment is the foundation upon which
all the *mitzvot* are built. After that comes the command,
"You shall not have. . . ." The corruption of one who
does not believe in God is greater than the corruption of
one who worships idols . . . as [the idol worshipers] also
believe in God, only they incorporate others with Him.

*A display of the Ten Commandments,
located on the grounds of the Texas
State Capitol in Austin, Texas.*

TEXT 7

THE LUBAVITCHER REBBE, RABBI MENACHEM MENDEL SCHNEERSON, *LIKUTEI SICHOT*
VOL. 8:302–303

יֵשׁ הַצָּעָה שֶׁהַמֶּמְשָׁלָה תִּתֵּן תְּמִיכָה לְתַלְמוּדֵי תּוֹרָה וְלִישִׁיבוֹת, אֲבָל כְּתָמִיד נִמְצָאִים . . . הַמִּשְׁתַּדְּלִים לְבַטֵּל תְּמִיכָה זוֹ מֵהַיְּשִׁיבוֹת וּלְבַטֵּל תַּלְמוּד תּוֹרָה מִפִּי תִּינוֹקוֹת שֶׁל בֵּית רַבָּן חַס וְשָׁלוֹם . . .

אוֹמְרִים שֶׁתְּמִיכָה כָּזֶה הִיא נֶגֶד הַקּוֹנְסְטִיטוּצְיָא. וְזֶה מוּזָר מְאֹד, כִּי אֲפִילוּ אֵלּוּ הָאוֹמְרִים שֶׁהַקּוֹנְסְטִיטוּצְיָא דּוֹחָה תַּלְמוּד תּוֹרָה שֶׁל תִּינוֹקוֹת שֶׁל בֵּית רַבָּן, וְאֵין לְהִשְׁתַּדֵּל שֶׁיַּעֲשׂוּ אַמֶענְדְמֶענְט (תִּיקוּן) בָּזֶה - בֶּטַח יוֹדְעוּ שֶׁאִם הַמֶּמְשָׁלָה מַסְכֶּמֶת לִתְמוֹךְ, וַהֲרֵי הִיא יוֹדַעַת אֶת הַקּוֹנְסְטִיטוּצְיָא, וַדַּאי שֶׁאֵין סְתִירָה בָּזֶה. וְהָאוּמְנָם עֲלֵיהֶם לְלַמֵּד אֶת בֵּית מִשְׁפָּט הָעֶלְיוֹן שֶׁל אַרְצוֹת הַבְּרִית הִלְכוֹת קוֹנְסְטִיטוּצְיָא דְאַרְצוֹת הַבְּרִית?

. . . יֶשְׁנָם גַּם . . . הָאוֹמְרִים שֶׁאִם הַיְּהוּדִים יְקַבְּלוּ הַתְּמִיכָה, תִּתָּנֶה הַמֶּמְשָׁלָה גַּם לַנּוֹצְרִים, וְיִחַזְקוּ בָּזֶה עֲבוֹדָה זָרָה, אֲשֶׁר בֶּן נֹחַ מוּזְהָר עָלֶיהָ. וְלָכֵן קַבָּלַת הַתְּמִיכָה אֲסוּרָה עַל פִּי שֻׁלְחָן עָרוּךְ, דְּוִלְפְנֵי עִוֵּר לֹא תִתֵּן מִכְשׁוֹל . . .

בְּפָּאבְּלִיק סְקוּלְס (בָּתֵּי סֵפֶר עֲמָמִים) לוֹמְדִים כַּמָּה וְכַמָּה מִקְצוֹעוֹת בְּאוֹפֶן וּבְסִגְנוֹן כָּזֶה אֲשֶׁר בְּמֵישָׁרִין וּבַעֲקִיפִין מַשְׁפִּיעִים עַל הַתַּלְמִיד לֵאמֹר . . . שֶׁאֵין בַּעַל הַבַּיִת הַמַּנְהִיג לְבִירָה זוֹ, וּמִזֶּה - צַעַד קָטָן לִכְפִירָה גְמוּרָה בְּבוֹרֵא עוֹלָם. וַהֲרֵי עַל הַכְּפִירָה הוּזְהֲרוּ בְּנֵי נֹחַ לְכָל הַדֵּעוֹת.

וְאוּלַי נָכוֹן יוֹתֵר שֶׁיִּלְמְדוּ בְּנֵי נֹחַ בְּבָתֵּי חִינּוּךְ מְשֶׁלָּהֶם מֵאֲשֶׁר בְּפָּאבְּלִיק סְקוּלְס, וְכַיָּדוּעַ דְּכוֹפֵר גָּמוּר גָּרוּעַ מֵעוֹבֵד עֲבוֹדָה זָרָה.

RABBI MENACHEM MENDEL SCHNEERSON
1902–1994

The towering Jewish leader of the 20th century, known as "the Lubavitcher Rebbe," or simply as "the Rebbe." Born in southern Ukraine, the Rebbe escaped Nazi-occupied Europe, arriving in the U.S. in June 1941. The Rebbe inspired and guided the revival of traditional Judaism after the European devastation, impacting virtually every Jewish community the world over. The Rebbe often emphasized that the performance of just one additional good deed could usher in the era of Mashiach. The Rebbe's scholarly talks and writings have been printed in more than 200 volumes.

There is a proposal that the government should provide [financial] support to Talmud Torahs and yeshivahs. But, as always, there are those . . . who are trying to counteract this support and prevent the Torah learning of Jewish children, God forbid. . . .

They argue that such support is against the Constitution. This is a strange argument, for even one who believes that the Constitution should take precedence over the Torah learning of Jewish children, and that no effort should be made to amend it in this regard, would certainly agree that if the government—which certainly knows what the Constitution says—agrees to provide this support, there is no conflict here. Is it their task to instruct the Supreme Court of the United States on constitutional law?

. . . They [also] argue that if Jewish schools receive this support, then Christian schools will receive it as well, with the result that one will be causing the strengthening of *avodah zarah*, which is forbidden to non-Jews [under the Noachide laws commanded by God to the whole of humanity]. Therefore, it is forbidden by Jewish law for Jews to accept this financial support, under the principle "Do not place a stumbling block before the blind." . . .

In public schools, many of the subjects are taught in a way that, both directly and indirectly, causes the student to conclude . . . that the world has no Master, which is a small step from completely denying the existence of the Creator of the World. Such denial is certainly a violation of the Noachide laws, according to all opinions. It may, in fact, be preferable that non-Jewish children are educated in their [Christian] schools rather than in public schools. As is known, a complete heretic is worse than an idol worshiper.

TEXT 8a

RABBI MEIR LEIBUSH WISSER, GENESIS 20:11

שֶׁגַּם אִם נִרְאֶה אִישׁ אוֹ עַם שֶׁהוּא פִילוֹסוֹף גָּדוֹל וְחָקַק לוֹ נִמוּסִים יְשָׁרִים,
וְהִרְגִּיל אֶת עַצְמוֹ בְּמִדּוֹת טוֹבוֹת . . . וְהוּא עוֹשֶׂה מִשְׁפָּט וּצְדָקָה, הַכֹּל עַל
פִּי עֲצַת שִׂכְלוֹ, בְּכָל זֶה לֹא נוּכַל לִבְטוֹחַ עַל הָאִישׁ הַהוּא אוֹ הָעָם הַהוּא
שֶׁבְּעֵת תְּסִיתֵהוּ תַאֲוָתוֹ לַעֲשׂוֹת רַע שֶׁתָּמִיד יִגְבַּר שִׂכְלוֹ עַל תַּאֲוָתוֹ . . .
אָז גַּם שִׂכְלוֹ יֵלֵךְ שׁוֹלָל לִרְצוֹחַ וְלִנְאוֹף וְלַעֲשׂוֹת כָּל רַע.
רַק כֹּחַ אֶחָד נִמְצָא בְּנֶפֶשׁ הָאָדָם אֲשֶׁר בּוֹ נוּכַל לִבְטוֹחַ שֶׁלֹּא נֶחֱטָא . . .
שֶׁהִיא יִרְאַת אֱלֹקִים . . . הַמַּשְׁקִיף עַל נִגְלֵהוּ וְנִסְתָּרָיו וְהַצּוֹפֶה אֶת כָּל
מַעֲשָׂיו. אָז גַּם עֵת יִגְבַּר עָלָיו יִצְרוֹ . . . יִזָּהֵר מֵעֲשׂוֹת רַע.

RABBI MEIR LEIBUSH WISSER (MALBIM) 1809-1879

Rabbi, Hebrew grammarian, and Bible commentator. Born in Ukraine, Rabbi Wisser served as rabbi in several prestigious communities across Europe. His fame reached as far as the Jewish community of New York which offered him the position of first Chief Rabbi of the city, an offer he rejected. He is best known for his commentary to the entire Bible which was unprecedented in its scope and thoroughness. He placed great emphasis on explaining the precise meaning of every word in the Bible.

We may observe a person or society who are great philosophers, have instituted a righteous way of life, have acclimated themselves with good character traits . . . and practice justice and charitable works—all in accordance with the reasoning of their intellect. Nevertheless, we cannot place our trust in that person or society that at such time when their passions will be roused, their intellect will conquer their passions. . . . On the contrary, their intellect itself may lead them along the path of immorality and murder and every type of evil.

There is only one force within the human soul that can insure against sin, and that is the fear of God . . . Who sees both what is revealed and what is hidden in the person and observes all the person's actions. Only this can ensure that at a time when a person's base inclinations overpower them, the person will . . . guard themselves from doing evil.

TEXT 8b

RABBI PINCHAS BIBERFELD, "OUR APPROACH TO HISTORY," IN *SEFER ZIKARON LERABBI YITSCHAK ISAAC HALEVI* (BENEI BERAK, 1964), PP. 351–352

זְכוּרַנִי כַּאֲשֶׁר בִּיקֵּר מָרָן הַקָּדוֹשׁ הַגָּאוֹן רַבִּי אֶלְחָנָן וַסֶרְמַן ה' יִנְקוֹם דָּמוֹ בְּבֶרְלִין וּבָא לְבֵית מִדְרָשֵׁנוּ . . . יְמֵי בִּיקּוּרוֹ שֶׁל מָרָן הַגְּרָ"א זצוק"ל חָלוּ לִהְיוֹת בְּפָרָשַׁת הַשָּׁבוּעַ וַיֵּרָא. הוֹסִיף מָרָן לְבָאֵר "וַיֹּאמֶר אַבְרָהָם כִּי אָמַרְתִּי רַק אֵין יִרְאַת אֱלֹקִים בַּמָּקוֹם הַזֶּה וַהֲרָגוּנִי עַל דְּבַר אִשְׁתִּי" (בְּרֵאשִׁית כ, יא) . . . הַכַּוָּונָה הָיְתָה בְּרוּרָה: בֶּרְלִין מָקוֹם שֶׁל תַּרְבּוּת טֶכְנִיקָה וְצִיוִוילִיזַצְיָה, אַךְ אִם אֵין יִרְאַת שָׁמַיִם, יֵשׁ לַחֲשׁוֹשׁ מִשּׁוּם רֶצַח.

הַיָּמִים הָיוּ רַק הַתְחָלַת יְמֵי שִׁלְטוֹן הָרֶשַׁע (שְׁנַת תרצ"ה אוֹ ו') וְטֶרֶם נִפְתְּחוּ עֵינֵי הַבְּרִיּוֹת לַעֲמוֹד עַל טִיב הַמַּהְפֵּכָה הָאֵיוּמָה שֶׁהִתְחוֹלְלָה בְּגֶרְמַנְיָה דְּאָז. דִּבְרֵי צַדִּיק הַדּוֹר פָּגְעוּ אָז בְּרִגְשׁוֹתַי וְהִרְהַרְתִּי: בָּא גָּאוֹן וְצַדִּיק מֵאֶרֶץ מִזְרָח אֵירוֹפָּאִית, בָּא וּמְבַקֵּשׁ לְבַשֵּׂר לָנוּ שֶׁכָּאן בְּאֶרֶץ "הַתַּרְבּוּת הַנְּאוֹרָה" יִרְצְחוּ בְּאוֹפֶן שְׁרִירוּתִי בְּנֵי אָדָם. כֵּיצַד יִתָּכֵן דָּבָר כָּזֶה? הֲלֹא בִּמְדִינַת חוֹק הַדְּבָרִים אֲמוּרִים? אֶלָּא שֶׁעֵינָיו שֶׁל הַגָּאוֹן הַצַּדִּיק הַזָּקֵן רָאֲתָה לְכַמָּה שָׁנִים בָּעָתִיד הַקָּרוֹב יוֹתֵר מֵאֲשֶׁר עֵינֵי הַצְּעִירוֹת יוֹתֵר . . .

RABBI PINCHAS BIBERFELD
1915–1999

Chief rabbi of Munich. Rabbi Biberfeld was born in Berlin, Germany. He received rabbinical ordination from Rabbi Dr. Yechiel Weinberg. In 1939, he immigrated with his family to Israel, and 11 years later founded the Zlatopol-Chortkov Kollel in Tel Aviv and served as its head for 30 years. In 1984, he returned to Germany where he served as chief rabbi of Munich.

I remember when Rabbi Elchanan Wasserman (may God avenge his blood) visited Berlin and spoke at our rabbinical seminary. . . . His visit was in the week in which the *parashah* of *Vayeira* is read, and he expounded on [Abraham's words to Abimelech], "Only there is no fear of God in this place, and they will kill me" (GENESIS 20:11). . . . The allusion was clear: Berlin may be a center of science and culture, but if there is no fear of Heaven, one should fear for one's life. . . .

This was in the first years of the Nazi regime—in 1935 or '36—and people had no inkling yet of where Germany was headed. I remember being personally insulted by the words of this *tsadik* of the generation. I thought to myself: A great sage and rabbi comes from Eastern Europe to tell us that here, in this civilized and enlightened country, human beings will be murdered with impunity? How is this possible? Is this not a country in which the rule of law prevails? But his sage eyes saw into the near future better than my much younger eyes. . . .

Berlin, ca. 1929. (Photo Credit: Roman Vishniac)

TEXT **8c**

THE LUBAVITCHER REBBE, RABBI MENACHEM MENDEL SCHNEERSON, *SICHOT KODESH*
5741, 3:107–110. TALK DELIVERED NISSAN 11, 5741 (APRIL 15, 1981)

ס׳אִיז יָדוּעַ תּוֹרַת הַבַּעַל שֵׁם טוֹב, אַז דֶער וָואס דֶערוִויסט זִיךְ וֶועלְכֶער
עִנְיָן עָם זָאל זַיין דַארְף עֶר דֶערְפוּן אָפְּלֶערְנֶען אַ הוֹרָאָה בְּנוֹגֵעַ צוּ זִיךְ,
וְעַל אַחַת כַּמָּה וְכַמָּה אַז עִנְיָן כְּלָלִי וָואס הָאט אוֹיפְגֶעטְרֵייסֶלְט דִי
גַאנְצֶע מְדִינָה הָאט אִין זִיךְ אַ הוֹרָאָה, אוּן נִיט אַ הוֹרָאָה אִין "מִדְרָשׁ"
אָדֶער אִין מַחְשָׁבָה - נָאר אַ הוֹרָאָה אִין מַעֲשֶׂה, וְאַדְרַבָּה - "הַמַּעֲשֶׂה
הוּא הָעִיקָר"...

וִוי הָאט גֶעקֶענְט מִלְכַתְּחִילָה פַּאסִירֶן אַז אַ מֶענְטְשׁ זָאל אָפְּטָאן אַזַא
זַאך וָואס אִיז אִינְגַאנְצֶן נִיט פַּארְשְׁטַאנְדִיק, ס׳אִיז נֶגֶד הַשֵּׂכֶל, נֶגֶד הָרֶגֶשׁ
וכו׳?!...אִיז יָדוּעַ דִי טַעֲנָה וָואס מ׳טַעֲנֶה׳ט, אַז דֶער שׁוֹרֶשׁ פוּן מַעֲשִׂים
בִּלְתִּי רְצוּיִים אִיז פַּארְבּוּנְדֶן מִיט עֲנִיּוּת, וָוארוּם וִויבַּאלְד עֶר אִיז בַּעֲנִיּוּת,
בְּמֵילָא בְּרֵיינְגֶט דָאס צוּ פַארְבִּיטֶערוּנְג, אוּן בִּשְׁעַת דָאס בְּרֵיינְגֶט צוּ
פַארְבִּיטֶערוּנְג בְּרֵיינְגֶט דָאס צוּ אַ רֶגֶשׁ שֶׁל נְקָמָה, וְכַיּוֹ"בַּ - וָואס דֶערְפוּן
קוּמֶען מַעֲשִׂים בִּלְתִּי רְצוּיִים.

זֶעט מֶען בְּפוֹעֵל, אַז אָט דֶער וָואס הָאט אָפְּגֶעטָאן אָט דֶער מַעֲשֶׂה - אִיז
נִיט קֵיין בֶּן עָנִי, נָאר אַדְרַבָּה - עֶר אִיז אוֹיפְגֶעוָואקְסָן אַלְס בֶּן עֲשִׁירוּת
וְלֹא עָצְבוֹ אָבִיו מִיָּמָיו, אוּן עֶס וַויַיזְט אוֹיס אַז מ׳הָאט פוּן אִים קֵיין זַאך
נִיט גֶעזְשַׁאלֶעוֶועט...דֶעם שׁוֹרֶשׁ פוּן הַנְהָגָה בִּלְתִּי רְצוּיִ׳ דַארְף מֶען
זוּכֶן נִיט אִין עֲנִיּוּת, נָאר עֶרְגֶעץ אַנְדֶערְשׁ ווּאוּ...

וְוִויבַּאלְד ס׳אִיז אוֹיסְגֶעשְׁטֶעלְט גֶעוָוארֶן אַז חִינּוּךְ אִיז גֶעגנּוּג אַז
מ׳קְלַייבְּט צוּזַאמֶען יְדִיעוֹת...נִיט פַּארְבּוּנְדֶן מִיט דֶער מַטָרָה פוּן
אַרָאפְבְּרֵיינְגֶען טוֹב אֲמִיתִּי פַּאר זִיךְ, אוּן טוֹב פַּאר דֶער אַרוּם, נִיט
פַּארְבּוּנְדֶן מִיט אוֹיסְפּוּרֶ֫עמֶען דֶעם יֵצֶר לֵב הָאָדָם...אַז דֶער חִינּוּךְ אִיז
נִיט דוּרְכְגֶענוּמֶען מִיט אֱמוּנָה כִּדְבָעֵי, אַז ס׳אִיז דָא אַ אֵיינֶער מִיט אַן "עַיִן
רוֹאָה וְאוֹזֶן שׁוֹמַעַת" - הָאט עֶר קֵיינְמָאל נִיט גֶעהֶערְט אִין אַן אוֹפֶן פוּן
דְּבָרִים הַיוֹצְאִים מִן הַלֵּב...נָאר מ׳גִיט אִים דִי מֶעגְלִיכְקֵייט אַז עֶר זָאל
צוּזַאמֶענקְלַייבְּן יְדִיעוֹת אוּן זָאל דָאס דֶערְנָאךְ קֶענֶען נוּצֶן אַז וִוי ס׳וֶועט
זַיין "יָשָׁר בְּעֵינָיו" אָט אַזוֹי אִיז "יַעֲשֶׂה".

There is a well-known teaching of the Ba'al Shem Tov, that when a person learns of a certain event, they should derive from it a lesson concerning their own conduct. Certainly, then, we should derive a lesson from the recent national event [the shooting of President Ronald Reagan by John Hinckley, Jr., on March 30, 1981]. that shook the entire country—not just a theoretical lesson, but one that applies in action. . . .

How did it happen that a person did such an irrational act? . . . There is a common argument that poverty is the root of all criminal action: poverty causes resentment, which causes feelings of vengefulness, which leads to criminal action.

But the person who perpetrated this crime came from a wealthy family, and his parents seem to have indulged his every need. . . . The root of his actions must be found elsewhere. . . .

The education that children receive today is focused on the accumulation of knowledge, without regard to the purpose toward which this knowledge should be directed—to creating true goodness for oneself, true goodness for one's surroundings, and to improve one's character and train oneself to behave in a moral manner. . . . The education is not permeated with the belief that there is a Higher Authority to whom one is responsible—an "Eye that sees and an Ear that hears." . . . As a result, the education the child receives is wholly self-serving, and they feel entitled to use this knowledge for any purpose they desire. . . .

TEXT 9

THE LUBAVITCHER REBBE, RABBI MENACHEM MENDEL SCHNEERSON,
CORRESPONDENCE, NISAN 26, 5724 (APRIL 8, 1964), WWW.CHABAD.ORG/2051611 ⊕

Some would argue . . . that the principle of separation of State and Church must be maintained at all costs, in order to prevent a resurgence of religious persecution so prevalent in the Middle Ages, when an established state religion denied equal, or any, rights to other religions, etc.

The fallacy of this argument should be quite obvious. By way of illustration: Suppose a person was ill at one time and doctors prescribed certain medication and treatment. Suppose that years later the same person became ill again, but with an entirely different, in fact quite contrary, malady. Would it be reasonable to recommend the same medication and treatment as formerly?

In medieval times the world suffered from an "excess" of religious zeal and intolerance. In our day the world is suffering from an excessive indifference to religion, or even from a growing materialism and atheism.

TEXT **10**

RABBI JOSEPH GLASER, CITED IN JONATHAN D. SARNA AND DAVID G. DALIN, *RELIGION AND STATE IN THE AMERICAN JEWISH EXPERIENCE* (NOTRE DAME, IN: UNIVERSITY OF NOTRE DAME PRESS, 2002), PP. 294–297

I must disagree with your opinion that there is some intrinsic value to individual Jews involved in the public lighting and blessing of the Hanukkiot. I think it might be just the opposite. Ultimately, the survival of Judaism depends on the home, which is where the Hanukkia should be lit. People coming to public places to observe (not really participate in) the ceremony are being involved in a kind of public, almost flamboyant religious exercise instead of a sacred home ritual.

**RABBI JOSEPH GLASER
1925–1994**

Born in Boston, Glaser was wounded twice as an infantryman in Europe during World War II. He graduated from UCLA in 1948 and received a law degree from the University of S. Francisco in 1951. From 1956 to 1959, he was the rabbi of Temple Beth Torah in Ventura, California, a Reform congregation. Later he became the executive vice president of the Central Conference of American Rabbis, the association of Reform rabbis.

Chabad of Philadelphia conducts the public menorah lighting in front of Independence Hall, 1974. (Photo Credit: Lubavitch Archives)

TEXT 11

I KINGS 19:11–13

> וְרוּחַ גְּדוֹלָה וְחָזָק מְפָרֵק הָרִים וּמְשַׁבֵּר סְלָעִים לִפְנֵי ה' לֹא בָרוּחַ ה' וְאַחַר הָרוּחַ רַעַשׁ לֹא בָרַעַשׁ ה'.
>
> וְאַחַר הָרַעַשׁ אֵשׁ לֹא בָאֵשׁ ה' וְאַחַר הָאֵשׁ קוֹל דְּמָמָה דַקָּה.
>
> וַיְהִי כִּשְׁמֹעַ אֵלִיָּהוּ וַיָּלֶט פָּנָיו בְּאַדַּרְתּוֹ וַיֵּצֵא וַיַּעֲמֹד פֶּתַח הַמְּעָרָה וְהִנֵּה אֵלָיו קוֹל . . .

A great, strong wind rent the mountains and shattered the rocks before God; but God was not in the wind. After the wind came a storm, but God was not in the storm. After the storm came fire, but God was not in the fire. After the fire came a small, still voice.

When Elijah heard this, he wrapped his face in his mantle, and he went out and stood at the entrance to the cave; and behold, the voice came to him. . . .

TEXT 12a

EXODUS 19:16–20 ⬚

וַיְהִי בַיּוֹם הַשְּׁלִישִׁי בִּהְיֹת הַבֹּקֶר וַיְהִי קֹלֹת וּבְרָקִים וְעָנָן כָּבֵד עַל הָהָר וְקֹל שֹׁפָר חָזָק מְאֹד וַיֶּחֱרַד כָּל הָעָם אֲשֶׁר בַּמַּחֲנֶה.

וַיּוֹצֵא מֹשֶׁה אֶת הָעָם לִקְרַאת הָאֱלֹהִים מִן הַמַּחֲנֶה וַיִּתְיַצְּבוּ בְּתַחְתִּית הָהָר.

וְהַר סִינַי עָשַׁן כֻּלּוֹ מִפְּנֵי אֲשֶׁר יָרַד עָלָיו ה' בָּאֵשׁ וַיַּעַל עֲשָׁנוֹ כְּעֶשֶׁן הַכִּבְשָׁן וַיֶּחֱרַד כָּל הָהָר מְאֹד.

וַיְהִי קוֹל הַשֹּׁפָר הוֹלֵךְ וְחָזֵק מְאֹד מֹשֶׁה יְדַבֵּר וְהָאֱלֹהִים יַעֲנֶנּוּ בְקוֹל.

וַיֵּרֶד ה' עַל הַר סִינַי אֶל רֹאשׁ הָהָר.

It came to pass on the third day when it was morning, that there were thunderclaps and lightning flashes, and a thick cloud was upon the mountain, and a very powerful blast of a shofar, and the entire nation that was in the camp trembled.

Moses brought the people out toward God from the camp, and they stood at the bottom of the mountain.

The entire Mount Sinai smoked because God had descended upon it in fire, and its smoke ascended like the smoke of the kiln, and the entire mountain trembled exceedingly.

The sound of the shofar grew increasingly stronger; Moses would speak and God would answer him with a voice.

And God descended upon Mount Sinai, to the top of the mountain.

TEXT 12b

EXODUS 34:1–3 🎏

וַיֹּאמֶר ה' אֶל מֹשֶׁה פְּסָל לְךָ שְׁנֵי לֻחֹת אֲבָנִים כָּרִאשֹׁנִים וְכָתַבְתִּי עַל הַלֻּחֹת
אֶת הַדְּבָרִים אֲשֶׁר הָיוּ עַל הַלֻּחֹת הָרִאשֹׁנִים אֲשֶׁר שִׁבַּרְתָּ.
וֶהְיֵה נָכוֹן לַבֹּקֶר וְעָלִיתָ בַבֹּקֶר אֶל הַר סִינַי וְנִצַּבְתָּ לִי שָׁם עַל רֹאשׁ הָהָר.
וְאִישׁ לֹא יַעֲלֶה עִמָּךְ וְגַם אִישׁ אַל יֵרָא בְּכָל הָהָר גַּם הַצֹּאן וְהַבָּקָר אַל יִרְעוּ
אֶל מוּל הָהָר הַהוּא.

God said to Moses: "Hew for yourself two stone tablets like the first ones. And I will write upon the tablets the words that were on the first tablets, which you broke.

"Be prepared for the morning, and in the morning you shall ascend Mount Sinai and stand before Me there on the top of the mountain.

"No one shall ascend with you, neither shall anyone be seen anywhere on the mountain; neither shall the sheep and the cattle graze facing that mountain."

TEXT 12c

RASHI, AD LOC.

הָרִאשׁוֹנוֹת עַל יְדֵי שֶׁהָיוּ בִּתְשׁוּאוֹת וְקוֹלוֹת וּקְהִלָּה, שָׁלְטָה בָּהֶן עַיִן רָעָה.
אֵין לְךָ מִדָּה יָפָה מִן הַצְּנִיעוּת.

Because the First Tablets were accompanied by commotion, noise, and crowds, the evil eye affected them [and they were destroyed]. For there is no greater virtue than modesty.

RABBI SHLOMO YITSCHAKI (RASHI), 1040–1105

Most noted biblical and Talmudic commentator. Born in Troyes, France, Rashi studied in the famed *yeshivot* of Mainz and Worms. His commentaries on the Pentateuch and the Talmud, which focus on the straightforward meaning of the text, appear in virtually every edition of the Talmud and Bible.

TEXT 13a

RABBI YOSEF CARO AND RABBI MOSHE ISSERLES, SHULCHAN ARUCH, *ORACH CHAYIM* 1:1

יִתְגַּבֵּר כָּאֲרִי לַעֲמוֹד בַּבּוֹקֶר לַעֲבוֹדַת בּוֹרְאוֹ . . . וְלֹא יִתְבַּיֵּישׁ מִפְּנֵי בְּנֵי אָדָם
הַמַּלְעִיגִים עָלָיו בַּעֲבוֹדַת הַשֵּׁם יִתְבָּרֵךְ.

Be strong as a lion to get up in the morning to serve your Creator . . . and do not be intimidated by those who mock your service of God.

RABBI YOSEF CARO (MARAN, *BEIT YOSEF*) 1488–1575

Rabbi Caro was born in Spain, but was forced to flee during the expulsion in 1492. His magnum opus, the Shulchan Aruch (Code of Jewish Law), has been universally accepted as the basis for modern Jewish law.

RABBI MOSHE ISSERLES (REMA) 1525–1572

Rema served as rabbi in Krakow, Poland, and is considered the definitive authority on Jewish law among Ashkenazic Jewry. Rema authored glosses on the Shulchan Aruch (known as the *Mapah*) and *Darchei Moshe*, a commentary on the halachic compendium *Arba'ah Turim*.

TEXT 13b

THE LUBAVITCHER REBBE, RABBI MENACHEM MENDEL SCHNEERSON,
IGROT KODESH 15:116

וּמַה נִּפְלָא, שֶׁנְּקוּדָה זוֹ דְתוֹקֶף הָרָצוֹן שֶׁלֹּא יֵבוֹשׁ מִפְּנֵי הַמַּלְעִיגִים, הִיא
הַתְחָלַת כָּל ד' חֶלְקֵי הַשֻּׁלְחָן עָרוּךְ. שֶׁמּוּבָן מִיַּד עַד כַּמָּה נוֹגֵעַ הָעִנְיָן
בְּקִיּוּם כָּל דִּינֵי תּוֹרָתֵנוּ תּוֹרַת חַיִּים . . . זֶהוּ עִנְיָנוֹ שֶׁל כָּל אֶחָד וְאַחַת
מִבְּנֵי יִשְׂרָאֵל, אֲשֶׁר תָּמִיד הָיוּ הַמְעַט מִכָּל הָעַמִּים, וְתָמִיד הָיוּ מְצוּיָנִים,
אֲפִילוּ בַּגָּלוּת הַיּוֹתֵר קָשָׁה, בְּכָל עִנְיְנֵיהֶם. וְרַק עַל יְדֵי הַנְהָגָה כָזוֹ, נִצָּבִים
הֵם וְקַיָּמִים עַד לְיָמֵינוּ אֵלֶּה, וּבְקָרוֹב יִזְכּוּ לִגְאוּלָה הַשְּׁלֵמָה וְהָאֲמִתִּית.

How amazing it is that this principle—the steadfast determination to "not be intimidated by those who mock one's service of God"—is the very beginning of all four sections of the Shulchan Aruch. So it is readily understood how crucial this is to the fulfillment of all the laws of our Torah, our guidance in life. . . .

This is what a Jew is all about. We have always been the "least numerous among the nations." But we always retained our distinctiveness in every area of our lives, even in the most difficult of our exiles. It is only due to this behavior that we survived to this day, and through which we will soon merit the true and complete redemption.

TEXT 14

RABBI MOSHE AMIEL, *DERASHOT EL AMI* 3:88–89

The *haskalah* movement popularized the slogan, "Be a human being in the street, and a Jew at home." Though this is but a sentence consisting of a few words, it perforated the very core of Judaism. . . .

In truth, this slogan is consistent with the *haskalah*'s borrowing of its values and frames of reference from outside sources. If Judaism is only a *religion*, then there is indeed no religion that encompasses the totality of the person. A "religion" suffices with a certain area of their personhood; the person's religion and the person's humanity remain two separate domains, neither of which encroaches on the other. If the religion is relegated to a place in the person's private life, concealed in the inner recesses of their home like contraband, it should be satisfied with that.

Yet how far the model is from the original, authentic Judaism: the Judaism that is *torat chayim*, the "teaching of life"; the Judaism that is the soul of the Jewish nation! As the soul permeates the entire body, so does the Torah permeate us from head to toe. "No place is void of Him" (ZOHAR, TIKUNIM 57); "Delve into [the Torah], delve into it, for all is in it" (ETHICS OF THE FATHERS, 5:21). There can be no differentiating between

RABBI MOSHE AVIGDOR AMIEL
1883–1946

Religious thinker and author. Rabbi Amiel was a student of Rabbi Chaim Soloveitchik and Rabbi Chaim Ozer Grodzinski. A chief ideologue of religious Zionism, he was elected chief rabbi of Tel Aviv in 1936. Amiel's first halachic publication was *Darchei Moshe*, followed by his three-volume *Hamidot Lecheker Hahalachah*. A renowned preacher, he published the homiletic works *Derashot El Ami* and *Hegyonot El Ami*.

the "human being" and the "Jew" in us. All that is human in us is Jewish.

TEXT 15

RABBI HERBERT WEINER, *9½ MYSTICS: THE KABBALA TODAY* (NEW YORK: TOUCHSTONE, 1997), PP. 191–196

I pressed my question from another angle and told him [the Rebbe] that I sensed a desire in Chabad to over-simplify, to strip ideas of their complexity merely for the sake of a superficial clarity. As a matter of fact, I blurted out, all his Hasidim seemed to have one thing in common: a sort of open and naive look in their eyes that a sympathetic observer might call *t'mimut* (purity) but that might less kindly be interpreted as emptiness or simple-mindedness, the absence of inner struggle.

I found myself taken aback by my own boldness, but the rebbe showed no resentment. He leaned forward. "What you see missing from their eyes is a *kera*!"

"A what?" I asked.

"Yes, a *kera*," he repeated quietly, "a split." The rebbe hesitated for a moment. "I hope you will not take offense, but something tells me you don't sleep well at night, and this is not good for 'length of days.' Perhaps if you had been raised wholly in one world or in another,

RABBI HERBERT WEINER
1919–2013

Born in Boston, Weiner graduated from the University of Massachusetts at Amherst in 1942. During World War II, he served as a radio officer in the Merchant Marine. In 1948, Weiner became the founding rabbi of Temple Israel of South Orange, N.J., a Reform congregation, and served there until his retirement in 1982. Weiner was the author of two books: *9½ Mystics*, and *The Wild Goats of Ein Gedi*, both of which were recipients of the National Jewish Book Award.

it might be different. But this split is what comes from trying to live in two worlds." . . .

Indeed, I thought, there is no split at Lubavitch. It offered its followers a world in which the mind was never confused by contradictions; where life was not compartmentalized; where the tensions between heart and mind, flesh and soul, God and His creation were all dissolved in the unity of a higher plan.

TEXT **16a**

MAIMONIDES, *MISHNEH TORAH*, LAWS OF CHANUKAH 3:3

> הִתְקִינוּ חֲכָמִים שֶׁבְּאוֹתוֹ הַדּוֹר שֶׁיִּהְיוּ שְׁמוֹנַת הַיָּמִים הָאֵלּוּ, שֶׁתְּחִלָּתָן
> כ"ה בְּכִסְלֵו, יְמֵי שִׂמְחָה וְהַלֵּל. וּמַדְלִיקִין בָּהֶן הַנֵּרוֹת בָּעֶרֶב עַל פִּתְחֵי
> הַבָּתִּים, בְּכָל לַיְלָה וְלַיְלָה מִשְּׁמוֹנַת הַלֵּילוֹת, לְהַרְאוֹת וּלְגַלּוֹת הַנֵּס.

RABBI MOSHE BEN MAIMON (MAIMONIDES, RAMBAM), 1135–1204
Halachist, philosopher, author, and physician. Maimonides was born in Cordoba, Spain. After the conquest of Cordoba by the Almohads, he fled Spain and eventually settled in Cairo, Egypt. There, he became the leader of the Jewish community and served as court physician to the vizier of Egypt. He is most noted for authoring the *Mishneh Torah*, an encyclopedic arrangement of Jewish law, and for his philosophical work, *Guide for the Perplexed*. His rulings on Jewish law are integral to the formation of halachic consensus.

The sages of that generation [of the Chanukah miracle] ordained that these eight days, beginning on the twenty-fifth of Kislev, should be days of rejoicing and praising God. Each and every evening of these eight nights we kindle the [Chanukah] lights in the doorways of our houses, to display and publicize the miracle.

TEXT **16**b

RABBI YOSEF CARO AND RABBI MOSHE ISSERLES, SHULCHAN ARUCH, *ORACH CHAYIM* 671:7

מַדְלִיקִין וּמְבָרְכִין (בְּבֵית הַכְּנֶסֶת) מִשׁוּם פִּרְסוּמֵי נִיסָא. וְאֵין אָדָם יוֹצֵא בְּנֵרוֹת שֶׁל בֵּית הַכְּנֶסֶת, וְצָרִיךְ לַחֲזוֹר וּלְהַדְלִיק בְּבֵיתוֹ.

The Chanukah lights are lit, and the blessings are recited over them, in the synagogue, in order to publicize the miracle. A person, however, does not fulfill their obligation with the lights of the synagogue, and should also light at home.

Children holding signs bearing a proud Jewish message at a Lag Ba'omer parade, 1973. (Photo Credit: Lubavitch Archives)

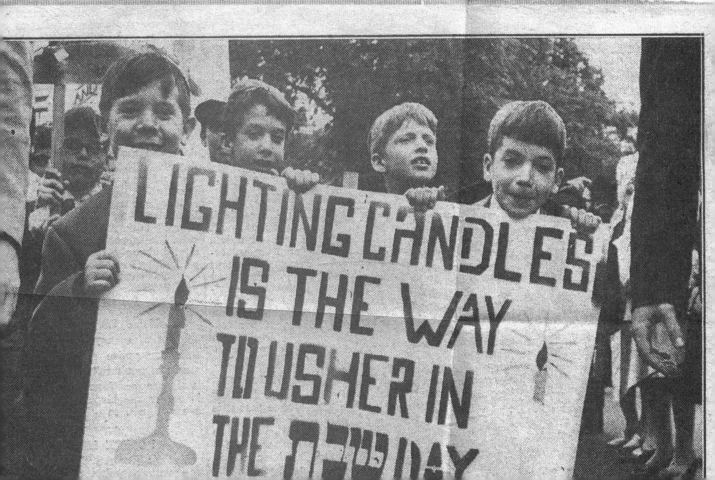

TEXT 17

RABBI LORD JONATHAN SACKS, "A JUDAISM ENGAGED WITH THE WORLD,"
PP. 9–14

The Jewish world today represents the working through of processes begun in mainland Europe long before the Holocaust. Faced with societies that did not accept them as Jews, a fateful choice framed itself in many Jewish minds: either to enter society and abandon their Jewishness, or to preserve their Jewishness at the cost of turning their back on society. There were, it seemed, just two options . . . assimilation or segregation. . . .

[Both] are a failure of nerve in the Judaic project. Can it really be that Judaism has nothing to contribute to society and to the world? Can it be that when Jews engage with the world they have to hide their identity, acting as if they were twenty-first-century equivalents of the Marranos of Spain, Jews in secret but not in public? Are Jewish faith and practice so fragile that they can only be sustained by being screened from all contact with other cultures?

It was once so but it is not so today. The Jewish situation has changed decisively. . . . Jews have sovereignty and independence in Israel, freedom and equality in the Diaspora. . . . We must stop feeling defensive about being Jewish and engage with the world with humility but without fear.

RABBI LORD JONATHAN SACKS, PHD
1948–

Former chief rabbi of the United Kingdom. Rabbi Sacks attended Cambridge University and received his doctorate from King's College, London. A prolific and influential author, his books include *Will We Have Jewish Grandchildren?* and *The Dignity of Difference*. He received the Jerusalem Prize in 1995 for his contributions to enhancing Jewish life in the Diaspora, was knighted and made a life peer in 2005, and became Baron Sacks of Aldridge in 2009.

TEXT 18a

EXODUS 28:31–35 ⊕

וְעָשִׂיתָ אֶת מְעִיל הָאֵפוֹד כְּלִיל תְּכֵלֶת . . .

וְעָשִׂיתָ עַל שׁוּלָיו רִמֹּנֵי תְּכֵלֶת וְאַרְגָּמָן וְתוֹלַעַת שָׁנִי עַל שׁוּלָיו סָבִיב
וּפַעֲמֹנֵי זָהָב בְּתוֹכָם סָבִיב.

פַּעֲמֹן זָהָב וְרִמּוֹן פַּעֲמֹן זָהָב וְרִמּוֹן עַל שׁוּלֵי הַמְּעִיל סָבִיב.

וְהָיָה עַל אַהֲרֹן לְשָׁרֵת וְנִשְׁמַע קוֹלוֹ בְּבֹאוֹ אֶל הַקֹּדֶשׁ לִפְנֵי ה' וּבְצֵאתוֹ
וְלֹא יָמוּת.

Make the [priestly] robe, completely of blue wool. . . .

And make on its hem pomegranates of blue, purple, and scarlet wool; and bells of gold between them all around. A golden bell and a pomegranate, a golden bell and a pomegranate, on the bottom hem of the robe, all around.

It shall be upon Aaron when he serves. Its sound shall be heard when he enters into the holy before God and when he leaves, lest he die.

TEXT 18b

TALMUD, MAKOT 24A–B

כְּבָר הָיָה רַבָּן גַּמְלִיאֵל וְרַבִּי אֶלְעָזָר בֶּן עֲזַרְיָה וְרַבִּי יְהוֹשֻׁעַ וְרַבִּי עֲקִיבָא מְהַלְכִין בַּדֶּרֶךְ, וְשָׁמְעוּ קוֹל הַמּוֹנָהּ שֶׁל רוֹמִי מִפְּלָטָהּ [בְּרִחוּק] מֵאָה וְעֶשְׂרִים מִיל. וְהִתְחִילוּ בּוֹכִין, וְרַבִּי עֲקִיבָא מְשַׂחֵק.

אָמְרוּ לוֹ: מִפְּנֵי מָה אַתָּה מְשַׂחֵק?

אָמַר לָהֶם: וְאַתֶּם, מִפְּנֵי מָה אַתֶּם בּוֹכִים?

אָמְרוּ לוֹ: הַלָּלוּ כּוּשִׁיִּים, שֶׁמִּשְׁתַּחֲוִים לָעֲצַבִּים וּמְקַטְּרִים לַעֲבוֹדַת כּוֹכָבִים, יוֹשְׁבִין בֶּטַח וְהַשְׁקֵט, וְאָנוּ בֵּית הֲדוֹם רַגְלֵי אֱלֹקֵינוּ שָׂרוּף בָּאֵשׁ, וְלֹא נִבְכֶּה?

אָמַר לָהֶן: לְכָךְ אֲנִי מְצַחֵק. וּמָה לְעוֹבְרֵי רְצוֹנוֹ כָּךְ, לְעוֹשֵׂי רְצוֹנוֹ עַל אַחַת כַּמָּה וְכַמָּה!

It happened that Rabban Gamliel, Rabbi Elazar ben Azariah, Rabbi Joshua, and Rabbi Akiva were traveling, when they heard the commotion of the mobs of Rome from a distance of one hundred and twenty *mil*. They began to weep, but Rabbi Akiva laughed.

Said they to him: "Why are you laughing?"

Said he to them: "Why are you weeping?"

Said they to him: "These barbarians, who prostrate themselves before statues and sacrifice to idols, dwell happy and secure, while we—the footstool of our God was consumed by fire. Shall we not weep?

Said he to them: "That is why I am laughing. If for the transgressors of God's will it is so, how much more so is it for those who do God's will."

TEXT 18c

THE LUBAVITCHER REBBE, RABBI MENACHEM MENDEL SCHNEERSON,
LIKUTEI SICHOT 16:341 🕮

פֿון כָּל הַנַּ"ל אִיז דָא אַ הוֹרָאָה מְיוּחֶדֶת פֿאַר דּוֹרֵנוּ זֶה - דָּרָא דְעִקְבְתָא
דִמְשִׁיחָא:

עֶס זײַנען פֿאַראַן אַזעלכע וואָס טַעֲנֶה'ן: הֵן אֱמֶת אַז מִצַּד דֶעם שְׁפַל
הַמַּצָּב פֿון אונזער דּור מוז מֶען זיך פֿאַרנעמען מיט הַרְבָּצַת הַתּוֹרָה
וְהַחֲזָקַת הַיַּהֲדוּת וְכוּ'; און מ'קען זיך ניט מִסְתַּפֵּק זײַן מיט זיצן אין די
אייגענע ד' אַמּוֹת (אֲפִילוּ אִין דִי ד' אַמּוֹת שֶׁל תּוֹרָה) און וואַרטן ביז
מ'וועט זיך וועְנדן צו אים און בֶּעטן עֶר זאָל מֵפִיץ זײַן תּוֹרָה וְכוּ' נָאר
מ'דאַרף אַרוֹיסגֵיין אין "דְרוֹיסן" אין חוצה און געפֿינען אידן "נִדָּחִים"
און פֿון זיי "מאַכן בַּעֲלֵי תְּשׁוּבָה" -

וואָס אִיז אָבֶּער דֶער הֶכְרֵח צו טאָן אָט די אַרבֶּעט מיט קוֹל רַעַשׁ גָּדוֹל?
פֿאַרוואָס אִיז אַזוֹי נוֹיטִיק צו אַרוֹיסגֵיין אִין גאַס און דאָרט אוֹיסרוּפֿן
בְּקוֹל רָם אַז אידן זאָלן לֵייגן תְּפִילִין, אָנקלאַפֿן מְזוּזוֹת אוֹיף די טִירן,
געבן צְדָקָה וְכַיּוֹצֵא בָּזֶה - אַ הַנְהָגָה וואָס מ'געפֿינט ניט אַ שְׁטוּרעם בָּזֶה
אין די פֿריִערדיקע דוֹרוֹת?

אִיז דֶער עֶנטפֶֿער אוֹיף דֶעם: לוֹיט אַלֶע סִימָנִים פֿון סוֹף מַסֶּכֶת סוֹטָה
זֶעט מֶען אַז מיר געפֿינען זיך אִיצט אין דָּרָא אִין דְעִקְבְתָא דִמְשִׁיחָא - אִין
דֶער דַּרְגָא הַיּוֹתֵר תַּחְתּוֹנָה - "שׁוּלֵי הַמְעִיל"; דאַרף מֶען וויסן זײַן, אַז
בְּשׁוּלֵי הַמְעִיל דאַרפֿן זײַן די "פַּעֲמוֹנִים" - אַז די כְּנִיסָה פֿון דֶעם סוּג
אִידן "אֶל הַקּוֹדֶשׁ", תַּחַת כַּנְפֵי הַשְּׁכִינָה אִיז אוֹיסגעשׁטעלט אִין אַן
אוֹפֿן פֿון "וְנִשְׁמַע קוֹלוֹ"; וְאַדְרַבָּה - דַּוְקָא אִין דֶעם "רַעַשׁ" פֿון עֲבוֹדַת
הַתְּשׁוּבָה אִיז דֶער תַּכְלִית הָעִלּוּי, כַּנַּ"ל.

נאָך אַן עִנְיָן אִין דֶעם:

בְּשָׁעַת מ'וועט אַז בַּיי "עוֹבְרֵי רְצוֹנוֹ" אִיז דָא "קוֹל הַמוֹנָה שֶׁל רוֹמִי" -
אַלֶע עִנְיָנִים פֿון לְעוּמַת זֶה וועְרן געטאָן ניט בְּחַדְרֵי חֲדָרִים נאָר מיט
דֶעם גְרעסטן פִּרְסוּם וְרַעַשׁ -

אִיז דֶער וועג צו מְבַטֵּל זײַן דֶעם שְׁטוּרעם פֿון סִטְרָא אַחֲרָא - "בְּמִינָה
וּדְגַמָתָה . . . מִינֵי' גוּבֵי' אַבָּא לִשְׁדֵי' בֵּי' נַרְגָּא", דאָס הֵייסט דוּרכדֶעם
וואָס אוֹיך די עֲבוֹדָה פֿון "עוֹשֵׂי רְצוֹנוֹ" אִיז אִין אַן אוֹפֿן פֿון "וְנִשְׁמַע קוֹלוֹ"
און דַּוְקָא אִין דֶעם אָרט וואו עֶס געפֿינט זיך "קוֹל הַמוֹנָה שֶׁל רוֹמִי";

אוּן דָאס וֶועט בְּרֶענגֶען צוּ "מַה לְעוֹבְרֵי רְצוֹנוֹ כַּךְ לְעוֹשֵׂי רְצוֹנוֹ עַל אַחַת
כַּמָה וְכַמָה" - אַז בַּיי אִידְן וֶועט זַיין "יוֹשְׁבִין בֶּטַח וְהַשְׁקֵט עַל אַדְמָתָם",
דוּרְךְ "יִתָּקַע בְּשׁוֹפָר גָדוֹל" דַוְקָא, דוּרְךְ דֶעם "קוֹל מְבַשֵׂר מְבַשֵׂר וְאוֹמֵר"
- מְבַשֵׂר הַגְאוּלָה בְּקָרוֹב מַמָשׁ.

This provides us with a special lesson for our generation—the generation of the "footsteps of Mashiach."

There are those who present the following argument: It
is true, they say, that due to the impoverished spiritual
state of our generation, we need to engage in the dissemination of Torah and the strengthening of Judaism.
We cannot settle for remaining in our own inner sanctum—be it even the inner sanctum of Torah—and wait
to be asked to teach Torah, etc. Rather, we must venture
out to "the outside," search out "lost" Jews, and "bring
them back into the fold."

Why, however, must this work be done with such commotion and noise? Why is it necessary to go out into
the street and loudly broadcast there, calling on Jews
to put on *tefilin*, affix *mezuzot* on their doorposts, give
charity, and so on? We don't find any precedent for such
tumultuous behavior in previous generations.

The answer to this argument is: According to all the
signs provided in the Talmud, we see that we are now
in the "generation of the footsteps of Mashiach"—the
lowest level, the "hem of the robe." We should therefore

remember that on the hem of the robe there need to be "bells," and that the "entering into the holy before God" of these Jews occurs in a manner of "its sound shall be heard." In fact, the "noise" that the return of these souls produces is a most lofty virtue.

Another point:

We see that, on the part of "the transgressors of God's will," there is "the commotion of the mobs of Rome"—in unholy matters, everything is done not in privacy, but with the greatest publicity and commotion. Therefore, the way to counteract the noise of the "other side" is with its own methodology, by fighting fire with fire. Meaning, that the efforts of "those who do God's will" is in a manner that "its sound shall be heard" in the very places where "the commotion of the mobs of Rome" asserts itself.

This will in turn bring about the fulfillment [of Rabbi Akiva's statement,] "If for the transgressors of God's will it is so, how much more so is it for those who do God's will." That the Jewish people will be settled on their land in security and tranquility, when "the great shofar blast would be sounded," and the "voice that announces, announces and proclaims" heralds the imminent Redemption.

KEY POINTS

1 In the 1970s, Chabad began erecting large Chanukah menorahs and conducting menorah lighting ceremonies in public places. Some Jewish organizations objected to this practice and even filed lawsuits against it, which eventually reached the Supreme Court of the United States.

2 The First Amendment of the U.S. Constitution forbids the government to enact any law "respecting an establishment of religion." Some understand this as precluding any government support of religion in any form. Other judges and legal scholars argue that an absolute "wall of seperation" in fact discriminates against religion, and violates the "Free Exercise" clause of the First Amendment.

3 Historically, the Jewish people suffered greatly when the government under which they lived was aligned with other religions. This led to a feeling that it is a Jewish interest to advocate an absolute "wall of separation" between religion and state.

4 History has shown us that the lack of a belief in a Higher Authority to whom a person is responsible for their actions leads to lawlessness and inhumanity exceeding the evils fueled by religious fanaticism. Hence the argument that we should advocate for more religion in the public sphere.

5 Tsnius—modesty and privacy—is an important Jewish value, especially in regard to things we hold special and sacred. On the other hand, Jewish pride is not only an important value in Judaism, but crucial to Jewish survival.

6 Judaism is not a "religion," but a way of being and living that embraces the totality of the person. A healthy Jewish identity does not create artificial divisions between our "private" and "public" self.

7 In a world where everything is about public display and attention-grabbing gimmickry, we need to "fight fire with fire" and utilize those very phenomena for holy purposes.

Visit
facebook.com/myJLI
to vote on the following question:

How public should we be about our Jewishness?

1 Religious belief is a personal matter and should remain that way.

2 Religion in the public sphere is dangerous for minority groups because it will lead to discrimination.

3 Jewish pride is essential for Jewish survival. We have survived because we have not hidden our identities and convictions.

Appendix

TEXT 19

MAIMONIDES, *MISHNEH TORAH*, LAWS OF KINGS 11:4 ⚏

וְזֶה גָּרַם לְאַבֵּד יִשְׂרָאֵל בַּחֶרֶב וּלְפַזֵּר שְׁאֵרִיתָם וּלְהַשְׁפִּילָם וּלְהַחֲלִיף
הַתּוֹרָה וּלְהַטְעוֹת רוֹב הָעוֹלָם לַעֲבֹד אֱלוֹהַּ מִבַּלְעֲדֵי ה'. אַךְ מַחְשְׁבוֹת
בּוֹרֵא עוֹלָם אֵין כֹּחַ בָּאָדָם לְהַשִּׂיגָם כִּי לֹא דְרָכֵינוּ דְּרָכָיו וְלֹא מַחְשְׁבוֹתֵינוּ
מַחְשְׁבוֹתָיו. וְכָל הַדְּבָרִים הָאֵלּוּ שֶׁל יֵשׁוּעַ הַנָּצְרִי וְשֶׁל זֶה הַיִּשְׁמְעֵאלִי
שֶׁעָמַד אַחֲרָיו אֵינָן אֶלָּא לְיַשֵּׁר דֶּרֶךְ לְמֶלֶךְ הַמָּשִׁיחַ וּלְתַקֵּן אֶת הָעוֹלָם כּוּלוֹ
לַעֲבוֹד אֶת ה' בְּיַחַד . . .

כֵּיצַד? כְּבַר נִתְמַלֵּא הָעוֹלָם כּוּלוֹ מִדִּבְרֵי הַמָּשִׁיחַ וּמִדִּבְרֵי הַתּוֹרָה וּמִדִּבְרֵי
הַמִּצְווֹת וּפָשְׁטוּ דְּבָרִים אֵלּוּ בְּאִיִּים רְחוֹקִים וּבְעַמִּים רַבִּים עַרְלֵי לֵב וְהֵם
נוֹשְׂאִים וְנוֹתְנִים בִּדְבָרִים אֵלּוּ וּבְמִצְווֹת הַתּוֹרָה אֵלּוּ אוֹמְרִים מִצְווֹת אֵלּוּ
אֱמֶת הָיוּ וּכְבָר בָּטְלוּ בַּזְּמַן הַזֶּה וְלֹא הָיוּ נוֹהֲגוֹת לְדוֹרוֹת וְאֵלּוּ אוֹמְרִים
דְּבָרִים נִסְתָּרוֹת יֵשׁ בָּהֶם וְאֵינָן כִּפְשׁוּטָן וּכְבָר בָּא מָשִׁיחַ וְגִלָּה נִסְתְּרֵיהֶם.
וּכְשֶׁיַּעֲמוֹד הַמֶּלֶךְ הַמָּשִׁיחַ בֶּאֱמֶת וְיַצְלִיחַ וְיָרוּם וְיִנָּשֵׂא מִיַּד הֵם כּוּלָן
חוֹזְרִין וְיוֹדְעִים שֶׁשֶּׁקֶר נָחֲלוּ אֲבוֹתֵיהֶם וְשֶׁנְּבִיאֵיהֶם וַאֲבוֹתֵיהֶם הִטְעוּם.

[Christianity] caused the Jews to be slain by the sword, their remnants to be scattered and humbled, the Torah to be altered, and the majority of the world to err and serve a god other than God. Yet the intent of the Creator of the world is not within the power of man to comprehend, for His ways are not our ways, nor are His thoughts our thoughts. Ultimately, all the teachings of Jesus of Nazareth, and those of the Ishmaelite who arose after him, are to prepare the way for the coming of the Messiah and the improvement of the entire world to serve God together. . . .

How so? The entire world has already become filled with the mention of the Messiah, Torah, and *mitzvot*. These matters have been spread to the furthermost islands and amongst many stubborn-hearted nations. They discuss these matters and the *mitzvot* of the Torah, saying, "These *mitzvot* were true, but were already negated in the present age and are not applicable for all generations." Others say, "They contain esoteric concepts that cannot be understood literally; the Messiah has already come and revealed their hidden truths." When the Messianic king will arise in truth, and will succeed in his mission and be elevated and exalted, they will all come back and realize that their ancestors endowed them with a false heritage and their prophets and ancestors caused them to err.

TEXT 20

RABBI MOSHE CORDOVERO, *EILIMAH RABBATI, MAAYAN* 1, *TAMAR* 1, CH 1

שֶׁאֱמוּנָה זוֹ הִיא מָקוֹר נוֹבֵעַ שְׁאָר כָּל הָאֱמוּנוֹת, שֶׁכּוּלָּם תְּלוּיוֹת בָּאֱלוֹהַּ הֱיוֹתוֹ נִמְצָא. וּמִי שֶׁיִּכְפּוֹר בָּזוֹ יִכְפּוֹר בְּכָל הַשְּׁאָר כּוּלָּם, וְלֹא נִשְׁאַר לוֹ שׁוּם חֵלֶק בְּשׁוּם אֱמוּנָה, כִּי יֵחָשֵׁב כִּבְהֵמָה שֶׁאֵין לְפָנֶיהָ אֶלָּא אֲכִילָה וּשְׁתִיָּה. וְיִגְרַע מְצִיאוּתוֹ מֵהָעוֹבֵד עֲבוֹדָה זָרָה: יוֹדֶה שֶׁיֵּשׁ אֱלוֹהַּ, אֶלָּא שֶׁטָּעָה מִי הוּא הָאֱלוֹהַּ, וְשָׂם לוֹ לֶאֱלוֹהַּ כְּפִי אֱמוּנָתוֹ וְדַעְתּוֹ.

RABBI MOSHE CORDOVERO (RAMAK), 1522–1570

Prominent kabbalist. Ramak belonged to the circle of Jewish mystical thinkers who flourished in 16th-century Safed. The name Cordovero indicates that his family originated in Córdoba, Spain. His most famous kabbalistic work is *Pardes Rimonim*.

The belief [in God] is the source from which all beliefs flow, as they are all predicated on the existence of God. One who denies this truth denies all faiths . . . and is like an animal who is beholden to nothing save its food and drink. Such a person is worse than one who serves idols: [the idolater] accepts that there is a God, and only errs regarding Who God is, and establishes a god for himself in accordance with his beliefs and understanding.

TEXT 21

RABBI NAFTALI TSVI YEHUDAH BERLIN, *HA'AMEK DAVAR*, DEUTERONOMY 29:17

אוֹ בְּאוֹפֶן אַחֵר שֶׁאֵינוֹ רוֹצֶה לַעֲבוֹד עֲבוֹדָה זָרָה, אֶלָּא שֶׁאֵינוֹ רוֹצֶה לְקַבֵּל עוֹל מַלְכוּת שָׁמַיִם גַּם כֵּן, אֶלָּא לִהְיוֹת חָפְשִׁי מֵעֲבוֹדַת כָּל אֱלוֹהַּ. וְהוּא בֶּאֱמֶת רַע וּמַר יוֹתֵר מֵעוֹבֵד עֲבוֹדַת כּוֹכָבִים, כֵּיוָן שֶׁאֵין עָלָיו שׁוּם עוֹל וְאֵינוֹ מַאֲמִין בְּדִין וּמִשְׁפָּט כְּלָל. אוֹ הוּא מֵיפֵר תּוֹרָה לוֹמַר שֶׁלֹּא נִיתְּנָה הַתּוֹרָה אֶלָּא כְּדֵי לְהַפְרִישׁ מֵאֱלִילִים, וְזֶהוּ הָרַעְיוֹן גָּרוּעַ מֵהַכֹּל.

Another type [of apostate] is one who does not want to serve alien gods, yet also refuses to accept the yoke of Heaven, desiring only to be free of the service of any god. In truth, this is far worse than idolatry, since this person accepts no authority over himself, and ultimately does not believe in law and judgment. This person might annul the entire Torah by arguing that the Torah's purpose is only to debunk idolatry. But this ideology is the worst of them all.

RABBI NAFTALI TSVI YEHUDAH BERLIN (NETSIV), 1816–1893

Head of the Volozhin yeshivah, Volozhin, Russia. Rabbi Berlin was born in Mir, Russia. He applied himself to his studies and was renowned for his extraordinary diligence. He is recognized for being one of the greatest scholars of his time. In 1854, he became the head of the yeshivah, one of the largest institutions of its kind, which he led for nearly forty years. He authored several works, including a commentary on the Talmud and halachic responses.

TEXT 22

THE LUBAVITCHER REBBE, RABBI MENACHEM MENDEL SCHNEERSON, *SICHOT KODESH*
5741 3:110, TALK DELIVERED NISSAN 11, 5741 (APRIL 15, 1981)

אוּן אָט דָאס וָואס עֶר הֶערט אַמָאל דֶערמָאנֶען דֶעם אוֹיבֶּערשְׁטֶן, אִיז
מֶען אִים מַסְבִּיר אַז ס'אִיז דָא דֶער עִנְיָן פוּן "סֶעפַּארֵיישָׁן" אַז ס'אִיז
אָפְּגֶעטֵיילְט חִינוּךְ פוּן לִימוּד פוּן דֶעם עִנְיָן פוּן אֱמוּנָה . . . אוּן מ'טוּט
דָאס נָאךְ אָן אִין אַן אִיצְטְלָא, אַז אִין דֶערוֹיף אִיז מְיוּסָד דֶער גַאנְצֶער
מַהֲלַךְ מְדִינָה זוּ - בִּשְׁעַת אַלֶע וֵוייסְן אַז דָאס אִיז הֵיפֶּךְ הַמְצִיאוּת.

דִי גַאנְצֶע מְדִינָה אִיז מְיוּסָד גֶעוָואנְרן דוּרְךְ דֶערוֹיף וָואס עֶס זַיינֶען
גֶעוֶוען מֶענְטְשְׁן וָואס מ'הָאט זֵיי נִיט גֶעלָאזְט זַיין מַאֲמִינִים אִין בּוֹרֵא
הָעוֹלָם וּמַנְהִיגוֹ מִיט'ן גַאנְצֶן שְׁטוּרֶעם, הָאבּן זֵיי גֶעדַארְפְט אַנְטְלוֹיפְן
פוּן דָארְטְן, זַיינֶען זֵיי גֶעקוּמֶען אַהֶערצוּ אִין אַרְצוֹת הַבְּרִית אוּן מְיַיסֵד
גֶעוֶוען דִי מְדִינָה - מִיט דֶער כַּוָּונָה אַז זֵיי זָאלְן קֶענֶען זַיין מַאֲמִינִים
אוּן דִינֶען דֶעם בּוֹרֵא עוֹלָם וּמַנְהִיגוֹ, וָואס "כָּל הָעַמִּים יֵלְכוּ אִישׁ בְּשֵׁם
אֱלֹקָיו".

הָאט מֶען דָאס אִיבֶּערְגֶעדְרֵייט, מֵהַפֵּךְ גֶעוֶוען, אוּן מְיַיסֵד גֶעוֶוען דֶעם
חִינוּךְ אוֹיף דֶערוֹיף אַז דֶער עִנְיָן פוּן דַת טָאר רַחֲמָנָא לִצְלַן - וִוי זֵיי זָאגְן
- נִיט דֶערמָאנְט וֶוערְן בְּבֵית סֵפֶר פוּן קִינְדֶער . . . וָוארוּם דָאס אִיז
אַנְטְקֶעגְן דִי יְסוֹדוֹת פוּן דֶער מְדִינָה.

When the child does hear any mention of the Almighty in school, it is immediately explained to them about the "separation"—that their education is completely separate from anything pertaining to faith. . . . All this is dressed in the notion that this country was founded upon the principle of this "separation," when everyone knows that the very opposite is the case.

This country was founded by people who were prevented from fully practicing their faith, and were therefore compelled to flee their countries of origin. They came here, to America, and founded this country, with the purpose in mind that they would be free to believe in and worship the Creator and Ruler of the world, "each people following in the path of their God."

This principle has now been turned upside down, to mean that the educational system is predicated on the principle that any mention of any religious value is forbidden . . . and that such mention is in opposition to the founding principles of this country.

Additional Readings

EXCHANGE BETWEEN RABBI JOSEPH GLASER AND RABBI MENACHEM MENDEL SCHNEERSON, ON PUBLIC MENORAHS

Central Conference of American Rabbis
Office of the Executive Vice President
April 25, 1978

Rabbi M. M. Schneerson
770 Eastern Parkway
Brooklyn, N.Y. 11213

Dear Rabbi:

It has come to my attention that Lubavitcher chassidim are erecting *Hanukkiot* and holding religious services in connection therewith on public property in various localities throughout the United States at Hanukkah time.

This is as much a violation of the constitutional principle of separation of church and state as is the erection of Christmas trees and creches depicting the birth of Jesus. It weakens our hand when we protest this intrusion of Christian doctrine into the public life of American citizens, and thus, it is really not worth the value received.

I would very much appreciate an opportunity to meet with you to discuss the matter further, and also to indulge a desire I have had for a long time to know you personally. I feel that we have many common interests, and want to explore them with you.

RABBI MENACHEM MENDEL SCHNEERSON
1902–1994

The towering Jewish leader of the 20th century, known as "the Lubavitcher Rebbe," or simply as "the Rebbe." Born in southern Ukraine, the Rebbe escaped Nazi-occupied Europe, arriving in the U.S. in June 1941. The Rebbe inspired and guided the revival of traditional Judaism after the European devastation, impacting virtually every Jewish community the world over. The Rebbe often emphasized that the performance of just one additional good deed could usher in the era of Mashiach. The Rebbe's scholarly talks and writings have been printed in more than 200 volumes.

My warmest good wishes for the remainder of the Pesach season.
Shalom,
  Rabbi Joseph B. Glaser

Central Conference of American Rabbis
Office of the Executive Vice President
May 31, 1978

Rabbi M. M. Schneerson
770 Eastern Parkway
Brooklyn, New York 11213

Dear Rabbi:

Following up on my letter of April 25 suggesting that we discuss religious observances, particularly the kindling of *Hanukkiot,* held on public property, I was pleased to receive a telephone call from your office inviting me to send our views for your consideration and response.

As believing Jews, Lubavitcher chasidim, Reform Jews, and others share the conviction that the *mitzvah* of kindling *Hanukkiot* should be fulfilled by all Jews. Likewise, that the lights should be placed in the windows, or even outside, of Jewish homes and synagogues "to proclaim the miracle," is a practice we encourage. All that we question is the necessity and

RABBI JOSEPH GLASER
1925–1994

Born in Boston, Glaser was wounded twice as an infantryman in Europe during World War II. He graduated from UCLA in 1948 and received a law degree from the University of S. Francisco in 1951. From 1956 to 1959, he was the rabbi of Temple Beth Torah in Ventura, California, a Reform congregation. Later he became the executive vice president of the Central Conference of American Rabbis, the association of Reform rabbis.

desirability of holding this or similar religious ceremonies on public property.

The *mitzvah* is fulfilled when *Hanukkiot* are lit on Jewish property. So there is no halachic necessity for doing so on public property. We believe public property religious observances are not only unnecessary, but undesirable. Allow me to explain why we feel that way.

As you know, the American Constitution provides for the separation of "church and state." The relative comfort of Jews in the United States has resulted in part from the application of that principle. By constant vigilance we Jews, and other Americans who believe that the full freedom of religion which church-state separation provides is important, have managed to minimize violation of the Constitutional principle. Of particular note in this context, we have had considerable success in recent decades in preventing Christmas displays, creches especially, on public property, and in preventing religious assemblies and prayer periods in public schools. Thus we and our children are not forced—as Jews in many nations are—to support Christianity through our taxes or to be exposed, and have our children exposed, to government sanctioned proselytizing. The civil courts have repeatedly agreed that we and our children need not be exposed to Christian observances which we find offensive.

Clearly Jewish religious observances and displays on public property are no less a violation of the doctrine of church-state separation than are Christian observances and displays. And when Jews seek to violate the Constitutional principle, we weaken our hand in our ongoing efforts to prevent Christian violations.

There is a second reason for our concern about Chabad's practice of holding Hanukkah observances on public property. For the reasons outlined above, in several communities Jews have objected to these observances. Heated debates in the Jewish community have spilled over into the general community and have been reported by the media. Surely the sad spectacle of Jews publicly fighting with other Jews is a *chillul hashem*. I must tell you in all candor that we continue to receive complaints about this particular Chabad practice, and thus I have no doubt that the disputations will continue and possibly even end up in court. Since you and we have no difficulty "proclaiming the miracle" via Hanukkah observance on private property, continued confrontation serves no positive Jewish purpose, and indeed is counter-productive.

Our request of you, then, is simply that in your role as leader of the Chabad Lubavitch movement, you direct a cessation of *Hanukkiot* lightings or other religious observances on public property. I would be happy to meet personally with you or your representatives to discuss the matter further.

Shalom,
Rabbi Joseph B. Glaser

By the Grace of G-d
3rd of Sivan, 5738
Brooklyn, N.Y.

Dr. Joseph B. Glaser
790 Madison Avenue
New York, N.Y. 10021

Greeting and Blessing:
This is to confirm receipt of your letter of May 31, and I regret the unavoidable delay in replying to it more promptly. In it you express your reservations about the kindling of *Hanukkiot* in public places on the grounds of (a) the principle of separation of church and state, and (b) it being "counter-productive."

Had I received your letter years ago, when this practice started, I would have had a more difficult task of defending it, for the simple reason that the expected positive results were then a matter of conjecture. But now, after the practice and the results have been observed for a number of years, my task is an easy one, since the general acclaim and beneficial results have far exceeded our expectations. The fact is that countless Jews in all parts of the country have been impressed and inspired by the spirit of Chanukah which had been brought to them, to many for the first time. Indeed, the eternal and always timely message of Chanukah—the victory of the outnumbered forces of light over the overwhelming forces of darkness that attempted to make Jews forget G-d's Torah and Mitzvoth (as we say in the prayer of "V'Al Hanissim") struck a responsive chord in the hearts of many Jews and strengthened their sense of identity with the Maccabbee of all ages.

This year, too, now that some six months have elapsed since Chanukah and reports have come in from various places where Chanukah Lamps were kindled publicly, the results have been most gratifying in terms of spreading the light of the Torah and Mitzvoth, and reaching out to Jews who *could not otherwise* have been reached, either because some of them are unaffiliated with any synagogue, or, though loosely affiliated, always thought that religious practices belong within the confines of a synagogue and do not relate to the personal everyday life of the individual. It was precisely through kindling the Chanukah Lamp in public places, during "ordinary" weekdays, with dignity and pride, that it was brought home to them that true Judaism is practiced daily, and that no Jew should feel abashed about it.

With regard to the "Constitutional" question, I can most assuredly allay your apprehensions on this score. I am fully certain that none of all those who participated in, or witnessed, the kindling of a Chanukah Lamp in a public place (and in all cases permission was *readily* granted by the authorities) felt that his or her loyalty to the Constitution of the USA had been weakened or compromised thereby. Indeed, many expressed surprise that this practice had not been inaugurated many years earlier, seeing that the U.S. Congress opens with a religious invocation by a representative of "one of the major religions" in this country; and, surely, the U.S. Congress, comprising each and every State of the Union, is *the* place where the Constitution of the USA should be most rigidly upheld. There is surely no need to belabor this point.

As for your stating that some Jews did object to the ceremony on Constitutional grounds, to my knowledge these were exceptional and isolated instances. Moreover, I dare say, that (entre nous) the objectors, though ostensibly citing the Constitution, were motivated by other sentiments; a plausible assumption, since they are identified with organizations that thwart every effort to get State aid for Hebrew Day Schools and Yeshivoth to alleviate their burden of the *secular*

department and other "non-religious" needs. Be it noted that the money that would have been received in such aid carries the motto, "In G-d We Trust!" It is lamentable that as a result of this attitude thousands of Jewish children have been *deprived* of their right to Jewish education. It is not surprising, therefore, to see such an appalling rate of intermarriage, nor is it surprising, however sad and deplorable, that the vast majority of intermarriages take place among the ranks of young people who have been deprived of Jewish education, for one reason or another.

In view of your expressed concern for the preservation of Judaism in this country and for the protection of our children against proselytizing, etc., I am encouraged to take advantage of this unexpected exchange of correspondence between us to express my ardent hope that you will use your influence to put an end to the *destructive* fight against State aid to parochial schools—at any rate insofar as the secular department is concerned, so as to enable Jewish Day Schools and Yeshivoth [to] open their doors to the maximum number of students, starting with the next school year and thereafter. For, only an adequate Jewish education can preserve our young generation and future generations from alienation, intermarriage and complete loss, G-d forbid.

I hope and pray that *everyone* who has a voice and influence in Jewish community affairs and is concerned for the preservation of Jews and Judaism in this country no less than for the preservation of the American way, will indeed act in the spirit of the basic principle of "this Nation *under G-d,* and government of the people, by the people, and *for* the people," including also the Jewish people, and do *everything* possible for the good of every Jewish child, that he and she remain Jewish, marry a Jew, and live Jewishly; and, of course, a good Jew is also a good American.

With prayerful wishes for an inspiring Yom Tov of Mattan Torah, and the traditional blessing to receive the Torah with joy and inwardness,

Sincerely yours,
M. Schneerson

Central Conference of American Rabbis
Office of the Executive Vice President
August 14, 1978

Rabbi M. M. Schneerson
770 Eastern Parkway
Brooklyn, New York 11213

Dear Rabbi Schneerson:

Thank you for your letter of the 3rd of Sivan which was delivered to me at Oxford University where I am doing some very interesting research in a comparative study of the Anglo-American and Jewish laws of self-incrimination. I graduated law school before entering the rabbinate and have maintained an interest in legal studies.

Knowing how busy you are and that your health has not been good, I deeply appreciate your taking the time to send me such a full reply. However, I can see that we are very much in basic disagreement.

You place a great deal of importance on the fact that the kindling of the *Hanukkiot* in public places has received general acclaim and that countless Jews in all parts of the country have been impressed. I must point out respectfully that constitutional matters are not decided by *vox populi* except in the extreme case where a constitutional amendment is being considered, and even then there are federalist safeguards. Constitutional law, which is what we are talking about, is a matter of principle and not of passing popularity. It follows that those who participated in, or witnessed, the kindling of a Hanukkah lamp in a public place feeling, as you say, that their loyalty to the Constitution of the United States had not been weakened or compromised thereby, are not the arbiters of such an issue. Neither are the authorities who you report readily granted permission for the kindling. Nor is the United States Congress which indeed, lamentably begins its sessions with a religious invocation. You are quite correct when you say that "surely the U.S. Congress, comprising each and every State of the Union, is *the* place where the Constitution of the U.S.A. should be most rigidly upheld." Unfortunately, all too often, that is not the case. Time after time, the United States Supreme Court, which *is* the place and the only place, where ultimately the U.S. Constitution is upheld, has struck down law after law passed by the Congress, as unconstitutional. This is also true in reference to acts of other governmental bodies, Federal, State and local, legislative and executive or administrative.

By the way, it is only very recently that the words "under God" were added to the Pledge of Allegiance, rather arrogantly, many of us thought, by President Eisenhower, whose understanding of the American process and constitutional principle was probably the least of all the presidents of the United States from George Washington to the present. No one took it very seriously, as it had no particular legal force, and no one really wanted to come out against God, which is part of the reason that your impression is that Jewish objection to the kindling of the *Hanukkiot* in public places is "to my knowledge . . . exceptional and isolated instances." We should add to that the fact that Jews do not like to oppose Jews in public and thus the far more substantial opposition than you realize exists has been muted up to now. If you are referring to Lincoln's Gettysburg address, it must be remembered that this was a personal affirmation of Lincoln, to which he was entitled, and for which I am grateful; Eisenhower, on the other hand, both cheapened and abused the phrase, and its underlying concept, when he promulgated it into the Pledge of Allegiance by Presidential decree. It is not correct to say that "the objectors, though ostensibly citing the Constitution, were motivated by other sentiments." I am one of those objectors and I must protest against such an allegation. It is my opinion that the principle of separation of Church and State, firmly imbedded in the United States Constitution, exalts religion by keeping the state out, and that any intermingling of religion and state cheapens, weakens and subordinates to the state religion. The lamentable experience throughout Europe is eminent proof of that, as testified to by Alexis de Tocqueville in his classic work *On Democracy in America*, which I urgently recommend you read. There, de Tocqueville, a French scholar of the 19th Century, glories in the vigorous and healthy state of religion in America and accounts for it by citing the sharp separation of religion and state in this country. He deplores the opposite situation in Europe. Further, if you would justify *Hanukkiot* kindling under the rubric of "civil religion," this, too, would be inappropriate. The proponents of civil religion clearly draw the line at sectarian prayer and practice of any sort, and what could be more sectarian than our Hanukkah, celebrating our national deliverance from Syria, our cultural reassertion, the miracle of the cruse of oil in our very own, highly exclusive Temple?

The matter of government support for religious schools, which you bring into our correspondence, has always been a most painful one for me. I feel very deeply about Jewish education and make every effort to strengthen it. I have supported Jewish day schools, and shall continue to do so, under all auspices, including the most Orthodox. But, for the reasons given above, I have steadfastly opposed any kind of direct, or dangerously indirect, government support. The moment the camel gets its nose under the tent, the inhabitants thereof are in trouble. The wall of separation between religion and state is like a dike; the slightest breach is a dangerous portent of a torrent to follow. Your own reasoning is a classic example thereof. You point to the prayers uttered in the halls of the Congress as justification for the kindling of *Hanukkiot* in public places, and then move right on to call for government subvention of religious based schools. Ultimately, this must lead to government intervention in matters theological and in the moral areas where religion must have full sway and unimpeded conscience. There can be no "deals" between secular power and religious authority. Inevitably, religious authority will be subordinated and crushed. To mingle religion and state is to pervert American democracy and to endanger American religion.

I want to assure you, dear Rebbe, that I believe in, worship and commune with God as deeply, as fervently, and as intensively as you do, and cherish and work for the perpetuation of Judaism as much and as indefatigably. It is for these reasons, as well as out of respect for the brilliance of the founding fathers of the United States of America, that I urge you to research the matter further and to reconsider your policy.

Finally, I must disagree with your opinion that there is some intrinsic value to individual Jews involved in the public lighting and blessing of the *Hanukkiot*. I think it might be just the opposite. Ultimately, the survival of Judaism depends on the home, which is where the *Hanukkiah* should be lit. People coming to public places to observe (not really participate in) this ceremony are being involved in a kind of public, almost flamboyant religious exercise instead of in a sacred home ritual. From that standpoint also, I think the matter should be reconsidered.

My very best wishes to you.

Shalom,

Rabbi Joseph B. Glaser

Jonathan D. Sarna and David G. Dalin, *Religion and State in the American Jewish Experience* (Notre Dame, IN: Notre Dame University Press, 1997), pp. 290–297
Reprinted with permission of the publisher

PRAYERS IN THE SCHOOLS, MENORAHS IN THE STREETS

RABBI JOSEPH TELUSHKIN

"Almighty God, we acknowledge our dependence upon Thee, and we beg Thy blessings upon us, our parents, our teachers, and our country."

This twenty-two-word prayer, composed in 1951 by the New York Board of Regents and recommended for daily use in New York State public schools, provoked debate not only in New York but also throughout the country. The debate culminated in a legal suit, *Engel v. Vitale,* which came before the Supreme Court in the early 1960s. In anticipation of the justices' deliberations as to whether such a prayer should be allowed in the country's public schools, twenty-two state governments signed an amicus curiae brief urging the Court to uphold the prayer's permissibility.

Public opposition to the prayer came largely, though by no means exclusively, from the organized Jewish community; secular organizations such as the American Civil Liberties Union, which had a disproportionately high percentage of Jewish members, were heavily involved in this battle as well. A brief urging the Court to outlaw all such prayers in public schools was submitted by the Synagogue Council of America, a national organization representing rabbis in the different denominations, and the National Jewish Community Relations Council representing Jewish communities throughout the United States. The brief's essential argument was that although the New York State prayer did not advocate a specific religion—it spoke rather of "Almighty God"—it still violated the First Amendment, which ordains that "Congress shall make no law respecting an establishment of religion." Although this constitutional provision is popularly understood as meaning that Congress is forbidden to establish a state religion (in the way

that the Church of England is that country's state religion), the Jewish organizations argued that a prayer promoting an "acknowledgment of dependence upon God and the invocation of His blessings" constitutes a preference for theistic religions that affirm a personal God, over nontheistic religions, such as Buddhism, which do not. Thus, although the prayer was not religiously specific (as it would be, for example, if it spoke of Jesus), it still promoted very specific religious ideas, notably "the existence of a personal God who can and will respond to prayer and grant the blessings prayed for." In the view of these organizations, such a prayer has no place in a public school. The government, they argued, is obliged not only to be neutral among competing faiths (e.g., not to favor Protestantism over Catholicism, or any form of Christianity over Judaism) "but also between religion and non-religion." The state, quite simply, has no business participating in any way in religious affairs. The signatories emphasized that their opposition to prayer in public schools had nothing to do with opposition to religion. Indeed, they had submitted this brief "on behalf of the coordinating bodies of 70 Jewish organizations, including the national bodies representing congregations and rabbis of Orthodox, Conservative, and Reform Judaism. The thousands of rabbis and congregations who have authorized submission of this brief can hardly be characterized as being on the side of those who oppose religion."

In the end, in a historic decision (1962), the Supreme Court ruled 6–1 that all prayers should be forbidden in public schools. (The newly appointed justice Byron White took no part in the case and therefore did not vote, while Justice Felix Frankfurter had suffered a cerebral stroke and was forced to retire from the bench before the decision could be announced.) Although the ruling acknowledged that the New York Board of Regents' prayer did not promote any one religion, still it promoted those religions that recognize "Almighty God," and therefore violated the First Amendment clause banning the establishment of any religion.

RABBI JOSEPH TELUSHKIN, 1948–

Rabbi and author. Joseph Telushkin received his ordination at Yeshiva University and a Jewish history degree at Columbia University. He has written many popular books about Judaism, including the best-selling *Jewish Literacy,* and *Rebbe,* a biography of the Lubavitcher Rebbe.

The ruling was widely hailed throughout the American Jewish community, many of whose older members recalled a time when readings from the New Testament were commonly conducted in public schools. The fact that the New York State prayer was decidedly nondenominational had not allayed the common Jewish fear that any opening in the wall between religion and state could eventually lead to the favoring of Christianity over other religions.

The most noted leader within the Jewish community who stood out almost alone in opposition to this commonly enunciated Jewish position was the Rebbe. Shortly after the ruling, the Rebbe argued that all legal means should be employed to obtain a reversal of the Court decision.[5] His passionate feelings on this issue received wide attention (see, for example, *The New York Times,* November 27, 1962), and many were surprised by the intensity of his response. One might have thought that the school prayer issue would have little resonance for him. After all, Lubavitcher Chasidim do not send their children to public schools but rather to Jewish day schools that start each morning with an extended prayer service. Those Jews who do attend public schools generally come from less traditional and often nonobservant backgrounds. To the Rebbe, though, this was precisely the point. The Jews who attend public schools often come from homes in which prayers are rarely, and in some cases never, recited. Yet, daily prayer is a requirement of Jewish law. Ideally, the prayers that are to be recited are those in the *siddur* (prayer book). But even if these prayers are not said, there is a great value in reciting any prayer addressed to God. Thus, reciting the "Almighty God" prayer composed by the Board of Regents fulfilled the requirement for some sort of prayer and, equally important, brought God into the daily life of Jewish children being raised in households where God might be infrequently discussed or invoked.

The Rebbe's support for prayers in public schools, and for public advocacy of a belief in God, also was influenced by other factors, most notably his early years in the aggressively atheistic and murderous Soviet Union, and his own later experience of living in Germany during the rise of Hitler and the Nazis (yet another antireligious ideology). From the Rebbe's perspective, school prayers had important spiritual and moral ramifications and benefits for both Jews and non-Jews. The same year, 1964, in which he issued a public letter in support of prayer in public schools, he also wrote a letter to Professor Velvel Greene of the University of Minnesota, the concluding paragraph of which underscored the importance of linking God and ethics: "If in a previous generation there were people who doubted the need of Divine authority for common morality and ethics, [and who believed instead] that human reason is sufficient authority for morality and ethics, our present generation has, unfortunately, in a most devastating and tragic way, refuted this mistaken notion. For it is precisely the nation which had excelled itself in the exact sciences, the humanities, and even in philosophy and ethics, that turned out to be the most depraved nation in the world. . . . Anyone who knows how insignificant was the minority of Germans who opposed the Hitler regime, realizes that the German cult was not something which was practiced by a few individuals, but had [been] embraced [by] the vast majority of the nation, who considered itself the 'super race.'"

Two years after the Supreme Court ruling, the Rebbe was asked whether he had reconsidered his position. He hadn't, except to note that time had "reinforce[d] my conviction of the vital need that the children in the public schools should be allowed to begin their day with the recitation of a nondenominational prayer, acknowledging the existence of a Creator and Master of the Universe, and our dependence upon Him."

In their brief to the Court, Jewish groups had specifically noted their opposition to mandating any sort of prayer acknowledging "dependence upon [a personal] God." But belief in a "personal God" before Whom all people are accountable is exactly what the Rebbe believed was required. What Jewish and non-Jewish children alike need—adults, too, for that matter—is understanding that "the world in which they live is not a jungle, where brute force, cunning, and unbridled passion rule supreme, but that it has a [Supreme Being] Who . . . takes a 'personal interest' in the affairs of each and every individual, and to Him everyone is accountable for [his or her] daily conduct."

The Rebbe went on to make reference to the rising rates of juvenile delinquency, noting that even if the government had sufficient police to keep an eye on every out-of-line child, that would not deter all crime. Further, even if marshaling so extensive a police force were possible, "this would not be the right way to remedy the situation. The remedy lies in removing the cause, not in merely treating its symptoms." And how was this to be done? "It is necessary to engrave upon the child's mind the idea that any wrongdoing is an offense against the divine authority and order."

Regarding the argument that the appropriate places for prayers are "houses of prayer" (synagogues and churches), the Rebbe noted that attendance at such services is not high, "both in regard to the number of worshippers and the frequency of their visits." Thus, "shifting the responsibility to the house of prayer will not correct the problem."

In his view, therefore, the problem of inculcating children with awareness of an "Eye that sees and an Ear that hears" cannot be solved through houses of worship alone, just as a criminal mentality cannot be eliminated through law enforcement agencies alone: "The crux of the problem lies in the success or failure of bringing up children to an awareness of a Supreme Authority, who is not only to be feared but also loved. Under existing conditions in this country, a daily prayer in the public schools is for a vast number of boys and girls the only opportunity of cultivating such an awareness."

The Rebbe offered a second argument as well, one intended to counter the overwhelming Jewish and liberal opposition to school prayers. Much of this opposition, whether it was stated explicitly or not, was rooted in a fear of Christianity. The concern was that any breakdown in the separation of church and state would lead to some form of Christian domination in the United States; after all, the large majority of Americans are Christians. For Jews, such a thought inevitably triggered the frightening recollection of the Jewish historical experience in medieval Europe during which a highly intolerant Christianity was the established state religion, and Jews suffered severe discrimination and persecution. For many Jews, therefore, an utterly secular America seemed preferable to one in which there was a state preference for religion in any form whatsoever.

To the Rebbe, such thinking was illogical, an example of people responding with a once-valid solution to an altogether new problem: "Suppose a person was ill at one time and doctors prescribed a certain medication and treatment. Suppose that years later, the same person became ill again, but with an entirely different, in fact quite *contrary*, malady. Would it be reasonable to recommend the same medication and treatment as formerly? . . . In medieval times, the world suffered from an 'excess' of religious zeal and intolerance. In our day, the world is suffering from an excessive indifference to religion, or even from a growing materialism and atheism." In other words, what is appropriate in an age of religious intolerance is less religion in the public sphere, what is appropriate in an age of indifference to religion is more religion.

But having acknowledged that, the Rebbe was not insensitive to Jewish fears of Christian domination, and the solution he proposed was a commonsensical one. Rather than respond to worries about Christian ascendancy by forbidding all prayers, he advocated that "a provision be made which would require the unanimous approval by the representatives of [different] religious denominations before a particular nondenominational prayer is introduced into the school."

In addition, and as a safeguard, it was only nondenominational prayers that the Rebbe endorsed, as such prayers united people in a feeling of responsibility before God. However, he strongly opposed Bible readings, since this could lead to readings drawn from religious texts that would make members of other religious groups uncomfortable.

For the organized Jewish communal leadership in the early 1960s, support for prayer and the affirmation of God in U.S. public schools was in itself a somewhat heretical notion, one it was happy to see outlawed by the Supreme Court. But the Rebbe stood steadfast in his opposition, though his arguments did not prevail.

Over the coming years, the Rebbe appears to have grown convinced that—at least for the foreseeable future—the Supreme Court was not going to allow such a prayer to be recited in public schools. In characteristic fashion, rather than give up entirely on the idea of bringing God into the classroom, the Rebbe sought out an alternative; in this case, becoming a supporter of a daily "moment of silence." The idea was that each school day would begin with a moment of quiet meditation. Such a moment, the Rebbe argued, would not compromise "the neutrality of the state, for this is not prayer, but silence."

He urged that the "moment" be instituted at the beginning of each day, thereby emphasizing its significance. There was a practical reason as well; if it came later in the day, many students would simply spend the minute reviewing something from the class period they had just concluded. However, if a child began the school day with such a moment, there would be a much greater likelihood that he or she would devote these sixty seconds, or at least part of them, to thinking about the big issues in life, devotion to parents, a general commitment to wanting to do good, "and belief in the Creator and the Ruler of the Universe."

Anticipating the objections secularists and other opponents of school prayers would offer to such a moment, the Rebbe then added that since each person has free will to think about whatever he or she wants, without suggestions from teachers, such a moment "does not represent an incursion of the state into the free exercise of religion by the individual."

This cause, too, has, as of yet, failed to fully clear court-based opposition. The next time, however, that the Rebbe undertook to support religion in the public square, he was no longer on the losing side.

The Lighting of Menorahs in the Public Square

Chabad's well-known focus on the public celebration of Chanukah started in the mid-1970s and was likely influenced, at least in part, by an unusual feature of contemporary American-Jewish life: In the United States, Chanukah is the third most widely observed Jewish holiday (after Passover and Yom Kippur), although in Jewish law it is less significant than the biblically based Sabbath, Sukkot, and Shavuot (Chanukah is a postbiblical holiday).

Because of Chanukah's proximity to Christmas, many Jewish parents in the United States and other Western countries observe it with special attention so that their children not feel deprived when they witness their Christian peers celebrating Christmas. Thus, many parents have turned the holiday, in part, into a Jewish form of the most widely observed Christian holiday. For example, Jewish children are given daily gifts throughout the holiday. By turning Chanukah into a fun-filled occasion, parents hope that their children will not feel they are missing out on Christmas trees and gifts "brought" by Santa Claus. And while this focus on gifts is certainly not an ideal religious response, it is, Jewishly speaking, preferable to the common alternative of bringing Christmas into Jewish homes. American-Jewish historian Jenna Weissman Joselit has documented that as recently as the 1960s, almost 40 percent of Chicago Jews "decorated their homes with Christmas trees."

The close proximity of the two holidays impacted Jewish behavior on a year-to-year basis. For many years, my father, Shlomo Telushkin, was the accountant for a Jewish company that produced Chanukah candles and decorations. He told me that the closer Chanukah fell to Christmas (under the Jewish calendar, which is lunar, Chanukah can start anywhere from late November to late December), the more business the company did.

With so many American Jews aware of Chanukah, whether they observed it or not, there was no way the Rebbe and Chabad *shluchim* would forgo the opportunity to reach out to Jews on this holiday.

The public lighting of a giant menorah originated in 1974 at the foot of Philadelphia's Liberty Bell, and was organized by the veteran Chabad *shliach* Rabbi Avraham Shemtov. A year later, Chabad *shliach* Rabbi Chaim Drizin in San Francisco lit a twenty-two-foot lamp in Union Square. The practice quickly spread, and in 1979, President Jimmy Carter ended a hundred days of self-imposed seclusion over the Iran hostage crisis by leaving the White House to light the Chabad menorah in front of the White House with Rabbi Shemtov. In those first years, some Jews expressed unhappiness about this entrance of Jewish observance into public places, but no *legal* challenges were mounted. The foreshadowing of the many courtroom battles that would soon ensue was first anticipated in a remarkable 1978 exchange of letters between the Rebbe and Rabbi Joseph Glaser, the longtime head of the Central Conference of American Rabbis (CCAR), the organization of Reform rabbis.

Rabbi Glaser initiated the first two letters. Their tone was respectful but demanding, and the issue addressed in both instances was Chabad's placement of menorahs on public property. Glaser's first letter (April 25, 1978) was written in a rather legalistic tone and opens rather curiously. (In a third letter, he noted that he had graduated law school before entering the rabbinate.) Though the lighting of public menorahs had been going on at that point since 1974, Glaser wrote as if he had only just heard about it:

> It has come to my attention that Lubavitcher Chasidim are erecting Hanukkiot and holding religious services in connection therewith on public property in various locations throughout the United States.
>
> This is as much a violation of the constitutional principle of separation of church and state as is the erection of Christmas trees and creches depicting the birth of Jesus. It weakens our hand when we protest this intrusion of Christian doctrine into the public life of American citizens and thus, it is really not worth the value received.

The relatively brief letter then shifted into a warmer tone:

> I would very much appreciate the opportunity to meet with you to discuss the matter further, and also to indulge a desire I have had for a long time to know you personally. I feel that we have many common interests, and want to explore them with you.
>
> My warmest good wishes for the remainder of the Pesach season.
>
> Shalom
>
> Rabbi Joseph B. Glaser

On May 31, Rabbi Glaser wrote again, this time after receiving a call from the Rebbe's office asking him to further delineate his views for the Rebbe's "consideration and response." On this occasion, Glaser set out to establish more of a common ground between Reform Judaism and Chabad, both of whose members do not necessarily think that the two groups have much in common:

> As believing Jews, Lubavitcher Chasidim, Reform Jews, and others share the conviction that the mitzvah of kindling Hanukkiot should be fulfilled by all Jews. Likewise, that the lights should be placed in the windows or even outside of Jewish homes and synagogue "to proclaim the miracle" is a practice we encourage. All that we question is the necessity and desirability of holding this or similar religious ceremonies on public property.

In a further effort to establish common ground, Glaser offered a rationale rooted in Jewish law (halacha) for his position: Since the obligation to light Chanukah candles is fulfilled when the menorah is lit on Jewish property, there is "no halachic necessity for doing so on public property." Glaser insisted, therefore, that in addition to being unnecessary, such an act also is undesirable. Jewish comfort in the United States has resulted in large part from the constitutionally guaranteed separation of church and state. This has enabled Jews and other supporters of separation to prevent "Christmas displays, crèches especially, on public property and [to prevent] prayer-periods in public schools." If Jews do not want to be exposed to Christian observances that they find "offensive"—in Glaser's words—then it is equally wrong for them to carry out Jewish religious rituals in the public square. Glaser further argued that continuing confrontations between Jews who disagreed with the celebration of menorah lightings on public property "serves no positive Jewish purpose, and indeed is counter-productive."

Near the letter's conclusion, we find the first indication that legal efforts to stop the Menorah Campaign might soon follow: "I must tell you in all candor that we continue to receive complaints about this particular Chabad practice, and thus I have no doubt that the disputations will continue and possibly even end up in court."

Glaser concludes his letter with an appeal to the Rebbe, in his role as leader, "to direct a cessation of *Hanukkiot* lightings or other religious observances on public property."

The Rebbe's response was dated barely a week later, 3 Sivan 5738 (June 8, 1978). It is written in a respectful tone, though he addresses Glaser, who signed his correspondence as *Rabbi* Joseph Glaser, as "Dr. Glaser," perhaps out of resistance to recognizing Glaser's rabbinic credentials, although by no means is this clear. To cite just one example, the Rebbe seemed very comfortable in addressing the prominent Reform clergyman Herbert Weiner as "Rabbi."

As the Rebbe saw it, Rabbi Glaser's critique was rooted in two objections: Chabad's behavior violates the principle of separation of church and state and also is counterproductive. He addressed the latter issue first:

> Had I received your letter years ago, when this practice started, I would have had a more difficult task of defending it, for the simple reason that the expected positive results were then a matter of conjecture. But now, after the practice and the results have been observed for a number of years, my task is an easy one, since the general acclaim and beneficial results have far exceeded our expectations. The fact is that countless Jews in all parts of the country have been impressed and inspired by the spirit of Chanukah which has been brought to them, to many for the first time.

Regarding Glaser's argument that any good gained from the public lightings could be achieved equally by lightings inside Jewish homes or at synagogues, the Rebbe noted that the actual experience of lighting candles in public places achieved its success specifically in "reaching out to Jews who *could not otherwise* have been reached, either because some of them are unaffiliated with any synagogue or, though loosely affiliated, always thought that religious practices . . . do not relate to the personal everyday life of the individual. It was precisely through kindling the Chanukah Lamp in public places during 'ordinary' weekdays . . . that it was brought home to them that true Judaism is

practiced daily, and that no Jew should feel abashed about it" (emphasis in original letter).

The Rebbe here might well have been tactfully alluding to the fact that though the Reform movement strongly encourages its adherents to light Chanukah candles, many members of Reform synagogues do not do so, certainly not for all eight days of the holiday. And, of course, there are many Jews—about half or more of the American-Jewish community at any given time—who maintain no synagogue affiliation at all and who, in the absence of these public lightings, will likely have no exposure to Chanukah.

Regarding the constitutional question, the Rebbe's tone turned slightly patronizing: "I can most assuredly allay your apprehension on this score. I am fully certain that none of those who participated in or witnessed the kindling of a Chanukah Lamp in a public place (and in all cases permission was *readily* granted by the authorities) felt that his or her loyalty to the Constitution of the U.S.A. had been weakened or compromised thereby . . . seeing that the U.S. Congress opens [its daily sessions] with a religious invocation . . . and surely the U.S. Congress, comprising each and every state of the Union, is *the* place where the Constitution of the U.S.A. should be most rigidly upheld."

The Rebbe then seized upon the issue of those opposed to the public lightings of menorahs as a springboard to discuss an issue that apparently concerned him even more: the widespread opposition of many Jews, Rabbi Glaser among them, who "thwart" every effort to secure government aid to enable Jewish day schools and yeshivot to cover the costs of their secular studies and other nonreligious needs (such as school lunches): "Be it noted that money that would have been received in such aid carries the motto, 'In God we trust.' It is lamentable that as a result of this attitude [opposition to public funding of religious schools], thousands of Jewish children have been *deprived* of their right to Jewish education."

Just as one suspects that Rabbi Glaser was quite aware that his earlier appeal to the Rebbe to direct his *shluchim* to cease public candlelightings would be rejected, the Rebbe now made an appeal to Glaser that, one suspects, he understood would go unheeded as well, though he framed his request in a respectful and friendly manner: "I am encouraged to take advantage of this unexpected exchange of correspondence between us to express my ardent hope that you will use your influence to put an end to the *destructive* fight against state aid to parochial schools, at any rate insofar as the secular department is concerned, so as to enable Jewish Day Schools and Yeshivot to open their doors to the maximum number of students."

The Rebbe concluded his letter with a blessing to Glaser for an inspiring Shavuot, the holiday that celebrates the giving of the Torah, and which would be observed in three days' time.

However, this was not the end of the correspondence. Rabbi Glaser was spending the summer at Oxford University researching Anglo-American and Jewish laws concerning self-incrimination, and he wanted the Rebbe to know that he was engaged in scholarly Jewish study. Just as he wanted "to assure you, dear Rebbe, that I believe in, worship and commune with God as deeply, as fervently, and as intensively as you do, and cherish and work for the perpetuation of Judaism as much and as indefatigably." Indeed, it was in light of the intensity of his commitment that he again urged the Rebbe to reconsider his positions.

The issue of governmental support for religious schools was one that deeply pained him, Glaser explained. He wanted to strengthen Jewish education but, for the reasons he had already offered, he ardently opposed government aid to parochial schools. He now introduced an additional argument, that such aid would, in the end, be catastrophic for the schools themselves: "The moment the camel gets its nose under the tent, the inhabitants thereof are in trouble. . . . The government will end up intervening in matters theological, and in the moral areas where religion must have full sway and unimpeded conscience."

Oddly, Rabbi Glaser's line of argument was reminiscent of certain ultra-Orthodox anti-Zionist groups in Israel who refuse all government aid to their schools, arguing that the government will then try to impose its views on them.

The rest of Rabbi Glaser's letter is a basic restatement and expansion of his views. He expresses his unhappiness that the U.S. Congress "lamentably begins its sessions with a religious invocation." Also, the insertion of the words "under God" in the Pledge of Allegiance pains Glaser. He points out that this addition to the Pledge came about only in the 1950s, during the administration of President Eisenhower, "whose understanding of the American process and constitutional principles was probably the least of all the presidents of the United States from George Washington to the present."

Finally, Glaser returns to the issue of the Chanukah menorahs, this time introducing a previously unstated argument. The Rebbe seems to believe, Glaser notes, that there is some "intrinsic value" in having Jews attend a public lighting and blessing of the Chanukah candles. But since "ultimately the survival of Judaism depends on the home," it is *there* that the menorah should be lit. Having people observing the ceremony in public constitutes a "flamboyant religious exercise instead of a sacred home ritual."

All true, perhaps, but the response one can imagine the Rebbe offering (he did not answer this letter) is that the alternative to people attending public lightings of Chanukah menorahs is not that they will light candles at home, but that they will not light them at all. In addition, as the Rebbe had earlier argued, it is certain, based on reports Chabad had received, that because of these public lightings, some spectators, perhaps many, had already started to light candles at home.

Rabbi Glaser and the Rebbe's letters and responses were primarily shaped by different concerns. For Rabbi Glaser, the most significant consideration was that American Jews have succeeded very well in an America in which religion and state are totally separate. Given that Jews are a small percentage of the population, it is best to keep things that way; otherwise, the Jewish situation could deteriorate rapidly: "The wall of separation between religion and state is like a dike: the slightest breach is a dangerous portent of a torrent to follow." However, Glaser's position was not dictated solely by this pragmatic consideration; for him, it was a matter of principle that the government involve itself in no way, financial or otherwise, in a religious ritual, even if all that was involved was permitting the ritual to be carried out on public grounds.

For the Rebbe, influenced yet again by his notions of love of all Jews, what was paramount was reaching Jews who were not being exposed to Judaism, in this instance offering them as a point of entry the joyous "festival of lights." The Rebbe also wanted to show the non-Jewish world—and through them, nonobservant Jews as well—an image of Jews who were willing to be very public about their religious commitment.

Over the following years, the public lighting of menorahs continued to grow. Professor Jonathan Sarna of Brandeis University has noted that since President Carter's participation in the Chabad menorah lighting, "Every president has recognized Chanukah with a special menorah-lighting ceremony, and limited his Christmas message to those who actually observe the holiday." In 1982, when President Ronald Reagan participated in the candlelighting ceremony at Lafayette Park, he referred to the menorah, erected by Chabad, as "the National Menorah," thereby, as historian Dr. Joshua Eli Plaut has noted, "equating its lighting with the National Christmas Tree lighting." Five years later, the largest menorah lighting of all occurred at the Sun Life Stadium in Miami, when Chabad *shliach* Rabbi Raphael Tennenhaus lit a menorah in front of seventy thousand people. That same year, 1987, the Rebbe transformed the campaign into an international one, pushing for public candlelightings throughout the world. Twenty-five years later, I attended a menorah lighting on a main street in Geneva, Switzerland, along with some four hundred other Jews, and which was witnessed by many non-Jews as well. "God gave each of us a soul, which is a candle that He gives us to illuminate our surroundings with His light," the Rebbe taught at a 1990 worldwide Chanukah satellite linkup. "We must not only illuminate the *inside* of homes, but also the outside, and the world at large."

Even as the public lightings of menorahs continued to grow from year to year, so, too, did the legal challenges of which Rabbi Glaser had warned the Rebbe. The most significant case occurred in Pittsburgh, and the legal battle provoked there was so fierce that it eventually ended up before the Pennsylvania Supreme Court (Allegheny County, 1989). The case addressed both the menorah and the Christian crèche. Over a period of some years, the city of Pittsburgh had permitted the Holy Name Society, a Catholic group, to place a crèche, depicting Jesus, Joseph, and Mary, on the Grand Staircase inside the Allegheny County courthouse. Alongside the crèche was a Latin banner proclaiming "Glory to God in the Highest." The Chabad menorah in Pittsburgh was no less public (it was eighteen feet high) but, unlike the crèche, it was placed outside, near the city-county building, where it stood alongside a forty-five-foot-high Christmas tree (the menorah was owned by Chabad, but the city stored and erected it each year). In 1986, the American Civil Liberties Union (ACLU) sued to stop the city from displaying both, arguing that the crèche and the menorah violated the Establishment Clause of the First Amendment. A lower court initially decided that Pittsburgh was within its right to display them, but then a higher court ruled that it was forbidden. In 1989, the case reached the U.S. Supreme Court, which issued a split decision, outlawing the placement of the crèche but permitting the displaying of the menorah alongside the Christmas tree. The court's reasoning was as follows: Because the crèche was positioned inside the Allegheny County courthouse, "the principle or primary effect" of the display was to advance religion, indeed a specific religion (and to do so inside a courthouse), but the case of the menorah that the city placed near a Christmas tree was not seen as *endorsing* the Jewish or Christian faith, just recognizing their status in U.S. society.

Subsequent to the Supreme Court ruling, challenges to the menorah lightings continued sporadically but started to diminish. At the same time, the acceptance of Chanukah within the United States continued to expand. In 1993, President Bill Clinton hosted Jewish schoolchildren for a candlelighting in the Oval Office, and eight years later, George W. Bush became the first president to host a Chanukah party at the White House; during the party, he himself lit the *shamash,* the central candle, which is then used to light the other candles.

Today, several thousand public menorah lightings under Chabad auspices take place throughout the world each year. An increasing number of non-Chabad and non-Orthodox groups carry out such lightings as well.

"Go out into the courtyard into the public domain," the Rebbe continued on that same Chanukah night,

"and create light which illuminates the entire outside world."

Rebbe: The Life and Teachings of Menachem M. Schneerson, the Most Influential Rabbi in Modern History (New York: HarperWave, 2014), pp. 255–270
Reprinted with permission of the publisher

AMERICAN JEWS AND CHURCH-STATE RELATIONS
THE SEARCH FOR "EQUAL FOOTING"

JONATHAN D. SARNA AND DAVID G. DALIN

The Constitutional Convention meeting in Philadelphia in 1787 received exactly one petition on the subject of religious liberty. The petitioner was Jonas Phillips, a German Jewish immigrant merchant, and what he requested—a change in the Pennsylvania state constitution to eliminate a Christological test oath—was outside of the convention's purview. But the sentiments expressed in the petition contain one of the earliest known American Jewish statements on religious liberty. "The Israelites," it declares, "will think themself happy to live under a government where all Religious societies are on an Equal footing."[1]

Eighteen days before Phillips penned his September 7 petition, the Constitutional Convention, meeting behind closed doors, accepted the provisions of Article VI: "no religious test shall ever be required as

a qualification to any office or public trust under the United States." Two years later, under pressure from six different states,[2] Congress passed a much more explicit guarantee of religious liberty as part of the First Amendment (ratified on December 15, 1791): "Congress shall make no law respecting an establishment of religion, or prohibiting the free exercise thereof." For Jews, however, these Constitutional provisions did not immediately translate into the kind of "Equal footing" that Jonas Phillips had sought. Indeed, the whole question of what equal footing means and how best to achieve it would continue to occupy American Jewish leaders for two full centuries. . . .

In the colonial period, Jews never expected to achieve complete religious equality. Given the right to settle, travel, trade, buy land, gain citizenship, and "exercise in all quietness their religion," they put up with blasphemy laws, Sunday laws, Christian oaths, church taxes, and restrictions on their franchise and right to hold public office. "They had not come to North America to acquire political rights," Jacob Marcus reminds us, and besides, as late as the 1760s "there

JONATHAN D. SARNA, PHD, 1955–

Historian. Dr. Sarna is the Joseph H. & Belle R. Braun Professor of American Jewish History and chair of the Hornstein Jewish Professional Leadership Program at Brandeis University, the chief historian of the National Museum of American Jewish History in Philadelphia, as well as a member of JLI's Academic Advisory Board. Sarna has written, edited, or co-edited more than 30 books. He is best known for his book *American Judaism: A History*, winner of the Jewish Book Council's "Jewish Book of the Year Award" in 2004. Dr. Sarna served as the chief course consultant for JLI's *To Be a Jew in the Free World*.

DAVID G. DALIN, PHD, 1949–

Historian. Dr. Dalin is a professor of history and politics at Ave Maria University in Florida. He is the author of numerous articles and books, including *The Myth of Hitler's Pope: How Pope Pius XII Rescued Jews from the Nazis*.

was not one American colony which offered political equality to all Christians."[3] . . .

The first decade and a half of American independence saw the parameters of religious liberty in the new nation steadily widen. New York, one of the most religiously pluralistic of the states, became in 1777 the first to extend the boundaries of "free exercise and enjoyment of religious profession and worship" to "all mankind," whether Christian or not (although it retained a limited antiCatholic naturalization oath). Virginia, in its 1785 Act for Religious Freedom (originally proposed by Thomas Jefferson in 1779), went even further with a ringing declaration "that no man shall be compelled to frequent or support any religious worship, place or ministry whatsoever . . . but that all men shall be free to profess and by argument to maintain, their opinions in matters of religion, and that the same shall in no wise diminish, enlarge or affect their civil capacities." The Northwest Ordinance, adopted by the Continental Congress in 1787, extended freedom of worship and belief into the territories north of the Ohio River. Finally, under the Constitution and the First Amendment, "no establishment" and "free exercise" became fundamental principles of federal law.[4]

America's two thousand or so Jews played no significant role in bringing these developments about. They received their rights on the federal level along with everybody else, not, as so often the case in Europe, as part of a special privilege or "Jew Bill." Religious liberty developed from de facto religious pluralism and a complex web of other social, ideological, political, and economic factors affecting the nation as a whole. For this reason, Jews were always able to couch their demands for religious equality in patriotic terms. In seeking rights for themselves on the state level, they appealed to principles shared by Americans of all faiths. . . .[5]

The first half-century following the adoption of the Constitution and First Amendment saw America's small Jewish communities engaged in a wide variety of local campaigns to achieve equal rights in the states. First Amendment guarantees, until the Supreme Court ruled otherwise in 1940, affected congressional legislation only; states remained free to engage in religious discrimination. . . . The most widely publicized of all religious-liberty cases took place in Maryland. According to that state's constitution, anyone assuming an "office of trust or profit" (including lawyers and jurors) was required to execute a "declaration of belief in the Christian religion" before being certified. Solomon Etting, one of the first Jewish merchants in Baltimore, petitioned in 1797 and 1802 to have this law changed, "praying to be placed on the same footing as other good citizens," but to no avail.[6] It took thirty years, a great deal of help from non-Jewish lawmakers, particularly Thomas Kennedy, and a state political realignment before the bill permitting Jews to subscribe to an alternate oath won final passage in 1826 by a narrow margin.[7]

Christian America or Religious America?

By 1840 Jews had won formal political equality in twenty-one of the twenty-six states. In the others, legal disabilities would shortly disappear, or would remain largely unenforced.[8] Yet, full equality still proved elusive, for church-state separation, the principle upon which Jews hinged so many of their hopes, turned out to mean different things to different people. Many Americans, especially in the wake of the Second Great Awakening, the religious revival that overtook the country in the early nineteenth century, had come to understand religious liberty in pan-Christian terms, as if the Constitution aimed only to place all Protestant denominations on an equal footing. Christianity, according to this argument, formed the basis of American society and was implicitly endorsed by the Constitution, even if not mentioned explicitly.[9] The legal case for this school of interpretation was made by Justice Joseph Story writing about the First Amendment in his famous *Commentaries on the Constitution*:

> *The real object of the amendment was, not to countenance, much less to advance Mahometanism, or Judaism, or infidelity, by prostrating Christianity; but to exclude all rivalry among Christian sects, and to prevent any national ecclesiastical establishment, which should give to an hierarchy the exclusive patronage of the national government.[10]*

This understanding of America as an essentially "Christian nation" carried wide appeal. Leading judges and lawyers, including James Kent of New York and Theophilus Parsons and Daniel Webster of Massachusetts, endorsed it, and it accorded with British precedent that recognized "the Christian religion . . . as constituting a part of the common law."[11] . . .

American Jews naturally opposed this "Christian America" interpretation of the First Amendment, and denied that Christianity formed part of the common law. They called instead for "equal footing" to all religions, Judaism included. Philadelphia Jews thus petitioned for the "rights of freemen, solemnly ascertained to all men who are not professed Atheists." Jacob Henry argued that "if a man fulfills the duties of that religion which his education or his Conscience has pointed to him as the true one; no person . . . has the right to arraign him at the bar of any inquisition" . . .

This sense of America as a broadly inclusive religious nation, while understandable as a response to "Christian America," was quite different from the theory of religion and state espoused by Thomas Jefferson and James Madison. Jefferson believed that religion was a personal matter not subject to government jurisdiction at all; we owe to him the famous interpretation of the First Amendment as "a wall of separation between church and state." Madison called in a similar vein for the "entire abstinence of the Government from any interference [with religion] in any way whatever."[12] The view that government should in a nondiscriminatory way support religion did, however, have firm roots in American tradition. The Northwest Ordinance of 1787 grouped religion with morality and knowledge as things "necessary to good government and the happiness of mankind." When the First Amendment was adopted, Samuel Huntington of Connecticut, speaking in Congress, quite explicitly sought "to secure the rights of conscience, and free exercise of the rights of religion, but not to patronize those who professed no religion at all." Several state constitutions and the writings of men like Benjamin Franklin all reinforced the same idea: that religion, defined in its broadest sense, benefits society and government alike.[13]

The fact that early American Jews embraced this tradition explains why, as a community, they never linked their rights to those of nonbelievers. Nor did they protest when several states, including Pennsylvania and Maryland, accorded Jews rights that nonbelievers were denied. Indeed, in one unusual petition in 1813, the Trustees of New York's Congregation Shearith Israel, seeking a share of the state's school fund, attacked the appropriation made to the New York Free School because it "encourage[d] parents in habits of indifference to their duties of religion." Siding with Presbyterians, Roman Catholics, Baptists, and Methodists against the school, they praised religious education as "the greatest foundation of social happiness," and argued on the basis of "the liberal spirit of our constitution," that funds should be made available to religiously sponsored charity schools as well. . . .[14]

Defenders of American Jewish Rights

By the middle decades of the nineteenth century, thanks to immigrants from Germany and Poland, the American Jewish population had grown substantially, reaching 15,000 in 1840 and almost 150,000 twenty years later. Jews now formed a sizable and self-conscious minority community, complete with its own institutions and leaders. . . .

Jews during this period looked to the First Amendment as a guarantor of Jewish rights and used it to legitimate their claims to equality. "The laws of the country," explained Isaac Leeser, editor of *The Occident* and the foremost traditionalist Jewish religious leader of his day, "know nothing of any religious profession, and leave every man to pursue whatever religion he pleases." . . . Religious liberty, to Leeser and most of his fellow Jews, meant "the right to worship God after the dictates of our own hearts." Nathaniel Levin, one of the leading Jewish citizens of Charleston, went out of his way to underscore this point when he delivered a public toast to religious liberty in 1859. "Separate man from religion in any of the duties of life," he declared, "and you degrade him to the level of the brute." Religious liberty, as he defined it, meant "liberty of conscience," and "freedom of thought" within a religious context.[15]

Having defined religious liberty in this way, mid-nineteenth-century Jews saw no need to protest that Congress and most state legislatures began their sessions with religious invocations. They simply insisted that Jews be invited to deliver such prayers as well—and in at least three cases rabbis were invited to do so. Similarly, when in 1861 Jews learned that only "regularly ordained minister[s] of some Christian denomination" could legally serve as regimental chaplains in the Union army, most did not object to the chaplaincy itself, although on its face it violated principles of strict church-state separation. Instead, they campaigned to have the law broadened to include rabbis, which, thanks to support from President Lincoln, it eventually was....[16]

The Shift to Separationism

The last third of the nineteenth century witnessed a momentous change in American Jewish attitudes toward issues of religion and state. Where before, as we have seen, the community generally adhered to a proreligion stance, supporting impartial government aid to *all* religions so long as Judaism was treated equally, now an increasing number of Jews spoke out unequivocally for a government free of *any* religious influence whatsoever, a secular state.

To some extent this reflected the changing spirit of the times. In the post-Civil War decades, James Turner has shown, agnosticism emerged as a respectable alternative to traditional religion: "Disbelief in God was, for the first time, plausible enough to grow beyond a rare eccentricity and to stake out a sizable permanent niche in American culture." Even more important, however, is the fact that Jews during this period found to their dismay that calls for religious equality fell more and more on deaf ears. The spiritual crisis and internal divisions that plagued Protestant America during this era—one that confronted all American religious groups with the staggering implications of Darwinism and biblical criticism—drove Evangelicals and liberals alike to renew their particularistic calls for a "Christian America." Evangelical leaders championed antimodernist legislation to protect the "Christian Sabbath," to institute "Christian temperance," to reintroduce Christianity into the schoolroom, and to write Christian morality into American law codes.... The implication, spelled out in 1867 by a writer in the *American Presbyterian and Theological Review,* was that non-Protestants could *never* win full acceptance as equals:

> *This is a Christian Republic, our Christianity being of the Protestant type. People who are not Christians, and people called Christians, but who are not Protestants dwell among us, but they did not build this house. We have never shut our doors against them, but if they come, they must take up with such accommodations as we have.... If any one, coming among us finds that this arrangement is uncomfortable, perhaps he will do well to try some other country. The world is wide; there is more land to be possessed; let him go and make a beginning for himself as our fathers did for us; as for this land, we have taken possession of it....*[17]

A proposed "Christian Amendment" designed to write "the Lord Jesus Christ" and the "Christian" basis of national life into the text of the Constitution attempted to ensure that these aims would be speedily realized. Then, in 1892, the Supreme Court in *Church of the Holy Trinity v. United States* declared that the United States actually was a "Christian Nation." The justice who wrote this decision, David Brewer, the son of a missionary, subsequently added insult to injury by defending his views in a published lecture, The United States—A Christian Nation (1905), where he relegated Judaism to the level of a tolerated creed....[18]

Jews, all too familiar with the antiJewish rhetoric of Christian romantics in Europe, became alarmed. As in the Old World so in the New, they thought, proponents of religion were allying themselves with the forces of reaction. "The Protestants come now and say defiantly that this is a Protestant country," Rabbi Max Lilienthal warned in a celebrated public address in 1870. "When I left Europe I came to this country because I believed it to be free." In search of a safe haven, many Jews now settled down firmly in the freethinking liberal camp; it seemed far more hospitable to Jewish interests. They also turned increasingly toward a more vehement response to "Christian America" claims—the doctrine of strict separation.[19]

Strict church-state separation was, of course, an old idea in America; its roots lay deeply embedded in colonial and European thought. As we have seen, the idea had been embraced by Thomas Jefferson and James Madison, who believed that the state should be utterly secular, religion being purely a matter of personal preference. While certainly not hostile to religion, they believed that religious divisions were salutary and that religious truth would be most likely to flourish in a completely noncoercive atmosphere. "Whilst we assert for ourselves a freedom to embrace, to profess, and to observe the religion which we believe to be of divine origin," Madison wrote in his *Memorial and Remonstrance* (1785), "we cannot deny an equal freedom to those whose minds have not yet yielded to the evidence which has convinced us." Jefferson refused to proclaim so much as a Thanksgiving Day lest he "indirectly assume to the United States an authority over religious exercises."[20] However, theirs was a decidedly minority view that fell into disfavor with the revival of national religious fervor early in the nineteenth century. It was only now, in the post-Civil War era and as a response to "Christian America" agitation, that strict separation attracted a school of new adherents. . . .

Jews became particularly ardent supporters of the Jefferson-Madison position. . . . Thus in 1868, Rabbi Max Lilienthal elevated complete church-state separation to one of the central tenets of American Judaism:

> [W]e are going to lay our cornerstone with the sublime motto, "Eternal separation of state and church!" For this reason we shall never favor or ask any support for our various benevolent institutions by the state; and if offered, we should not only refuse, but reject it with scorn and indignation, for those measures are the first sophistical, well-premeditated steps for a future union of church and state. Sectarian institutions must be supported by their sectarian followers; the public purse and treasury dares [sic] not be filled, taxed and emptied for sectarian purposes.[21]

Lilienthal's Cincinnati colleague, Rabbi Isaac Mayer Wise, proclaimed a year later that "the State has no religion. Having no religion, it cannot impose any religious instruction on the citizen, adult or child."[22] This soon became the predominant American Jewish position on church-state questions, seconded by one Jewish organization after another. During the latter decades of the nineteenth century, they opposed "religious legislation" in any form, and applauded liberal efforts to "secularize the State completely."[23]

To be sure, as Shlomith Yahalom has shown, Jewish advocates of church-state separation stopped short of supporting the blatantly anti-religious planks advocated by some separationist organizations. Calls by the Liberal League, the American Association for the Advancement of Atheism, and others for taxation of church property, elimination of chaplains from the public payrolls, abolition of court and inaugural oaths, and removal of the phrase "In God We Trust" from the currency never won serious Jewish support, even from those who seconded their larger objectives.[24] Indeed, the Central Conference of American Rabbis, in attacking religious legislation in 1892, went out of its way to recognize at the same time "the value of religious sentiment." Similarly, Rabbi David Philipson, a champion of strict separation, (naively) records his "amazement" at finding that the American Secular Union, which he had been invited to address on church-state separation, "was practically an irreligious organization." One speaker, he writes, so outraged him, "that . . . I cast my manuscript aside" and spoke instead "on religion and the Bible."[25]

Eager to foster voluntary adherence to religion, even as they sought to combat any form of state religion, American Jews steered a middle course. They embraced separationism in theory as the best and most legitimate defense against a Christian-dominated state, but as a practical matter they were much more circumspect and pragmatic, generally keeping in mind other competing considerations and speaking up only in those instances when they believed Jewish interests to be genuinely at risk.

The Battle over Religion in the Public Schools

The issue that stood at the heart of church-state debates in late nineteenth and twentieth-century America and affected American Jews significantly concerned the emotional question of religion in the public schools. . . . Whatever their claims to the contrary, the schools then were culturally Protestant: "They associated Protestant Christianity with republicanism, with economic progress, and with virtue."[26] Curricula and textbooks were, consequently, rife with material that Catholics and Jews found offensive. As early as the 1840s, New York Jews are known to have protested the use of such textbooks in the public schools, but to no avail; the board of education, controlled by Protestants, refused to declare stories about the "Son of God" or readings from the New Testament out of bounds. As a result, Jews who could afford to do so sent their children to Jewish schools—which flourished not only in New York but in every major city where Jews lived.[27]

But not for long. As public schools, under pressure from Catholics and others, became more religiously sensitive, Jews flocked to them for they were free, convenient, often educationally superior, and usually far more commodious than their Jewish counterparts. Furthermore, public schools had in a short time become symbols of American democracy: "temples of liberty," Julius Freiberg of Cincinnati once called them, where "children of the high and low, rich and poor, Protestants, Catholics and Jews, mingle together, play together, and are taught that we are a free people, striving to elevate mankind, and to respect one another."[28] As such, the schools came to have an insurmountable advantage over "sectarian" schools; Jews perceived them as an entree to America itself and supported them as a patriotic duty. By the mid-1870s, most Jewish day schools had closed, replaced by Sabbath, Sunday, and afternoon supplementary schools.

By the 1870s and 1880s, then, a growing number of Jewish leaders had begun to espouse the ideal of nonsectarian, religiously-neutral public school education. To attend public schools and to guard them from sectarianism became not just a matter of Jewish communal interest, but a patriotic obligation as well. In carrying out this "obligation," however, Jews frequently came into conflict with their Protestant and Catholic neighbors. Many schools, for example, began the day with morning religious exercises "usually including, in whole or in part, reading of the King James version of the Bible, reciting of some form of prayer, and singing of hymns." In several states such devotions were even mandated by state law, on the theory that public schools should not be "godless," and that while "sectarianism" was constitutionally enjoined, religion (which usually meant Protestantism) was not.[29] A Texas court, in a 1908 opinion, upheld this view, and defended it with an argument that many at the time found convincing:

> Christianity is so interwoven with the web and woof of the state government that to sustain the contention that the Constitution prohibits reading of the Bible, offering prayers, or singing songs of a religious character in any public building of the government would produce a condition bordering upon moral anarchy.[30]

The problem faced by American Jews was how to dissent from this approach without embracing the very "godlessness" that so many devout Christians sought to preclude. Since the public school symbolized American ideals, Jews wanted their children to be treated in accordance with what they believed those ideals demanded. They wanted the public schools to make their children "Americans," not Christians. It was not enough, then, that most states, particularly in the twentieth century, made provisions for students who wished to be excused from religious exercises, for coercion was not the major issue.[31] Instead, as so often before, the issue was one of religious equality. Jews sought to have schools and other public institutions that would be "undisturbed," in the words of Rabbi Max Lilienthal, "by sectarian strife and bigoted narrowmindedness." . . .[32] "Opposition to sectarianism," explained one Jewish pamphleteer in 1906, "is not an indication of hostility to Christianity but of devotion to American ideals."[33]

Much as they opposed sectarianism in the public schools, many Jews in this period sympathized with Christian fears that schools devoid of religion might become secular and "godless." They searched, therefore, for some way of reconciling their belief in church-state separation with their conviction that education needed to be (in Max Lilienthal's words) "thoroughly . . . preeminently and essentially Godful." Lilienthal himself urged educators to stress the importance of "good deeds and actions." Teach young people "to cling to that sacred covenant of mutual love, mutual good will, and forbearance . . . ," he wrote, "and you will make our schools Godful and truly religious in the noblest sense of the word."[34] Rabbi Bernhard Felsenthal, a Reform rabbi in Chicago, called for "instruction in unsectarian ethics."[35] This, however, did not satisfy the more Orthodox editors of the *American Hebrew*. Calling it "absurd to ask that the State should support schools and identify them with agnosticism," they called on government to teach not just bland ethics but:

the three great religious facts upon the verity of which all religions are united, viz:

1. The existence of God,
2. The responsibility of man to his Maker,
3. The immortality of the soul.

These principles did not, to their mind, conflict with church-state separation for they were "nonsectarian" and represented a religious consensus. Foreshadowing arguments that would be widely heard a century later, they warned that it would be "just as wrong to associate the schools with implied agnosticism as with any sectarianism."[36]

The twentieth century brought with it no resolution to the public school problem. Fueled in part by mainstream Protestants who saw public schools as a vehicle for Americanizing the immigrants and stemming their own movement's decline, pressure to strengthen the religious component of state-sponsored education heightened. Jewish pupils suffered particularly acutely, for both prayers and Bible readings tended to be cast in a Protestant mold; in some cases, they even included New Testament passages that doomed Jews to eternal damnation. Determined to protect Jewish children, the Reform Movement's Central Conference of American Rabbis (CCAR), in 1906, established a standing committee on church and state to collect information and work for Jewish rights.[37]

Initially, the committee focused all its attention on battling "sectarianism in the public schools." It marshaled evidence to prove that "morning religious exercises" in most public schools involved "Protestant religious worship," and argued that, as such, the exercises were both offensive and un-American. . . . [H]owever, unity dissolved when the question turned to what function the public schools *should* play in the realm of religion and ethics. Indeed, the issue became the subject of spirited debate at the Central Conference's annual convention in 1911.[38]

The same kind of debate took place over the so-called Gary Plan, initiated in Gary, Indiana in 1913, permitting released time during the school day for moral and religious instruction outside of school property. Many rabbis were opposed to the plan, despite its nationwide popularity, fearing that once the wall between church and state was breached "the religion of the majority will receive general sanction." One rabbi went so far as to urge his colleagues to line up with the Free Thinking Society and fight the Gary Plan tooth and nail. Other rabbis, such as Samuel Schulman of New York . . . voiced support for the plan, with certain changes. The CCAR, he proclaimed, "should not content itself merely with the negative attitude of insisting upon the complete separation of church and state, but should, wherever it can, constructively and helpfully meet all efforts made for the improvement of ethical and religious education in the nation."[39]

As one of the leading American rabbis of his day, Schulman actually sought to change the whole tenor of church-state thinking within the American Jewish community. In a private letter to Samson Benderly, director of New York's Bureau of Jewish Education, he explained why:

In America, we have a unique and therefore, very delicate problem. We, of course, want to keep religion, Bible reading, hymn singing out of the public schools. At the same time we know that there is not enough efficient moral and religious education in the country. . . . Jews make a mistake in thinking only of themselves and assuming always a negative and critical attitude. They must supplement that negative attitude with a constructive policy. Otherwise, they will soon be classed in the minds of the Christian men and women in this country with the free-thinkers and with those who have no interest in the religious education of the youth. That, of course, is undesirable both because it is contrary to our genius as Jews and also contrary to the real spirit of Americanism, which while not ecclesiastical, and separates Church from State, has always been religious.[40]

Many of the leading figures in Reform Judaism, including Rabbi Julian Morgenstern, came to agree with Schulman, and in 1926, in a highly significant and much disputed policy departure, the Dismissal Plan, a modified version of the Gary Plan that called on schools to "reduce their time schedule by . . . one hour or more at the end of the school day," won CCAR approval, in the hope that parents would devote the time gained to their children's religious education. . . . Louis Marshall was prepared to go even further. He believed that released time *during* the school day was constitutional and "highly commendable," and urged his fellow Jews to support the idea, fearing that "unless something of this sort is done, we shall have a Godless community."[41]

Fears of godlessness, however, were soon drowned out by renewed fears of Christianization, as evidence mounted that released-time programs were being abused . . . Teachers in some communities pressured students to attend religious classes; in others, Jewish students were taunted for studying apart from everybody else. . . . The dilemma that American Jews faced, especially in the 1940s, was whether, given these abuses, released-time programs should be opposed everywhere, even at the risk of seeming "godless," or whether in the interests of Jewish education, as well as goodwill and interfaith harmony, only the abuses themselves should be attacked, not the program as a whole.

Rabbis themselves were divided on the issue: in one memorable case, the Northern California Board of Rabbis opposed a released-time bill, while the Southern California Board supported it! Conservative and Orthodox rabbis tended to be more sympathetic to such plans than Reform rabbis, although the Conservative Rabbinical Assembly went on record in 1946 against any form of religion in the public schools, released time included. And even in Reform congregations, the issue sometimes pitted rabbis opposed to released time on principle against congregants who pragmatically sought to make the plan work, if only for the sake "of good public relations."[42]

The Supreme Court decision in *McCollum v. Board of Education* (1948), declaring unconstitutional released-time plans that used public-school classrooms for religious instruction during regular school hours, strengthened the hands of those in the Jewish community who favored a high wall of separation between church and state. The Synagogue Council of America (representing Orthodox, Conservative, and Reform rabbinic and congregational associations) as well as the organizations associated with the National Community Relations Advisory Council (NCRAC), founded in 1944 as the national coordinating body in the field of Jewish community relations (representing the American Jewish Committee, the American Jewish Congress, the Anti-Defamation League of B'nai B'rith, the Jewish Labor Committee and the Jewish War Veterans), had all filed *amicus curiae* (friends of the court) briefs in the case supporting the McCollums. This raised some eyebrows since the McCollums were atheists, but most Jewish organizations felt that Jews had a compelling interest in the case, especially given the abuses that released-time programs entailed. When the Supreme Court declared that "both religion and government can best work to achieve their lofty aims if each is left free from the other within its respective sphere," the organizations felt vindicated.[43] A month after the decision, the Synagogue Council of America and NCRAC, allied in a Joint Committee on Religion and the Public Schools (later the Joint Advisory Committee on Religion and the State), issued an important statement of principles embodying the new spirit that *McCollum* had unloosed. "The maintenance and furtherance of religion are the responsibility of the synagogue, the church and the home," the statement declared. It proceeded to condemn not only religious education and sectarian observances in the public schools, but also all government aid (other than lunches, medical, and dental services) to denominational schools.[44]

Major Jewish organizations scarcely deviated from this position in the ensuing decades; indeed, it represented somewhat of a Jewish consensus for over a generation. During these years, the Supreme

Court became increasingly involved in church-state problems—a consequence of *Cantwell v. Connecticut* (1940) that applied "the liberties guaranteed by the First Amendment" to the states under terms of the Fourteenth Amendment—and Jewish organizational activities, as a result, shifted ever more toward the legal arena. The American Jewish Committee, the Anti-Defamation League of B'nai B'rith, and the American Jewish Congress became particularly active in this realm—especially the latter, whose Commission on Law and Social Action, directed for many years by attorney Leo Pfeffer, maintained "an absolutist approach to the First Amendment." Pfeffer's view that "complete separation of church and state is best for the church and best for the state, and secures freedom for both" seemed to most Jews to be both logically consistent and historically convincing.[45]

The Supreme Court appeared increasingly to agree. In a critical decision, *Engel v. Vitale* (1962), it outlawed state-composed prayers as constituting an impermissible establishment of religion. The particular prayer involved was a nondenominational one composed by the New York Board of Regents and actually approved by several rabbis, including Rabbi Menachem Schneerson, the Lubavitcher Rebbe, who argued that "it is necessary to engrave upon the child's mind the idea that any wrongdoing is an offense against the divine authority and order."[46] But the overwhelming majority of American Jews, along with many liberal Christians, applauded the decision, notwithstanding the firestorm of protest from Evangelicals, and hailed it "as an affirmation of the position they had long espoused." The same kind of reactions greeted the Court's complementary decision a year later, in *Abington Township School District v. Schempp* (1963), outlawing all devotional reading of the Bible in the public schools, including the practice of reciting the Lord's Prayer.[47] In the case of *Lee v. Weisman*, decided in 1992, the Court extended this principle to hold that a state may not sponsor prayers at public school graduation ceremonies either.[48]

With these decisions, the long agonizing battle over the character of America's public schools—a battle that, as we have seen, really reflected divergent views over the character of the nation as a whole—largely came to an end. Jewish organizations continued to keep a vigilant watch lest religion reenter classrooms through the back door via mandated teaching of "creationism" or other devices, and the Supreme Court on several occasions found it necessary to reiterate, as it did in *Wallace v. Jaffree* (1985), that state encouragement of school prayer was unconstitutional.[49] But the central focus of church-state controversy now shifted from the public schools to public funding of religious schools. And on this issue Jews found themselves seriously divided.

State Aid to Parochial Schools

Unlike other church-state issues that aroused Jewish concern, state aid to parochial schools did not involve the question of Jewish equality. Where Sunday closing laws and prayer in the public schools clearly disadvantaged Jews and could be fought on the basis of Jewish group interests as well as minority rights, state aid to parochial schools was offered to Christian and Jewish schools alike. The issue, then, was not the "equal footing" demand insisted upon since the days of Jonas Phillips, but rather the "wall of separation" axiom upon which Jews had built so much of their twentieth-century church-state philosophy. The debate, which began in earnest in the 1960s, pitted advocates of principle, who felt that any breach in the "wall of separation" would affect America and its Jews adversely, against proponents of pragmatism, who argued for an accommodationist policy benefiting Jewish day schools, interfaith relations, and American education as a whole. . . .

The growth of parochial schools, Catholic and Jewish alike, during the 1940s, coupled with heightened national concern over the quality of primary education, led to renewed pressure on behalf of state and federal measures to grant limited assistance to parochial schools on the basis of the "child benefit theory," the idea, supported by the Supreme Court, that state aid could be extended to parochial-school children so long as "the school children and the state alone are the beneficiaries."[50] As early as 1945, the Central Conference of American Rabbis had expressed concern over this development. In the wake of *Everson v. Board of Education of Ewing Township* (1947), an important case that permitted states to fund the cost of transporting students to parochial schools, this concern turned into real alarm. "The wall of separation between the church and state is surely being breached," Rabbi Joseph Fink, chairman of the Committee on Church and State, exclaimed. He called on his colleagues to do all that they could to uphold the status quo. For a time, leading Jewish organizations and religious bodies, including the Orthodox, united behind the 1948 Synagogue Council-NCRAC statement broadly opposing *all* government aid to parochial schools. Beginning in the 1950s, however, demands for a reevaluation of this policy sounded from a variety of quarters.[51]

In 1952, Will Herberg, author of *Judaism and Modern Man* and considered at the time "a fresh voice in the world of modern religious thought," published in *Commentary* magazine a widely-read article urging Americans of all faiths to rethink their views on the problem of church and state given the new pluralistic realities of American life. Herberg was especially harsh on his fellow Jews. "Judging by their public expressions," he wrote, "they seem to share the basic secularist presupposition that religion is a 'private matter'—in the minimizing sense of 'merely private'—and therefore peripheral to the vital areas of social life and culture." He urged Jews to "rid themselves of the[ir] narrow and crippling minority-group defensiveness," called for interreligious harmony, and insisted that Jews had little to fear from proposals to extend limited federal aid to parochial schools.[52]

Six years later, Rabbi Arthur Gilbert reiterated some of these same concerns in an address to the annual Convention of the Central Conference of American Rabbis, in which he challenged his rabbinic colleagues to rethink their knee-jerk commitment to strict separationism, and the secular bias upon which it was predicated. "Our record is stuck in its groove," he warned, and he specifically attacked Reform opposition to the use of public funds to pay for the transportation of parochial-school children. Drawing from his own experience at the Anti-Defamation League of B'nai B'rith, he called for policy positions "that appear to be more realistic and respond in a more sophisticated fashion to the temper and needs of today's society." . . .[53]

In the years that followed, calls for change sounded in more and more circles. Professors Jakob J. Petuchowski of Hebrew Union College and Seymour Siegel of the Jewish Theological Seminary spoke out in support of state aid to parochial schools and advocated abandonment of the whole separationist agenda in favor of a more proreligious, "equal-footing" stance. Siegel, attacking defenders of the "non-existent wall of separation" who "brain-washed" the Jewish community, charged that a secular state and "desacralized" society were alien to both Americanism and Judaism. Echoing Will Herberg, he described Supreme Court rulings banning Bible reading and prayer from the public schools as bad law and bad public policy.[54] Immanuel Jakobovitz, then the rabbi of the prestigious Fifth Avenue Synagogue in New York and later Chief Rabbi of the British Empire, came to similar conclusions from an Orthodox perspective. In a stinging dissent, he attacked the New York Board of Rabbis for its support of the Supreme Court's decision in *Engel,* and expressed his "dismay at the alliance between teachers of Judaism and the spokesmen of secularism and atheism."[55]

Writing in *Commentary* in 1966, Milton Himmelfarb, another critic of separationism as well as a staunch advocate of state aid to parochial schools, posed a more pragmatic argument for change:

> It is time we actually weighed the utility and cost of education against the utility and cost of separationism. All the evidence in America points to education, more than anything else, influencing adherence to democracy and egalitarianism. All the evidence points to Catholic parochial education having the same influence. . . . Something that nurtures a humane, liberal democracy is rather more important to Jews than twenty-four-karat separationism.[56]

Orthodox leaders fully agreed, insisting that aid to parochial schools was "good for Torah," "good for the Jews," and "good for America." It was, they argued, "both constitutional and equitable" for the government to share the cost of secular programs, since the government required such programs, set standards for what they should contain, and derived benefit from the well-educated citizens they produced.[57]

In 1965, when Congress debated the Elementary and Secondary Education Act that included "child benefit" money earmarked for special educational services in parochial and private schools, intraJewish divisions came out into the open. Jewish spokesmen testified on both sides of the issue, and as a result of the debate the National Jewish Commission on Law and Public Affairs (COLPA) was formed to support aid to parochial schools and to promote the rights and interests of the "observant Jewish community."[58]

Since then, the Jewish community has consistently spoken with two voices on programs to assist secular education in parochial schools. Most Jewish organizations continue to condemn the programs on "no establishment" grounds. Any breach in the "wall of separation between church and state," they fear, will ultimately work to the detriment of Jews and America as a whole. A minority of Jewish organizations, meanwhile, staunchly defend such programs on pragmatic and "free exercise" grounds. The tangible benefits that would result from federal aid to parochial education, they insist, would more than compensate for any potential problems.

"Overhauling Our Priorities"

The creation of COLPA and the attendant calls for a new American Jewish policy on church-state questions carried implications that went far beyond the issue of aid to parochial schools. A growing minority came to agree with Rabbi Walter Wurzberger, a leading Modern Orthodox rabbi and onetime president of the Synagogue Council, that the time had come for a "thorough overhauling" of Jewish priorities on *all* church-state issues. In place of what Wurzberger spoke of as "obsessive preoccupation with the Establishment Clause," they called for far greater attention to "free exercise" claims. They especially sought support for initiatives that could make it easier for Jews to observe their religious traditions.[59]

Surprisingly, the religious tradition that most frequently found its way into the courts concerned public displays of the menorah (candelabrum), symbol of the relatively minor Jewish holiday of Chanukah usually celebrated in December. The issue as popularly understood involved a basic question: should government property be devoid of *any* religious symbols, or should it be open to *all* religious symbols? What made the issue complex was the widespread public celebration of Christmas, the only American legal holiday from which Jews, as non-Christians, felt emotionally excluded. Jews had long protested sectarian celebrations of Christmas, especially in public schools, and in more recent years they had also fought to remove such Christmas symbols as the cross and the crèche from public property, arguing (as opponents of menorah displays also did) that these amounted to an impermissible establishment of religion. The Supreme Court in the controversial case of *Lynch v. Donnelly* (1984) partially overruled this objection, declaring that the crèche, at least in the company of other "secular" Christmas symbols, was constitutionally unobjectionable. The question, then, was whether the menorah too was unobjectionable and whether, if so, Jews should ask for it to be placed on public property alongside the permissible symbols of Christmas.[60]

Most Jewish organizations, unhappy with the *Lynch* decision, continued to believe that religious symbols of any sort should be kept off public property on First Amendment grounds. Some Orthodox groups, however, and particularly the Chabad (Lubavitch) organization, took an opposite stance. They insisted that menorahs *should* be placed on public property both as a Jewish response to Christmas and as a symbol of religious pride.[61] In *Allegheny County v. ACLU of Pittsburgh* (1989), the Supreme Court partially vindicated this view, upholding the placement of a menorah on public property, next to a Christmas tree, on the grounds that "both Christmas and Chanukah are part of the same winter-holiday season, which has attained secular status in our society."

Within the Jewish community, however, debate continued focusing on a much deeper issue. Supporters of the publicly displayed menorah argued that the public square should be filled with a multitude of religious symbols. These, they believed, would foster respect for religion, stimulate Jewish observance, and help fight assimilation. Opponents, meanwhile, feared that displays of religious symbols on government property would foster fanaticism and intolerance. Confining such symbols to private property, they felt, was the best guarantee of church-state separation and the rights of religious minorities.

Similar debates have swirled around other Jewish attempts to reorder church-state priorities. In one celebrated case, *Goldman v. Weinberger* (1986), an Orthodox Jewish Air Force officer named Simcha Goldman contested the military's uniform dress requirements that barred him from wearing a yarmulke while serving on duty. The Supreme Court ultimately ruled against Goldman, but the fact that his case was supported on "free exercise" grounds by COLPA, the American Jewish Committee, and other Jewish organizations pointed to a renewed emphasis on freedom *for* religious practices.[62] Related "free exercise" cases, most of them confined to lower courts, have involved everything from issues of Sabbath and holiday observance, to the religious rights of Jews incarcerated in prison, to divorce-law protection for women whose husbands refused to issue them a traditional Jewish divorce (*get*).[63] No matter how different the circumstances in each case, however, the ultimate goal has generally been the same: "to remove the obstacles which face adherents of minority religions in the exercise of their religious rights."[64]

Conclusion

In the two hundred years since Jonas Phillips pleaded with the Constitutional Convention for religious freedom, the condition of Jews in America has improved dramatically. They have won full legal equality under federal law and in each of the states; they face few if any hardships from Christian Sunday laws; and their children, at least in most places, can attend state-sponsored public schools without fear of intimidation on religious grounds. Most of these improvements derive, directly or indirectly, from the principles set forth in the Constitution itself, particularly the "no establishment" and "free exercise" clauses of the First Amendment.

What these clauses mean, however, has remained a subject of continuing controversy. Does the First Amendment imply that America is a Christian nation (as some Evangelicals claim), a religious nation, or a secular nation? Does it envisage a government guaranteeing equality to *all* religions, one divided by a high wall from *any* religion, or one occupying some middle ground? And what happens when the "no establishment" and "free exercise" clauses conflict with one another? Which takes precedence?

American Jews have never been of one mind on these questions. While quite generally opposed to those who would Christianize the country or discriminate on religious grounds, they have been far less certain about what their communal priorities should be: religion in American life or governmental secularism? Accommodation to religion or separation from it?

Historically . . . American Jews have supported a wide range of positions on church-state relations; indeed, over the long span of American Jewish history there has been far less communal consensus on the subject than generally assumed. Fearing the persecutory potential of the Christian state, on the one hand, and the possible antireligious animus of the secular state, on the other, many American Jews have sought a middle ground, a quest that has thus far proved elusive. But if there has been no community-wide consensus on specific policies and approaches, there has, at least, been a common vision, one that links Jonas Phillips with his modern-day counterparts. It is the search for "equal footing," the conviction that America should be a land where people of all faiths are treated alike.

Excerpted from *Religion and State in the American Jewish Experience* (Notre Dame, IN: Notre Dame University Press, 1997), pp. 1–38
Reprinted with permission of the publisher

Endnotes

[1] Reprinted in Morris U. Schappes, ed., *A Documentary History of the Jews in the United States, 1654–1875* (New York, 1971), 68–69, and with minor differences in Bernard Schwartz, *The Roots of the Bill of Rights* (New York, 1980), 439–440.
[2] The states were Pennsylvania, New Hampshire, New York, Virginia, North Carolina, and Maryland (minority position); see Schwartz, *Roots of the Bill of Rights*, 1167.

[3] Jacob R. Marcus, *The Colonial American Jew* (Detroit, 1970), 226, 511-512; see also Abram Vossen Goodman, *American Overture: Jewish Rights in Colonial Times* (Philadelphia, 1947).

[4] Stanley F. Chyet, "The Political Rights of the Jews in the United States: 1776–1840," *American Jewish Archives* 10 (1958): 14–75; Oscar and Mary Handlin, "The Acquisition of Political and Social Rights by the Jews in the United States," *AJYB* 56 (1955): 43–98; Conrad H. Moehlman, *The American Constitutions and Religion* (Berne, Ind., 1938); many of these documents are reprinted in Sarna, Kraut, and Joseph, *Jews and the Founding of the Republic*, 85–102.

[5] Jonathan D. Sarna, "The Impact of the American Revolution on American Jews," *Modern Judaism* 1 (September 1981): 149–160.

[6] Quoted in Isaac M. Fein, *The Making of an American Jewish Community* (Philadelphia, 1971), 26.

[7] See E. Milton Altfeld, *The Jew's Struggle for Religious and Civil Liberty in Maryland* (Baltimore, 1924) and Edward Eitches, "Maryland's Jew Bill," *American Jewish Historical Quarterly* 60 (March 1971): 258–279.

[8] Chyet, "Political Rights of the Jews in the United States," 80

[9] Robert T. Handy, *A Christian America* (New York, 1971); Borden, *Jews, Turks, and Infidels*, 53–74; see also James R. Rohrer, "Sunday Mails and the Church-State Theme in Jacksonian America," *Journal of the Early Republic* 7 (Spring 1987): 60.

[10] Joseph Story, *Commentaries on the Constitution of the United States* (Boston, 1833) as reprinted in John F. Wilson and Donald L. Drakeman, *Church and State in American History* (Boston, 1987), 92–93; for a modern view, see Leonard W. Levy, "The Original Meaning of the Establishment Clause of the First Amendment," in *Religion and the State: Essays in Honor of Leo Pfeffer*, ed. James E. Wood, Jr. (Waco, Tex. 1985), 43–83.

[11] On Kent, see *People v. Ruggles*, 8 Johns Rep. (N.Y.) 294 (1811), and John Webb Pratt, *Religion, Politics, and Diversity: The Church-State Theme in New York History* (Ithaca, N.Y., 1967), 138. On Parsons, see Nathan Dane, *A General Abridgement and Digest of American Law* (Boston, 1823-29), 2:337 as quoted in Borden, *Jews, Turks, and Infidels*, 12. On Webster, see *Vidal v. Girard's Executors*, 2 How. 127 (1844), and Jonathan D. Sarna, "The Church-State Dilemma of American Jews," in *Jews in Unsecular America*, ed. Richard John Neuhaus (Grand Rapids, Mich., 1987), 10–11. For British precedent, see *Shover v. The State*, 5 Eng: 259 as quoted by Bernard J. Meislin, "Jewish Law in America," in *Jewish Law in Legal History and the Modern World*, ed. Bernard S. Jackson (Leiden, 1980), 159.

[12] See Jefferson's letter to the Danbury Baptists (1802) and Madison's letter to Rev. jasper Adams (1832), reprinted in Wilson and Drakeman, *Church and State in American History*, 78–81. For the background to Jefferson's letter, see Constance B. Schulz, "'Of Bigotry in Politics and Religion': Jefferson's Religion, the Federalist Press, and the Syllabus," *Virginia Magazine of History and Biography* 91 (January 1983): 73–91, esp. 85.

[13] *Annals of the Congress of the United States*, compiled by Joseph S. Gales, Sr. (1834) as reprinted in Wilson and Drakeman, *Church and State in American History*, 76; Sarna, "Church-State Dilemma of American Jews," 11.

[14] The petition is reprinted in *PAJHS* 27 (1920): 92–95.

[15] *The Occident* 16 (1859): 580. See Naomi W. Cohen, *Encounter With Emancipation: The German Jews in the United States, 1830–1914* (Philadelphia, 1984), 77: "The Jewish pioneers for religious equality generally asked for government neutrality on matters of religion . . . a neutral-to-all-religions rather than a divorced-from-religion state."

[16] Bertram W. Korn, *Eventful Years and Experiences* (Cincinnati, 1954), 98–124; idem, *American Jewry and the Civil War* (New York, 1970), 56–97.

[17] *American Presbyterian and Theological Review* 5 (July 1867): 390–391.

[18] Borden, *Jews, Turks, and Infidels*, 62–74; Cohen, *Encounter With Emancipation*, 98–100, 254–256.

[19] David Philipson, *Max Lilienthal* (New York, 1915), 121; the above paragraphs are adapted from Sarna, "Church-State Dilemma of American Jews," 13–14.

[20] James Madison, *A Memorial and Remonstrance: To the Honorable the General Assembly of the Commonwealth of Virginia* (1785), and Thomas Jefferson to the Rev. Mr. Millar (1808), both reprinted in Wilson and Drakeman, *Church and State in American History*, 69, 79; see Robert M. Healey, "Jefferson on Judaism and the Jews: 'Divided We Stand, United, We Fall!'" *AJH* 73 (June 1984): 359–374, and more broadly, William Lee Miller, *The First Liberty: Religion and the American Republic* (New York, 1986), 5–150.

[21] Reprinted in Philipson, *Max Lilienthal*, 456–457, cf. 109–125.

[22] Quoted in Heller, *Isaac M. Wise*, 620.

[23] "Commending the 'Congress of Liberals,'" reprinted in *Where We Stand*, 14-15.

[24] Yahalom, "American Judaism and the Question of Separation between Church and State," esp. 257–264; Stokes, *Church and State in the United States* 3:592–595.

[25] *CCARYB* 3 (1893): 45; David Philipson, *My Life as an American Jew* (Cincinnati, 1941), 76.

[26] Kaestle, *Pillars of the Republic*, 93; Lloyd P. Gartner, "Temples of Liberty Unpolluted: American Jews and Public Schools, 1840–1875," in *A Bicentennial Festschrift for Jacob Rader Marcus*, ed. B. W. Korn (Waltham, Mass. and New York, 1976), 161; see Robert Michaelson, *Piety in the Public School* (New York, 1970).

[27] Hyman B. Grinstein, *The Rise of the Jewish Community of New York, 1654–1860* (Philadelphia, 1945), 235–236; Joseph R. Brandon, "A Protest against Sectarian Texts in California Schools in 1875," *Western States Jewish History* 20 (April 1988): 233–235; Alexander M. Dushkin, *Jewish Education in New York City* (New York, 1918), 46–50. Catholics, of course, were vehement in their opposition to the Protestant character of the public schools. On this issue, the *New York Herald* noted with amusement, Jews and Catholics were united for the first time in 1,840 years; see Diane Ravitch, *The Great School Wars: New York City, 1805–1873* (New York, 1974), 53.

[28] Quoted in Gartner, "Temples of Liberty Unpolluted," 180.

[29] Ibid., 177, 182; William E. Griffiths, *Religion, the Courts, and the Public Schools: A Century of Litigation* (Cincinnati, 1966), 1–92.

[30] *Church v. Bullock*, 104 Texas 1, 109 SW 115 (1908), quoted in Griffiths, *Religion, the Courts, and the Public Schools*, 50.

[31] Griffiths, *Religion, the Courts, and the Public Schools*, 72–92; see, however, Henry Berkowitz's memoir of religious coercion in the Pittsburgh public schools quoted in Cohen, *Encounter With Emancipation*, 92.

[32] Philipson, *Max Lilienthal*, 123.

[33] Ephraim Frisch, *Is the United States A Christian Nation? A Legal Study* (Pine Bluff, Ark., 1906).

[34] *American Israelite*, September 19, 1873.

[35] *The Nation* 34 (January 12, 1882): 34.

36 *American Hebrew,* March 2, 1888, SO, 51, 59; Cohen, *Encounter with Emancipation,* 95.

37 The committee was established on the basis of a 1904 proposal by Rabbi Joseph Krauskopf; see *CCARYB* 14 (1904): 32. Its first publication was entitled, significantly, *Why the Bible Should Not Be Read in the Public Schools* (1906). See Lance J. Sussman, "Rhetoric and Reality: The Central Conference of American Rabbis and the Church-State Debate, 1890–1940," in *In Celebration: An American Jewish Perspective on the Bicentennial of the United States Constitution,* ed. Kerry M. Olitzky (Lanham, Md., 1989), 72–100; and Eugene Lipman, "The Conference Considers Relations Between Religion and the State," in *Retrospect and Prospect,* ed. Bertram W. Korn (New York, 1965), 114–128.

38 *CCARYB* 16 (1906): 153; 21 (1911): 259, 262.

39 Nathan Schachner, "Church, State and Education," *AJYB* 49 (1947–48): 29; *CCARYB* 25 (1915): 426, 428; 35 (1925): 60.

40 Samuel Schulman to Samson Benderly, December 9, 1915, Schulman Papers 1/5, American Jewish Archives, Cincinnati, Ohio.

41 Reznikoff, *Louis Marshall, Champion of Liberty,* 970–971.

42 *CCARYB* 51 (1941): 121; 53 (1943): 75; *AJYB* 48 (1946–1947): 129.

43 *McCollum v. Board of Education,* 333 U.S. 203 at 383; Naomi W. Cohen, *Not Free to Desist: A History of the American Jewish Committee, 1906–1966* (Philadelphia, 1972), 440; *CCARYB* 58 (1948), 104–106.

44 *AJYB* 50 (1948–1949): 221–223. According to the official history of the Synagogue Council, this position could "be fairly said to represent the majority opinion, almost the official opinion of American Jewry," quoted in Murray Friedman, *The Utopian Dilemma* (Washington, D.C., 1985), 29.

45 Leo Pfeffer, "Is the First Amendment Dead?" reprinted in Naomi W. Cohen, "Schools, Religion and Government-Recent American Jewish Opinions," *Michael* 3 (1975): 373; Pfeffer, *Church, State, and Freedom,* 728; see Pfeffer's "An Autobiographical Sketch," in *Religion and the State: Essays in Honor of Leo Pfeffer,* ed. Wood, 487–533. On the Supreme Court's involvement in the question of religion and the public schools, with copies of relevant decisions, see Miller and Flowers, *Toward Benevolent Neutrality: Church, State, and the Supreme Court,* 378–452.

46 "Letter from the Lubavitcher Rabbi (1964)," quoted in Cohen, "Schools, Religion, and Government," 364; Pratt, *Religion, Politics, and Diversity: The Church-State Theme in New York History,* 290.

47 *AJYB* 64 (1962–63): 110; Cohen, "Schools, Religion, and Government," 348.

48 On *Lee v. Weisman,* see Terry Eastland, ed., *Religious Liberty in the Supreme Court: The Cases That Define the Debate Over Church and State* (Washington, D.C., 1993), 439–467; and Leonard W. Levy, *The Establishment Clause: Religion and the First Amendment,* 2d ed. (Chapel Hill, N.C., 1994), 200–204.

49 Pfeffer, *Church, State, and Freedom,* 342, 350; *Wallace v. Jaffree,* 105 S.Ct. 2479.

50 *Cochran v. La. State Board of Education,* 281 U.S. 370 at 375.

51 *CCARYB* 55 (1945): 92; 57 (1947): 122; *AJYB* 50 (1948–1949): 222.

52 Will Herberg, "The Sectarian Conflict Over Church and State," *Commentary* 14 (November 1952): 450–462; David G. Dalin, "Will Herberg in Retrospect," *Commentary* 86 (July 1988): 38–43.

53 *CCARYB* 68 (1958): 55, 57.

54 Seymour Siegel, "Church and State," *Conservative Judaism* 17 (Spring/Summer 1963): 1–12.

55 Cohen, *Jews in Christian America,* 177–178.

56 Milton Himmelfarb, "Church and State: How High a Wall," *Commentary* 42 (July 1966), reprinted in his *The Jews of Modernity* (New York, 1973), 171; see also Seymour Siegel, "Church and State," *Conservative Judaism* 17 (1963): 1–12; idem, "Church and State: A Reassessment," *Sh'ma* 1 (December 11, 1970), reprinted in *Listening to American Jews,* ed. Carolyn T. Oppenheim (New York, 1986), 130–134; and Jakob J. Petuchowski, "Logic and Reality," *The Jewish Spectator,* September 1962, 20.

57 Quoted in Sheldon J. Harr, "Church, State, and the Schools: A Jewish Perspective" (Rabbinic thesis, HUC-JIR, 1973), 83–84.

58 Cohen, "Schools, Religion, and Government," 378–379; *AJYB* 67 (1966): 128, 139–141.

59 Walter Wurzberger, "Separation of Church and State Revisited," *Face to Face* 8 (Fall 1981): 8; see Noah Pickus, "Before I Built a Wall—Jews, Religion and American Public Life," *This World* 15 (Fall 1986): 28–42; see also Friedman, *The Utopian Dilemma,* esp. 87–98.

60 Jonathan D. Sarna, "Is Judaism Compatible with American Civil Religion? The Problem of Christmas and the National Faith," in *Religion and the Life of the Nation,* ed. Rowland A. Sherrill (Urbana, Ill., 1990), 152–173.

61 See, for example, *American Israelite,* December–January 1987; Yosef Friedman, ed., *And There Was Light* (New York, 1988).

62 *Goldman v. Weinberger,* 106 S.Ct. 1310.

63 For examples see Bernard J. Meislin, *Jewish Law in American Tribunals* (New York, 1976) with updates in *Jewish Law Annual,* and Louis Bernstein, *Challenge and Mission: The Emergence of the English Speaking Orthodox Rabbinate* (New York, 1982), 184–210. J. David Bleich has surveyed Jewish divorce in American law in "Jewish Divorce: Judicial Misconceptions and Possible Means of Civil Enforcement," *Connecticut Law Journal* 16 (Winter 1984): 201-289.

64 Wurzberger, "Separation of Church and State Revisited," 8.

IS MONOTHEISM HAZARDOUS TO LIFE?

RABBI TZVI FREEMAN

Hey Rabbi:

It seems to me that monotheism is a solution to nothing. Before monotheism, we had barbarians. After monotheism, we had barbarians. Monotheistic barbarians.

Before monotheism, we had wars in the name of a whole pantheon of gods. After monotheism, we had wars in the name of a supreme god.

It's one thing when you go to war with "Our god is bigger than your god." Those wars, bad as they were, were local. It's another when you declare "Ours is the only god!" Those are the wars that can destroy the world.

Or is that the entire goal of monotheism—to wipe all disbelievers off the face of the earth?

—Kinda Angry

Hey Kinda:

You're right. Monotheism is a dangerous belief.

Perhaps one of the most dangerous beliefs there is. Because it leaves no room for anything else. You could destroy the world with this belief.

There's another dangerous belief. That's belief in the human being. One who worships human intellect as the measure of all things has also proven himself capable of destroying the world with his beliefs. Because a human's mind cannot help but be bribed by his own ego.

For either of these beliefs—the belief in human beings and the belief in One G-d—to safely enter our world, the two concepts had to be married together.

RABBI TZVI FREEMAN, 1955–

Rabbi, computer scientist, and writer. A published expert, consultant, and lecturer in the field of educational technology, Rabbi Freeman held posts at the University of British Columbia and the Digipen School of Computer Gaming. Rabbi Freeman is the author of *Bringing Heaven Down to Earth* and *Men, Women & Kabbalah*. He is a senior editor at Chabad.org.

For monotheism to work, a crucial fact about this One G-d must be accepted: That He is in love with this world He has made, and especially with the people He has placed upon it.

For human intellect to function safely, we must first accept that there is something beyond intellect, something eternally and immovably good and life-affirming Who determines what is true and what is not, what is right and what is wrong.

Look through the annals of history and you will see it: When this sort of belief has guided men and women, whatever religion they followed, those people brought peace, wisdom and progress into the world.

Today, we desperately need this marriage of beliefs. With it, we can heal our world.

Two Themes of Beginning

Take a look at the opening of Genesis and you will see these two themes.

There are actually two narratives of creation there: The first is centered on the theme of G-d as Creator, the second focused on the theme of Adam, the first human being, created "in the divine image."

Take one narrative without the other, and you've lost everything. If G-d leaves no room for man, or man leaves no room for G-d, you've got one lousy story ahead of you.

Even in the first narrative alone, take a closer look: G-d creates and then He declares each thing He makes to be good. When it's all done, it's declared "very good."

That's an essential part of the narrative: The Creator appreciates His creation. It has purpose and meaning to Him.

No, this world was not created for some apocalyptic finale, neither was its magnificence formed only to dissipate into ionized gas. It was created, as Isaiah says, "not for desolation, but to be lived upon." And to find divine meaning in that life.

G-d loves life. Life is G-dly. The two, of necessity, go hand in hand.

The *Alef-Bet* of Creation

An ancient Midrash says the same in the language of a parable.[1]

It says that the G-d chose to create the world beginning with the second letter of the alphabet, rather than the first. Why? Because if the world began with the first letter, it would be a world that allowed for only one singularity. Nothing else would have meaning. It would be a meaningless, dark world.

So instead He created it beginning with the second letter—the letter *beit* of *Breishit*. Only later, when He gave the Torah, did He begin with the first letter—the letter א *alef* of אנכי *Anochi*.

That way, there would first be a something, a world, and then we would discover the meaning of that world.

What is that meaning?

That even when there is a world, there is truly only One; there is nothing else but Him. Because this world is the ultimate mystery of the divine, and it is up to us to unveil that mystery—by cherishing life, nurturing life, and doing all the best things we can with life. By cherishing His world.

Two Kinds of One

That's the real meaning of "G-d is One."[2]

Some people think that's a statement of belief in a supreme deity—one who is so big, He has exclusive rights over everything. Which means that nothing has real value.

Maybe you've heard the story of the rabbi who, in discussion with a self-professed atheist, said, "The god that you don't believe in, I also don't believe in."

Because these people haven't really escaped the paradigm of polytheism. They are still orbiting within its gravitational pull. They see the world around them as something entirely separate from the G-d that created it.

That's not the meaning of "G-d is One."

"G-d is one" is a statement about the essential fabric of our reality. It's a statement that "in the heavens above and on the earth below, there is nothing else but Him." And that can only be so if this world He has created has divine meaning.[3]

"G-d is one" tells you: Look at this amazing creation you inhabit. Listen to the majestic harmony of a billion trillion parts. Peer upon the infinite wisdom that lies within each of its details. Discover G-d here. Because in the all the things that He has made, there is a wondrous paradox—that within the endless diversity of all opposites breathes a perfect oneness.

Blind Faith vs. Solid Faith

How do people come to these bizarre conclusions about G-d and what He wants from them? How could you have a god who created a world and wants to see its destruction?

Because their beliefs are based on their own need for power.

When the god you worship is based on your need for power, or even on your sense of reason, that god can never be bigger than you. You are, after all, its foundation. So the bigger this god becomes, you will always be bigger than it.

This kind of belief is in the same category as "blind faith." Blind faith is an instinct to just follow, to allow your ego to be swallowed into a much greater whole—and thereby become an even greater ego.

And that leaves the whole world at your disposal.

The way out is to begin from the opposite end. Begin with a sense that this reality is not predicated on your existence, but upon a singularity that transcends all things and is found within all of them.

When you really get that, it's only natural to ask, "If so, what am I doing here? What is this world doing here? What is this all about? What is the meaning?" And you search for meaningful answers.

If you think about these questions with a clear mind, looking at this amazing world about you, you'll certainly realize that the Creator of this world desires diversity.

And that's what Jews believe—that in the messianic era there will still be many nations. "No nation shall raise a sword against another. They will learn war no more."[4] They won't all become Jews.[5] They will be good people, keeping the basic laws of civil human behavior—known as the "laws of Noah."[6]

And in those times, as Maimonides writes, "the entire occupation of the world will be to know G-d."[7] All these nations will see the oneness of the divine in each thing, each from their unique perspective.

Faith, Love & G-d

That sense, that capacity to start with a point beyond yourself, is called *emunah*. Some translate that as "belief," but they miss the point.

Emunah is an intuitive knowledge of a reality that is much greater than you. It is a knowledge that is beyond our sense of reason, because it is capable of escaping the ego.

So that if you have true *emunah* you feel truly small. You feel that your entire existence is not to "just be," but for a purpose.

With faith predicated on ego and power, there is no room for others. With *emunah*, there is space for everyone. There is a sense of mission, a commitment to life, and to finding meaning in all things.

That's something accessible to all people. Whatever trappings your monotheism may take on, if you truly believe in G-d's oneness, that oneness will include a love for life, for living beings, and especially for your fellow human beings. Because if you truly love G-d, you love that which G-d loves.[8]

Reprinted with permission of the Judaism website—Chabad.org

Endnotes

[1] Midrash Rabbah, Genesis 1:14; Zohar, beginning of Parashat Vayigash; *Maamar V'HaBriach Hatichon* 5658; *Maamar Chayav Inish* 5718.
[2] Deuteronomy 6:4.
[3] See *Maamar Havaye Li B'ozrei* 5717, chapter 11b.
[4] Isaiah 2:4. Mica 4:3.
[5] See Maimonides, *Mishneh Torah*, Laws of Kings, chapters 11-12. Elucidated in *Likutei Sichot*, volume 23, page 179. See there, especially footnote 76.
[6] Talmud, Sanhedrin 56a.
[7] Ibid.
[8] See *Hayom Yom*, Nissan 28.

Acknowledgments

There is no comfort in a colorless and bland peace. Friction births the spark of ingenuity that advances a nation and alters its destiny. The mettle of unity is tested in how we endure our disputes and how we come out on the other side. So although we are told that "G-d found no better vessel to hold blessing for the Jewish people other than peace" (Mishnah, Uktsin 3:12), it is a plain fact that dispute and argument is as old as the Jewish nation itself. The discordant groups and doctrinal debates that pepper our history made us who we are today.

Great Debates in Jewish History offers a glimpse at six pivotal debates that engulfed the Jewish people at different periods of our long history. In this course, we examine the background, motives, ideologies, key events, and aftermath of these flare-ups. We seek the underlying ideologies that led to each clash, study how the two sides interacted with each other and lived through the tension, discuss the consequences of the debate, and explore by what means these disputes were resolved. Thereby, we discover how these debates shaped much of Jewish life today. We also leave with valuable lessons for navigating today's wide-ranging diversity among different communities, advocacy groups, denominations, and philosophies.

The course was conceived and developed with guidance and direction from **Professor Lawrence H. Schiffman,** Judge Abraham Lieberman professor of Hebrew and Judaic studies at the Skirball Department of Hebrew and Judaic Studies, and director of the Global Network for Advanced Research in Jewish Studies at New York University. Professor Schiffman is a devoted friend of JLI and a member of its Academic Advisory Board. The JLI curriculum team was fortunate to draw on Professor Schiffman's vast erudition and expertise to develop a scholarly and relevant learning experience. His guidance has been invaluable in the framing, research, writing, and publication of this course.

The development of Lesson 6 was greatly aided by two dear friends of JLI. **Professor Jonathan Sarna** is the Joseph H. & Belle R. Braun Professor of American Jewish History at Brandeis University, and chief historian of the National Museum of American Jewish History. Dr. Sarna is also a member of JLI's Academic Advisory Board. His generous communication of his expertise in American Jewish history helped us develop Lesson 6. **Mr. Nathan Lewin** is a noted American attorney who has engaged in litigation for more than 45 years. His personal and professional experiences, which he relayed to us, relating to the topic of Lesson 6, were informative and important.

We extend our thanks to **Rabbi Mordechai Dinerman** for his coordination with Professor Schiffman in developing this course, for his editorial oversight over course development, and for his work on Lessons 1, 2, 4 and 5. We thank **Rabbi Lazer Gurkow** for his work on Lessons 2 and 5, **Rabbi Dr. Shmuel Klatzkin** for his work on Lesson 3, **Rabbi Eli Raksin** for his work on Lesson 4, **Rabbi Shmuel Super** for his work on Lesson 3, and **Rabbi Yanki Tauber** for his work on Lesson 6.

We extend our appreciation to **Rabbi Naftali Silberberg**, who, along with **Rabbi Mordechai Dinerman,** directs the JLI Curriculum Department and the Flagship editorial team; to **Rabbi Dr. Shmuel Klatzkin**, JLI's senior editor; and to **Rabbi Zalman Abraham**, who skillfully provides the vision for strategic branding and marketing of JLI course offerings.

Rabbis Avraham Bergstein, Yakov Gershon, Lazer Gurkow, and Motti Schochet provided research assistance for this course, and **Rabbi Yisrael Glick** assisted in writing Lesson 5. **Rabbi Zalman Gordon, Rabbi Shimon Posner, Rivkah Slonim, Rabbi Yisrael Rice,** and **Rabbi Avrohom Sternberg**, members of the JLI Editorial Board, provided countless useful suggestions that enhanced the course and ensured its suitability for a wide range of students.

Rivki Mockin streamlined the curriculum process and ensured the smoothness and timeliness of the product, and **Chana Dechter,** JLI Flagship's administrator and project manager, contributed immeasurably to the production and professionalism of the entire project. **Mendel Schtroks, Raizel Shurpin** and **Shternie Morosow** designed the textbooks with taste, expertise, and patience. **Chany Tauber** researched and selected the images for the textbook. **Mendel Sirota** directed the book publication and distribution. **Zushi Greisman, Ya'akovah Weber, Sarah Hinda Appelbaum** and **Rachel Witty** enhanced the quality and professionalism of the course with their proofreading.

Baila Pruss, Mushka Pruss and **Chany Tauber** designed the aesthetically pleasing PowerPoints, and **Moshe Raskin** and **Getzy Raskin** produced the videos for this course. The video scripts were masterfully written by **Rabbi Yaakov Paley**.

We are immensely grateful for the encouragement of JLI's visionary chairman, and vice-chairman of *Merkos L'Inyonei Chinuch*—Lubavitch World Headquarters, **Rabbi Moshe Kotlarsky**. Rabbi Kotlarsky has been highly instrumental in building the infrastructure for the expansion of Chabad's international network, and is the architect of scores of initiatives and services to help Chabad representatives across the globe succeed in their mission. We are blessed to have the unwavering support of JLI's principal benefactor, **Mr. George Rohr**, who is fully invested in our work, continues to be instrumental in JLI's monumental growth and expansion, and is largely responsible for the Jewish renaissance that is being spearheaded by JLI and its affiliates across the globe.

The commitment and sage direction of JLI's dedicated Executive Board—**Rabbis Chaim Block, Hesh Epstein, Ronnie Fine, Yosef Gansburg, Shmuel Kaplan, Yisrael Rice,** and **Avrohom Sternberg**—and the countless hours they devote to the development of JLI, are what drive the vision, growth, and tremendous success of the organization.

Finally, JLI represents an incredible partnership of more than 1,400 *shluchim* and *shluchot* in more than one thousand locations across the globe, who contribute their time and talent to further Jewish adult education. We thank them for generously sharing feedback and making suggestions that steer JLI's development and growth. They are our most valuable critics and our most cherished contributors.

Inspired by the call of the **Lubavitcher Rebbe**, of righteous memory, it is the mandate of the Rohr JLI to **provide a community of learning** for all Jews throughout the world where they can participate in their precious heritage of Torah learning and experience its rewards. May this course succeed in fulfilling this sacred charge!

On behalf of the Rohr Jewish Learning Institute,

RABBI EFRAIM MINTZ
Executive Director

RABBI YISRAEL RICE
Chairman, Editorial Board

Rosh Chodesh Elul, 5777

The Rohr Jewish Learning Institute

AN AFFILIATE OF MERKOS L'INYONEI CHINUCH,
THE EDUCATIONAL ARM OF THE CHABAD LUBAVITCH MOVEMENT

822 EASTERN PARKWAY, BROOKLYN, NY 11213

JLI INTERNATIONAL

Rabbi Avrohom Sternberg
CHAIRMAN

Rabbi Dubi Rabinowitz
DIRECTOR

Rabbi Berry Piekarski
ADMINISTRATOR

Mendel Schtroks
CONTENT MANAGER

Rabbi Yosef Yitzchok Noyman
ADMINISTRATOR, JLI ISRAEL
IN PARTNERSHIP WITH MIVTZA
TORAH—ISRAEL

Rabbi Israel Ashkenazi
DIRECTOR, JLI ISRAEL

Rabbi Eli Wolf
ADMINISTRATOR, JLI IN THE CIS
IN PARTNERSHIP WITH THE
FEDERATION OF JEWISH
COMMUNITIES OF THE CIS

Rabbi Shevach Zlatopolsky
EDITOR, JLI IN THE CIS

Dr. Arye Olman
TRANSLATOR, RUSSIAN

Rabbi Nochum Schapiro
REGIONAL REPRESENTATIVE,
AUSTRALIA

Rabbi Avraham Golovacheov
REGIONAL REPRESENTATIVE,
GERMANY

Rabbi Shmuel Katzman
REGIONAL REPRESENTATIVE,
NETHERLANDS

Rabbi Avrohom Steinmetz
REGIONAL REPRESENTATIVE,
BRAZIL

NATIONAL JEWISH RETREAT

Rabbi Hesh Epstein
CHAIRMAN

Mrs. Shaina B. Mintz
ADMINISTRATOR

Bruce Backman
Rabbi Menachem Klein
COORDINATORS

Rabbi Shmuly Karp
SHLUCHIM LIAISON

Mrs. Chana Dechter
Rabbi Mendel Rosenfeld
Aliza Landes
SERVICE AND SUPPORT

JLI LAND & SPIRIT
ISRAEL EXPERIENCE

Rabbi Shmuly Karp
DIRECTOR

Mrs. Shaina B. Mintz
ADMINISTRATOR

Rabbi Yechiel Baitelman
Rabbi Dovid Flinkenstein
Rabbi Chanoch Kaplan
Rabbi Levi Klein
Rabbi Mendy Mangel
Rabbi Sholom Raichik
STEERING COMMITTEE

SHABBAT IN THE HEIGHTS
Rabbi Shmuly Karp
DIRECTOR

Mrs. Shulamis Nadler
SERVICE AND SUPPORT

Rabbi Chaim Hanoka
Rabbi Zalman Marcus
STEERING COMMITTEE

MYSHIUR
ADVANCED LEARNING INITIATIVE

Rabbi Shmuel Kaplan
CHAIRMAN

Rabbi Levi Kaplan
DIRECTOR

TORAHCAFE.COM
ONLINE LEARNING

Rabbi Levi Kaplan
DIRECTOR

Rabbi Mendy Elishevitz
Rabbi Elchonon Korenblit
WEBSITE DEVELOPMENT

Moshe Levin
CONTENT MANAGER

Avrohom Shimon Ezagui
FILMING

MACHON SHMUEL
THE SAMI ROHR RESEARCH INSTITUTE

Rabbi Avrohom Bergstein
DEAN

Rabbi Zalman Korf
ADMINISTRATOR

Rabbi Moshe Miller
Rabbi Gedalya Oberlander
Rabbi Chaim Rapoport
Rabbi Chaim Schapiro
RABBINIC ADVISORY BOARD

Rabbi Yakov Gershon
RESEARCH FELLOW

FOUNDING DEPARTMENT HEADS

Rabbi Mendel Bell
Rabbi Zalman Charytan
Rabbi Mendel Druk
Rabbi Menachem Gansburg
Rabbi Meir Hecht
Rabbi Yoni Katz
Rabbi Chaim Zalman Levy
Rabbi Benny Rapoport
Dr. Chana Silberstein
Rabbi Elchonon Tenenbaum
Rabbi Mendy Weg

Faculty Directory

ALABAMA

BIRMINGHAM
Rabbi Yossi Friedman 205.970.0100

MOBILE
Rabbi Yosef Goldwasser 251.265.1213

ALASKA

ANCHORAGE
Rabbi Yosef Greenberg
Rabbi Mendy Greenberg 907.357.8770

ARIZONA

FLAGSTAFF
Rabbi Dovie Shapiro 928.255.5756

ORO VALLEY
Rabbi Ephraim Zimmerman 520.477.8672

PHOENIX
Rabbi Zalman Levertov
Rabbi Yossi Friedman 602.944.2753

SCOTTSDALE
Rabbi Yossi Levertov 480.998.1410

TUCSON
Rabbi Yehuda Ceitlin 520.881.7956

ARKANSAS

LITTLE ROCK
Rabbi Pinchus Ciment 501.217.0053

CALIFORNIA

AGOURA HILLS
Rabbi Moshe Bryski
Rabbi Yisroel Levine 818.991.0991

BAKERSFIELD
Rabbi Shmuli Schlanger
Mrs. Esther Schlanger 661.331.1695

BEL AIR
Rabbi Chaim Mentz 310.475.5311

BERKELEY
Rabbi Yosef Romano 510.396.4448

BURBANK
Rabbi Shmuly Kornfeld 818.954.0070

CARLSBAD
Rabbi Yeruchem Eilfort
Mrs. Nechama Eilfort 760.943.8891

CHATSWORTH
Rabbi Yossi Spritzer 818.718.0777

CONTRA COSTA
Rabbi Dovber Berkowitz 925.937.4101

CORONADO
Rabbi Eli Fradkin 619.365.4728

ENCINO
Rabbi Aryeh Herzog 818.784.9986
Chapter founded by Rabbi Joshua Gordon, OBM

FOLSOM
Rabbi Yossi Grossbaum 916.608.9811

FREMONT
Rabbi Moshe Fuss 510.300.4090

GLENDALE
Rabbi Simcha Backman 818.240.2750

HUNTINGTON BEACH
Rabbi Aron Berkowitz 714.846.2285

LA JOLLA
Rabbi Baruch Shalom Ezagui 858.455.5433

LAGUNA BEACH
Rabbi Elimelech Gurevitch 949.499.0770

LOMITA
Rabbi Eli Hecht
Rabbi Sholom Pinson 310.326.8234

LONG BEACH
Rabbi Abba Perelmuter 562.621.9828

LOS ANGELES
Rabbi Leibel Korf 323.660.5177

MARINA DEL REY
Rabbi Danny Yiftach-Hashem
Rabbi Dovid Yiftach............310.859.0770

NORTH HOLLYWOOD
Rabbi Nachman Abend............818.989.9539

NORTHRIDGE
Rabbi Eli Rivkin............818.368.3937

OAKLAND
Rabbi Dovid Labkowski............510.545.6770

OJAI
Rabbi Mordechai Nemtzov............805.613.7181

PACIFIC PALISADES
Rabbi Zushe Cunin............310.454.7783

PALO ALTO
Rabbi Yosef Levin
Rabbi Ber Rosenblatt............650.424.9800

PASADENA
Rabbi Chaim Hanoka............626.564.8820
Rabbi Sholom Stiefel............626.539.4578

RANCHO MIRAGE
Rabbi Shimon H. Posner............760.770.7785

RANCHO PALOS VERDES
Rabbi Yitzchok Magalnic............310.544.5544

RANCHO S. FE
Rabbi Levi Raskin............858.756.7571

REDONDO BEACH
Rabbi Yossi Mintz
Rabbi Zalman Gordon............310.214.4999

S. CLEMENTE
Rabbi Menachem M. Slavin............949.489.0723

S. CRUZ
Rabbi Yochanan Friedman............831.454.0101

S. DIEGO
Rabbi Rafi Andrusier............619.387.8770
Rabbi Motte Fradkin............858.547.0076

S. FRANCISCO
Rabbi Shlomo Zarchi............415.752.2866

S. LUIS OBISPO
Rabbi Chaim Leib Hilel............805.229.1836

S. MATEO
Rabbi Yossi Marcus............650.341.4510

S. MONICA
Rabbi Boruch Rabinowitz............310.394.5699

S. RAFAEL
Rabbi Yisrael Rice............415.492.1666

SOUTH LAKE TAHOE
Rabbi Mordechai Richler............530.314.7677

THOUSAND OAKS
Rabbi Chaim Bryski............805.493.7776

TUSTIN
Rabbi Yehoshua Eliezrie............714.508.2150

VENTURA
Rabbi Yakov Latowicz............805.658.7441

WEST HOLLYWOOD
Rabbi Mordechai Kirschenbaum............310.275.1215

WEST LOS ANGELES
Rabbi Mordechai Zaetz............424.652.8742

YORBA LINDA
Rabbi Dovid Eliezrie............714.693.0770

COLORADO

ASPEN
Rabbi Mendel Mintz............970.544.3770

DENVER
Rabbi Yossi Serebryanski............303.744.9699

FORT COLLINS
Rabbi Yerachmiel Gorelik............970.407.1613

HIGHLANDS RANCH
Rabbi Avraham Mintz............303.694.9119

LONGMONT
Rabbi Yakov Borenstein............303.678.7595

VAIL
Rabbi Dovid Mintz............970.476.7887

WESTMINSTER
Rabbi Benjy Brackman............303.429.5177

CONNECTICUT

FAIRFIELD
Rabbi Shlame Landa............203.373.7551

GREENWICH
Rabbi Yossi Deren
Rabbi Menachem Feldman............203.629.9059

NEW LONDON
Rabbi Avrohom Sternberg............860.437.8000

STAMFORD
Rabbi Yisrael Deren
Rabbi Levi Mendelow 203.3.CHABAD

WEST HARTFORD
Rabbi Shaya Gopin 860.232.1116

WESTPORT
Rabbi Yehuda L. Kantor 203.226.8584

DELAWARE

WILMINGTON
Rabbi Chuni Vogel 302.529.9900

DISTRICT OF COLUMBIA

WASHINGTON
Rabbi Levi Shemtov
Rabbi Shua Hecht 202.332.5600

FLORIDA

ALTAMONTE SPRINGS
Rabbi Mendy Bronstein 407.280.0535

BAL HARBOUR
Rabbi Dov Schochet 305.868.1411

BOCA RATON
Rabbi Zalman Bukiet
Rabbi Arele Gopin 561.994.6257
Rabbi Moishe Denburg 561.526.5760

BOYNTON BEACH
Rabbi Yosef Yitzchok Raichik 561.732.4633

BRADENTON
Rabbi Menachem Bukiet 941.388.9656

BROWARD CO.: SOUTHWEST
Rabbi Aryeh Schwartz 954.252.1770

CAPE CORAL
Rabbi Yossi Labkowski 239.963.4770

CORAL GABLES
Rabbi Avrohom Stolik 305.490.7572

CORAL SPRINGS
Rabbi Yankie Denburg 954.471.8646

DELRAY BEACH
Rabbi Sholom Ber Korf 561.496.6228

FLEMING ISLAND
Rabbi Shmuly Feldman 904.290.1017

FORT LAUDERDALE
Rabbi Yitzchok Naparstek 954.568.1190

FORT MYERS
Rabbi Yitzchok Minkowicz
Mrs. Nechama Minkowicz 239.433.7708

HALLANDALE BEACH
Rabbi Mordy Feiner 954.458.1877

HOLLYWOOD
Rabbi Leizer Barash 954.965.9933
Rabbi Leibel Kudan 954.801.3367

KENDALL
Rabbi Yossi Harlig 305.234.5654

LAKELAND
Rabbi Moshe Lazaros 863.510.5968

LONGWOOD
Rabbi Yanky Majesky 407.636.5994

MAITLAND
Rabbi Sholom Dubov
Rabbi Levik Dubov 470.644.2500

MIAMI
Rabbi Chaim Lipskar 786.368.9040

N. MIAMI BEACH
Rabbi Eily Smith 786.247.7222

OCALA
Rabbi Yossi Hecht 352.291.2218

ORLANDO
Rabbi Yosef Konikov 407.354.3660

ORMOND BEACH
Rabbi Shmuel Konikov 386.672.9300

PALM BEACH GARDENS
Rabbi Dovid Vigler 561.624.2223

PALM CITY
Rabbi Shlomo Uminer 772.288.0606

PALMETTO BAY
Rabbi Zalman Gansburg 786.282.0413

PEMBROKE PINES
Rabbi Mordechai Andrusier 954.874.2280

PLANTATION
Rabbi Pinchas Taylor 954.644.9177

PONTE VEDRA BEACH
Rabbi Nochum Kurinsky 904.543.9301

SARASOTA
Rabbi Chaim Shaul Steinmetz 941.925.0770

SATELLITE BEACH
Rabbi Zvi Konikov 321.777.2770

SOUTH PALM BEACH
Rabbi Leibel Stolik 561.889.3499

SOUTH TAMPA
Rabbi Mendy Dubrowski 813.922.1723

SUNNY ISLES BEACH
Rabbi Alexander Kaller 305.803.5315

S. AUGUSTINE
Rabbi Levi Vogel 904.521.8664

TALLAHASSEE
Rabbi Schneur Oirechman 850.523.9294

VENICE
Rabbi Sholom Ber Schmerling 941.493.2770

WESTON
Rabbi Yisroel Spalter 954.349.6565

WEST PALM BEACH
Rabbi Yoel Gancz 561.659.7770

GEORGIA

ALPHARETTA
Rabbi Hirshy Minkowicz 770.410.9000

ATLANTA
Rabbi Yossi New
Rabbi Isser New 404.843.2464

ATLANTA: INTOWN
Rabbi Eliyahu Schusterman
Rabbi Ari Sollish 404.898.0434

CUMMING
Rabbi Levi Mentz 310.666.2218

GWINNETT
Rabbi Yossi Lerman 678.595.0196

MARIETTA
Rabbi Ephraim Silverman 770.565.4412

HAWAII

PRINCEVILLE
Rabbi Michoel Goldman 808.647.4293

IDAHO

BOISE
Rabbi Mendel Lifshitz 208.853.9200

ILLINOIS

CHAMPAIGN
Rabbi Dovid Tiechtel 217.355.8672

CHICAGO
Rabbi Meir Hecht 312.714.4655
Rabbi Yosef Moscowitz 773.772.3770
Rabbi Levi Notik 773.274.5123

DES PLAINES
Rabbi Lazer Hershkovich 224.392.4442

ELGIN
Rabbi Mendel Shemtov 847.440.4486

GLENVIEW
Rabbi Yishaya Benjaminson 847.998.9896

HIGHLAND PARK
Mrs. Michla Schanowitz 847.266.0770

NAPERVILLE
Rabbi Mendy Goldstein 630.778.9770

NORTHBROOK
Rabbi Meir Moscowitz 847.564.8770

OAK PARK
Rabbi Yitzchok Bergstein 708.524.1530

PEORIA
Rabbi Eli Langsam 309.692.2250

ROCKFORD
Rabbi Yecheskel Rothman 815.596.0032

SKOKIE
Rabbi Yochanan Posner 847.677.1770

VERNON HILLS
Rabbi Shimmy Susskind 847.984.2919

WILMETTE
Rabbi Dovid Flinkenstein 847.251.7707

INDIANA

INDIANAPOLIS
Rabbi Avraham Grossbaum
Rabbi Dr. Shmuel Klatzkin 317.251.5573

IOWA

BETTENDORF
Rabbi Shneur Cadaner............................563.355.1065

KANSAS

OVERLAND PARK
Rabbi Mendy Wineberg............................913.649.4852

KENTUCKY

LOUISVILLE
Rabbi Avrohom Litvin............................502.459.1770

LOUISIANA

METAIRIE
Rabbi Yossie Nemes
Rabbi Mendel Ceitlin............................504.454.2910

MARYLAND

ANNAPOLIS
Rabbi Nochum Light............................443.321.9859

BALTIMORE
Rabbi Velvel Belinsky............................410.764.5000
Classes in Russian

BEL AIR
Rabbi Kushi Schusterman............................443.353.9718

BETHESDA
Rabbi Sender Geisinsky............................301.913.9777

COLUMBIA
Rabbi Hillel Baron
Rabbi Yosef Chaim Sufrin............................410.740.2424

FREDERICK
Rabbi Boruch Labkowski............................301.996.3659

GAITHERSBURG
Rabbi Sholom Raichik............................301.926.3632

OLNEY
Rabbi Bentzy Stolik............................301.660.6770

OWINGS MILLS
Rabbi Nochum H. Katsenelenbogen............................410.356.5156

POTOMAC
Rabbi Mendel Bluming............................301.983.4200
Rabbi Mendel Kaplan............................301.983.1485

ROCKVILLE
Rabbi Moishe Kavka............................301.836.1242

MASSACHUSETTS

BOSTON
Rabbi Yosef Zaklos............................617.297.7282

CAPE COD
Rabbi Yekusiel Alperowitz............................508.775.2324

LONGMEADOW
Rabbi Yakov Wolff............................413.567.8665

NEWTON
Rabbi Shalom Ber Prus............................617.244.1200

SUDBURY
Rabbi Yisroel Freeman............................978.443.0110

MICHIGAN

ANN ARBOR
Rabbi Aharon Goldstein............................734.995.3276

BLOOMFIELD HILLS
Rabbi Levi Dubov............................248.949.6210

GRAND RAPIDS
Rabbi Mordechai Haller............................616.957.0770

WEST BLOOMFIELD
Rabbi Elimelech Silberberg............................248.855.6170

MINNESOTA

MINNETONKA
Rabbi Mordechai Grossbaum
Rabbi Shmuel Silberstein............................952.929.9922

S. PAUL
Rabbi Shneur Zalman Bendet............................651.998.9298

MISSOURI

CHESTERFIELD
Rabbi Avi Rubenfeld............................314.258.3401

S. LOUIS
Rabbi Yosef Landa 314.725.0400

NEVADA

LAS VEGAS
Rabbi Yosef Rivkin 702.217.2170

SUMMERLIN
Rabbi Yisroel Schanowitz
Rabbi Tzvi Bronchtain 702.855.0770

NEW JERSEY

BASKING RIDGE
Rabbi Mendy Herson
Rabbi Mendel Shemtov 908.604.8844

CLINTON
Rabbi Eli Kornfeld 908.623.7000

FAIR LAWN
Rabbi Avrohom Bergstein 201.362.2712

FORT LEE
Rabbi Meir Konikov 201.886.1238

FRANKLIN LAKES
Rabbi Chanoch Kaplan 201.848.0449

HASKELL
Rabbi Mendy Gurkov 201.696.7609

HOLMDEL
Rabbi Shmaya Galperin 732.772.1998

MADISON
Rabbi Shalom Lubin 973.377.0707

MANALAPAN
Rabbi Boruch Chazanow
Rabbi Levi Wolosow 732.972.3687

MOUNTAIN LAKES
Rabbi Levi Dubinsky 973.551.1898

MULLICA HILL
Rabbi Avrohom Richler 856.733.0770

OLD TAPPAN
Rabbi Mendy Lewis 201.767.4008

PASSAIC
Rabbi Yitzchak Sebbag
Dr. Michael Akerman 973.246.5251

RANDOLPH
Rabbi Avraham Bekhor 973.895.3070

ROCKAWAY
Rabbi Asher Herson
Rabbi Mordechai Baumgarten 973.625.1525

RUTHERFORD
Rabbi Yitzchok Lerman 347.834.7500

SCOTCH PLAINS
Rabbi Avrohom Blesofsky 908.790.0008

TEANECK
Rabbi Ephraim Simon 201.907.0686

TENAFLY
Rabbi Mordechai Shain 201.871.1152

TOMS RIVER
Rabbi Moshe Gourarie 732.349.4199

WEST ORANGE
Rabbi Mendy Kasowitz 973.486.2362

WOODCLIFF LAKE
Rabbi Dov Drizin 201.476.0157

NEW YORK

BEDFORD
Rabbi Arik Wolf 914.666.6065

BINGHAMTON
Mrs. Rivkah Slonim 607.797.0015

BRIGHTON BEACH
Rabbi Moshe Winner 718.946.9833

BROOKVILLE
Rabbi Mendy Heber 516.626.0600

CEDARHURST
Rabbi Zalman Wolowik 516.295.2478

COMMACK
Rabbi Mendel Teldon 631.543.3343

DOBBS FERRY
Rabbi Benjy Silverman 914.693.6100

EAST HAMPTON
Rabbi Leibel Baumgarten
Rabbi Mendy Goldberg 631.329.5800

ELLENVILLE
Rabbi Shlomie Deren 845.647.4450

FOREST HILLS
Rabbi Yossi Mendelson 917.861.9726

GREAT NECK
Rabbi Yoseph Geisinsky 516.487.4554

KINGSTON
Rabbi Yitzchok Hecht 845.334.9044

LARCHMONT
Rabbi Mendel Silberstein 914.834.4321

LONG BEACH
Rabbi Eli Goodman 516.897.2473

NYC KEHILATH JESHURUN
Rabbi Elie Weinstock 212.774.5636

RUTHERFORD
Rabbi Yitzchok Lerman 347.834.7500

NYACK
Rabbi Chaim Zvi Ehrenreich 845.356.6686

OCEANSIDE
Rabbi Levi Gurkow 516.764.7385

OSSINING
Rabbi Dovid Labkowski 914.923.2522

OYSTER BAY
Rabbi Shmuel Lipszyc
Rabbi Shalom Lipszyc 347.853.9992

PARK SLOPE
Rabbi Menashe Wolf 347.957.1291

PORT WASHINGTON
Rabbi Shalom Paltiel 516.767.8672

PROSPECT HEIGHTS
Rabbi Mendy Hecht 347.622.3599

RIVERDALE
Rabbi Levi Shemtov 718.549.1100

ROCHESTER
Rabbi Nechemia Vogel 585.271.0330

ROSLYN
Rabbi Yaakov Reiter 516.484.8185

SCARSDALE
Rabbi Avrohom Butman 914.527.2077

SEA GATE
Rabbi Chaim Brikman 917.975.2792

SOUTHAMPTON
Rabbi Chaim Pape 917.627.4865

STATEN ISLAND
Rabbi Mendy Katzman 718.370.8953

STONY BROOK
Rabbi Shalom Ber Cohen 631.585.0521

SUFFERN
Rabbi Shmuel Gancz 845.368.1889

WESTBURY
Rabbi Mendy Brownstein 516.850.4486

YORKTOWN HEIGHTS
Rabbi Yehuda Heber 914.962.1111

NORTH CAROLINA

ASHEVILLE
Rabbi Shaya Susskind 828.505.0746

CARY
Rabbi Yisroel Cotlar 919.651.9710

CHAPEL HILL
Rabbi Zalman Bluming 919.630.5129

CHARLOTTE
Rabbi Yossi Groner
Rabbi Shlomo Cohen 704.366.3984

GREENSBORO
Rabbi Yosef Plotkin 336.617.8120

RALEIGH
Rabbi Pinchas Herman
Rabbi Lev Cotlar 919.637.6950

WILMINGTON
Rabbi Moshe Lieblich 910.763.4770

OHIO

BEACHWOOD
Rabbi Shmuli Friedman 216.370.2887

BLUE ASH
Rabbi Yisroel Mangel 513.793.5200

COLUMBUS
Rabbi Yitzi Kaltmann 614.294.3296

DAYTON
Rabbi Nochum Mangel
Rabbi Shmuel Klatzkin 937.643.0770

OKLAHOMA

OKLAHOMA CITY
Rabbi Ovadia Goldman 405.524.4800

TULSA
Rabbi Yehuda Weg.................918.492.4499

OREGON

PORTLAND
Rabbi Mordechai Wilhelm.................503.977.9947

SALEM
Rabbi Avrohom Yitzchok Perlstein.................503.383.9569

PENNSYLVANIA

AMBLER
Rabbi Shaya Deitsch.................215.591.9310

BALA CYNWYD
Rabbi Shraga Sherman.................610.660.9192

LAFAYETTE HILL
Rabbi Yisroel Kotlarsky.................484.533.7009

LANCASTER
Rabbi Elazar Green.................717.368.6565

MONROEVILLE
Rabbi Mendy Schapiro.................412.372.1000

NEWTOWN
Rabbi Aryeh Weinstein.................215.497.9925

PHILADELPHIA: CENTER CITY
Rabbi Yochonon Goldman.................215.238.2100

PITTSBURGH
Rabbi Yisroel Altein.................412.422.7300 EXT. 269

PITTSBURGH: SOUTH HILLS
Rabbi Mendy Rosenblum.................412.278.3693

RYDAL
Rabbi Zushe Gurevitz.................267.536.5757

WYNNEWOOD
Rabbi Moishe Brennan.................610.529.9011

RHODE ISLAND

WARWICK
Rabbi Yossi Laufer.................401.884.7888

SOUTH CAROLINA

COLUMBIA
Rabbi Hesh Epstein
Rabbi Levi Marrus.................803.782.1831

MYRTLE BEACH
Rabbi Doron Aizenman.................843.448.0035

TENNESSEE

CHATTANOOGA
Rabbi Shaul Perlstein.................423.490.1106

MEMPHIS
Rabbi Levi Klein.................901.754.0404

TEXAS

ARLINGTON
Rabbi Levi Gurevitch.................817.451.1171

AUSTIN
Rabbi Mendy Levertov.................512.905.2778

BELLAIRE
Rabbi Yossi Zaklikofsky.................713.839.8887

DALLAS
Rabbi Mendel Dubrawsky
Rabbi Moshe Naparstek.................972.818.0770

FORT WORTH
Rabbi Dov Mandel.................817.263.7701

FRISCO
Rabbi Mendy Kesselman.................214.460.7773

HOUSTON
Rabbi Dovid Goldstein
Rabbi Zally Lazarus.................281.589.7188
Rabbi Moishe Traxler.................713.774.0300

HOUSTON: RICE UNIVERSITY AREA
Rabbi Eliezer Lazaroff.................713.522.2004

LEAGUE CITY
Rabbi Yitzchok Schmukler.................281.724.1554

MISSOURI CITY
Rabbi Mendel Feigenson.................832.758.0685

PLANO
Rabbi Mendel Block
Rabbi Yehudah Horowitz.................972.596.8270

S. ANTONIO
Rabbi Chaim Block
Rabbi Levi Teldon 210.492.1085

THE WOODLANDS
Rabbi Mendel Blecher 281.719.5213

UTAH

SALT LAKE CITY
Rabbi Benny Zippel 801.467.7777

VERMONT

BURLINGTON
Rabbi Yitzchok Raskin 802.658.5770

VIRGINIA

ALEXANDRIA/ARLINGTON
Rabbi Mordechai Newman 703.370.2774

FAIRFAX
Rabbi Leibel Fajnland 703.426.1980

NORFOLK
Rabbi Aaron Margolin
Rabbi Levi Brashevitzky 757.616.0770

TYSONS CORNER
Rabbi Chezzy Deitsch 703.829.5770
Chapter founded by Rabbi Levi Deitsch, OBM

WASHINGTON

BELLINGHAM
Rabbi Yosef Truxton 617.640.8841

MERCER ISLAND
Rabbi Elazar Bogomilsky 206.527.1411

SPOKANE COUNTY
Rabbi Yisroel Hahn 509.443.0770

WISCONSIN

KENOSHA
Rabbi Tzali Wilschanski 262.359.0770

MADISON
Rabbi Avremel Matusof 608.231.3450

MILWAUKEE
Rabbi Mendel Shmotkin 414.961.6100

WAUKESHA
Rabbi Levi Brook 925.708.4203

PUERTO RICO

CAROLINA
Rabbi Mendel Zarchi 787.253.0894

ARGENTINA

PALERMO NUEVO
Rabbi Mendy Grunblatt 54.11.4771.8228

ISEJ
Rabbi Yoel Migdal 54.11.4961.0621

ALTO PALERMO
Rabbi Pinhas Sudry 54.1.4822.2285

OLLEROS
Rabbi Yaakov Birman 54.11.4774.5071

ESCUELA Y COMUNIDAD WOLFSOHN TABACINIC
Rabbi Mendy Gurevitch 55.11.4545.7771

OR MIZRAH
Rabbi Mendi Mizrahi 54.11.4963.1221

CABALLITO SUR
Rabbi Shloimi Setton 549.11.5325.0849

SALTA
Rabbi Rafael Tawil 54.387.421.4947

MACHON OR CHAYA
Mrs. Chani Gorowitz 54.11.4865.0445

AUSTRALIA

NEW SOUTH WALES

DOUBLE BAY
Rabbi Yanky Berger
Rabbi Yisroel Dolnikov 612.9327.1644

DOVER HEIGHTS
Rabbi Motti Feldman 612.9387.3822

NORTH SHORE
Rabbi Nochum Schapiro
Mrs. Fruma Schapiro 612.9488.9548

VICTORIA

ELSTERNWICK
Rabbi Chaim Cowen................................614.3330.8584

MOORABBIN
Rabbi Elisha Greenbaum.........................614.0349.0434

WESTERN AUSTRALIA

PERTH
Rabbi Shalom White...............................618.9275.2106

AZERBAIJAN

BAKU
Mrs. Chavi Segal................................994.12.597.91.90

BELARUS

BOBRUISK
Mrs. Mina Hababo...............................375.29.104.3230

MINSK
Rabbi Shneur Deitsch
Mrs. Bassie Deitsch..............................375.29.330.6675

BELGIUM

BRUSSELS
Rabbi Shmuel Pinson............................375.29.330.6675

BRAZIL

CURITIBA
Rabbi Mendy Labkowski.......................55.41.3079.1338

S. PAULO
Rabbi Avraham Steinmetz.....................55.11.3081.3081

CANADA

ALBERTA

CALGARY
Rabbi Mordechai Groner.........................403.281.3770

EDMONTON
Rabbi Ari Drelich
Rabbi Mendy Blachman..........................780.200.5770

BRITISH COLUMBIA

RICHMOND
Rabbi Yechiel Baitelman..........................604.277.6427

VANCOUVER
Rabbi Dovid Rosenfeld...........................604.266.1313

VICTORIA
Rabbi Meir Kaplan................................250.595.7656

MANITOBA

WINNIPEG
Rabbi Shmuel Altein..............................204.339.8737

ONTARIO

LAWRENCE/EGLINTON
Rabbi Menachem Gansburg.....................416.546.8770

MISSISSAUGA
Rabbi Yitzchok Slavin............................905.820.4432

NIAGARA FALLS
Rabbi Zalman Zaltzman..........................905.356.7200

OTTAWA
Rabbi Menachem M. Blum.......................613.843.7770

RICHMOND HILL
Rabbi Mendel Bernstein.........................905.770.7700

GREATER TORONTO REGIONAL OFFICE & THORNHILL
Rabbi Yossi Gansburg............................905.731.7000

THORNHILL WOODS
Rabbi Chaim Hildeshaim.........................905.881.1919

WATERLOO
Rabbi Moshe Goldman............................226.338.7770

YORK MILLS
Rabbi Levi Gansburg.............................416.551.9391

QUEBEC

MONTREAL
Rabbi Ronnie Fine
Pesach Nussbaum................................514.738.3434

TOWN OF MOUNT ROYAL
Rabbi Moshe Krasnanski
Rabbi Shneur Zalman Rader.....................514.739.0770

WESTMOUNT
Rabbi Yossi Shanowitz
Mrs. Devorah Leah Shanowitz...................514.937.4772

SASKATCHEWAN

REGINA
Rabbi Avrohom Simmonds.......................306.585.1359

SASKATOON
Rabbi Raphael Kats................................306.384.4370

CAYMAN ISLANDS

GRAND CAYMAN
Rabbi Berel Pewzner..............................717.798.1040

COSTA RICA

S. JOSÉ
Rabbi Hershel Spalter
Rabbi Moshe Bitton............................506.4010.1515

COLOMBIA

BOGOTA
Rabbi Chanoch Piekarski....................57.1.635.8251

CROATIA

ZAGREB
Rabbi Pinchas Zaklas..........................385.1.4812227

DENMARK

COPENHAGEN
Rabbi Yitzchok Loewenthal..................45.3316.1850

ESTONIA

TALLINN
Rabbi Shmuel Kot................................372.662.30.50

FRANCE

PARIS
Rabbi Avraham Pevzner....................33.1.40.38.02.02

CANNES
Rabbi Yehouda Lewin........................33.4.92.98.67.51

BOULOGNE
Rabbi Michael Sojcher......................33.6.20.44.07.63

MARSEILLE
Rabbi Eliahou Altabe........................33.6.11.60.03.05
Rabbi Menahem Mendel Assouline............33.6.64.88.25.04

GEORGIA

TBILISI
Rabbi Meir Kozlovsky........................995.32.2429770

GERMANY

BERLIN
Rabbi Yehuda Tiechtel......................49.30.2128.0830

HAMBURG
Rabbi Shlomo Bistritzky..................49.40.4142.4190

HANNOVER
Rabbi Binyamin Wolff......................49.511.811.2822

COLOGNE
Rabbi Menachem M. Schtroks..............49.178.4444.770

DUSSELDORF
Rabbi Chaim Barkahn........................49.173.2871.770

GREECE

ATHENS
Rabbi Mendel Hendel........................30.210.323.3825

GUATEMALA

GUATEMALA CITY
Rabbi Shalom Pelman........................502.2485.0770

ISRAEL

ASHKELON
Rabbi Shneor Lieberman....................054.977.0512

BALFURYA
Rabbi Noam Bar-Tov........................054.580.4770

CAESAREA
Rabbi Chaim Meir Lieberman..............054.621.2586

EVEN YEHUDA
Rabbi Menachem Noyman....................054.777.0707

GANEI TIKVA
Rabbi Gershon Shnur 054.524.2358

GIV'ATAYIM
Rabbi Pinchus Bitton 052.643.8770

KARMIEL
Rabbi Mendy Elishevitz 054.521.3073

KFAR SABA
Rabbi Yossi Baitch 054.445.5020

KIRYAT BIALIK
Rabbi Pinny Marton 050.661.1768

KIRYAT MOTZKIN
Rabbi Shimon Eizenbach 050.902.0770

KOCHAV YAIR
Rabbi Dovi Greenberg 054.332.6244

MACCABIM-RE'UT
Rabbi Yosef Yitzchak Noiman 054.977.0549

NES ZIYONA
Rabbi Menachem Feldman 054.497.7092

NETANYA
Rabbi Schneur Brod 054.579.7572

RAMAT GAN-KRINITZI
Rabbi Yisroel Gurevitz 052.743.2814

RAMAT GAN-MAROM NAVE
Rabbi Binyamin Meir Kali 050.476.0770

RAMAT YISHAI
Rabbi Shneor Zalman Wolosow 052.324.5475

RISHON LEZION
Rabbi Uri Keshet 050.722.4593

ROSH PINA
Rabbi Sholom Ber Hertzel 052.458.7600

YEHUD
Rabbi Shmuel Wolf 053.536.1479

JAPAN

TOKYO
Rabbi Mendi Sudakevich 81.3.5789.2846

KAZAKHSTAN

ALMATY
Rabbi Shevach Zlatopolsky 7.7272.77.59.49

KYRGYZSTAN

BISHKEK
Rabbi Arye Raichman 996.312.68.19.66

LATVIA

RIGA
Rabbi Shneur Zalman Kot
Mrs. Rivka Glazman 371.6720.40.22

LITHUANIA

VILNIUS
Rabb Sholom Ber Krinsky 370.6817.1367

LUXEMBOURG

LUXEMBOURG
Rabbi Mendel Edelman 352.2877.7079

MOROCCO

CASABLANCA
Rabbi Levi Banon 212.5.22.26.90.37

NETHERLANDS

THE HAGUE
Rabbi Shmuel Katzman 31.70.347.0222

AMSTERDAM
Rabbi Jaacov Zwi Spiero 31.652.328.065

ALMERE
Rabbi Moshe Stiefel 31.36.744.0509

HEEMSTEDE-HAARLEM
Rabbi Shmuel Spiero 31.23.532.0707

NIJMEGEN
Rabbi Menachem Mendel Levine 31.621.586.575

ROTTERDAM
Rabbi Yehuda Vorst 31.10.265.5530

PANAMA

PANAMA CITY
Rabbi Ari Laine
Rabbi Gabriel Benayon 507.223.3383

PARAGUAY

ASUNCION
Rabbi Levi Feigelstock 595.21.228.669

RUSSIA

ASTRAKHAN
Rabbi Yisroel Melamed 7.851.239.28.24

BRYANSK
Rabbi Menachem Mendel Zaklas 7.483.264.55.15

CHELYABINSK
Rabbi Meir Kirsh 7.351.263.24.68

MOSCOW: MARINA ROSHA
Rabbi Mordechai Weisberg 7.495.645.50.00

NIZHNY NOVGOROD
Rabbi Shimon Bergman 7.920.253.47.70

OMSK
Rabbi Osher Krichevsky 7.381.231.33.07

PERM
Rabbi Zalman Deutch 7.342.212.47.32

ROSTOV
Rabbi Chaim Danzinger 7.8632.99.02.68

S. PETERSBURG
Rabbi Zvi Pinsky 7.812.713.62.09

SAMARA
Rabbi Shlomo Deutch 7.846.333.40.64

SARATOV
Rabbi Yaakov Kubitshek 7.8452.21.58.00

TOGLIATTI
Rabbi Meier Fischer 7.848.273.02.84

UFA
Rabbi Dan Krichevsky 7.347.244.55.33

VORONEZH
Rabbi Levi Stiefel 7.473.252.96.99

SINGAPORE

SINGAPORE
Rabbi Mordechai Abergel 656.337.2189
Rabbi Netanel Rivni 656.336.2127
Classes in Hebrew

SOUTH AFRICA

CAPE TOWN
Rabbi Levi Popack 27.21.434.3740

JOHANNESBURG
Rabbi Dovid Masinter
Rabbi Ari Kievman 27.11.440.6600

SWEDEN

MALMO
Rabbi Shneur Kesselman 46.707.366.770

STOCKHOLM
Rabbi Chaim Greisman 468.679.7067

SWITZERLAND

BASEL
Rabbi Zalmen Wishedsky 41.41.361.1770

LUZERN
Rabbi Chaim Drukman 41.41.361.1770

THAILAND

BANGKOK
Rabbi Yosef C. Kantor 6681.822.9541

UKRAINE

DNEPROPETROVSK
Rabbi Dan Makagon 380.504.51.13.18

NIKOLAYEV
Rabbi Sholom Gotlieb 380.512.37.37.71

ODESSA
Rabbi Avraham Wolf
Rabbi Yaakov Neiman .... 38.048.728.0770 EXT. 280

ZHITOMIR
Rabbi Shlomo Wilhelm 380.504.63.01.32

UNITED KINGDOM

BOURNEMOUTH
Rabbi Bentzion Alperowitz............................44.749.456.7177

CARDIFF
Rabbi Michoel Rose 44.792.866.9536

CHEADLE
Rabbi Peretz Chein 44.161.428.1818

LEEDS
Rabbi Eli Pink..44.113.266.3311

LONDON
Rabbi Mendel Cohen......................................44.777.261.2661
Rabbi Nissan D. Dubov..................................44.208.944.1581
Rabbi Mendy Korer 44.794.632.5444
Rabbi Dovid Katz..44.207.624.2770
Rabbi Yisroel Lew...44.207.060.9770

MANCHESTER
Rabbi Levi Cohen 44.161.792.6335
Rabbi Shmuli Jaffe...44.161.766.1812

JEWISH LEARNING INSTITUTE

The Jewish Learning Multiplex
Brought to you by the Rohr Jewish Learning Institute

In fulfillment of the mandate of the Lubavitcher Rebbe, of blessed memory,
whose leadership guides every step of our work,
the mission of the Rohr Jewish Learning Institute is to transform
Jewish life and the greater community through the study of Torah,
connecting each Jew to our shared heritage of Jewish learning.

While our flagship program remains the cornerstone of our organization,
JLI is proud to feature additional divisions catering to specific populations,
in order to meet a wide array of educational needs.

THE ROHR JEWISH LEARNING INSTITUTE,
a subsidiary of *Merkos L'Inyonei Chinuch,*
is the adult education arm of the Chabad-Lubavitch Movement.

Torah Studies provides a rich and nuanced encounter with the weekly Torah reading.

MyShiur courses are designed to assist students in developing the skills needed to study Talmud independently.

IN PARTNERSHIP WITH CHABAD ON CAMPUS

This rigorous fellowship program invites select college students to explore the fundamentals of Judaism.

IN PARTNERSHIP WITH CTEEN: CHABAD TEEN NETWORK

Jewish teens forge their identity as they engage in Torah study, social interaction, and serious fun.

The Rosh Chodesh Society gathers Jewish women together once a month for intensive textual study.

TorahCafe.com provides an exclusive selection of top-rated Jewish educational videos.

This yearly event rejuvenates mind, body, and spirit with a powerful synthesis of Jewish learning and community.

Participants delve into our nation's rich past while exploring the Holy Land's relevance and meaning today.

Select affiliates are invited to partner with peers and noted professionals, as leaders of innovation and excellence.

THE SAMI ROHR
RESEARCH INSTITUTE

Machon Shmuel is an institute providing Torah research in the service of educators worldwide.